THE AMERICAN VEIN

THE AMERICAN VEIN

Directors and Directions in Television

Christopher Wicking and
Tise Vahimagi

A Dutton Paperback

E. P. Dutton
New York

This edition of
THE AMERICAN VEIN
First printed 1979 by E.P. Dutton, a division of Elsevier-Dutton Publishing Co., Inc.
All rights reserved. Printed in the U.S.A.
Copyright © 1979 by Christopher Wicking
and Tise Vahimagi
Reprinted by arrangement with Talisman Books, London.

No part of this publication may be reproduced or transmitted in any form or by any means, including photocopy, recording or any information storage and retrieval system now known or to be invented, without permission in writing from the publisher, except by a reviewer who wishes to quote brief passages in connection with a review written for inclusion in a magazine, newspaper or broadcast.

Library of Congress Catalog Card Number: 79-52675
ISBN: 0-525-05420-0 (cloth)
ISBN: 0-525-47603-2 (DP)
Published simultaneously in Canada by Clarke, Irwin & Company Limited, Toronto and Vancouver

10 9 8 7 6 5 4 3 2 1

Contents

Chapter One/ Kings of the Stardust Ballroom

Chapter Two/ I Also Do The Catering

Chapter Three/ Made it Ma, Top of the World!

Chapter Four/ Elephants' Graveyard

Chapter Five/ How Do You Get to Carnegie Hall?

Chapter Six/ Not Just a Poor Player

Chapter 7/ Paso Por Aqui

Acknowledgments

This book would have seemed more like a monograph without the following individuals and companies:

-Jack Cook at Warner Bros TV gave us the keys to the basement and Altman's career took on some sort of shape, while a key period and major company began to seem even more important.
-Simon Foster at Universal/MCA gave us the total picture of the contemporary affairs of the company, as well as much encouragement, and a belief that the book would be useful to the industry as well as to lunatic afficionados; sadly, much material relating to the earlier period of the company's history had been junked.
-Howard Karshan, plus Grace Kelly and the other friendly faces in the Viacom office made it easy as pie to figure out that company's and much of CBS's network activities.
-Alan Howden at the BBC and Vivien Maccoby, with their immaculate records were also invaluable.
-Ron V. Borst unearthed many evasive credits, synopses and opinions from his virtually bottomless files.
-Jack Edmund Nolan's pioneering TVresearch contributed to the book in many ways, particularly via his extremely perceptive column in the pages of *Films in Review.*
-Dave Shaw contributed not only enthusiasm but also the resources of a veritable computer bank of a memory.
-André De Toth and Cedric Francis (with their recollections of working with Warner Bros.), together with Adrian Caddy of Richard Price Associates, gave generously of their time.
-*The American Vein* might still have remained an idea in our heads, were it not for our publishers Kevin Gough-Yates and Margaret Tarratt. They have wrung it out of us into print, credit by credit, and should therefore receive some themselves. We thought they were late-comers to TV only to find that they too were secret teleastes of long standing with records which helped us as well.
-While Brenda, Mitchel and Sara-Lisa Wicking variously made lists, grabbed credits off the screen, typed, enthused—and also did the catering.

Christopher Wicking and Tise Vahimagi
London, September 1978

Introduction

The growth of American TV began in the late 1940s, when its origins as an extension of the commercial interests of radio were naturally reflected in its form. News bulletins, current affairs broadcasts, comedy and music shows with radio stars transferred (and sometimes failed to transfer) from one box to another. A joke of the time had an old man shown TV for the first time exclaim 'Gee, it's just like radio with pictures'.

Initially the new medium was an enemy of cinema, the Hollywood studios regarding it as a threat to their own carefully controlled monopoly of artists and audience alike. But TV's need to transmit more and more material as its popularity grew, along with its commercial success, slowly sucked Hollywood. Here was another way to make a buck. Small, independent companies began to churn out a small-screen equivalent of 'B' westerns, thrillers and other juvenile-oriented productions until, in time, **The Range Rider** and **The Cisco Kid** series supplanted Johnny Mack Brown and Rocky Lane.

Still, there was little reason for film critics or enthusiasts to pay much attention to what was happening in the hybrid medium. The events which began to cause notice to be paid all emanated from live TV dramas: **Marty, Twelve Angry Men, The Caine Mutiny Court Martial, Patterns, The Miracle Worker, Requiem for a Heavyweight.** They were written by TV's first new generation of artists (writers Rod Serling, Paddy Cheyevsky, Reginald Rose) and directed by Sidney Lumet, John Frankenheimer, Arthur Penn. This was where the action was. When these TV productions were re-made as films, when the directors moved from small to large screen, they were generally welcomed for their vision and promise, but the work they left behind remained to this day, unexplored.

Tyro cineastes of the 1960s, emboldened by what has become known as 'Cahierism' were all busily checking out American cinema, from its pantheon to its bargain basements, appraising, or, in the case of those who had been weaned on it uncritically (as the mother's milk of entertainment, myth and fantasy), reappraising everything that moved, from PATHS OF GLORY to FRONTIER GUN, VIVA ZAPATA to DETOUR, SEVEN MEN FROM NOW to ZORRO'S FIGHTING LEGION.

They were helped considerably by a slim but magical volume—*Vingt Ans de Cinéma Américain*—a typically French round up of American directors from A for Aldrich (but also Arnold, Jack) to Z for Zinnemann (but not, strangely in retrospect, Zugsmith, Albert). This appeared a full two years before the *Film Culture* issue devoted to Andrew Sarris's Americanisation of 'auteurism', and therefore seven years before it was expanded into *The American Cinema* in book form. Whether or not Tavernier, Boisset, Coursodon and Wagner set Sarris to work, their catholic view was inspirational.

It was also becoming apparent that film and TV had something in common. For on returning home from a sortie into some grindhouse for, say, Samuel Fuller's CRIMSON KIMONO, **The Dick Powell Theatre** segment on TV was by the very same Sam. When RIDE THE HIGH COUNTRY was followed two weeks later by THE DEADLY COMPANIONS and it became clear that in Sam Peckinpah there was a major new talent unheralded by critics, it was with surprise and pleasure that, again, **Dick Powell Theatre** presented a Peckinpah piece.

Plainly, thought the cineaste, though a difference in scale, ambition and framework separated large and small screens, TV itself had become a valid extension of American cinema in its broadest sense.

Nearly twenty years later, Robert Altman, James Frawley, Lamont Johnson, Sydney Pollack, Bob Rafelson, Michael Ritchie, Stuart Rosenberg, Mark Rydell, Richard Sarafian, Franklin Schaffner and Steven Spielberg are the most famous of those directors who have followed Peckinpah out of TV film—but their formative work is still virtually unknown and, to the majority of all but the most rabid teleastes, unseen.

Not only that, but TV continues to be reviled and ignored.

*

When we embarked on *The American Vein* (a mad enough thing to do, based as we are in England, and far from the source material) we aimed at a true comprehensiveness: to produce a mixture of Sarris and *Vingt Ans*—a book with silly categories, a few puns and analyses, but above all a complete picture of the work of the practitioners of telefilm. We quickly realised that we would have to amend 'comprehensive' to 'representative', for relying on our own records, and those of American companies and organisations with an English branch office, has meant that there are inevitably many gaps. We had, too, planned to include full details of the work of non-film TV directors (the Penns, the Lumets) but not enough information has been unearthed to make this valid. We were cheered (if saddened too) to learn, however, that the UCLA Television Arts Department has similar problems. With records lost and kinescopes (prints) no longer existing, TV history is beginning to look as tattered as that surrounding the pioneer days of cinema.

This book, then, is like a map of Alaska some 20 years ago. The shape of the country was known, to be sure, major rivers, mountain ranges and so forth.

But the details? Their absence was what prompted the explorer to set out. It has only recently been correctly mapped.

We have filled in many details, but there are many more left empty. The very nature of 'authorship' is arguable. While we have taken an auteurist principle, concentrating on directors, we have done it from convenience rather than total conviction. We had hoped to include a section on writers, who would seem to us to be capable of 'authorship', along with that on producers, but again, the sheer lack of detail prevented any true career guides from emerging. Another difficulty arises from the complete unavailability of the older TV material. Where so many movies can be seen on TV, or hired on 16mm, including rivetting classics like GANGS INCORPORATED and THE LAW WEST OF THE PECOS, it is virtually impossible, unless a TV network feels like obliging, to see any of the classic (or non-classic) TV productions of the past. To demand to see something you have to know what programmes to ask for—and, hopefully, an inundation of requests by enthusiasts to see Budd Boetticher's **Mavericks,** Robert Altman's **Alfred Hitchcock Presents,** Don Siegel's **Frontier** pilot, might generate a growing awareness that such works exist to be seen.

Among the many Laws which man has thought up to explain the world in which he lives, there are incontrovertible ones (like Boyle's, presumably) along with the fun ones (Parkinson's and Murphy's). The one we like best is Sturgeon's Law (coined by the brilliant science-fiction writer Theodore Sturgeon). As paraphrased by his young colleague, Harlan Ellison, the Law states: ' "94 Percent Of Everything Is Shit". Puddings, plays, poetry, parties, pistols, people. That is, ninety-four percent of everything is merely average. Merely sufficient. There is only six percent of grandeur in the universe anywhere!'

There is of course another truism, if not a Law: 'Nobody ever set out to make a bad movie' (or, by extension, TV show).

This book operates in the Twilight Zone between those two concepts.

Christopher Wicking and Tise Vahimagi
September 1978

List of Abbreviations

TV credits are somewhat confusing to set out, for of course there are *series* titles **(Maverick)** as well as titles of individual segments/episodes *(Shady Deal At Sunny Acres).* These are written with the year of production preceeding them (1957: **Maverick**/*Shady Deal at Sunny Acres).* If discussed in the text, minus the series titles, the segment will still be written *Shady Deal at Sunny Acres.* Telefilms, movies-of-the-week, any productions which are known solely under their own titles are written **The New Maverick.** Titles for feature films, as distinct from telefilms, read: THE MAGNIFICENT AMBERSONS.

dir.	directed by
wr.	written by
cr.	created by
st.	story by
aka.	also known as
pr.	produced by
exec. pr.	executive producer
assoc. pr.	associate producer
co-.	credit shared with other or others.
hyphenate	the combination of more than one function, eg. writer-director-producer.
miniseries	a multi-segment, but otherwise one-off/short term production, such as the **Best Seller** adaptations.
pilot	the original production upon which the series was based and sold to the TV network.
segment	an episode of a series.
multiples	segments in a series with which the individual person was known to have worked but whose titles have not been traced.
pt.	part, ie. in a 2 part segment of a series or as part of a miniseries.

Chronology of Television

1948

The demise of the big Hollywood studio empire begins with their defeat in *US v. Paramount et al.* **Texaco Star Theatre** is the bright star of the day, helping Milton Berle become 'Mr. Television'. **Kraft Television Theatre** is under way, and soon **Philco Playhouse** premieres (with *Dinner at Eight*) along with **Studio One** (signing-in with *The Storm*). These series open the gateway to what will emerge as the great '50s drama anthology boom. Westerns from the radio and movie ranges also make their first TV appearances, with the start of **The Lone Ranger, Hopalong Cassidy** and **Gene Autry.**

1949

The advent of the thriller anthology series, including **Suspense** and **Lights Out,** bring out the crime actioners: **The Big Story, Man Against Crime,** and **Martin Kane, Private Eye** (all of which are produced 'live') are the pioneers. DuMont network's **Captain Video,** pioneering the TV s-f hero, joins the juvenile adventure slot. **The Life of Riley,** featuring Jackie Gleason, marks the beginning of what will soon become a standard diet for TV—the situation-comedy.

1950

Comedy team of Jerry Lewis and Dean Martin strike oil on **Colgate Comedy Hour. The Sid Caesar-Imogene Coca Show,** now titled **Your Show of Shows** reaches new peak in TV popularity. More anthology series appear, in the form of **Lux Video Theatre** and **Robert Montgomery Presents,** to offer further opportunities for new writers and directors. Production of episodic action series continues, with **Danger, Ellery Queen, Big Town** and **I Cover Times Square.**

1951

I Love Lucy is filmed in a small Hollywood studio, and shortly becomes the most popular sit-com of the decade. **Goodyear Playhouse** and **Schlitz Playhouse** make their debut in the anthology series department. More episodic action is supplied by the series **Mr. District Attorney, Racket Squad** and **Foreign Assignment** (later to become **Foreign Intrigue**). **The Range Rider, The Cisco Kid** and **Flash Gordon** meanwhile aim at the younger market.

1952

Jack Webb launches **Dragnet** (on film), which he creates, produces, directs, and stars in. This unique series will become the foundation-stone for the many that will follow. Classic documentary **Victory at Sea** is telecast via NBC, with music supplied by Richard Rodgers. **Omnibus** opens the gates to 90-minute anthology drama. Other crime series appear with plots culled from the movies and radio, **Gangbusters, Boston Blackie** and **Dangerous Assignment,** but none have the staying power of **Dragnet.**

1953

Goodyear Television Playhouse and Delbert Mann score with Paddy Chayfesky's *Marty,* which Mann will direct again for the big-screen two years later. ZIV produces **I Led Three Lives,** a propaganda-based series conforming to current issues stirred up by Senator Joseph McCarthy. The first Directors' Guild of America Award for TV is presented to Robert Florey for *The Last Voyage,* a segment of **Four Star Playhouse** (which had premiered the year before). The **You Are There** series, a breeding ground for many talents, makes its debut. Western series, **Action in the Afternoon,** signs in its unusual base of production being Philadelphia. The **Adventures of Superman** series begins a five-year run, some of which will be filmed in colour. **U.S. Steel Hour, G.E. Theater, Hallmark Hall of Fame** and **Camera Three** join the ranks of the anthology series.

1954

ABC-TV gets Disney and Warner Brothers under contract for tele-production. Reginald Rose's play, *Twelve Angry Men,* strikes a successful chord on **Studio One. Producer's Showcase** premieres, with the Otto Preminger produced and directed *Three by Coward.* More shows turn from 'live' to film. **Climax** debuts with Raymond Chandler's *The Long Goodbye,* starring Dick Powell; this series begins 'live' but will eventually go to film. Roy Kellino receives the DGA Award for *The Answer,* telecast on **Four Star Playhouse.** Juvenile canine capers make their mark with **Lassie and Rin-Tin-Tin,** and prepare for a long stay. The highly-polished **Medic** series appears and receives critical acclaim for its tough approach to hospital drama. **Father Knows Best** settles in for a long run in the growing sit-com field.

1955

Gunsmoke debuts in late '55, launching the era of the 'adult western'. This series will remain strong in the viewer-ratings until it is made redundant by the network some twenty years later. **You'll Never Get Rich** appears, and Nat Hiken gets an Emmy; in 1959 the show will go into syndication as **Sgt. Bilko. Screen Directors' Playhouse** makes its debut, and one of the series highlights is John Ford's *Rookie of the Year.* **Alfred Hitchcock Presents** joins the popular ranks of **Matinée Theatre, Highway Patrol, Science Fiction Theatre** and Disney's **Davy Crockett.** Franklin Schaffner receives Emmy for Best Director of a 'live' show, **Ford Star Jubilee's** *Caine Mutiny Court Martial,* while Rod Serling and Gore Vidal receive acclaim for their *Patterns* **(Kraft Theatre)** and *Visit to a Small Planet* **(Philco-Goodyear** series), respectively. **Warner Brothers Presents** starts a series of rotating shows: **Casablanca, Cheyenne** and **King's Row.** Fox also start their **20th Century Fox Hour,** via **CBS,** and Metro their **MGM Parade,** via ABC.

1956

Cheyenne, emerging from the Warner Brothers' series, signals the massive rush into TV western production. **Playhouse 90** debuts; its second telecast episode being Serling's masterful *Requiem for a Heavyweight.* Hundreds of pre-1948 feature films are bought for Television. Although most every 'live' show has now turned to film, the George Roy Hill-directed *A Night to Remember* (for **Studio One)** goes out 'live' (using some 31 sets and 107 actors) and is amazingly *repeated* just 35 days later. **Dick Powell's Zane Grey Theatre** comes in for its six-year run.

1957

Robert Stevens picks up an Emmy for his *The Glass Eye* segment of **Alfred Hitchcock Presents.** Long-timers **Perry Mason, Wagon Train, Have Gun Will Travel, Maverick** and **M Squad** make their premiere. The latter show is a particularly hard-hitting police drama, anticipating the pattern of brutality to be laid down by Quinn Martin's **The Untouchables.** Disney's **Zorro** makes its mark on the small-screen as a well-produced children's show. A two-part **Studio One** episode, *The Defender* (starring Ralph Bellamy, William Shatner and Steve McQueen), is telecast—it will later become a milestone in TV drama, as **The Defenders** series.

1958

Naked City debuts, and scores with its original use of actual New York locations. *Little Moon of Alban* (on **Hallmark Hall of Fame**) and *The Days of Wine and Roses* (on **Playhouse 90**) notch up exceptional drama for anthology series. The former episode wins an Emmy for director George Schaefer. **Studio One** finally moves its base to Hollywood, and **Kraft Theatre** closes its final curtain. Richard L. Bare receives the DGA Award for his *All Our Yesterdays* segment of **77 Sunset Strip.** Charles Marquis Warren creates **Rawhide,** and launches it on its eight-year trail. *Eddie* (for **Alcoa Goodyear)** gets Jack Smight the Emmy for Best Director. Sam Peckinpah makes his mark on **Dick Powell's Zane Grey Theatre** and **The Rifleman.**

1959

Desilu Playhouse telecasts what will be a memorable two-part episode—*The Untouchables.* The episode wins the DGA Award of the Year for director Phil Karlson. Jack Webb produces a unique, but short-lived, series, **Pete Kelly's Blues.** Rod Serling creates **The Twilight Zone,** the first adult-market fantasy anthology series. **Bonanza** is launched, and will become the second longest running western on TV. Emmy awarded to Robert Mulligan for Best Director on *The Moon and Sixpence* **(Hallmark Hall of Fame). Playhouse 90** bows out.

1960

The Untouchables series stirs violence in action shows, while anti-violence groups stir into action. George Schaefer receives both DGA and Emmy awards for *Macbeth,* on **Hallmark Hall of Fame. The Flintstones** mark the first made-for-TV animation show. Peckinpah creates **The Westerner,** which he also produces, directs and writes.

1961

The Defenders, created by Reginald Rose, debuts. The series breaks new ground within the confines of a continuing format, often dealing with controversial issues. For Best Director on various **Defenders** episodes, Franklin Schaffner receives an Emmy. Notable for fine medical drama, **Ben Casey** and **Dr. Kildare** climb high in the ratings. **The Dick Van Dyke Show, Hazel** and **Mister Ed** lead the comedy field. **The Untouchables** is under close scrutiny from the Italian-American and anti-violence groups; *A Lion Walks among Us* (segment of **Bus Stop**) and western series **Whispering Smith** are spotlighted for excessive violence. The often impressive **Dick Powell Theatre** and Nat Hiken's **Car 54—Where Are You?** make their premiere. **General Electric Theatre,** after a nine-year run, comes to an end.

1962

The Beverly Hillbillies sweeps the sit-com prizes for CBS. **The Virginian** launches TV's first 90-minute western. Military-based shows become popular, and include **The Gallant Men, Combat, McHale's Navy** and **Ensign O'Toole.** *The Price of Tomatoes* episode of **Dick Powell Theatre** wins David Friedkin the DGA Award. **Sam Benedict** debuts as another hard-hitting drama series with a legal background. Stuart Rosenberg gains an Emmy for his direction on *The Madman* segment of **The Defenders.**

1963

A 45-minute legal drama series, **Arrest and Trial,** appears. **East Side/West**

Side depicts social workers in a series that also breaks new ground; some southern US stations refuse to telecast certain episodes because of prominent black rôles. Tom Gries receives an Emmy award for his *Who Do You Kill?* segment of **East Side/West Side.** Teachers are depicted in **Mr. Novak**—this series also has its controversial moments. Leslie Stevens's **The Outer Limits** takes control of TV-sets, and offers above-average s-f for almost two years. **The Fugitive,** creating a new concept in series drama, starts running. **Bob Hope Chrysler Theatre, Kraft Suspense Theatre,** and **The Richard Boone Show** sign-in. **Cheyenne, Have Gun-Will Travel** and **The Untouchables** sign-off.

1964

The Man From UNCLE premieres, and immediately amasses a cult-following. Universal's **See How They Run** premieres as the first made-for-TV movie, in the slot originally intended for Don Siegel's **The Killers** (which is re-routed directly to the big-screen). The DGA Award goes to Lamont Johnson for the **Profiles in Courage** pilot, *The Oscar Underwood Story.* The Emmy goes to Paul Bogart for *The 700 Year Old Gang* segment of **The Defenders.** Bizarre sit-coms gain popularity, with the advent of **The Munsters, The Addams Family, My Living Doll** and **Bewitched. Peyton Place** begins its marathon run, and will hold viewers for the next five years.

1965

Sit-coms get even more weird, and prolific, with **My Mother the Car, Hogan's Heroes, F Troop, I Dream of Jeannie** and Mel Brooks's **Get Smart. I Spy** debuts, and scores as a racial vanguard, featuring two heroes—one black and one white. **Bob Hope Chrysler Theatre** episode *The Game* wins Sydney Pollack an Emmy for Best Director. **Trials of O'Brien** premieres, and features a Peter Falk characterisation that will surface again some six years later, though in a different format.

1966

Star Trek on its 3-year 'mission', opens up a new realm of science-fiction—inside and outside the TV studios. Unlikely daytime Gothic soap-opera **Dark Shadows** appears, eventually clicks, and embarks on what will result in 1000 episodes. Spies and agents dominate the small-screen, featuring **Mission: Impossible, T.H.E. Cat, The Girl from UNCLE,** and (most popular of all) ABC's **Batman** series. **Family Affair** joins the sit-com gallery, and remains for many years. A kaleidoscopic comedy series, **The Monkees,** captures viewers with its unique TV style.

1967

The Smothers Brothers Comedy Hour enters to reach new levels of controversy for an unprepared CBS. **High Chaparral** makes its mark as a well-produced, intelligent western series. Quinn Martin's **The Invaders** begins, setting a new course of paranoia in the s-f genre. George Schaefer receives the DGA Award for *Do Not Go Gentle into that Good Night* and Paul Bogart wins an Emmy for *Dear Friends,* both episodes of **CBS Playhouse. The Fugitive** finally stops running. Jack Webb revives **Dragnet** after an eight year hiatus.

1968

Rowan and Martin's **Laugh-in** scores high in the ratings with its imaginative approach to comedy. **Julia** scores as the first sit-com to feature a black heroine. The debut of the 90-minute **Name of the Game** series (along with **The Virginian**) produces the most expensively-made, per episode, series on TV. David Greene awarded Emmy as Best Director for *The People Next Door,* telecast on **CBS Playhouse.** The trend moves toward police shows, and **Hawaii Five-O, The Mod Squad** and Jack Webb's **Adam-12** settle down for a long stay. **I Spy** terminates.

1969

Medical shows continue to spark prime-time interest, with **Marcus Welby MD** and **Medical Center. The Bold Ones** and **Room 222** supply the drama—the former is an umbrella title for 4 rotating series, a format gaining popularity. Paul Bogart collects an Emmy for his *Shadow Game* episode of **CBS Playhouse.** Harold Robbins's **The Survivors** pre-dates the star-cast miniseries trend that will rise to success some six years later. **Smothers Brothers Comedy Hour** gets too hot to telecast and CBS are forced to cancel the series. A Universal pilot/tele-feature, **Night Gallery,** offers a compendium of weird tales directed by three notable talents, including the remarkable Steven Spielberg.

1970

The Mary Tyler Moore Show makes its debut; the MTM anvil will later strike several spin-off series. **The Immortal** and **Night Gallery** supply the fantastic on an original level, the latter series unfolding from Universal's rotating **Four-In-One** series. The **McCloud** series also starts from the **Four-In-One** stable. An Emmy for Best Director is awarded to Daryl Duke for *The Day the Lion Died* segment of **The Bold Ones: The Senator.**

1971

All in the Family begins, breaks several TV taboos, and scores high in the ratings; it also marks the movement toward script-purchase of successful British sit-coms. **Brian's Song** scores high marks and **The Night Stalker** racks up the greatest-ever viewer attendance in the tele-feature category. Also cast from the same mould, Spielberg's **Duel** goes on to achieve greater glory as a 'theatrical' feature. **Columbo, Longstreet** and **Cannon** usher in a fashion for off-beat detectives. The innovative **Alias Smith and Jones** series rides in. The long-running **Green Acres** moves out.

1972

The Hands of Cormac Joyce marks **Hallmark Hall of Fame's** 100th production for TV. **Mystery Movie** continues the rotating series trend with 90-minute segments of **Banacek** and **MacMillan and Wife.** With inspiration from the feature-movie, **M*A*S*H** becomes a highly popular, fast-paced comedy series. Warner Brothers open new territory with their **Kung Fu** series, releasing the flood-gates to scores of imitators. **The Waltons** rake the ratings with a new slant on family soap-opera.

1973

Six Million Dollar Man series begins, sweeping in a trend for semi-human heroes; the viewer-ratings happily endorse the movement. **Kojak** is the other big hit of the season, creating a hero with several dimensions of emotion in a series concept that towers above contemporaries. Jerry Thorpe receives Emmy for **Kung Fu** segment *An Eye for an Eye.* The exceptionally-polished **Police Story** debuts, offering greater scope for police drama via an anthology format. The new **Shaft** series features a black hero made popular on the big-screen. Emmy awarded to Robert Butler for Best Director on **The Blue Knight–Part III. Bonanza** sees its final episode.

1974

Police Woman spins off from **Police Story,** and goes on to achieve equal success as own series. Spin-offs from theatrical features gain momentum; **Paper Moon, Madigan** and **Planet of the Apes** reign as small-screen examples. Jack Smight's **Frankenstein: The True Story** tele-feature ranks as one of the most ambitious and well-produced films in the genre.

1975

The success of **Rich Man, Poor Man** begins the era of the miniseries. **Baretta,**

The Rockford Files, Ellery Queen and **Starsky and Hutch** all succeed in the popularity and quality departments. Full scale movement of the police actioner is in progress; it will later burn itself out on two counts: over-production and excess violence. **Happy Days** enters the sit-com field to rise as top network comedy show. **Gunsmoke** dies after 20 years on TV, a victim of policy rather than preference. Rod Serling dies, after a 25-year career as one of Television's most inventive and prolific writers.

1976

Bionic Woman premieres to partner **Six Million Dollar Man** at the top of the success scale. Furthering the popularity of miniseries, NBC launch the **Best Sellers** series. **Charlie's Angels** appears and introduces a lightweight drama series with more cheesecake than drama. Immediate popularity, however, secures the future of **Charlie's Angels** on network TV. Tele-feature **21 Hours at Munich** cements the turn toward dramatic re-enactment of contemporary world events. NBC-TV telecasts Hollywood classic GONE WITH THE WIND over two consecutive evenings.

1977

ABC-TV network hits ceiling by telecasting 12 hours of **Roots** over an unprecedented 8 consecutive evenings. Both miniseries **Roots** and former network underdog ABC receive wide acclaim. **How the West Was Won,** as series of 2-hour specials, makes a strong attempt at reviving the TV western. Following heavy 'watchdog' pressure, networks demand cut-down of violent shows resulting in cut-down of ratings all around. The majority of TV production is aimed for the 'prime-time' family audience—with severe losses on all sides. The very last episode of **The Mary Tyler Moore** show goes out.

1978

Universal/MCA pour exceptionally large sums into preparation of future TV-film production, aiming primarily at tele-features and miniseries. Following a seventeen-year hibernation, John Newland revives psychic phenomena series **One Step Beyond,** retitling it **The Next Step Beyond.** Once-popular **Six Million Dollar Man** series winds down as final segment goes out. Actioner **Kojak** leaves his mean streets after commanding a five-year following. Both shows, however, qualify themselves for a new lease of life via re-runs in syndication, due to each logging up over 5 years of episodes.

THE AMERICAN VEIN

Kings of the Stardust Ballroom

These directors are the aristocrats of American TV. While many have flirted with movies, deserted the movies, may in time leave for the movies, the small screen has been a successful and artistically valid creative framework, and their names on the titles are a virtual guarantee of quality. While, in this first attempt to shine a light on them, only a fraction of their output has been studied, the evidence is that closer scrutiny will yield rich deposits of excellence.

Edward Abroms

1971: **Columbo**/*Short Fuse.* 1972: **Night Gallery**/*Something In the Woodwork;* **Alias Smith and Jones**/*The Ten Days that Shook Kid Curry;* **MacMillan and Wife**/*The Fine Art of Staying Alive;* **Columbo**/*The Most Dangerous Match;* **Griff**/*All the Lonely People, Don't Call Us, We'll Call You.* 1974:**Get Christie Love**/*Death on Delivery;* **Police Story**/*The Witness.* 1975:**Cannon**/*Search & Destroy;* **Switch**/*Before the Holocaust;* **Doc Elliot**/*The Runner;* **Doctor's Hospital**/*Vital Signs, Watchman Who Will Guard Thy Sleep?, Swandive, But Who Will Bless Thy Daughter Norah?* 1976: **Ellery Queen**/*Adventure of the Half Hearted Huckster;* **Feather and Father Gang**/*Flight to Mexico;* **Kojak**/*Law Dance;* **Six Million Dollar Man**/*The Fires of Hell.* 1977: **Switch**/*Switch Hitter;* **Kojak**/*Lady in the Squad Room, Caper on a Quiet Street;* **Six Million Dollar Man**/*Target Steve Austin.* 1978: **Kojak**/*The Halls of Terror.*

Abroms illustrates the way TV can function positively in terms of generating and encouraging talent in much the same way that the motion picture studio system did. Like Robert Wise, Mark Robson, Phil Karlson etc, Abroms was an editor (**Berlin Affair, Ransom for a Dead Man, One of Our Own, Kojak** segments) before being given the opportunity to direct. He has worked exclusively within the series arena. *Search and Destroy* is a slightly unusual **Cannon** segment in that it is almost watchable, rough around the edges, eschewing the wholly conventional set ups that even people like William Hale, who should know better, seem content to tolerate. *Lady in the Squad Room* and *Caper on a Quiet Street* are of a far higher standard, but then so too is the whole **Kojak** series.

The Witness segment of **Police Story** suggests that Abroms's work should be searched for with anticipation. It is marvellously written (by Ken Pettus), and is a bleak and uncompromising piece of work which emanates from an anthology. It is far tougher, and less circumscribed than segments featuring recurring characters. Prowl car cops Don Meredith and new partner Robert Lee Jarvis get wind of the imminent entry to town of some Eastern mobster to take over the rackets. But who is he? Not even his name is known—and those informants who might know won't tell, so fearful are they of reprisals. The investigation becomes obsessive for Meredith, though it is virtually a sub-plot to the more urgent cases on the desk. Slowly facts materialise—a name is known—but so powerful is the man, that he doesn't even have a record in the vehicle registration department until, in a wholly surprising climax, Meredith is killed. Mr Big who is never seen, will, we are sure, never be apprehended.

Around this central narrative is woven the 'education' of Jarvis the new partner who is surprised and shocked by the way Meredith treats the rule book. He'll let small time drug pedlars continue to operate in return for information. He has the kind of intimate cameraderie with those on the other side of the law which is, in truth, the only way some cases ever get solved. Most of his phone calls are from informants and, charmingly, his wife knows them all and chats on about their vacations, family problems, etc. truly sharing in the life. She is altogether another kind of partner. Thus Meredith is presented as a dedicated cop, but also as a rounded human being. His death is shocking, for his whole life has been a fool's errand. If, ultimately, the top echelon of criminals is beyond the law, what hope is there for a policeman?

The gradual chipping away at the edifice of secrecy and fear surrounding 'Mr. Big' is effectively suspensful, while the education of the new partner is resolved by bringing the narrative full circle. With Meredith dead, Jarvis effectively picks up his mantle; he has inherited his spirit and is seen desperately plea-bargaining with a drug pusher for information which will lead him further. He is fully street-wise by now, but also conscious of the battle lines of the war in which he has now fully joined.

Reza Badiyi

1968: **Get Smart**/*Ice Station Siegfried;* **The Good Guys**/*They Eat by Night, The Courtship of Miles Butterworth.* 1969:**Mission Impossible**/*The Visitors, Blind, Hit;* **Hawaii Five-O**/*Savage Sunday.* 1970:**Mission Impossible**/*The Field, The Ghost Story, Casino, Lovers' Knot, Homecoming.* 1972:**The Eyes of Charles Sand**; **Banyon**/*The Murder Game.* 1973:**Faraday & Co**/*A Matter of Magic;* **N.Y.P.D.**/*'L' is for Love and Larceny;* **Six Million Dollar Man**/*Operation Firefly.* 1974: **Six Million Dollar Man**/*Little Orphan Airplane, The Coward, The Last of the Fourth of Julys.* 1975: **Joe Forrester**/*Firepower.* 1976: **Serpico**/*The Country Boy, The Serbian Connection;* **Holmes and Yoyo**/*Yoyo takes a Bride, The Cat Burglar;* **The Rockford Files**/*The Becker Connection, Crack Back;* **Baretta**/*Crazy Annie, Open Season, Who Killed Cock Robin?, Por Nada.* 1977:**Man from Atlantis**/*The Killer Spores;* **Baretta**/*Just for Laughs;* **The Rockford Files**/*The Dwarf in the Helium Hat, The Dog and Pony Show, The Second Chance;* **Switch**/*Net Loss;* **Hawaii Five-O**/*Tread the King's Shadow.*

Early comedy credits suggest that Badiyi's roots are within the sit-com syndrome, and there are those who would say the connection continues into **Six Million Dollar Man** and **Fantastic Journey.** Certainly **Rockford Files** has the attractively wry humour of Garner/Huggins/Cannell, and Badiyi has directed five segments.

Yet from what we've seen, Badiyi's work here *uses* comedy, but doesn't purvey it, and *The Becker Connection* and *Crack Back* virtually play down the usual humour to the point of non-existence, so that what wisecracks there are come out with more despair than gaiety.

In *The Becker Connection,* a standup comic is playing to an utterly heartless house and when series regular Stuart Margolin leaps on the stage afterwards (it's supposed to be a talent show), he proceeds to mindlessly do the act he last performed at a prison concert, recounting a string of witless jokes about warders and prison conditions which have no application, point or humour to the current audience, all of which is funny, but chillingly so. The overall mood of this segment is sour, and *Crack Back* becomes even darker in tone, as well as in appearance.

The heavy breathing phone calls and postal pornography bring it close to the world of Raymond Chandler. Overall, both segments indicate far more of a controlling directorial influence than is usual in the series. Having yet to come across the marvellously-titled *Dwarf in the Helium Hat* and Badiyi's other, later segments, it is impossible to know for sure whether the differences are indeed those of influence and personal vision, or merely part of an overall change of format.

Elsewhere, *Killer Spores, Savage Sunday, Firepower* and *The Serbian Connection* have shown that Badiyi can get close to series characters in a human and affecting manner, and has an eye that can divest an action sequence of cliché and substitute telling detail instead.

Whilst it is obviously too early to be certain, Badiyi has revealed enough that is fresh and distinctive to make us confident that a worthwhile body of work is being established.

Paul Bogart (1919-   )

1961: **The Defenders/***The Prowler.* 1962: **The Defenders/***The Collosus, Everybody Else Is Dead, A Man against Himself, The Seven Ghosts of Simon Gray.* 1963:**The Defenders/***Claire Cheval Died in Boston, Old Lady Ironsides, The Secret, Moment of Truth, Yankee Come Home.* 1964: **The Defenders/***The Non-Violent, Death on Wheels, King of the Hill, The 700 Year Old Gang, A Voice Loud and Clear.* 1965:**The Defenders/***Impeachment, The Prosecutor, Turning Point;* **Coronet Blue/***A Time to be Born;* **The Trials of O'Brien/***Dead End on Flugel Street, Leave it to Me;* **Get Smart/***Now You See Him, Now You Don't.* 1966:**Bob Hope Chrysler Theatre: Enigma/***Storm Crossing;* **Hawk/**(+ series pr.), *The Theory of the Innocent Bystander;* **Ages of Man; Mark Twain Tonight.** 1967:**CBS Playhouse/***Dear Friends,* **The Final War of Ollie Winter.** 1968:**Secrets; The House without a Christmas Tree.** 1969:**CBS Playhouse/***Shadow Game;* **Look Homeward Angel;The Country Girl.** 1970:**In Search of America; Double Solitaire.** 1971: **The Thanksgiving Treasure; Nichols/***The Siege, Paper Badge.* 1974:**Tell Me Where it Hurts; The Adams Chronicles.** 1975:**Winner Take All.** 1976:**Alice** (pilot).

While MARLOWE and CLASS OF 44 left cineastes feeling disappointed, THE SKIN GAME, a masterly treatment of the Peter Stone script (analysed by Richard Corliss in his book *Talking Pictures*) is one of the finest American movies of the '70s, coming close to both Ben Jonson's *The Alchemist* and Preston Sturges's 'humours' of the '40s. Bogart's identification with this film clearly demands that due attention is paid to his other work, which is, inconveniently, mainly TV.

From **The Defenders** (and, in all likelihood, other Herbert Brodkin series of the early '60s) to telefeatures such as **Winner Take All** (with Shirley Jones as a housewife with a compulsive gambling problem) Bogart has continuously been in the vanguard of TV quality, taking over from the Schaffners, Pollacks and Roy Hills those assignments which most resemble 'Art' on TV. Biographical information about Bogart is at a premium, but it is highly likely that his career began much earlier and that he therefore played a role in the heady days of live TV.

The quality of such work as *Dear Friends* and *Shadow Game* (each won him an Emmy) paved the way for the 'movie of the week' syndrome and, ultimately, the miniseries. Any in-depth investigation of the last two decades of American TV must pay attention to Bogart's contributions. They will unquestionably reveal other achievements to rank with THE SKIN GAME. Indeed, his work on **Nichols** may have got him the job.

Robert Butler

1961: **Have Gun Will Travel**/*El Paso Stage;* **Detectives**/*Personal Enemy.* 1962: **Untouchables**/*Elegy* 1963:**Defenders**/*Bagman.* 1964: **The Fugitive**/*Man in a Chariot;* **Arrest and Trial**/*Birds of a Feather.* 1965: **Mister Roberts**/*Physician, Heal Thyself, Which Way did the War Go?* (3 pts.), *Getting There is Half the Fun, Don't Look Now but Isn't That the War?;* **Hogan's Heroes**/*The Informer, Hold that Tiger, Kommandant of the Year, The Late Inspector General, Happy Birthday Adolf;* **Defenders**/*A Matter of Law and Disorder;* **Fugitive**/*Last Second of a Bad Dream;* **I Spy**/*Sophia, It's All Done with Mirrors;* **Star Trek**/*The Cage* (1st pilot). 1966: **Star Trek**/*Menagerie* (co-dir); **Batman**/*Hi Diddle Riddle, Fine Feathered Finks, Instant Freeze, The Ring of Wax;* **Fugitive**/*Strokes of Genius;* **Virginian**/*Day of the Scorpion.* 1967: **Cimarron Strip**/*Without Honor, The Judgement;* **Felony Squad**/*Live Coward Dead Hero;* **Gunsmoke**/*Prairie Wolfer.* 1968: **Gunsmoke**/*Manson;* **Mission Impossible**/*The Mind of Stefan Miklos;* **Lancer**/*Death Bait, Lifeline, Shadow of a Dead Man.* 1971: **Death Takes a Holiday; Nichols**/*Bertha.* 1972: **Columbo**/*Double Shock;* **Hawaii Five-O**/*Percentage;* **Gunsmoke**/*The Sodbusters;* **Kung Fu**/*The Ancient Warrior, The Stone, Chains, Sun and Cloud Shadow.* 1973: **Columbo**/*Publish or Perish;* **The Blue Knight** (3rd pilot). 1975: **Strange New World.** 1976: **James Dean; Mayday at 40,000 Feet.** 1977: **In the Glitter Palace.** 1978: **Lacy and the Mississippi Queen.**

There seem to be two Robert Butlers—one who can win the 1973 Emmy for **The Blue Knight** and bring a tough, angular style to cop shows and westerns—the other who has fun cavorting with **Hogan's Heroes, Mister Roberts** and **Batman** and who has hit the big screen with four Disney features (GUNS IN THE HEATHER, THE BAREFOOT EXECUTIVE, THE COMPUTER WORE TENNIS SHOES and

NOW YOU SEE HIM, NOW YOU DON'T). His **Gunsmokes, Fugitives** and **Kung Fus** are among the best of his series work, but he has never hung around any show for long.

The Emmy has helped him earn more interesting, one-off telefeatures such as **In the Glitter Palace,** a much-praised murder thriller which becomes a sympathetic investigation into lesbianism; **James Dean,** a memory of the actor's years in New York written by his friend and fellow-student, William Bast (played by Michael Brandon, with Stephen McHattie as Dean); **Lacy and the Mississippi Queen,** Disneyesque, but mature; all show the empathy Butler has developed with his actors and his evocative visual sense.

There is one piece of amazing trivia for those who relish such things. In 1966, Butler directed *The Cage,* as a pilot for **Star Trek.** It failed to sell; a second pilot followed successfully. *The Cage* was used as the basis for the two-part segment titled *Menagerie,* Marc Daniels directing the new footage.

In 1974, Daniels directed **Planet Earth,** another Gene Roddenberry pilot project which failed to sell. So in 1975, Butler clocked in to use Daniels's footage in the second pilot **Strange New World.**

Marvin Chomsky

1967: **Wild Wild West**/*Night of the Iron Fist, Night of the Vipers, Night of the Undead;* **Gunsmoke**/*9:12 to Dodge, Railroad.* 1968: **Star Trek**/*And the Children Shall Lead, Day of the Dove, All Our Yesterdays.* 1969: **Hawaii Five-O**/*Three Dead Cows at Makapu* (2 pts); **Gunsmoke**/*The Innocent;* **Then Came Bronson** (multiples). 1970: **The Name of the Game**/*So Long Baby and Amen, A Capitol Affair, Beware of the Watchdog;* **Assault on the Wayne. World of Disney**/*The Wacky Zoo of Morgan City.* 1971: **Mrs. Sundance; Mongo's Back in Town. Banyon**/*Just Once, Think of Me Kindly.* 1972: **Cade's County**/*Slayride* (pilot), *Jessie;* **The Bold Ones: The Doctors**/*A Purge of Madness;* **Hawaii Five-O**/*Pig in a Blanket;* **Family Flight; Fireball Forward.** 1973: **Female Artillery; The Magician** (pilot). 1974: **The FBI Story**/*The FBI vs Alvin Karpis Public Enemy No. 1.* 1975: **Brinks—the Great Robbery; The FBI Story**/*Attack on Terror—The FBI vs. the Ku Klux Klan;* **Kate McShane**/(pilot); **A Matter of Wife and Death.** 1976: **Law and Order; Little Ladies of the Night; Roots** (pts 3, 4, 6). 1977: **Big Hawaii (Danger in Paradise)**/(pilot); **Holocaust.**

Helmsman of the engaging and undervalued EVEL KNIEVEL, Chomsky's TV work is both proficient (the weird niceties of **Wild Wild West,** through the best of the last season's **Star Treks**) and hit or miss (the unspeakable boredom of **Brinks** and the uneasy encounter with watered-down Scorsese, **Little Ladies of the Night).**

His undeniable energy, an apparent predilection for female-oriented subjects and, when the material complements it, a streak of the bizarre, all suggest a non-conformist fretting under the strains of the system yet not entirely able to sever the shackles.

However his work on **Roots** and now the controversial **Holocaust** have elevated him to the top of the tree. His shows have always been ones to watch, in the hope that they hit more often than they miss. There can be no excuse for Chomsky not exercising desire and klaut in choosing, or instigating, the best possible subjects—and with such freedom we would expect many hits.

Robert Collins

1969: **Marcus Welby M.D.** (wr)/*The Homecoming, The Soft Phrase of Peace, The Foal* (co wr), *Fun and Games and Michael Ambrose* (co wr). 1970: **Marcus Welby M.D.**/*The Home of Alquiet* (dir only), *Another Buckle for Wesley Hill* (wr/dir). 1971: **Marcus Welby M.D.**/*A Taste of Salt* (wr/dir); **Dan August** (wr)/*The Meal Ticket.* 1972: **The Bold Ones: The Doctors** (wr)/*A Standard for Manhood, A Nation of Human Pincushions.* 1974: **Police Story**/*The Wyatt Earp Syndrome* (wr dir); **Police Woman**/*(multiples–cr-wr/dir).* 1975: **Medical Story**/*Quality of Mercy* (wr/dir). 1976: **Serpico**/*The Deadly Game* (pilot–wr dir). 1977: **The Life and Assassination of the Kingfish.**

Keeping alive the tradition of successfully graduating from the writer's cubicle to the director's chair, Robert Collins forceably demonstrates how much more unique and personal is the 'vision' of the writer/director hyphenate—certainly in TV where the dictum is it is cheaper to 'Get it right in the typewriter'. Having already conceived the style, the feel, the attitude, the point of view, from an intimate position before going onto the floor to shoot, the subsequent transition from the page to the screen is obviously made smoother and more unified when the same man puts down the pen and picks up the megaphone.

Naturally, another kind of talent is necessary. Many writers don't have it; nor do they have the ability to view their own pages objectively, to compromise and work within the pressure cooker in which a director lives. Collins's work brilliantly advocates the trend's advancement.

The Wyatt Earp Syndrome shows cop Harry Guardino's obsession with his work and the almost pathological dedication and idealism which motivates it. He is seen to be as 'positively' psychotic as any 'negatively' psychotic criminal. He knows he can't strike a natural balance, knows he needs help. Nobody, least of all his wife (Kim Darby), can give him this, for the only real 'help' would, by extension, be the eradication of crime and then there would be no further need for cops. He is trapped in his condition. The irony is that he is an excellent officer. The bleak conclusion is the inevitability of the marriage breaking. Guardino, therefore, becomes even more enmeshed in his personally 'unhealthy' yet socially invaluable state.

The Deadly Game, the **Serpico** pilot, was far less interesting on a story level, yet conversely, something of a narrative breakthrough, as well as showing

Collins firmly in touch with developments on the big screen (and with the klaut to get away with it on the small screen) for there were more interesting diversions in these 90 minutes than in some entire series.

As the movie SERPICO had originally told the important part of this real life officer's story, Dino di Laurentiis's ripoff of his own feature property rather desperately had to 'flashback' to the events leading up to those already depicted in the book and the movie. While this was OK for Collins, those who followed up with the series segments were incredibly constrained by the holier-than-thou persona evinced by David Birney in the title role (a persona given an unfortunately Christ-like dimension by Birney's beard and St Bernard eyes). It was not surprising that the series abruptly folded.

Collins makes us look behind the veneer of 'realism' to the primal qualities associated with drama throughout the ages ('good' vs. 'evil') and about which we feel morally confused. Where Siegel, in DIRTY HARRY used these confusions to brilliant effect (and Eastwood has continued to explore them), Collins seems to be attempting to *ease* the confusion, by very gently reminding us that 'good' *is* better—though it has its price. Where Serpico/Birney became insufferable in the hands of other directors, in Collins's work he became genuinely moving. With lots of FRENCH CONNECTION-type waiting around and inaction, there are marvellous scenes with Bert Young (a minor villain, but the only character to whom Serpico can relate). Posing as a 'connection', Serpico uses the inertia to examine himself. There is location shooting in a misty New York dockscape, and unintelligible dialogue scenes shot on the end of long lenses. *The Deadly Game* seems like a stylistic experiment on the one hand, and an unusually radical exploration of a state of being. The close affinities with *The Wyatt Earp Syndrome* reveal Collins's coherent personality.

The Quality of Mercy segment of **Medical Story** falls chronologically between the other two shows, and is both more conventional and more powerful, revealing the depth of Collins's talent. The opening eight minutes is a remarkable sequence, shot entirely from a subjective point of view. A man suffers a heart attack at home and is given immediate aid by ambulance men. He is taken to hospital, admitted, taken to the operating theatre, and seemingly pounding heart-beats become a funeral throb and change to staccato bongos. The wavering focus is cliché but because there are no cuts to other angles the artist's single-minded obsession is indicated. The segment becomes a model of crusading American drama, the 'ripped from today's headlines' school being at heart, a cry of rage about the state of public medicine, the strain on hospital staff, the cruelty to the patients and the gap separating this level from the capitalist luxury of private medicine. The detached, almost meditative rhythms of **Serpico** here give way to pulsating crescendos.

Life and Assassination of the Kingfish indicates that the ambiguity of *The Wyatt Earp Syndrome* has returned, for this is a version of the life of Huey Long, which has itself already inspired ALL THE KING'S MEN and A LION IN THE STREETS. More please!

Fielder Cook (1923-)

1955: **Kraft Television Theatre** (series asst. pr.) *Patterns.* 1955/1957: **Alcoa-Goodyear Hour; Kaiser Aluminum Hour; Studio One; Theatre Guild on the Air (US Steel Hour); Playhouse 90; Dupont Show of the Week; The Director's Company**/(all multiples). 1959: **Rendezvous**/*In an Early Winter.* 1961: **Ben Casey**/pilot, *To the Pure, An Expensive Glass of Water, The Sound of Laughter, My Good Friend Krikor, A Few Brief Lines for Dave, Pavanne for a Gentle Lady.* 1962: **Ben Casey**/*And If I Die, A Certain Time, A Certain Time a Certain Darkness, The Sweet Kiss of Madness;* **The Fifty Minute Hour; Focus; Going My Way** (pilot). **The Defenders**/*The Bedside Murder.* 1963: **The Eleventh Hour**/(pilot); **Espionage**/*A Camel to Ride;* **Television Playhouse** [GB]/*To Bury Caesar* co. dir. + pr.). 1965: **Mr. Roberts**/*Bookster's Honeymoon* (pilot). 1966: **Brigadoon.** 1969: **Hallmark Hall of Fame**/*Teacher, Teacher;* **Mirror Mirror off the Wall.** 1970: **The Price.** 1971: **World Premiere**/*Sam Hill: Who Killed the Mysterious Mr. Foster?;* **The Homecoming; Goodbye Raggedy Ann.** 1972: **The Waltons**/(pilot). 1973: **From the Mixed up Files of Mrs. Basil E. Frankweiler.** 1974: **Miles to Go Before I Sleep.** 1975: **World Premiere**/*This is the West That Was.* 1976: **Hallmark Hall of Fame**/*Beauty and the Beast;* **Judge Horton and the Scottsboro Boys.**

For over a quarter of a century, Cook has been in the first flight of TV talent, but in any true critical sense is known only for PATTERNS (aka PATTERNS OF POWER), the theatrical adaptation of a play he first directed for TV, and BIG HAND FOR THE LITTLE LADY (aka BIG DEAL IN DODGE CITY), which—while generally delighting purists—was criticised for betraying TV origins. The George C. Scott **Beauty and the Beast,** which surfaces on occasions as a theatrical feature, was also made for TV. These three pieces are all that is generally available of Cook's work for study.

He has a marvellous way with actors, and may prove to be a kindred spirit to George Cukor in consistently arraying 'civilised entertainments' before us. Projects such as *Sam Hill: Who Killed the Mysterious Mr. Foster?* (a comedy-western with Ernest Borgnine as an apparently goofy lawman, and Bruce Dern as the bad guy) and *This is the West That Was* (with Ben Murphy as Wild Bill Hickok and Kim Darby as Calamity Jane, who 'invents' Hickok's romantic and heroic deeds) indicate that the flavour—and witty deceptions—of BIG HAND FOR A LITTLE LADY are some kind of trademark. **Goodbye Raggedy Ann** (with Mia Farrow and Martin Sheen, about a prospective suicide in the Hollywood dream community) and **Judge Horton and the Scottsboro Boys** (a dramatisation of a notorious historical case of bigotry) keep Cook alive in the PATTERNS vein—turning over the stones of American institutions.

A strong streak of American 'emotionalism' also runs through Cook's work. He made **The Waltons** pilot, and had an extensive stint on **Ben Casey** (including, again, the pilot). The latter indicates that the style for that legendary medical series (with Vince Edwards in the title role and Sam Jaffe as the immortal 'Dr. Zorba'), which helped launch such careers as Sydney Pollack's, owes a great deal to Cook.

Here, therefore, is a career every bit as significant as that of Frankenheimer or Lumet—Cook's only mistake would seem to have been to *stay* in the medium and he seems one of the most important figures for study right now.

Robert Day (1922-   )

[GB] 1955: **Rendezvous/***The Big Miracle, Next Time You'll See Venice.* 1956: **Adventures of Robin Hood/***Too Many Robins, The Youthful Menace, The Quickness of the Hand, Pepper, Too Many Earls;* **The Buccaneers/***The Hand of the Hawk, Dead Man's Rock, Ghost Ship, Conquest of New Providence.* 1957: **Adventures of Robin Hood/***The Fire, The Mark, To be a Student, The Rivals, The Road in the Air;* **OSS** (untitled segments); **The Buccaneers/***Blood Will Tell, Conquistador, Cutlass Wedding, The Spy Abroad;* **The Highwayman/***The Chimneysweep.* 1958: **Adventures of Robin Hood/***Goodbye Little John, Brother Battle.* 1964: **Danger Man/***Fish on the Hook.* 1965: **The Avengers/***From Venus with Love, Never Never Say Die, Return of the Cybernauts, The £50,000 Breakfast, The Positive-Negative Man, Mission-Highly Improbable.* 1966: **Human Jungle/***The 24 Hour Man.* [US] 1968: **The Invaders/***The Peacemaker, The Miracle;* **Wonderful World of Disney/***The Secret of the Pond* (2 pts). 1969: **Ironside/***Good Will Tour;* **Lancer/***Cut the Wolf Loose, Welcome to Genesis.* 1970: **Ritual of Evil; The Bold Ones: The Senator/***A Continual Roar of Musketry;* **The Name of the Game/***The Battle at Gannon's Bridge;* **The House on Greenapple Road; Paris 7000/***Elegy for Edward Shelby.* 1971: **Banyon/**(pilot); **Mr. and Mrs. Bo Bo Jones; In Broad Daylight; The Name of the Game/***Seek and Destroy;* **Twin Detectives.** 1972: **The Sixth Sense/***The eyes That Wouldn't Die, The Shadow in the Well, With This Ring, I Thee Kill;* **Ghost Story/***Touch of Madness, Time of Terror;* **The Reluctant Heroes.** 1973: **The Great American Beauty Contest; Tenafly/***Joyride to Nowhere;* **Of Men and Women/***The Interview;* **Barnaby Jones/***A Little Glory, A Little Death;* **McCloud/***The Colorado Cattle Caper.* 1974: **Sunshine/***Jill.* 1975: **Switch/**pilot; **Kojak/***A House of Prayer a Den of Thieves;* **Death Stalk; The Trial of Chaplain Jensen.** 1976: **Kingston The Power Play; Having Babies.** 1977: **Logan's Run/**(pilot). 1978: **Dallas/***Digger's Daughter, Bar-B-Q.*

Day was a victim of the dreary British feature scene of the mid-60s, which was totally unable to accommodate tough and gutsy, already American-oriented directors. His Tarzan movies helped redefine the mythic Ape Man for the then-contemporary scene and are fine genre movies—to this day still unappreciated by critics only too willing to revere lesser but more fashionable American works.

Day had already been supplementing his career with **Danger Mans** (admittedly the most successful of all British mid-Atlantic series hybrids) **Human Jungles** etc. It was only sensible for him to ply his trade where this kind of TV drama originated.

Day surfaced on the other side of the Atlantic with **Ironsides** and **Lancers**—but was simultaneously lost from view of British eyes. Few of his shows have crossed back across the water. *A House of Prayer a Den of Thieves* (with Eileen Brennan, Lonny Chapman, Jeff Corey and Vincent Guardenia—a far cry from Dawn Addams, Terence Longden, Peter Bowles and Martin Miller, for instance—the cast of the British *Fish on the Hook*) is simply **Kojak**—high enough praise— but the most recent of Day's projects to appear, the **Logan's Run** pilot, is merely a lazy exercise, already tramelled by format problems that beset the series and a lack of conceptual vigour which were instrumental in sinking it after a period of treading water.

Worth checking out are **Reluctant Heroes** (curiously, the title of a smash British stage comedy of the early 1950s) a much more successful **MASH** ripoff; **Banyon,** a 1930s private-eye pastiche in similar serio-comic mood; **House on Greenapple Road**—Janet Leigh and Julie Harris in a flashback-oriented murder thriller; **Ritual of Evil,** an unduly restrained occult story with Louis Jourdan and Anne Baxter; **Death Stalk**—DELIVERANCE with women, escaped cons seizing the wives of the couples vacationing on the rapids, which happily revives echoes of TARZAN THE MAGNIFICENT, a similarly venal pursuit adventure.

There is also a preponderance of 'domestic' style themes (**Great American Beauty Contest, Mr. and Mrs. Bo Bo Jones, Having Babies**) which suggest an eye for 'America' and a fascination with its institutions. At first sight, they appear to be out of character, but, in fact, they are a step closer to reality via human comedy—a characteristic which ran through Day's British feature work.

His career is too disparate and 'convenient' to suggest that Day is always or even, often, engaged on a personal level. When he is, however, sparks certainly fly.

Daryl Duke

1966: **Wojeck**/*Thy Mother a Lady Lovely and Bright, Chocolate Fudge with Walnuts.* 1970: **The Bold Ones: The Senator**/*The Day the Lion Died, George Washington Told a Lie, To Taste of Death but Once;* **The Doctors**/*Giants Never Kneel;* **The Prosecutors**/*If I Should Wake before I Die, Memo from the Class of '76;* **Four-in-One: Night Gallery**/*The Last Laurel;* **The Psychiatrist**/*Such Civil War in my Love and Hate.* 1972: **Ghost Story**/*House of Evil, Doorway to Death;* **Banacek**/*No Sign of the Cross;* **The Bold Ones: The Doctors**/*A Standard for Manhood, Time Bomb in the Chest.* 1973: **The President's Plane is Missing.** 1974: **Cry for Help; Harry O**/*Reasons to Kill (2 pts);* **If I Had a Million.** 1975: **They Only Come out at Night.** 1976: **Griffin and Phoenix: A Love Story.**

Duke went to America after a successful career in Canadian TV, and in 1972 notched up a cult success with his feature PAYDAY; he has yet to follow it up with another—a disappointment for his big screen admirers.

They should obviously turn to his TV work—**Cry for Help,** certainly, with Robert Culp as a cynical phone-in DJ who does a Groucho with his callers, until a young girl rings in to say that she is about to kill herself. An update of MISS LONELYHEARTS, a race against time suspenser, a world not too far removed from PAYDAY. Its brilliance is matched on the big screen by episodes in ALICE DOESN'T LIVE HERE ANYMORE, but few places else.

The President's Plane is Missing is Washington-disaster-suspense; **They Only Come Out at Night** a reportedly routine police drama with Jack Warden, **Griffin and Phoenix** (Peter Falk and Jill Clayburgh) that horror-of-horrors, two terminally-ill lovers looning through their last days.

These shows (and **The Bold Ones** segments—Duke was the 1970 Emmy winner for *The Day the Lion Died)* have at least some of the insights of PAYDAY.

Jerrold Freedman

1969: **Trial Run** (assoc. pr.). 1970: **Four In One: The Psychiatrist**/*God Bless the Children* (wr. pr.), *The Private World of Martin Dalton* (pr.), *Par for the Course* (co.-wr./pr.); **The Bold Ones: The Protectors** (series pr.), *A Thing not of God* (dir.); **The Bold Ones: The Senator**/*A Single Blow of a Sword* (wr. only); **Night Gallery**/*Room with a View;* **Harpy** (dir.). 1971: **Night Gallery**/*The Flip Side of Satan, Witches' Feast, Dr Stringfellow's Rejuvenator, Professor Peabody's Last Lecture, Marmalade Wine* (+wr). 1973: **Bloodsport** (+wr); **A Cold Night's Death**; **Kojak**/*One for the Morgue* (wr only). 1974: **The Last Angry Man.** 1976: **Kojak**/*I Was Happy where I Was* (co-st only).

A Cold Night's Death is one of the finest telefilms of the '70s, a splendid psychological thriller with a chilling sting in the tail,written by the excellent Christopher Knopf. The opening shot is an extremely long take, travelling over vast snowy wastes which seem to last forever. We come at last to a research station, where someone is sending a radio message. Somebody is out to get him, they're nearly here, and otherwise incoherent babblings. End of scene. Robert Culp and Eli Wallach arrive the next day; they are research scientists investigating the effects of intense cold and sensory deprivation. They are here to relieve the incumbent. The cameras prowl through the centre as they explore, heading always for the radio room; suspense builds. Inside, is the man who was sending the message, frozen to death at the radio. The window is wide open, but the door is unlocked, and the question is why did he simply sit there and freeze? There are no other people within miles. The conclusion is that he simply cracked up, a victim of the effects he, and now Culp and Wallach, are studying, using chimpanzees and other smaller animals. The suspicion remains however that 'something' lurks around the place (we are perhaps reminded of THE THING itself).

Normal routine takes over, each man gets on with his assignments, and slowly on the other's nerves. We watch the process which killed their predecessor happening again. Doors are mysteriously locked and opened, a new chimpanzee is found dead, each man suspects that the other is going mad, trying to kill him, as, wonderfully well written, acted and directed, events build to a truly grotesque, yet marvellously logical conclusion. If anything can be a masterpiece on TV, this is.

All his credits turn out to be rich; from producing/writing **The Bold Ones** (including two Steven Spielberg segments) directing strange (but largely comic) **Night Gallerys**, and of course KANSAS CITY BOMBER, the reviled Raquel Welch movie, which is actually a fascinating piece of work, especially when Freedman's other TV work is borne in mind, for **Bloodsport**—a cool, yet angry attack on sports fetishism, with Ben Johnson as a father determined that his son shall be a football star—shares a common point of view and an oblique style (in contrast to **Cold Night's Death).** There is very little conventional drama in either of these sport films, which is perhaps why BOMBER was so disliked. Looked at as a pair they each make more sense. Freedman's style—*cinéma verité*—admittedly asks a lot of an audience, his abrupt transitions and changes of pace could become irritating if you are unsympathetic. But as The Archers (Powell & Pressburger) said, 'It is better to miss Paris than hit Margate'.

Alvin Ganzer

1956: **Casablanca/***Satan's Veil;* **Four Star Playhouse/***Silhouette of a Killer.* 1959: **Laramie/***Lonesome Gun;* **Twilight Zone/***What You Need, The Hitch-hiker, The Fever.* 1960: **Twilight Zone/***Nightmare as a Child;* **Route 66/***The Quick and the Dead.* 1961: **Hawaiian Eye/***Girl On a String, Princess from Manhattan;* **Route 66/***The Beryilium Eater, An Absence of Tears, Effigy in Snow.* 1963: **Temple Houston/***The Siege at Thayer's Bluff, The Third Bullet.* 1964: **Man from UNCLE/***The Deadly Games Affair, The Girls from Navarone Affair.* 1965: **Man from UNCLE/***Hong Kong Shilling Affair, The Deadly Decoy Affair, The Re-Collectors Affair;* **Lost in Space/***Welcome Stranger;* **Wild Wild West/***The Night that Terror Stalked the Town.* 1967: **Cimarron Strip/***The Hunting, Till the End of Night.* 1971: **The Name of the Game/***The Broken Puzzle.* 1972: **Ironside/***Another Shell Game.* 1973: **Ironside/***The Taste of Ashes.* 1974: **Police Woman/***The Company, Once a Snitch;* **Ironside/***The Last Cotillion.* 1975: **Joe Forrester/***Bus Station, Powder Blue.* 1976: **The Hardy Boys/***Mystery of King Tut's Tomb.* 1977: **Quincy/***Hit and Run at Danny's;* **Nancy Drew Mysteries/***The Ghostwriter's Cruise.*

These piecemeal credits reflect the holes in our research rather than a stutteringly eccentric career. Ganzer seems to be one of the most dynamic of the hitherto-anonymous names who labour in the series vineyards. *The Company* and *The Snitch* are rich, dense, powerful police shows, with a tough, uncompromising view of the world. If this was present in **Casablanca, Hawaiian Eye** and the other earlier shows, Ganzer's work would, whatever its individual touches, be ideal material for sociologists to study the shifting patterns in relationships with the law (as seen by TV). The presence of **Lost in Space** and **Man from UNCLE** among Ganzer's output suggest we curb our enthusiasm. Those **Police Womans** are so good, however, that we are tempted to err on the side of folly.

Bernard Girard

1954/1955: **Your Are There**/*The Completion of the First Trans-Continental Railroad, P. T. Barnum Presents Jenny Lind, Lou Gehrig's Greatest Day, The Final Performance of Sarah Bernhardt, Dewey's Victory at Manila, The Assassination of Julius Caesar, The First Modern Use of Penicillin, Napoleon's Return from Elba, The Discovery of Radium, December 7 1941, The Boston Massacre, Washington Crosses the Delaware, The Rescue of American Prisoners from Santo Tomas, Eli Whitney Invents the Cotton Gin, The Hoax of the Cardiff Giant, The Chicago Fire, The Heroism of Clare Baston, The Capture of John Wilkes Booth, The Great Comstock Silver Strike, Stanley Finds Livingstone, The Lost Battalion, The Resolve of Patrick Henry, The Berlin Air Lift, The Recovery of the Mona Lisa.* 1957: **M Squad**/*The Palace Guard, Diamond Hard;* **Wagon Train**/*The Charles Avery Story.* 1958: **Zane Grey Theatre**/*Stage for Tucson, Death Watch, The Fearful Courage.* 1959; **Adventures in Paradise**/*The Archer's Ring, The Forbidden Sea, Mission to Manila;* **Johnny Staccato**/*Murder in Hi-Fi.* 1961:**Alcoa Theatre**/*Pattern of Guilt, Seven Against the Sea.* 1962: **Alfred Hitchcock Hour**/*Ride the Nightmare, Hangover, The Matched Pearl, Ten O'Clock Tiger, A Piece of the Action.* 1963: **Great Adventure**/*The Pathfinder, The Outlaw and the Nun;* **Alfred Hitchcock Hour**/*Blood Bargain, An Out for Oscar, Run for Doom, The Dividing Wall.* 1964: **Rawhide**/*Moment in the Sun* (+ wr.); **The Virginian**/*Riff Raff, The Exiles;* **Alfred Hitchcock Hour**/*The Water's Edge;* **Kraft Suspense Theatre**/*That He Should Weep for Her.* 1965: **One Step Down.** 1970: **Hunters are for Killing.** 1972: **The Sixth Sense**/*If I Should Die before I Wake.*

It was exciting being a tele-viewer when Girard was rising to the top of the tree—the fascinating **You Are There** historical reconstructions (' . . . this is the way it happened, the only difference is that you are there . . .!'), **M Squad, Wagon Train, Zane Grey Theatre, Johnny Staccato, Alfred Hitchcock Hour** multiples flowing freely. He made the interesting feature RIDE OUT FOR REVENGE in 1957, but not until DEAD HEAT ON A MERRY-GO-ROUND did he break into big screen activity, and that splendidly tight, austere, elliptic thriller has sadly been followed by nothing to equal its stature. In the last decade, Girard has become an elusive, mysterious figure, with few TV credits and features to his name.

William A. Graham

1955: **Kraft Theatre**/(multiples). **US Steel Hour**/multiples. **Bell Telephone Hour**; **Omnibus**/multiples. 1960: **The Witness**/*Charles 'Lucky' Luciano, Louis 'Lepke' Buchalter, Al Capone.* 1961: **Naked City**/*The Face of the Enemy, The Deadly Guinea Pig, The Apple Falls not far from the Tree, C3H5(NO3)3, To Dream Without Sleep;* **Route 66**/*Eleven, the Hard Way, From an Enchantress Fleeing.* 1962: **Naked City**/*Stop the Parade a Baby is Crying;* **Checkmate**/*Remembrance of Crimes Past, Rendezvous in Washington;* **Sam Benedict**/*Maddon's Folly.* 1963: **Naked City**/*Golden Lads and Girls;* **Kraft Suspense Theatre**/*The Hunt.* 1964: **Kraft Suspense Theatre**/*Doesn't Anyone Know Who I Am?;* **The Rogues**/*The Computer Goes West;* **The Fugitive**/*Wings of an Angel, Storm Centre.* 1965:**The FBI**/*All the Streets Are Silent, Slow March up a Steep Hill, The Monster, The Exiles, Image in a Cracked Mirror, To Free My Enemy;* **The Big Valley**/*Palms of Glory.* 1966: **ABC Stage 67**/*The People Trap* (aka **The Last Generation**); **World Premiere**/*The Doomsday Flight;* **Batman**/*True or False Face—Super Rat Race;* **Run for your Life**/*Committee for the 25th;* **The Blue**

Light (segments released as I DEAL IN DANGER). 1967: **Ironside**/*Eat Drink and Be Buried;* **The Outsider; Custer**/*Legend of Custer* (2 pts). 1968: **The Name of the Game**/*Fear of High Places;* **Perilous Voyage; The Intruders** (aka **Death Dance at Medalia** and **Incident at Medalia**). 1969: **Trial Run; Then Came Bronson** (pilot/movie); **World Premiere**/*Act of Piracy.* 1971: **Congratulations It's a Boy!; The Thief; Marriage: Year One; The Magic Carpet.** 1972: **Jigsaw** (pilot/movie); **Honky.** 1973: **Birds of Prey; Police Story** (pilot); **Mr Inside and Mr. Outside; Shirts/ Skins.** 1974: **Trapped Beneath the Sea; When the Lilies Bloom.**1976: **Sounder Part 2; Shark Kill.** 1976: **Minstrel Man; 21 Hours at Munich.** 1971: **The Amazing Howard Hughes.** 1978: **Cindy.**

While there are a handful of purely formula titles in the Graham list, he has managed to maintain successfully the standards of the New York anthology dramas which were his initial TV assignments before he went to Hollywood after the demise of the New York scene in the early '60s. **The Fugitive** and **The FBI**, benefited from the in-the-streets style of **Naked City,** while his background at Yale University (majoring in English) may be partly responsible for the more 'literate' qualities which distinguish his work in such series.

When TV began to compete for the movie audience with 'made for TV features' in the late '60s Graham turned with more regularity to the Hollywood version of the anthology dramas of his New York origins. Throughout the '70s he has been able to work exclusively within this field, and maintain consistently interesting and ambitious work as he bends and twists the formulas.

Doomsday Flight is a bomb-aboard-the-plane thriller, lifted several notches above the norm by its Rod Serling script. **The Intruders** is, rare for Graham, a western, neatly creating a similar kind of tension, 'the bomb' here being Jesse James and the Younger Brothers who are on their way to town. There is tension too at the heart of **Trapped Beneath the Sea**—the rescue of an experimental submarine although it is 'defused' by being set within the flashback structure of an enquiry into the incident. **Birds of Prey** with David Janssen as an airwatch helicopter pilot, is among the best of Graham's suspense-orientated projects.

But there is another, more off-beat, side to his work. **Then Came Bronson** was the pilot for the series with Michael Parks as a dropout reporter taking to the road on his motor cycle as a solo EASY RIDER. **The Thief** has Richard Crenna turn to crime to meet his gambling debts. **Shirts/Skins** explores the macho mystique most cogently articulated in John Updike's novel *Rabbit Run.* Best of all is **The Amazing Howard Hughes** for, with writer John Gay, Graham has surpassed the typical biopic, coming up instead with an elliptic, elusive, enthralling series of kaleidoscopic vignettes which manage to describe the nature of the weird millionaire far more persuasively than any more obvious investigation would have done. The final sequence, is particularly affecting, with the emaciated Hughes being carted in and out of cars, buildings, planes, hotel rooms by a troupe of aides. Their contact for all its physicality is as remote and meaningless as all his relationships.

Walter Grauman (1922-)

1955/1958: **Matinee Theatre/**(dir+pr multiples) 1957: **Colt 45/***Rebellion, The Young Gun.* 1958: **Alcoa Theatre/***High Class Type of Mongrel.* 1959:**The Untouchables/**(series pr +) *Underground Railway, The Noise of Death, One-Armed Bandit, The White Slavers.* 1960: **The Untouchables/** (series pr +) *Head of Fire Feet of Clay, The Antidote, The Mark of Cain, Nicky.* 1961: **Goodyear Playhouse/***(multiples).* 1962: **Naked City/***Hold for Gloria Christmas, The Prime of Life;* **Route 66/***Poor Little Kangaroo Rat;* **New Breed/**(dir + pr multiples). 1963: **Empire (Big G)/***Ballard Number One;* **The Fugitive/***Fear in a Desert City;* **Twilight Zone/***Miniature.* 1964: **The Fugitive/***Crack in a Crystal Ball, Ballad for a Ghost;* **Eleventh Hour/**(multiples). 1965: **The Fugitive/***Landscape with Running Figures* (2 pts). 1966: **The Blue Light/**(series exec pr); **The Fugitive/***Angels Travel on Lonely Roads.* 1967: **Felony Squad/**(series exec pr). 1968: **Felony Squad/***The Counterfeit Cop.* 1969: **Daughter of the Mind; Lancer/***Catch a Wild Horse.* 1970: **Crowhaven Farm; The Old Man who Cried Wolf.** 1971: **Dead Men Tell no Tales; Paper Man; They Call it Murder.** 1972: **Streets of San Francisco/**(pilot), *The First Day of Forever, 45 Minutes from Home, Tower beyond Tragedy, Whose Little Boy Are You?, A Collection of Eagles, The Bullet, A Room with a View, Deathwatch, The House on Hyde Street.* 1974: **Manhunter/**(pilot). 1975: **Force Five.** 1976: **Most Wanted/**(pilot), *The Ten Percenter;* **Tales of the Unexpected/***No Way Out;* **Streets of San Francisco/***The Cannibals.*

As TV guides only rarely print more than actor credits, and as **The Untouchables** waited for the end-titles to list the creative personnel, it was an interesting test for auteur hunters to watch that series. It is easy to recognise a style retrospectively; we looked forward to testing our understanding. Whenever a segment unfolded that was, surely, helmed by a Karlson, or a Wendkos, or a Garnett, it always turned out to be Walter Grauman.

The best of Grauman's **The Untouchables** also have fine scripts (Ben Maddow, *Head of Fire Feet of Clay, The Noise of Death,* David Zelag Goodman, *The Antidote)* and combine a serpentine and unconstricting visual sense, with lowering close-ups which *do not* dominate the scene. In these shows, even the occasional David Lean-like kinky angle actually works. It is likely that Grauman was one of the first to create a perfectly judged style which could justly be considered 'pure TV'.

Grauman could also make lines like 'There's one thing I like about you Ness—you're the one copper who never told me to keep my nose clean' and 'I heard! They just locked me up, they didn't cut off my ears' zing like Damon Runyon. Another line, from the wife of a racketeer: 'When he dies I'm going down on the street and commit a mortal sin so I can go to Hell and marry him all over again' which, as read (by an actress who actually seems to care), and as directed by Grauman, comes over as wonderfully moving, so deep is the love expressed. It indicates, perhaps, the director's main achievement with the series—to make us sympathise with the lowlife, so that it is of more than academic interest that Ness and Co. have a set of dubious morals and get them in the end.

Grauman also did some fine work on **The Fugitive,** particularly

Landscape with Running Figures. **Crowhaven Farm, Dead Men Tell no Tales** (with elements of Hitchcock in NORTH BY NORTHWEST mood) and **The Streets of San Francisco** pilot are perhaps the best of his recent telefilms. He seems to have settled into far too cosy a relationship with the Quinn Martin company (a relationship going back through **Fugitive** to **Untouchables**); it is to be hoped that he doesn't inhale too much of the lacklustre fumes which have settled over that hitherto excellent part of the TV world. His past career is justified—he helped initiate an art—it would be good if his future were as definite.

David Greene

1959: **Five Fingers**/*A Shot in the Dark.* 1961: **The Defenders**/*The Last Six Months, The Locked Room.* 1962: **Twilight Zone**/*A Piano in the House;* **The Defenders**/*A Book for Burning;* **Man of the World**/*Masquerade in Spain;* **Sir Francis Drake**/*Queen of Scots, The Lost Colony of Virginia, The Garrison, Mission to Paris, Escape, The Doughty Plot, King of America.* 1963: **Espionage**/*Medal for a Turned Coat, Once a Spy . . . , The Gentle Spies, He Rises on Sunday and We on Monday, To the Very End;* **The Defenders**/*Judgement Eve, The Last Illusion, Metamorphosis, Poltergeist;* **The Saint**/*The Pearls of Peace.* 1964: **Studio 64**/*The Happy Moorings;* **The Defenders**/*The Thief, The Uncivil War.* 1965: **For the People**/*To Prosecute all Crimes;* **The Defenders**/*Fires of the Mind, Hero of the Day, A Taste of Ashes;* **Coronet Blue**/*A Dozen Demons, Six Months to Mars, Tomoyo, The Flip Side of Timmy Devon, Saturday.* 1968: **CBS Playhouse**/*The People Next Door.* 1975: **Ellery Queen**/ *pilot , The Adventure of Auld Lang Syne.* 1976: **Rich Man Poor Man**/pts 1, 2, 3, 8 & 9; **Roots**/pts 1 & 2. 1977: **Lucan**/(pilot); **The Trial of Lee Harvey Oswald.**

Whereas British directors from Hitchcock to Yates establish careers at home then streak off for the more creatively conducive climate of America, Greene turned this syndrome inside out. A RADA trained actor, he became involved with TV while touring in Canada and began directing (one such project, unlikely as it sounds today, involved Lorne Greene as Othello). He established his reputation in America with his work on **The Defenders.** He spent most of the '60s commuting between America and Britain, seeking feature work. His winning the 1968 Emmy for *The People Next Door* was the final thrust into big screen work, and critics were finally alerted to this 'new talent' with THE SHUTTERED ROOM, an outstanding fantasy film (from a story by H. P. Lovecraft) which was more about the 'demons of the mind' than the beasts in the attic. THE STRANGE REPORT (one of the most accomplished British films since the war) and I START COUNTING (inferior, but only by Greene's standards) seemed likely to take him on to even better things. Instead, the career began to flounder—and Greene went back to American TV.

He is now re-established; he directed blockbusting **Rich Man Poor Mans** and the early segments of **Roots.** The **Lucan** pilot worked wonders through its casting (Ned Beatty and Stockard Channing); Greene's eye for beautifully formal composition and his skill and subtlety with actors, however, did not manage to break through the essential formula nature of the series. **The Trial of**

Lee Harvey Oswald is a glorious failure—a brave attempt to speculate, dramatise, exorcise the traumas surrounding the Kennedy assassination, in a way wholly unique to TV. Yet structural faults, conceptual confusion and the final and hypocritical 'we do not know the answers, we are only posing the questions' cop-out made the viewer frustrated and irritated with the programme, rather than angry about the circumstances surrounding the 'trial'. Even so, Greene held it together remarkably well—the audacious re-enacting of the assassination, on the actual spot (who knows, with some of the original crowd) made the eyes boggle anew at the extraordinary 'license' of America itself. Other magic moments mark the show for some curious distinctions and one should surely not look to Greene to explain its deficiencies.

Now on the feature trail again (with GRAY LADY DOWN) he will presumably continue to bounce between large and small screens. His appearances on either are always to be greeted with cheers.

William Hale

1964: **Bob Hope Chrysler Theatre: Enigma**/*After the Lion Jackals.* 1966: **The Time Tunnel**/*The Day the Sky Fell Down, Crack of Doom, Death Trap, Robin Hood;* **Run for Your Life**/*The Rediscovery of Charlotte Hyde.* 1967: **The Time Tunnel**/*Death Merchant;* **The Invaders**/*The Spores;* **Lancer**/*The Escape, The Great Humbug, Juniper's Camp, Julie, The Fixit Man, A Person Unknown;* **World Premiere**/*How I Spent My Summer Vacation* (aka DEADLY ROULETTE). 1968: **The Invaders**/*The Captive, The Possessed, The Organisation, The Vise, The Pursued;* **Felony Squad**/*The Deadly Junkman.* 1969: **The FBI**/*The Swindler* (+ multiples). 1970: **Night Gallery**/*Since Aunt Ada Came to Stay, The Diary;* **The Bold Ones: The Protectors**/*Draw a Straight Man.* 1971: **Cannon**/*No Pockets in a Shroud;* **Night Gallery**/*A Midnight Visit to the Blood Bank.* 1973: **Kojak**/*The Girl in the River* (co dir), *Siege of Terror, Web of Death* (co dir); **Streets of San Francisco**/*Betrayed, Before I Die, Crossfire;* **Caribe**/*The Assassin.* 1974: **Streets of San Francisco**/*One Last Shot, Labyrinth, Ten Dollar Murder;* **Hawaii Five-O**/*The Killer Who Wouldn't Die;* **Nightmare**; **The Great Niagara**.1975: **Streets of San Francisco**/*Poison Snow, School of Fear, Men Will Die, Most Likely to Succeed;* **Bert D'Angelo Superstar**/*Requiem for a Rip-Off;* **Crossfire**. 1977: **Red Alert**.

Hale's would seem to be a sadly abortive career overall—for he first came to the attention of the serious student with low budget features like GUNFIGHT IN ABILENE and DEADLY ROULETTE which held promises for the future. Lo and behold, the admired DEADLY ROULETTE turns out to be *How I Spent My Summer Vacation* one of the first of Universal's made-for-TV movies; it is, therefore, an even more remarkable effort. This genuinely bizarre mixture of caper/thriller/whodunwot deserves a much higher reputation than that of cult favourite. It shows how good Hale can be, as does the more recent **Red Alert,** a disaster-thriller set in a nuclear power plant (and shot in the Houston Space Lab and the NASA Mission Control Centre) which builds into its tension a valid critique of the nuclear system. Hale's other telefeatures (**Nightmare** with

Richard Crenna, a variant on REAR WINDOW, has one reaching for one's nails; **The Great Niagara** with Richard Boone in conflict with sons Michael Sacks and Randy Quaid over his obsession with conquering the Falls; **Crossfire,** an undercover cop melo) are all also worth catching.

For the majority of his TV time, Hale has been locked into series segments, making it harder for enthusiasts to seek out his work, but providing many moments of delight when one of his pieces surfaces. *Siege of Terror* is one of the tightest, tautest **Kojaks**, with Harvey Keitel holed up with hostages in a siege situation; the opening robbery, chase and crash is wonderful action stuff. *Labyrinth* is another siege story, but while the action works well, the narrative itself is derivative. Other **Streets of San Francisco** segments confirm however that when Hale is let loose in the urban jungle, some classic action can result.

With the development and extension of telefeatures, Hale should be able to consolidate his position and press beyond the high standards he has already set himself.

Daniel Haller (1929-)

1971: **O'Hara–US Treasury**/*Operation: Pay-Off;* **Sarge**/*An Accident Waiting to Happen, The Silent Target* (aka *Drake's Castle), Ring Out, Ring In;* **Owen Marshall, Counselor at Law**/*18 Years Next April, Voice from a Nightmare, Run Carol Run;* **Rod Serling's Night Gallery**/*I'll Never Leave You—Ever.* 1972: **The Sixth Sense**/*Face of Ice;* **Owen Marshall, Counselor at Law**/*Charlie Gave Me Your Number, They Got to Blame Somebody;* **Ironside**/*Shadow Soldier, The Best Laid Plans.* 1973: **Owen Marshall, Counselor at Law**/*'N' is for Nightmare, The Sin of Susan Gentry, The Attacker, Subject: The Sterilization of Judy Simpson;* **Ironside**/*The Last Payment;* **Toma**/*Crime without Victim.* 1974: **Kojak**/*A Souvenir from Atlantic City;* **Ironside**/*Fall of an Angel;* **Sunshine**/*A Song for Montana* (2 pts), *Buy the Book, Have a Nice Day, A Houseboat is Not a Home, Father Nature, Intensive Care.* 1975: **Kojak**/*A Wind from Corsica,* **The Desperate Miles.** 1976: **Sara**/*Grandpa's Girl;* **McNaughton's Daughter**/*Love is a Four-Letter Word;* **Kojak**/*A Grave too Soon, Deadly Innocence.* 1977:**Rosetti and Ryan**/*Is There a Lawyer in the House;* **Kingston: Confidential**/*Dateline-Fear City;* **Family Classics**/*Black Beauty* (5 pts). 1978: **Buck Rogers** (1st pilot).

The remarkable art director of the Roger Corman/Vincent Price/Edgar Allan Poe series turned director himself with DIE MONSTER DIE, a fair debut, but subsequent features (DUNWICH HORROR etc.) failed to confirm his talent. Rather than wait and, perhaps court failure, he settled into TV. Of his available work, the **Kojak** segments are standouts, particularly *Souvenir from Atlantic City* and *A Grave too Soon.* His entry into the miniseries league, with *Black Beauty,* was panned by the trade, but for its budgetary limitations and narrative constrictions rather than for Haller's failure. He may well move on and his work become more generally known. He should console himself while out on the streets that his segments are way above average.

Joseph Hardy

1973: **Toma**/*Rockabye.* 1974: **A Tree Grows in Brooklyn.** 1975: **The Silence; Last Hours Before Morning.** 1976: **Executive Suite**/*The Secret, The Trap* (both co-dir with Charles Dubin). 1978: **The Paper Chase** (pilot); **Return Engagement.**

Last Hours Before Morning is a fascinating 'little' thriller, which is set in the '40s and aims to capture the mood of bleak despair associated with the period. It succeeded. **The Silence** is equally intriguing—the script by Stanley Greenberg is based on 70 hours of taped conversations with the real James Pelosi (played in the film by Richard Thomas) who was given the 'silent treatment' by fellow West Point cadets for allegedly cheating in an examination. The form it takes is a re-construction of the original conversations, which cut in and out to illustrate and elucidate the events being discussed, as Greenberg (Cliff Gorman), tries to find the 'truth' in order to effectively write the film. The result is very austere, clever rather than intelligent. But Hardy certainly establishes a formal awareness, which marks him out from many of his contemporaries, and informs **Paper Chase.**

Harvey Hart (1928-)

1961: [CANADA] **Playdate**/*Masterpiece;* [GB] **Late Night Theatre**/*The Night they Killed Joe Howe.* 1963: **Alfred Hitchcock Hour**/*Terror at Northfield.* 1964: **Seaway**/*The Sparrows;* **Alfred Hitchcock Hour**/*Triumph.* 1965: **Alfred Hitchcock Hour**/*Power of Attorney, Lonely Place, Death Scene, Something with Claws, Dark Intruder;* **Laredo**/*I See by Your Outfit, Rendezvous at Arillo.* 1966: **Star Trek**/*Mudd's Women;* **Bob Hope Chrysler Theatre: Enigma**/*Don't Wait for Tomorrow;* **Court Martial**/*Let Slip the Dogs of War, No Wreath for an Angel, Judge Them Gently.* 1968: **The Name of the Game**/*The Taker.* 1969: **The Survivors**/*Chapter 2;* **The Young Lawyers.** 1970: **Dan August**/*The Murder of a Small Town, The Color of Fury, In the Eyes of God.* 1973: **Columbo**/*By Dawn's Early Light.* 1974: **Murder or Mercy?; Panic on the 5:22; Can Ellen Be Saved?** 1975: **Columbo**/*Now You See Him, A Deadly State of Mind, Forgotten Lady.* 1976: **Street Killing.** 1977: **The City; Goldenrod; Prince of Central Park.**

Another member of American TV's Canadian contingent who has been adding his creative flavour to the prolific Hollywood blender, Hart arrived shortly after the 'boom years' (1958-1962). He has steadily worked his way through some fairly notable small-screen series (besides garnering critical interest for his feature BUS RILEY'S BACK IN TOWN which he lost with THE SWEET RIDE). Latterly he has been among the top echelon of directors for telefeatures.

The Hitchcock Hour initially seemed to suit his palate and in 1965 (the year of BUS RILEY) he shot a segment called *Dark Intruder* from a script by Barre

Lyndon, which was to serve as a pilot for a proposed fantasy series, **The Black Cloak.** *Dark Intruder* failed to spark off the series and was released to theatres as a 59 minute 'feature', where it became fodder. Other regulation segments—*Terror at Northfield* from a Leigh (BIG SLEEP, RIO BRAVO) Brackett script, *Power of Attorney* and *Death Scene,* both written by James Bridges, are more representative of the show's outstanding qualities. Hart progressed through a variety of other Universal series, confirming a reputation as a director who produced the right effect only when his scripts had a strong enough cause.

This strain continues with the telefeatures. **Panic on the 5:22** has three lowlife characters attempting an armed robbery on board a special commuter railcar for wealthy New York business folk; the juxtaposition of character and class allows for some excellent mental and physical skirmishes between the two factions. **Murder or Mercy?** is a courtroom melo dealing with euthanasia (did Melvyn Douglas kill his wife with an overdose of morphine?) which reunited Hart with Bradford Dillman, one of the stars of **Court Martial.** Michael Parks (Hart's star in BUS RILEY) plays the leader of a dangerous religious sect in **Can Ellen Be Saved?** On less 'ripped from today's headlines' levels, **Goldenrod** is a rodeo tale set in Hart's Canadian homeland, and **Prince of Central Park** neatly edges away from whimsy in a tale of two children who desert their foster home to live in Central Park, and find Ruth Gordon to befriend them.

While Hart's uneasy fusion of style and content persists, his shows demonstrate that when the heart is in the right place uneasiness can become an oddly disturbing virtue.

Richard T. Heffron

1970: **The Bold Ones: The Lawyers**/*The Rockford Riddle, The People against Ortega, Hall of Justice.* 1971: **Do You Take This Stranger?** 1972: **Banacek**/*The Two Million Clams of Cap'n Jack.* 1973: **Banacek**/*No Stone Unturned;* **Toma**/*(pilot);* **Outrage.** 1974: **The Morning After; California Kid; Locusts.** 1975: **The Rockford Files** (pilot); **Death Scream; The Honorable Sam Houston.**

An apparently small body of work eminently worthy of closer study (Heffron's feature OUTLAW BLUES having already earned him some cult attention).

The **Toma** and **Rockford Files** pilots(both for the Roy Huggins outfit) are the quintessence of these two quirky and rarely deficient series, but it is Heffron's blend of anger and dramatic confrontation of emotional 'issues' which zap you. **Outrage** builds from teenage provocation of a middle-class Robert Culp to a sinister DEATH WISH revenge drama. **Death Scream** digs into a murder case where the victim screams for help for half an hour but receives no help (both stories based on real-life incidents) while **The Morning After** is a brilliant study of alcoholism, with Dick Van Dyke (of all people) in the Ray Milland part, the horrors made all the more pungent through the script of that fantasy-master Richard Matheson.

The California Kid is more laid-back, but, perhaps even more successfully, reprises recurring themes from Heffron's earlier shows: Martin Sheen out for revenge on Vic Morrow, a venal sheriff who hates speed-freaks (and virtually executed Sheen's brother). With more genre elements than the other, more 'respectable' shows, Heffron is able to make his points, and score stylishly as well as more subtly. If proof is needed of the efficaciousnes of the telefeature, Heffron provides it.

Jeremy Paul Kagan

1971: **Nichols**/*All in the Family.* 1972: **Columbo**/*The Most Crucial Game;* **The Bold Ones: The Doctors**/*The Love Affair.* 1974: **Unwed Father; Judge Dee and the Monastery Murders.** 1975: **Katherine** (+ wr).

HEROES has established Kagan as a new big screen director. It confirms the promise of his TV work. The mad outsider played in HEROES by Henry Winkler has a predecessor in **Unwed Father,** where Joseph Bottoms fights everyone in sight for the custody of his illegitimate child whilst girlfriend Kay Lenz wants to have it adopted. With Beverly Garland, Kim Hunter and Joseph Campanella also in the cast, Kagan shows he can pick—and use well—fine actors. **Katherine** written by Kagan, is another emotionally oriented subject. It stars Henry Winkler again, along with Sissy Spacek and Art Carney. Earlier work on the rewarding **Nichols, Bold Ones** and **Columbo** series, together with the oddball **Judge Dee and the Monastery Murders** (a period mystery with a seventh century Chinese detective) are pleasures worth encountering.

Lee H. Katzin

1965: **Rat Patrol**/*The Kill or Be Killed Raid, The Life against Death Raid;* **Wild Wild West**/*Night of the Steel Assassin;* **Branded**/*The Greatest Coward of Them All.* 1966: **Bonanza**/*The Greatest Coward on Earth;* **Mission Impossible**/*The Traitor, Snowball in Hell, Shock, The Widow.* 1967: **Hondo**/*. . . . And the Apaches* (pilot), *. . . And the Superstition Massacre;* **Felony Squad**/*A Blueprint for Dying.* 1968: **It Takes a Thief**/*When Good Friends Get Together.* 1969: **Mission Impossible**/*The Astrologer, The Photographer, The Counterfeiter.* **Along Came a Spider.** 1972: **Visions; Voyage of the 'Yes'; MacMillan and Wife**/*Man without a Face.* 1973: **Ordeal; The Stranger.** 1974: **Space 1999**/*Breakaway* (pilot). 1975: **Last Survivors; Sky Heist.** 1976: **The Quest**/(pilot); **Man from Atlantis**/(pilot). 1977: **Relentless.** 1978: **Bastard.**

Katzin's forte appears to be a certain kind of outrageousness, a larger than life excess, which he both intensifies with an aggressively formal style, yet tempers with a surface realism. The various raids in **Rat Patrol** are an example; **Rat Patrol** was denounced for its 'gratuitous' treatment of the war in the days before **MASH** and **What Did You Do in the War Daddy?** made such an approach acceptable. The often deliciously absurd convolutions of **Mission Impossible** are another instance with their bizarre justifications for Watergate-type 'interference'. It is easy to cite more: the lunacy of **Wild Wild West** (which was never a western, always a serial oriented fantasy) and, latterly, after Katzin had flirted with features (WHATEVER HAPPENED TO AUNT ALICE, LE MANS, THE SALZBURG CONNECTION), **Along Came a Spider,** where Suzanne Pleshette has a bizarre 'foolproof' scheme for revenge against Ed Nelson: **Sky Heist** is another superbly clever caper. Katzin's pilots also show his skills: the obviously fantastical **Space 1999, Man from Atlantis,** and **The Stranger**—astronaut Glenn Corbett on the run on an alien planet.

While all this may be 'lightweight', it is rarely thin 'escapism'. Katzin seems to delight in the freedom offered by such material, and is a superb craftsman. With meticulously plotted and paced narratives, he moves with a wicked precision. His professionalism takes on the quality of subversive technique. Is Katzin trying to offer barbed critiques of society through our responses? Does he merely take a puppet-master's pleasure in fashioning such entertainments? Those who care about answers to such questions should watch Katzin closely.

Bob Kelljan

1975: **Starsky and Hutch**/*Snowstorm, Pariah.* 1976: **Starsky and Hutch**/*Vampire.* 1977: **Charlie's Angels**/*Terror on Ward One, Angels on Ice;* **Dog and Cat**/(pilot); **Starsky and Hutch**/*Starsky and Hutch Are Guilty, The Plague;* **Wonder Woman**/*The Man Who Could Move the World.*

Hitherto Kelljan has been known solely to fantastique freaks for his COUNT YORGA—VAMPIRE features. Their virtues were to bring the myth of the undead to modern Los Angeles and, by contrasting it with the drug and acid cultures, make it seem almost normal, yet make the world in general even more disturbing. Their relatively low budgets also meant that the 'crude' techniques possible became virtues when compared to the formal elegance of Fisher or Corman, which is appropriate surely only in period work.

The first sample of Kelljan's TV work to surface in the UK was the *Vampire* segment of **Starsky and Hutch**—leading one to mourn for the lunacies of typecasting; it left one pleasantly surprised by the way cop thriller met horror movie. The ubiquitous John Saxon played the 'vampire'—and either through a particularly ambiguous script (by Michael Grais and Mark Foster) or through critical inattentiveness, no explanation was given to explain the vampiric action. Though neither Kelljan nor Saxon attempted to match the goosepimples stirred by **The Night Stalker,** the sheer change from the drugbusts and hijacks of the series was a relief and, on a pure action level, Kelljan handled the confrontation at the climax with great panache.

Kelljan's other stuff is comparatively conventional, from the story end. Yet there is a generally recurring situation in his work, that of a strong nameless antagonist with powerless goodguys unable to handle his threat.

In the **Dog and Cat** pilot, Lou Antonio's partner is killed and the assailant—a mad-eyed hit man who generates the kind of lunatic power of Andy Robinson in DIRTY HARRY—spends the rest of the running time sniping away at everyone in the main plot. By virtue of his madness, the threat reaches an even higher level of fear than normal. In *Starsky and Hutch Are Guilty,* a pair of S. and H. lookalikes are framing them for corrupt practices. In all three segments, an apparently friendly associate is manipulating the mayhem, thereby compounding the chaos, while in *Terror on Ward One* an unknown rapist almost reaches the 'phantom' level of *Vampire.*

While such storylines are hardly out of the ordinary in the genre, it is significant that Kelljan seems to be specialising in them. Certainly the *emphasis* he places on the vulnerability of his heroes, the almost supernatural omnipotence with which the unknown villains are imbued, indicates a director fully aware of the paranoia of our time. Kelljan's style—unclichė, unfussy, unpretentious—suggests a director with confidence in himself and in his material. He throws off a restless energy which, if harnessed to material which allows a more personal involvement (Kelljan also wrote the Count Yorga movies) and a more individual exploration of themes, might produce some memorable work, which captures both modern and primal terrors in a disturbing and powerful way. Kelljan should be watched closely, but not for **Wonder Woman.**

Bruce Kessler

1967: **The Monkees**/*The Chaperone, Monkees at the Circus, I've Gotta Little Song Here, Alias Mickey Dolenz.* 1968: **Adam 12**/*Log 33.* 1969: **It Takes a Thief**/*Guess Who's Coming to Rio;* **Adam 12**/*Loan Sharks.* 1970: **Alias Smith and Jones**/*Return to Devil's Hole;* **McCloud**/*Horse Stealing on Fifth Avenue.* 1974: **Marcus Welby MD**/*Loser in a Dead Heat;* **McCloud**/*The Gang that Stole Manhattan, This Must be the Alamo, Shivaree on Delancey Street.* 1975: **Switch**/*The Cruise Ship Murders, Big Deal in Paradise, The Man Who Couldn't Lose;* **Ironside**/*The Faded Image;* **Baretta**/*Count the Days I'm Gone, And Down Will Come Baby;* **McCloud**/*Five Guns for New York;* **Get Christie Love**/*A Few Excess People, From Paris with Love, Too Many Games in Town.* 1976: **Rockford Files**/*Return to the 39th Parallel;* **Baretta**/*That Sister Ain't no Cousin;* **Quincy**/*Hot Ice Warm Heart;* **McCloud**/*McCloud Meets Dracula.* 1977: **Switch**/*Camera Angles.*

Thanks to the purchasing and programming departments of the British TV companies, very few of Kessler's segments have been screened in the U.K. We assign him to the Ballroom on the strength of an excellent **McCloud**—*This Must be the Alamo*—and a topgrade **Rockford Files**—*Return to the 39th Parallel,* both of which indicate that the promise of his feature HELLS ANGELS 69 is, at least, matched in his TV work. Possibly it has been excelled. The absence of tele-features or miniseries in Kessler's credits might mean that he has been unlucky, or simply that he is content to work on the kind of high level shows which so far constitute his output. Most of them have their roots in humour **(The Monkees, Alias Smith and Jones)** or have a built-in level of humour **(McCloud, Switch, Rockford Files, Baretta)** and allow for a cool, laidback, knowing sensibility for fun—and sometimes make a few points—in their grooves. If this were the total sum of Kessler's contribution, it adds up to quite a lot. Who could ask for more?

Randal Kleiser

1973: **Marcus Welby MD**/*Fear of Silence.* 1974: **Marcus Welby MD**/*Designs, A Fevered Angel, To Father a Child;* **Lucas Tanner**/*Bonus Baby.* 1975: **Marcus Welby MD**/*The Strange Behaviour of Paul Kelland.* 1976: **Starsky and Hutch**/*Nightmare, Giveaway on the Docks;* **The Boy in the Plastic Bubble.**

The Boy in the Plastic Bubble is Kleiser's most substantial telefilm. It draws on his **Marcus Welby** medical background for a story, based on case studies, of a boy born without natural resistance to infection who must therefore live his life in the germ-free 'bubble' developed by NASA. The film concentrates on the boy as an adolescent (John Travolta), his love affair with the girl next door (Glynis O'Connor), and his final decision to risk life outside the protected environment. The end (has his body developed enough immunity? Will he die from his first cold?) remains a mystery as he casts safety away for pleasure and communion. Kleiser's handling, full of naturalistic humour, plays down all mawkishness; it draws analogies between the boy's environment and conditions endured by astronauts (Buzz Aldrin, first man on the moon, visits him at one point). The 'great step for mankind' is paralleled by Travolta's first, unprotected step beyond his bubble. On the basis of this one film, we would predict further interesting work from Kleiser. For both this and the *Nightmare* segment of **Starsky and Hutch** (David Soul, shot full of drugs, in a state of hallucination) show that he can bring off-beat qualities to TV frameworks.

John Korty (1936-   )

1970: **Riverrun.** 1971: **The People.** 1973: **The Autobiography of Miss Jane Pitman, Class of '63, Go Ask Alice.** 1975: **Farewell to Manzanar.**

'Director-writer-cameraman-animator-editor' says Korty's entry in the *International Television Almanac,* and he seems to confound those no-hopers who prefer to believe that quirky individuality has no place in American TV. Korty's first film, the documentary LANGUAGE OF FACES won honours at 10 international festivals, while his cartoon BREAKING THE HABIT (smoking) was nominated for an Oscar. THE ELECTRIC FLAG dealt in 15 minutes with the making of a candidate and the making of THE CANDIDATE—Michael Ritchie's feature—in its investigation of the role of TV and film in the running of a political candidate.

Korty's first feature (a low budget independent job based in San Francisco) is perhaps part of the LANGUAGE OF FACES syndrome—an audaciously ambitious view of fifty years of a marriage. FUNNYMAN, his next, equally low budget, equally independent feature, is less ambitious in scale but not in theme—nothing less than a study of the wellsprings of comedy, via the character of comedian Peter Bonerz who has the inevitable 'Hamlet' complex. This idea, which has bedevilled many a talent, is treated by Korty with a wry, genuinely sympathetic air. The only problem, on reflection, is that in his stand-up scenes, Bonerz isn't very funny, and the audience cannot tell whether he is supposed to be or not to be. It is a serious flaw, but not deep enough to make one despair. One looked forward to more Korty movies with much the same sympathy as he shows to the characters in them.

Korty's other feature work has been for TV, but only **The Autobiography of Miss Jane Pitman** has turned up in Britain. Just as with Spielberg or Peckinpah, one laments the lack of attention that has been paid to his TV work. It is even more regrettable in this case, for Korty's projects sound unique.

The People, adapted from a Zenna Henderson sci-fi novel, takes Kim Darby, as a new schoolteacher, into a strange, isolated community where there is no human emotion or happiness; it is apparently paying for some past sins. **Class of '63** is soap-opera material transcended by Korty's understanding of the human animal. **Go Ask Alice** is based on the diary of a real-life teenager who became a 15-year-old junkie. **Farewell to Manzanar** deals with the internment of all Japanese—including those American-born—during the hysteria generated by the war in the Pacific—and the fears that the 'aliens' would assert their true colours by destroying American society. Real Japanese play the central family on which Korty focusses during their incarceration at Camp Manzanar.

While in cold print all of these sound as though they could become tracts or styleless messages, Korty shows that his concern is for people and not with a mere parade of their problems. These six telefeatures—along with whatever else may follow—make up a body of work which, had it been conceived or released theatrically, would have earned Korty an enviable reputation.

Bernard L. Kowalski

1960: **The Westerner**/*Mrs Kennedy.* 1961: **Perry Mason**/*The Case of the Posthumous Painter, The Case of the Injured Innocent, The Case of the Missing Melody, The Case of the Pathetic Patient, The Case of the Renegade Refugee.* 1965: **The Trials of O'Brien**/*Bargain Day on the Street of Regret, The Trouble with Archie;* **The Virginian**/*The Claim;* **Rat Patrol** (series pr) + *The Chase of Fire Raid;* **Wild Wild West**/*The Night the Wizard Shook the Earth.* 1966: **Rawhide** (series co-pr) + *The Enormous Fist, Corporal Dasovik, The Book;* **The Monroes**/*The Intruders;* **Mission Impossible**/ (pilot); *Fakeout, A Spool there Was;* **Gunsmoke**/*Quaker Girl.* 1971: **Black Noon; Women in Chains; Terror in the Sky.** 1972: **Banacek**/*A Million the Hard Way;* **Streets of San Francisco**/*The Thirty Year Pin;* **Columbo**/*Death Lends a Hand, Fade into Murder;* **The Woman Hunter; Two for the Money; The New Healers.** 1973: **The Storm; She Cried Murder; Columbo**/*An Exercise in Fatality;* **Banacek**/*If Max Is so Smart Why Doesn't He Tell Us Where He Is?, The Vanishing Chalice;* **Tenafly**/*The Window that Wasn't.* 1974: **Rockford Files**/*The Case Is Closed;* **In Tandem** (pilot for **Movin' On**). 1975: **Sunshine**/*Leave It to Weaver;* **Banacek**/*Fly Me If You Can Find Me;* **Baretta** (series exec pr) + *He'll Never See Daylight, Woman in the Harbour, If You Can't Pay the Price, The Mansion, Ragtime Billy Peaches, The Goodbye Orphan Annie Blues, Photography by John Doe.* 1977: **Baretta**/*Guns and Brothers;* **Flight to Holocaust; Risko.**

There is a touch of the Katzins about Kowalski—but the one is a sleek panther and the other a big wild bear. While 'outrageousness' figures quite prominently in the Kowalski credits (uniting him with Katzin in identical or similar projects—**Rat Patrol, Wild Wild West, Mission Impossible,** or **Banacek,** the latter with its format of incredible crimes solved by the imperturbable, eponymous hero, George Peppard) this is as much stylistic as thematic. **Flight to Holocaust** for instance is a mini-disaster movie, with a plane crashing into the side of a skyscraper; can the passengers be rescued before the craft falls to the street below? The young team who volunteer to carry out the rescue are plainly hopeful of getting a series—but to date they haven't. Kowalski blithely waves a dismissive hand to the looney narrative and turns in a positive *succés du style* of rushing, swooping, tracking, probing, craneing, crawling camerawork. **The Storm**—written and produced by Sterling Silliphant—is very similar. This one has a young team (of doctors) hoping for a series and winning the approval of a small town when disaster strikes and they come to the rescue.

Elsewhere, **Women in Chains** (wild and woolly women's prison melo), **Black Noon** (mad horror/western with WITCHES OF SALEM and HIGH PLAINS DRIFTER nudging each other uncomfortably), **Two for the Money** (detectives Robert Hooks and Stephen Brooks tracking down a mass-murderer who has evaded capture for ten years), carry a wacky charge. It must be said however that **The Woman Hunter** is an abomination.

In the series vein, Kowalski has naturally had to temper his inclinations to the mood of the shows. When both fit easily, fine work results: *Death Lends a Hand,* with a Levinson & Link script and an excellent performance by Robert Culp is one of the best **Columbos**—Kowalski's cameras prowl and stalk to good effect. *Fade into Murder* shows the series on decline, but relishes a wonderfully relaxed hammy performance by William Shatner as a ludicrous matinee idol actor.

Kowalski often acts as a series producer, and exercises a far greater degree of control and determination than is usual. Many would feel that **Rawhide,** whose 1966 season he co-produced with the late Bruce Geller (a creative partnership spanning **The Westerner, Mission Impossible** and **Mannix**), was amongst the best of '60s series TV, representing therefore a Kowalski highspot. To addicts of the bizarre though, **Baretta** is the tops. Kowalski, functioning also as executive producer, directed seven segments in the first season, three of them right up front, and thereby set the style. With Robert Blake's feisty persona to play with, Kowalski came into his own, and in *If You Can't Pay the Price* came up with one of the most oddball, yet most satisfying of all series segments.

Hardly anything happens in a conventional manner (the mood is rather reminiscent of Howard Zieff's feature SLITHER), and what does happen is terribly slow—but extremely freaky and certainly 'outrageous' in the best sense of the term—for with Blake camping out in his car across the street from a racketeer's mansion in order to get the goods on a drugs shipment, a series of elliptic sequences and resonant relationships are triggered off. Co-written by 'John Thomas James', the segment is the quintessence of the Roy Huggins narrative-style brought refreshingly up to date. That such a segment ever got made is further proof of the extraordinarily rich vein of material just waiting to be mined.

Kowalski's contribution to all this is incalculable—but crucial.

Seymour 'Buzz' Kulik (1922-   )

1954/1957: **You Are There; Lux Video Theatre; Climax; Playhouse 90** (multiples). 1958: **Have Gun-Will Travel**/*The Manhunter, A Score for Murder;* **Perry Mason**/*The Case of the Pint-Sized Client.* 1959: **Perry Mason**/*The Case of the Dangerous Dowager.* 1960: **Twilight Zone**/*King Nine Will Not Return, The Trouble with Templeton;* **Naked City**/*Bullets Cost Too Much;* **Have Gun-Will Travel**/*The Fatalist, Saturday Night, Crowbait, The Sanctuary.* 1961: **The Defenders** (pilot), *The Accident, Death across the Counter, The Point Sharer, The Quality of Mercy, The Riot, The Trial of Jenny Scott, The Young Lovers;* **Have Gun-Will Travel**/*A Quiet Night in Town (2 pts), Duke of Texas, The Cure;* **Twilight Zone**/*Static, A Hundred Yards over the Rim, The Mind and the Matter.* 1962: **Dick Powell Theatre**/*The Court Martial of Captain Wycliffe, The Great Anatole;* **The Defenders**/*Blood County, The Iron Man;* **Naked City**/*The Man Who Bit the Diamond in Half.* 1963: **The Great Adventure**/*Wild Bill Hickock, The Great Diamond Mountain;* **Twilight Zone**/*Jess-Belle, On Thursday We Leave for Home;* **Kraft Suspense Theatre**/*The Case against Paul Riker* (2 pts); **The Richard Boone Show**/*The Stranger.* 1964: **The Defenders**/*The Fine Line;* **Ready for the People; Kentucky Jones**/(series exec prod). 1970: **Brian's Song.** 1971: **Owen Marshall, Counsellor at Law**/(pilot). 1973: **Portrait...A Man Whose Name Was John; Pioneer Woman; Incident on a Dark Street.** 1974: **Bad Ronald; Remember When?** 1975: **Matt Helm** (1st pilot+pr); **Babe; Cage without a Key.** 1976: **The Feather and Father Gang** (pilot), *Never Con a Killer;* **The Lindberg Kidnapping Case.** 1977: **Kill Me if You Can.** 1978: **Ziegfeld: The Man and his Women** (+ pr).

When the Mulligans, Lumets and Frankenheimers were whisked away from live TV for feature careers, talents like Kulik took over in the vanguard of 'important' drama. With the demise of live TV, Kulik and others moved directly to telefilm. Kulik was able to respond to **Have Gun Will Travel** (his *Quiet Night in Town* is a rare two-parter, and has Sydney Pollack in an acting role) and **Twilight Zone** *(A Hundred Yards over the Rim* is a classic segment; three astronauts crash on another planet; they fight among themselves until only one is left; he staggers to the rim to see a signpost—'Las Vegas. 5 miles' which reminds one of PLANET OF THE APES). He is, however, more closely identified with **The Defenders.** Kulik directed the pilot and nine subsequent segments. With scripts by Reginald Rose, the series's creator (for Kulik—the *pilot, The Accident, Death across the Counter, The Quality of Mercy, The Trial of Jenny Scott),* Kulik and his colleagues made the series a landmark and created the ideal compromise between film techniques and the standards of live drama.

After a number of features which Kulik failed to handle in big screen terms (WARNING SHOT, VILLA RIDES, TO FIND A MAN, SHAMUS), he has become entrenched once more as a king of the hill. His work on the award winning **Brian's Song** obviously helped. Writer William Blinn dramatised the friendship between Brian Piccolo (James Caan) and Gale Sayers (Billy Dee Williams), the Chicago Bears football players, which ended with Piccolo's death from cancer at the age of 26. Many observers found this unbearable, but along with LOVE STORY, it established a small screen fascination with terminal illness no less pervasive than the rush to 'committed' series drama which followed **The Defenders.**

Kulik has now amassed a string of important telefilm credits. The three-hour **Vanished,** from Fletcher Knebel's novel—a political suspense story with Richard Widmark as the US President facing an international crisis when a top advisor is kidnapped. **Remember When?**—a SUMMER OF '42 ripoff by the same author, Herman Raucher, **Cage without a Key**—a return to social problems with an exposé of juvenile detention centres; plus three biographical dramas: **Babe** (athlete Babe Didrikson), **The Lindberg Kidnapping Case** and **Ziegfeld: The Man and his Women.**

To show his catholic range, or lack of any real commitment, Kulik has flirted with lighter-hearted material such as the pilots for **Matt Helm** and **The Feather and Father Gang.**

Michael Landon

1969: **Bonanza** (wr) *A Dream to Dream, Six Black Horses* (co-wr). 1973: **Love Story**/*Love Came Laughing* (dir), *The Roy Campanella Story* (dir). 1974/1977: **Little House on the Prairie** (exec pr + dir) *pilot, Harvest of Friends, Mr Edward's Homecoming, The Award* (wr only), *Plague* (wr only), *The Lord Is My Shepherd* (+ wr), *To See the World, Journey into Spring* (+ wr 2 pts), *The Music Box, Castoffs, Whisper Country, To Run and Hide, The Wolves, My Ellen* (+ wr).

Having survived the indignities of being a Teenage Werewolf, Landon settled into **Bonanza** for its marathon fourteen year run as Little Joe Cartwright the young son, the rebel, the one who learned the lessons of life in those segments which detailed the development of his character. During this period he began to write segments. When the series finally folded in 1973, he found a new on-screen identity, as Charles Ingalls. He also found a new role—as executive producer on the same show, **Little House on the Prairie**—a series based on a successful series of children's books. Landon also directed the pilot, and has continued to write and direct throughout the series's run.

An interesting phenomenon, was that **Little House** played in prime-time spots, and in the late '70s was often a lonely bastion of traditional 'family values'. It was sneered at unfairly by intellectuals who think art must reflect *their* values. The series does present its audience—particularly its younger members—with the kind of veiled morality once the standard backbone of Hollywood features. The series confronts the obvious traumas of life head-on as well as conflicts, bigotry, prejudice—and relates them to a Thoreau-like vision of the world. It is hard, in fact, to sneer once the rhythms and sensibility of the series are appreciated. But some of our most accepted critics are slaves to fashion. Landon's segments are the most honestly felt. As a director, his skill at visual storytelling has developed with the years; the conviction which he brings to the emotions on display give his work a quality which often approaches the quivering intensity of feeling of Frank Borzage.

Robert Michael Lewis

1971: **MacMillan and Wife**/*Till Death Do Us Part, An Elementary Case of Murder.* 1972: **MacMillan and Wife**/*Cop of the Year, Night of the Wizard, Blues for Sally M;* **The Astronaut**. 1973: **Kung Fu**/*The Nature of Evil;* **The Alpha Caper; A Message to My Daughters; Money to Burn.** 1974: **Pray for the Wildcats; The Day the Earth Moved; Kung Fu**/*The Devil's Champion.* 1975: **The Invisible Man** (pilot); **Guilty or Innocent: The Sam Sheppard Murder Case.** 1976: **Serpico**/*Everyman Must Pay His Dues.*

Money to Burn finds E. G. Marshall as a convict using the prison print shop to counterfeit money, while ex-cons on the outside rob the treasury building to swop the phoney bills for money which has been withdrawn from circulation and is due to be burned. **Alpha Caper** is a very similar story, with Henry Fonda as a probation officer using ex-cons to rob a bullion shipment. **Pray for the Wildcats** has another older-generation lead—Andy Griffith—manipulating the lives of three advertising executives (William Shatner, Robert Reed and Marjoe Gortner), and climaxes as the quartet takes off on a motor cycle trek. This trio of themes and variations makes Lewis's other work worth exploring. Overall, his style is still tentative, heavily dependant on his material. But when this is ingenious he shows himself as a potentially distinctive talent.

Robert Markowitz

1976: **Delvecchio**/*One Little Indian, Board of Rights;* **Serpico**/*Trumpet of Time.* 1977: **The Deadliest Season; The Story Teller.**

One of the brightest of the younger talents, Markowitz's *Trumpet of Time* concentrated on the problems attendant on **Serpico's** goodness and nobility in a venal world (losing his girl friend, etc.) and left him walking the dog back to a lonely apartment. The curious Levinson and Link project, **The Story Teller,** was preceded by **The Deadliest Season,** a much-praised 'provocative drama' about the vicious nature of modern ice hockey and the events on the rink which lead Michael Moriarty to being arrested and tried for murder. With Friedman's **Blood Sport** and KANSAS CITY BOMBER, it is one of the few films to look at the nature of professional sport. It helped end the first phase of Markowitz's TV career, for he followed **The Story Teller** with his first feature, VOICES which was shot in New Jersey.

Robert Ellis Miller (1927-)

1959: **M Squad**/*Death Is a Clock;* **Perry Mason**/*The Case of the Prudent Prosecutor.* 1961: **Desilu Playhouse**/*Two Counts of Murder, Martin's Folly.* 1962: **Alcoa Premiere**/*Five Six Pick Up Sticks, Voice of Charlie Pont;* **The Twilight Zone**/*The Changing of the Guard.* 1963: **The Virginian**/*To Make This Place Remember;* **Route 66**/*You Can't Pick Cotton in Tahiti;* **Burke's Law**/*Who Killed Snooky Martinelli?, Who Killed His Royal Highness?;* **Naked City**/*On the Battlefront Every Minute Is Important, One Two Three, Rita Rakahowski.* 1964: **The Virginian**/*Vengeance Is the Spur;* **The Reporter**/*How Much for a Prince?;* **The Richard Boone Show**/*Welcome Home, Dan;* **The Rogues**/*The Project Man.* 1965: **Bob Hope Chrysler Theatre**/*One Embezzlement and Two Margharitas, Wind Fever.* 1976: **Just an Old Sweet Song.**

Whether Miller has 'made it' is a moot point, for with the exception of THE HEART IS A LONELY HUNTER his features have veered more towards the fey and foolish. They lack the emotional conviction necessary to make them work, and smack instead of the meretricious. His sensitivity and flair for dealing with life's outcasts animated his early '60s TV work, whether in anthology drama or in superior series like **Route 66** and **Naked City**—where titles like *You Can't Pick Cotton in Tahiti* and *One, Two, Three, Rita Rakahowski* were the norm. They expressed the freedom and enthusiasm which the production of the shows encouraged and allowed people like Miller to demonstrate their talent. It also gave them the confidence to strike away from the medium which had nurtured them.

Allen H Miner

1959: **M Squad**/*The $20 Plates;* **Wagon Train**/*The Ricky and Laurie Bell Story, The Maggie Hamilton Story;* **Tightrope**/*Bullets and Ballet.* 1960: **Wagon Train**/*The Doctor Willoughby Story, The Flint McCulloch Story;* **Desilu Mystery Theatre**/*The Night the Phone Rang;* **The Untouchables**/*The Tri-State Gang.* 1961: **Wagon Train**/*The Hunter Mallory Story, The Ella Lindstrom Story* (+ wr), *The Elizabeth McQueeny Story;* **Naked City**/*The S.S. 'American Dream'.* 1962: **Desilu Western Theatre**/*The Day the Town Stood Up* (+ co-wr); **Wagon Train**/*The Charles Maury Story;* **Perry Mason**/*The Case of the Double Entry Mind, The Case of the Stand-In Sister, The Case of the Fickle Filly, The Case of the Bluffing Blast, The Case of Constant Doyle.* 1965: **The Legend of Jesse James**/*The Widow Fay, The Judas Boot.* 1966: **The Loner**/*Mantrap;* **Mission Impossible**/*The Frame.* 1971: **The Catcher.**

One of the more curious (and inexcusable) omissions from Sarris's THE AMERICAN CINEMA is Allan H. Miner, who should have made it into the 'Expressive Esoterica' section for his tremendous rewarding trio of westerns—GHOST TOWN, BLACK PATCH and THE RIDE BACK. They were major Miner. Here quite plainly was a talent every bit as promising as early Peckinpah—but without the relatively high budgets, scope and colour of DEADLY COMPANIONS and RIDE THE HIGH COUNTRY. Miner essayed the tight composition, big closeup style of a Phil Karlson.

For our purposes, because of the features, he should perhaps be in the 'Elephants' Graveyard' section—but there is reason to believe that he actually began his career in TV. With such excellent westerns as *The Day the Town Stood Up* and *The Flint McCulloch Story* to his credit, we would like to think so for in the western genre (occasionally having a hand in the writing), Miner was able to transcend formula, and use the frameworks for personal expression of a high order.

There are great gaps in our filmography. Miner may have been contracted to the Four Star company (whose records have been closed to us), but the gap between 1966 and the lone credit of 1971 is inexplicable. **The Catcher,** an unknown quantity to us, sounds like an attempt to bring western themes into the urban thriller with an ex-cop turned bounty hunter. This strain may run through **M Squad** and **Tightrope** segments, but memory reminds us that *The Tri-State Gang* though Miner, *was* minor.

Miner is, in all likelihood, a TV equivalent of Edgar G. Ulmer—which wouldn't be at all bad.

David Moessinger

1969: **Marcus Welby MD**/*Enid* (wr only). 1970: **Marcus Welby MD**/*The House of Alquist* (co-wr only), *Cynthia* (wr only). 1971: **The Bold Ones: The Lawyers**/*In Sudden Darkness* (wr/dir); **Marcus Welby MD**/*Portrait of Debbie* (wr only); **Alias Smith and Jones**/*How to Rob a Bank in One Hard Lesson* (wr only). 1972: **Alias Smith and Jones**/*Bushwhack!* (wr only). 1973: **Marcus Welby MD**/*Nguyen* (wr/dir). 1975: **Police Woman**/*The Hit* (wr/dir), *Bait* (wr/dir). 1976: **Serpico**/*Danger Zone* (wr only), *One Long Tomorrow* (dir only); **Fantastic Journey**/*Riddles* (dir only). 1977: **Quincy**/*Let Me Light the Way* (wr/dir); **Logan's Run**/*Scavenger Hunt* (dir only).

Like Robert Collins, Moessinger is one of the newer breed of writer/directors; their careers have many parallels. They share an interest in medical matters (**Marcus Welby**—*The House of Alquist* was directed by Collins, **Quincy**) as well as a connection with **Police Woman** (which Collins 'created'), and **Serpico** whose pilot Collins wrote and directed. While Moessinger's work is less consistently engrossing than that of Collins, *Let Me Light the Way* shook the **Quincy** format out of its blandness and gave star Jack Klugman (who also wrote the original story) a genuine reason for expressing passionate concern, which is his brilliant forte. He created a disturbingly real and frightening segment revolving around a rape case. If Moessinger can continue to wear two hats, and find himself engaged and committed in a similar fashion on other programmes, he will be one of the best talents around.

John Llewellyn Moxey (1920-)

[GB] 1955: **Play of the Week**/*The Pay Off;* **London Playhouse**/*Waterloo, A Garden in the Sea, The Man Who Liked Christmas.* 1956: **Television Playhouse**/*Morning Departure, The Pay Off, The Man in the Dock, The Silver Cord, The Doctor's Dilemma;* **Play of the Week**/*The Climbers, Adam's Apple.* 1957: **Television Playhouse**/*The Long Wait;* **Play of the Week**/*Views Observed, Miss Mabel.* 1958: **Play of the Week**/*Myself When Young, Disturbance, The Big Knife;* **Television Playhouse**/*The Fourposter, Strictly for the Sparrows.* 1959: **Armchair Theatre**/*No Gun No Guilt, Parole, Wedding Day, The Scent of Fear, Love and Money, Lysette.* 1961: **Play of the Week**/*The Ring of Truth, Soldier in the Snow, Over the Bridge, Any Other Business;* **Armchair Theatre**/*Strangers in the Room;* **Television Playhouse**/*Winner Takes the Lady.* 1963: **The Saint**/*The Elusive Ellshaw;* **Play of the Week**/*I Can't Bear Violence, The Funambulists, The Teachers;* **Television Playhouse**/*Return to the Regiment;* **Man of the World**/*The Enemy, In the Picture;* **The Odd Man**/*The Sheep 'Neath the Snow;* **The Cheaters**/*Intent to Defraud.* 1964: **Play of the Week**/*The Corsican Brothers, Dance of Death, Tarnish on a Golden Boy, Guilty Party, A Tricycle Made for Two;* **The Saint**/*Jeanine, The Imprudent Politician;* **Gideon's Way**/*State Visit, The Nightlifers.* 1965: **The Baron**/*Red Horse Red Rider, Epitaph for a Hero, The Legions of Ammak, Samurai West;* **Play of the Week**/*A Fearful Thing, Finesse in Diamonds;* **Gideon's Way**/*The Golden Frog;* **Sunday Playhouse**/*A Tall Stalwart Lancer.* 1966: **The Saint**/*The Smart Detective, The Russian Prisoner;* **Armchair Theatre**/*The Wager, Dead Silence;* **Blackmail**/*Care and Protection;* **The Avengers**/*Who's Who?* 1967: **The Saint**/*The Best Laid Schemes;* **The Tormentors**; **The Champions**/*The Iron Man.* [US] 1967: **Dial M for Murder**, **N.Y.P.D.**/*Finger Man, Murder for Infinity, Cruise to Oblivion.* 1968: **Laura**; **Hatful of Rain**; **Judd for the Defense** (2 segments); **Run for Your Life**/*The Exchange* (final segment); **Mannix**/*Night Out of*

Time, A View of Nowhere, Pressure Point. 1969: **Mission Impossible**/*The Glass Cage, Doomsday, The Banker* (2 pts); **Mannix**/*End Game;* **Name of the Game**/*An Agent of the Plaintiff, Lady on the Rocks.* 1970: **The House that Wouldn't Die; Mannix**/*A Ticket to the Eclipse;* **Name of the Game**/*The Tradition;* **San Francisco International Airport.** 1971: **The Last Child; The Night Stalker; The Death of Me Yet; Taste of Evil; Escape; The Hardcase.** 1972: **Home for the Holidays; Ghost Story**/(pilot); **The Bounty Man; Kung Fu**/*The Squaw Man, Empty Pages of a Dead Book, Night of the Owls Day of the Doves, The Passion of Chen Yi.* 1973: **Genesis II; Enter Horowitz.** 1974: **Where Have All the People Gone; The Day They Took the Babies Away; The Strange and Deadly Occurrence.** 1975: **Conspiracy of Terror; Charlie's Angels** (pilot); **Foster and Laurie.** 1976: **Smashup on Inter State 5; Tales of the Nunundaga.** 1977: **Panic in Echo Park.**

Robert Day and then-just-plain John Moxey both left England for Hollywood TV in the late '60s. At that time, Day had made many more movies, Moxey having run up a huge list of TV credits, for he had been active in live 'serious drama' as well as the hybrid **Saints** and **Gideon's Ways** telefilms. Even without film, he brought a film maker's visual sense to his live and taped dramas, some of which were excellent. They commended him to producer David Susskind, who hired Moxey to tape the TV remakes of **Laura, Hatful of Rain** and **Dial M for Murder.** With actors like Sandy Dennis, Michael Parks, Herschel Bernardi, Peter Falk, Don Stroud, in **Hatful of Rain,** it is not surprising that Moxey decided to pack up and leave England.

The two sides of American TV—the prestigious and the pulp—have become emmeshed in his subsequent career. He is more journeyman than genius. But when the right projects surface, Moxey turns in a thrilling job. **The Night Stalker** is classic genre TV—far more frightening than **Duel,** and in many respects a finer piece of work. Written by Richard Matheson, it is a modern vampire story set in Las Vegas, with Darren McGavin as Kolchak, an ex-New York journalist desperate for a scoop to lift him back to the big time. He slowly realises that the macabre and mysterious murders taking place must be attributed to a vampire. Nobody, of course, believes him—until in a genuinely chilling climax, the vampire is laid traditionally to rest. There is much more to the story than this, both in Matheson's loving script and Moxey's set-pieces; there is detail and ensemble acting. The effect on the small screen is, on first viewing, shattering. The project inspired a sequel **(The Night Strangler)** and the **Kolchak: The Night Stalker** series, none of which Moxey directed and none of which can lick the original's boots.

In a fantasy vein Moxey made **The House that Wouldn't Die** (with Barbara Stanwyck), the similar **Strange and Deadly Occurrence** (Robert Stack and Vera Miles encounter a haunted house), **Home for the Holidays** (a deranged killer loose at a family reunion), **Taste of Evil** (Ms Stanwyck again and a Jimmy Sangster script) plus science-fiction oriented subjects like **The Last Child** where, in a 1984-totalitarian state, only one child is permitted per couple; Michael Cole and Janet Margolin are imprisoned for breaking the law and they escape and flee to Canada. **Genesis II** is a Gene Roddenberry future view, and

Where Have All the People Gone? is a post-radioactive disaster movie.

Moxey has made over twenty telefeatures. The best of his non-fantasies are **Foster and Laurie** and **Smashup on Interstate 5,** which have identical structures. Foster and Laurie (Dorian Harewood and Perry King) were real-life New York cops who were ambushed and killed in 1972. The film begins with the killing, then flashes back to episodes in their lives, showing us the people behind the statistics. Similarly, **Smashup** has the spectacular multi-vehicle pile-up as an opening sequence and takes us back into the lives and problems of a handful of the victims. An extra suspense dimension is now added for when we come out of the flashbacks, we don't know which of the characters will live or die. This story viewpoint was first used by Moxey in **San Francisco International Airport** and though, by **Smashup** the form and technique had been fine honed, clichés were, unfortunately, rife in the flashbacks. Moxey has proved that he is one of the most accomplished contemporary talents and deserves close study.

Gary Nelson (1936-)

1962: **Have Gun-Will Travel**/*Memories of Monica Alice.* 1963: **Have Gun-Will Travel**/*The Debutante, Cage at McNaab, The Savages, Two Plus One.* 1964: **Run Buddy Run**/*The Death of Buddy Overstreet, Down on the Farm, Grand Hotel, Buddy Overstreet Forgive Me.* 1966: **Get Smart**/*The Spy Who Met Himself, Strike While the Agent Is Hot, The Mild Ones, The Mysterious Dr. T., The King Lives?, The Hot Line, Die Spy.* 1967: **Gomer Pyle**/*Win a Date, Two on the Bench.* 1968: **The Good Guys**/*Two's a Crowd.* 1969: **Hawaii Five-O**/*The Joker is Wild Man Wild.* 1971: **The Partners** (pilot) *Here Come the Fuzz, Desperate Ours, Abra Cadaver, Waterloo at Napoleon, How Many Carats in a Grapefruit?, To Catch a Crooke.* 1973: **Kojak**/*Requiem for a Cop;* **MacMillan and Wife**/*Two Dollars on Trouble to Win;* **Toma**/*The Cain Connection, Indictment;* **Faraday and Co**/*Say Hello to a Dead Man* (pilot). 1974: **Police Story**/*Fathers and Sons.* 1975: **MacMillan and Wife**/*No Hearts No Flowers;* **Medical Story** (pilot); **The Invisible Man**/*Stop When Red Lights Flash;* **The Boy Who Talked to Badgers.** 1976: **Panache.** 1977: **Washington: Behind Closed Doors** (6 pts).

Requiem for a Cop, Two Dollars on Trouble to Win, especially *Fathers and Sons,* suggested that Nelson was a director to watch with interest. **Washington: Behind Closed Doors** proved it conclusively. There are two mysteries—why did it take Nelson so long to break out of spoof-comedy? How much more good stuff has he done that we haven't yet seen?

He began as an assistant director, and—so a publicity story of the time went—was promoted to director on *Memories of Monica* and given bride-to-be Judi Meredith as a guest star, as a wedding present by the **Have Gun-Will Travel** production. This technical background in the day-to-day mechanics of production, rather than in writing or editing may prove to be a limiting factor, making him unduly dependent on scripts and sympathetic producers. If

Washington alone was the criterion, doubts about Nelson might be valid. But his other fine segments indicate that he has both technical flair and a point of view, while his comedy background is also an asset. We confidently expect Nelson to remain in the forefront of quality work.

Fans of the feature SANTEE will be pleased to know that their man is neither an oddball, a one-shot or a newcomer.

Sam O'Steen

1974: **I Love You, Goodbye.** 1975: **Queen of the Stardust Ballroom.** 1976: **High Risk Whatever Happened to Rosemary's Baby?**

Queen of the Stardust Ballroom was a latterday **Marty**—and the performances of Maureen Stapleton and Charles Durning as the middle-aged lovers who meet at the Stardust Ballroom survive the glue inherent in the situation. O'Steen was responsible for the overall success of what was, ultimately, a triumph of style and performance over the best instincts of the audience.

Doubts creep in with **I Love You, Goodbye,** a first-draft for **Ballroom,** which has Hope Lange deserting her family to seek greater 'meaning'. It is OK though didactic. **High Risk** is a polished, yet empty caper movie (with circus artists using their skills to pull the big one) and . . . **Rosemary's Baby** a most obvious—and therefore clumsy, disappointing—sequel to the extraordinary Polanski original.

The jury is, as they say, still out. Yet the court reporter, at the risk of future derision, predicts a favourable verdict—sentimentalist that he is.

Leo Penn

1963: **Dr. Kildare**/*The Hand That Hurts The Hand That Heals, Please Let My Baby Live.* 1964: **77 Sunset Strip**/*Bonus Baby;* **Alfred Hitchcock Hour**/*Anyone for Murder?;* **Ben Casey**/*Justice to a Microbe;* **Slattery's People**/*Question: Is Laura the Name of the Game?, Question: Which One Has the Privilege?.* 1965: **I Spy**/*No Exchange on Damaged Merchandise, A Cup of Kindness;* **Voyage to the Bottom of the Sea**/*The Cyborg;* **Lost in Space**/*There Were Giants in the Earth;* **Slattery's People**/*Question: What Did You Do All Day Mr. Slattery?, Question: What's a Requiem for a Loser?, Question: What Time Is the Next Bandwagon?.* 1966: **I Spy**/*So Long Patrick Henry, Dragon's Teeth;* **The Girl from UNCLE**/*The Little John Doe Affair;* **Run for your Life**/*A Game of Violence, The Day Time Stopped, Baby the World's on Fire;* **Star Trek**/*The Enemy Within.* 1967: **Custer**/*Death Hunt, Dangerous Prey;* **The Virginian**/*Stacey;* **Ironside**/*Leaf in the Forest;* **Iron Horse**/*The Prisoners.* 1968: **The Virginian**/*The Heritage, Six Graves at Socorro Creek;* **Gunsmoke**/*The Prisoner.* 1969: **Lancer**/*Blind Man's Bluff, Zee.* 1970: **Marcus Welby MD**/*A Very Special Sailfish, The Worth of a Man, A Woman's Place.* 1971: **Marcus Welby MD**/*I'm Really Trying, Once There Was a Bantu Prince, I Can Hardly Tell You Apart, The White Cane, Don't Ignore the Miracles;* **Hawaii Five-O**/*Nine Ten You're Dead, R & R & R.* 1972: **Cannon**/*The Stakeout, Press Pass to the Slammer;* **Ghost Story**/*The Summer House;* **Owen Marshall, Counselor at Law**/*A Piece of God.* 1973: **Marcus**

Welby MD/*Don't Phase Me Out, The Comeback, Each Day a Miracle, A Joyful Song, The Tall Tree;* **Kojak**/*Die Before They Wake, Therapy in Dynamite;* **Owen Marshall, Counselor at Law**/*Child of Wednesday;* **Columbo**/*Any Old Port in a Storm.* 1974: **Kojak**/*The Best Judge Money Can Buy;* **Owen Marshall, Counselor at Law**/*I've Promised You a Father . . . ;* **Little House on the Prairie**/*Ma's Holiday, The Voice of Thinker Jones, Money Crop;* **Marcus Welby MD**/*Save the Last Dance for Me, Public Secrets;* **Lucas Tanner**/*Winners and Losers, The Noise of a Quiet World.* 1975: **Cannon**/*To Still the Voice, Wedding March, Melted Man;* **Doctors Hospital**/*Point of Maximum Pressure.* 1976: **The Bionic Woman**/*Jaime's Mother;* **Sara**/*The Mountain Man;* **Marcus Welby MD**/*Vanity Case.* 1977: **Kojak**/*Cry for the Kids, The Queen of Hearts is Wild, Take Out Death;* **Switch**/*Hemline Heist, Eyewitness, The Hundred Thousand Ruble Rumble, Fleece of Snow;* **Best Sellers: Dark Secret of Harvest Home** (5 pts). 1978: **Best Sellers: Testimony of Two Men** (2 pts).

A real toiler of the small screen, Penn has worked his way through class shows and trash shows. His segments stand up among the best of the former, and bring a certain emotional gloss to the unvarnished surfaces of the latter. Until **Dark Secret of Harvest Home** there is nothing in his work that an outsider would consider important or outstanding.

Yet for twenty-five years, Penn's sensibility has, with remarkable consistency, been able to give an extra edge of television 'humanism' to series TV. On a most upfront level, **Dr. Kildare, Ben Casey, Marcus Welby MD, Little House on the Prairie, Doctors Hospital, Lucas Tanner** and **Sara** are dangerously close to triple-hankie country. Penn *believes,* very strongly, in the material to hand, and makes the viewer believe in it too. What might have been tripe becomes moving. He even discovered humanity in a **Cannon** script (*The Wedding March*—both frightening and tender) which puts him in a class of one.

The *Cry for the Kids* segment of **Kojak** is a disturbing view of juvenile crime and extends to an almost horrific association with gangsterism (shades of Sidney Kingsley's play DEAD END). While this is admittedly familiar ground (in a generalised fashion, Barry Shear's *Welcome to the Gardens* covers the same territory), Penn is concentrating on a single character, not a group. It is a hard-hitting statement on mob teenage recruitment, which is processed through Penn's emotion filter and comes out even more disturbing. The busy parents who have no time for the embryonic hood, are presented as normal 'caring' people and some of the hoods don't like what they're doing. It shows a world of chaos and, while obviously the script has the chapter and verse, set in other hands it might have seemed purely conventional melo.

Penn may not be anyone's idea of an auteur but it seems to us that his view of the world is consistent throughout his career. Not all his shows are of great significance; he represents, let us say, a John Cromwell, or a Henry King of the small screen, someone whose basic attitudes to life and character animate the creative inventions of other people and bring them to the viewer's attention with force and love. It is not absurd to suggest that Penn is 'mainstream' TV at its most excellent—and, as such, he has made the Ballroom a better place.

Daniel Petrie (1920-)

1961: **The Defenders**/*The Crusader.* 1963: **East Side/West Side** (multiples). 1964: **Seaway**/*Shipment from Marseille, The Last Voyage;* **For the People**/*Guilt Shall Not Escape or Innocence Suffer;* **Suspense**/*Sam Gifford.* 1965: **The Defenders**/*No Knock, Silent Killer, Whitewash.* 1969: **Silent Night Lonely Night; Marcus Welby MD**/*Fun and Games and Michael Ambrose, The Legacy, Homecoming.* 1970: **Ironside**/*Eden Is the Place We Leave;* **Marcus Welby MD**/*Don't Kid a Kidder, Epidemic;* **Four-in-One: San Francisco International Airport**/('untitled' episode). 1971: **The City; A Howling in the Woods; MacMillan and Wife**/*Husbands Wives and Killers;* **Hec Ramsey** (pilot); **The Bold Ones: The Lawyers**/*The Hyland Confession;* **The Man and the City**/*A Very Special Girl.* 1972: **Moon of the Wolf; Banyon**/*Completely Out of Print;* **Ironside**/*Programmed for Panic;* **Trouble Comes to Town; Man and the City**/*Hands of Love.* 1973: **MacMillan and Wife**/*Death of a Monster . . . Birth of a Legend.* 1974: **The Gun and the Pulpit; Mousey.** 1975: **Returning Home.** 1976: **Sybil** (2 pts). 1977: **Eleanor and Franklin: The White House Years.**

From THE IDOL to THE BETSY, Petrie's features have enabled critics to indulge their favourite form of analysis—mocking and scoffing. His TV work is another thing entirely. The critics do not watch it and when they do, they ignore the director. In fact, it indicates once more that it is not simply the sizes of the respective screens which are different. Petrie *is* a TV director. Indeed, there is a strong thematic unity in the majority of his TV work, the theme of 'service'. **The Defenders, East Side/West Side** and **For the People** first involved him with urban social problems. He was still making such shows six years later with **Man and the City, Ironside** and **The Bold Ones.** In the tele-features, Kirk Douglas is a biology teacher in **Mousey; Returning Home** is a remake of THE BEST YEARS OF OUR LIVES (the men have served their country—how will it now serve them?). In **Trouble Comes to Town,** smalltown sheriff Lloyd Bridges is torn between serving the (racist) community or the memory of (and his debt to) the man who saved his life, by taking care of the man's son, who is black. **Eleanor and Franklin: The White House Years** obviously presents Roosevelt as a man serving the people of the United States, as well as serving as a husband (with dreary results).

Petrie's best is **The Gun and the Pulpit,** an extraordinary example of thematic glut. Petrie shapes the film into three basic areas of 'service'; the gunfighter initially serves only himself, then dons the garb of a dead priest and pretends to serve the church. The two elements are finally drawn together when he serves the whole frontier town, both as gunfighter and priest. Only a refugee from a bygone age such as Marjoe Gortner could have convincingly pulled off the part.

Moon of the Wolf boldly ventures (into werewolf/**Night Stalker** country) where one would think someone like Petrie would fear to tread. **A Howling in the Woods** is also spine-tingle time, while **Sybil** is a mammoth vehicle for Joanne Woodward to revamp THREE FACES OF EVE whilst adding a myriad more faces. It is written by Stewart Stern, screenwriter of REBEL WITHOUT A CAUSE as well as, more significantly, RACHEL, RACHEL and SUMMER WISHES—WINTER DREAMS, both for Joanne Woodward.

Whatever Petrie's sins are on the big screen, there are virtues galore on the small one; he has a nervous, actor-oriented style augmented by flashes of visual panache, like the weird, long, long tracking shot opening of **Gun and the Pulpit.** Although he can tend towards the pompous and the tendentious, overall Petrie has, true to his own theme, served TV well.

David Lowell Rich (1923-)

1956: **Studio One** (multiples); **CBS Workshop** (multiples); **Big Town**/(multiples); **The Big Story**/(multiples). 1957: **M Squad**/Shakedown. 1958: **Maverick**/*Yellow River;* **M Squad**/*The Black Mermaid, Chicago Bluebeard, The System.* 1959: **77 Sunset Strip**/*Eyewitness;* **M Squad**/*Model in the Lake.* 1960: **Wagon Train**/*The Tiburcio Mendez Story;* **General Electric Theatre**/*The Secret Life of John Chapman;* **Zane Grey Theatre** (multiples). 1961: **Route 66**/*The Opponent, Like a Motherless Child, City of Wheels, How Much a Pound is Albatross?, Incident on a Bridge;* **Naked City**/*The Day it Rained Mink, A Run for the Money, The Multiplicity of Herbert Konish.* 1962: **Route 66**/*Two on the House, A Feat of Strength, Kiss the Maiden all Forlorn, 1800 Days to Justice, Between Hello and Goodbye, One Tiger to a Hill, Journey to Nineveh, Suppose I Said I Was the Queen of Spain;* **Naked City**/*The One Marked Hot Gives Cold;* **Alfred Hitchcock Hour**/*To Catch a Butterfly* (+ pr). 1963: **Route 66**/*A Gift for a Warrior, The Voice at the End of the Line, Somehow it Gets to Be Tomorrow, Man out of Time;* **Twilight Zone**/*Of Late I Think of Cliffordville;* **Naked City**/*Go Fight City Hall;* **Arrest and Trial**/*Roll of the Dice, A Shield Is for Hiding Behind, Inquest into a Bleeding Heart.* 1964: **Kraft Suspense Theatre**/*Leviathan Five, Won't it Ever Be Morning?, March from Camp Tyler;* **Bob Hope Chrysler Theatre**/*See How They Run, Wings of Fire, Guilty or Not Guilty.* 1965: **Laredo**/*Yahoo!, Three Guns to Texas.* 1967: **The Borgia Stick.** 1968: **Marcus Welby MD** (pilot). 1969: **Mission Impossible**/*Underground;* **Set This Town on Fire.** 1970: **Berlin Affair; Ironside**/*Check, Mate and Murder* (2 pts); **The Sheriff; The Mask of Sheba.** 1971: **Owen Marshall: Counselor at Law**/*Legacy of Fear;* **Marcus Welby MD**/*Tender Comrade, Ask Me Again Tomorrow;* **Ransom for Alice.** 1972: **Ghost Story**/*Alter Ego;* **All My Darling Daughters; Brock's Last Case; The Judge and Jake Wyler; Lieutenant Schuster's Wife; Profane Comedy.** 1973: **The Horror at 37,000 Feet; Satan's School for Girls; The Crime Club; Beg Borrow or Steal; Death Race; Runaway.** 1974: **Aloha Means Goodbye; The Chadwick Family.** 1975: **Bridger—The Fortieth Day** (+ pr); **You Lie so Deep My Love** (+ pr). 1976: **The Daughters of Joshua Cabe Return.** 1977: **A Family Upside Down.**

Rich's career is a microcosmic history of two decades of American TV. The younger brother of John Rich, he began with live TV in New York, then cut his celluloid teeth with the undemanding, yet highly influential **Maverick, M Squad** and **77 Sunset Strip.** In the early '60s he became identified with the social-realist strain, and virtually defined the twin peaks of a new kind of aware TV, **Naked City** and particularly **Route 66**—in its own way, an EASY RIDER ten years ahead of its time. With the decline of such series in the middle of the decade and the growing dependence on one-shot anthology drama as the medium's sop to 'respectability', Rich continued in the forefront of such activity. But with the arrival of the MOVIE OF THE WEEK, one would have expected him to have experienced greater freedom of material: there has, instead, been a decline in his fertility, imagination and ambition. By any standards **The Daughters of Joshua Cabe Return** is execrable.

The Borgia Stick however, (THE BIG HEAT meets THE PARALLAX VIEW) and **Brock's Last Case** (Richard Widmark, a 'retired' city detective involved with rural crime) have Rich in good form. Whatever the virtues of some of the late-period pieces, things like the crusading *Go Fight City Hall, Suppose I Said I Was the Queen of Spain, Somehow It Gets to Be Tomorrow* and others of their ilk define Rich's way with players and eye for location shooting more memorably. His decline into easy formulae is a disappointment, when it is clear that he is capable of near excellence.

Sutton Roley

1960: **77 Sunset Strip**/*Tiger by the Tail;* **Wagon Train**/*The Cathy Eckhart Story.* 1962: **Have Gun-Will Travel**/*The Exiles.* 1964: **Gunsmoke**/*Aunt Thede.* 1965: **Big Valley**/*The River Monarch;* **The Man from UNCLE**/*The Summit 5 Affair;* **Lost in Space**/*The Oasis, The Sky Is Falling, Wish Upon A Star, One of Our Dogs Is Missing.* 1966: **Voyage to the Bottom of the Sea**/*The Phantom, Dead Man's Doubloons, The Return of the Phantom.* 1967: **The Invaders**/*Quantity Unknown, The Innocents.* 1968: **Mannix**/*To the Swiftest Death;* **Lost in Space**/*The Anti-Matter Man, The Space Croppers.* 1969: **Mission Impossible**/*The Cardinal, Underwater, Crackup.* 1970: **Mission Impossible**/*Blast.* 1971: **Sweet Sweet Rachel.** 1973: **Snatched.** 1975: **Satan's Triangle.** 1976: **Hawaii Five-O**/*Double Exposure, A Capitol Crime;* **Baretta**/*They Don't Make 'Em Like They Used to.* 1977: **Kojak**/*A Strange Kind of Love;* **Starsky and Hutch**/*Death in a Different Place;* **Switch**/*Butterfly Mourning, The 12th Commandment, The Things That Belong to Mickey Costello;* **Hawaii Five-O**/*Elegy in a Rain Forest;* **Lucan**/*One Punch Wolfson, The Lost Boy.*

Maybe Roley's always been good, but only recently has it seemed so. We will certainly be looking back (and forward) with interest—for some of his recent shows have been extraordinarily good—*Death in a Different Place,* one of the finest of all **Starsky and Hutch** segments; *A Strange Kind of Love,* a tremendously good **Kojak;** *Elegy in a Rain Forest* the best recent **Hawaii;** the best two **Lucan's.**

His style (detractors be warned . . .) is reminiscent of Sidney Furie's, shooting through knotholes and bead curtains in the urban wasteland, using wide-angle, distorting lenses and long takes outdoors. While this may sound irritating, allied to a genuine care, concern and anger for outcasts and losers (be they criminals, deviants or *enfants sauvages),* these elements of his style mesh to brilliant effect, for they are not *used* for effect. They draw the audience visually into an equally caring frame of mind—concern and anger rise in the viewer—ultimately it *understands.*

Boris Sagal (1923-   )

1958: **77 Sunset Strip**/*The Well-Selected Frame.* 1959: **Johnny Staccato**/*The Nature of the Night, The Shop of the Four Winds, The Wild Reed;* **Adventures in Paradise**/*Hangman's Island.* 1961: **The Defenders**/*Perjury;* **The Twilight Zone**/*The Silence, The Arrival.* 1962: **Alfred Hitchcock Hour**/*The Test;* **Sam Benedict**/*Hannigan, Nor Practice Makes Perfect.* 1963: **Dundee and Culhane**/*The Turn the Other Cheek Brief, The Dead Man's Brief;* **Naked City**/*An Economy of Death.* 1965: **A Man Called Shenandoah**/*Survival;* **Dr Kildare**/*Catch a Crooked Mouse.* 1966: **T.H.E. Cat**/(series' producer); *To Kill a Priest, The Sandman, King of Limpets, Payment Overdue, Crossing at Destino Bay.* 1968: **Cimarron Strip**/*Nobody.* 1969: **Night Gallery** (pilot co-dir); **Destiny of a Spy; UMC** (pilot). 1970: **Hauser's Memory; Four-in-One: San Francisco International Airport**/*Situation Red, Hostage, Emergency Alert.* 1971: **McCloud**/*The Disposal Man;* **Hitched** (aka **Westward the Wagon**). 1972: **Columbo**/*The Greenhouse Jungle.* 1973: **Columbo**/*Candidate for Crime;* **The Snoop Sisters**/*Fear is a Free Throw;* **Deliver Us from Evil; Madigan**/*The Lisbon Beat, The Naples Beat.* 1974: **Ironside**/*Amy Prentiss:* (aka *The Chief);* **Indict and Convict; Three for the Road; A Case of Rape.** 1975: **The Dream Makers; Man on the Outside** (pilot) for **(Griff); The Oregon Trail; The Greatest Gift; The Runaway Barge** (+ pr); **The Harness; Mallory: Circumstantial Evidence.** 1976: **Rich Man Poor Man**/pts 4, 5, 6 & 7. 1977: **The Moneychangers** (6 pts). 1978: **Eisenhower: The War Years.**

Up to the late '60s, Sagal's TV career combined a certain black humour with a tough, sometimes sadistic view of genre affairs. **T.H.E. Cat,** for instance, which he produced and oft-times directed, was an almost totally amoral caper series (with Robert Loggia as a cool, cat burglar apparently carrying out breathtaking stunts organised by Paul Baxley) with no sense of 'reality', of 'significance', or 'responsibility'. To those that think 'that's the nature of escapist TV', we make the obvious point that no series or programme exists in an existential vacuum. However much they fail, most shows *try* to be 'real', or 'significant' or—if they are like **T.H.E. Cat**—'responsible'.

Destiny of a Spy, however, began to take Sagal down a different road. One of the first genuine tele-movies, it is a bleak and rather heartless spy story, influenced by Le Carré to be sure, but carrying its own strange charge. As the '70s have wound on, it has become clear that Sagal is, in fact, a most bizarre misanthrope, turning out yet more bleak and heartless shows which carry the same strange electric charge. **Hauser's Memory** is more accessible than others, being a fast, baffling, sci-fi extension of **Destiny of a Spy,** (David McCallum has a memory transplant and finds himself in a ruthless world full of extremely nasty characters . . .).

Hitched is an unduly sour western (its European title, **Westward the Wagon**—the singular—being at first sight a comment on TV budgetary restrictions); **Indict and Convict,** an unusually sour courtroom melo (with the D.A. a chief suspect in a double murder case); **A Case of Rape,** given the subject matter, could hardly be less than an unusually sour view of human relationships.

Two of Sagal's tele-features stand out for an especially uncompromising view of life—**The Dream Makers** and **The Greatest Gift.** The first stars James Franciscus as a university teacher who becomes involved in the music business he's bright eyed and bushy tailed, a tailor-made young executive; he relishes the creative power and the physical buzz he gets from the job after years of leading an imitation of life. But . . . a payola scandal sends him down the tubes—and he never manages to crawl out). The film starts with Franciscus driving a cab, and his passenger pulling a gun, demanding his money. Everything else is a flashback—and when we return, there is no reprieve—he is killed. It is senseless, meaningless, purposeless. The point is that he got that joy, that amazing high; he *knew* he was good and simply couldn't go back to teaching.

The Greatest Gift initially appears to be a typical slice of Americana, seen through the eyes of a growing adolescent, the son of rural preacher, Glenn Ford, and wife, Julie Harris. The style of the film, however, continually undercuts the normal rosy glow with which such stories are conventionally told, and in another 'senseless' climax, Ford is killed by the menacing Harris Yulin who, as sheriff, escapes legal retribution. The boy, Lance Kerwin, determines on personal revenge—stalks Yulin, has him in his gun sights, but cannot pull the trigger. With sister and mother, he drives off to a 'new' life. The overwhelming feeling is of hopelessness, of the meanness and arbitrary hand of fate.

The remorseless unveiling of such emotional trauma operates on a very depressing but consistently personal level. Sagal has been able to use genre and TV formula in a subversive and disturbing way. His is one of the most distinctive of contemporary voices.

George Schaefer (1920-)

1958: **Little Moon of Alban.** 1960: **Macbeth.** 1961/1966: **Hallmark Hall of Fame** (multiples). 1968: **Victoria Regina.** 1969: **The Magnificent Yankee.** 1972: **A War of Children.** 1973: **A Time for Love** (co-dir). 1974: **F. Scott Fitzgerald and 'The Last of the Belles'.** 1976: **Truman at Potsdam, Amelia Earheart.**

With a background in Yale Drama School and ten years producing and directing for the theatre, Schaefer's TV work is heavily influenced by theatrical conventions. **Macbeth,** released as a feature in Europe, seemed impossibly arch and clumsy on the big screen, Maurice Evans's tragic figure grotesque and hugely wrong. It was more powerful on TV and in that context, a noble and an important event. Indeed, Schaefer won the Emmy for it.

F. Scott Fitzgerald and 'The Last of the Belles', fourteen years later, revealed however that Schaefer's style was still heavily dependent on the text and on the player. As the text was by James Costigan, the players Richard Chamberlain and Blythe Danner, and the project itself an ambitious one (intercutting the real-life Scott and Zelda in 1928, and a dramatisation of the story *The Last of the Belles* with its own stylisation of the couple's courtship)a 'lack' of rich visual resource was hardly noticed. A greater stylist than Schaefer would have more successfully woven the present/past, reality/illusion web.

James Costigan was the writer of **A War of Children,** an altogethe tougher, more involving drama which took its impulse from the Catholic v Protestant conflict in Northern Ireland; it detailed the remorseless, perniciou growth of hatred, in a hitherto 'untouched' family.

Whilst Schaefer is content to work with closeups and dialogue, he i concerned to pick away at surface generalities and search for the emotiona 'truth'. He is to be followed therefore less for his visual sensibility than as a guid to a humane and telling understanding; his work is an orchestration of 'quality'

Barry Shear (1923-)

1964: **Tom, Dick & Mary**/*A Lesson in Living.* 1966: **Man from UNCLE**/*The Minus X Affair;* **The Gi from UNCLE**/*The Dog Gone Affair, The Faustus Affair.* 1967: **The Girl from UNCLE**/*The Mouli Ruse Affair, The UFO Affair, The Low Blue C Affair, The Phi-Beta Killer Affair, The Carpathian Cape Affair.* 1968: **Julia**/*The Interview;* **Ironside**/*I, The People, A Drug on the Market;* **Tarzan**/*End of Challenge, Alex the Great, Trek to Terror.* 1969: **Night Gallery** pilot (co-dir); **The Name of th Game**/*Keep the Doctor Away;* **Ironside**/*Seeing Is Believing, Goodbye to Yesterday.* 1970: **Th Name of the Game**/*The Enemy before Us* (+ pr), *I Love You Billy Baker* (2 pts, + pr), *The Man Wh Killed a Ghost.* 1971: **The Sixth Sense**/*The Heart That Wouldn't Stay Buried;* **MacMillan an Wife**/*The Easy Sunday Murder Case;* **The Name of the Game**/*A Sister from Napoli* (+ pr); **Alias Smit and Jones**/*The Day they Hanged Kid Curry, Dreadful Sorry Clementine, The Bounty Hunter, Th Reformation of Harry Briscoe;* **Hawaii Five-O**/*King Kanehaneha Cloak Blues.* 1972: **Short Walk t Daylight; Jigsaw**/*Kiss the Dream Goodbye;* **Cool Million**/*The Abduction of Bayard Barne Search*/*The 24 Carat Hit;* **Ellery Queen: Don't Look Behind You.** 1973: **Jarrett; McCloud**/*Butc Cassidy Rides Again.* 1974: **McCloud**/*The Barefoot Girls of Bleecker Street;* **Get Christi Love!**/*Emperor of Death Street;* **Ironside**/*Class of '40;* **Police Woman**/*The Trick Book* (2 pts), *Silk Flanagan;* **Punch and Judy.** 1975: **Strike Force; Joe Forrester**/*Welcome to the Gardens;* **Polic Women**/*Silence;* **Starsky and Hutch** (pilot). 1976: **The Feather and Father Gang**/*Welcome Hom Vince, Here a Spy There a Spy, For the Love of Sheila;* **Streets of San Francisco**/*In Case of Madnes* **Baa Baa Black Sheep**/*The Deadliest Enemy of All* (2 pts), *Devil in the Slot;* **City of Angels**/*Th Losers.* 1977: **San Pedro Beach Bums** (pilot); **Lucan**/*How Do You Run Forever?.*

WILD IN THE STREETS brought Shear up front; ACROSS 110th STREET was welcome reminder he deserved that critical attention; DEADLY TRACKERS (whic he took over when Samuel Fuller was fired) was a convenient excuse to forge him again. His TV work is, however, consistently remarkable, and whilst h appears to be content to work with formula shows (there are very few tele features in his credits) he seems able to invest them with an almost immediatel recognisable quality.

One theme which recurs with a certain frequency is that of home, roots, th past. *Class of '40* is murder at a college reunion; *How Do You Run Foreve* presents wild child **Lucan** with a set of parents who give him a home, love an stability, and then wrenches them all away. Most impressively (and in one of th finest pieces of genre TV) *The Enemy before Us* takes **Name of the Gam** series regular Tony Franciosa back to his roots in New York's Little Italy.

fuses brilliantly the personal story of his return and his relationships with his stepbrother (Martin Balsam) and his stepmother (Katina Paxinou) with the segment's 'plot' about dope-pushing and crime on the streets. In this, one found (or heard) Orson Welles and the credit 'as the voice of Thomas Wolfe' reinforcing the messages of YOU CAN'T GO HOME AGAIN.

The crime-on-the-streets theme with a concern and emotional sympathy for ethnic cultures, values and problems, recurs in such segments as *Welcome to the Gardens* where cop-on-the-beat **Joe Forrester** becomes involved with a Chicano gang war in a slum area. Though veering too heavily towards a do-gooding liberalism, the show successfully meshed vibrant characters and performances and a true emotional portrait of underprivileged people with the formula mechanics of the series. *The Trick Book,* a two-part **Police Woman,** is a curious Jekyll and Hyde of a show. Part one is almost wholly brilliant, a mosaic of converging themes and developing patterns, as Angie Dickinson (posing as a hooker) and Earl Holliman investigate the murder of an upmarket brothel keeper, whose trick book (list of client's names) has been stolen. Blackmail, murder, 'two cultures', and hypocrisy fuse in a surgical dissection of apparently respectable society. Jack Gilford is encouraged to a beautiful performance as a seedy, ageing private eye who suddenly senses riches to be within his grasp. Unaccountably, part two is almost routine. Seen as a whole, the power of the first part carries the show through to the end. *Silence,* another **Police Woman** segment, is another great show. Television is television is television, however, and Shear then came up with *Silky Flanagan*—an extremely silly, lightweight and pointless segment.

Throughout his TV career, flippancy has rubbed shoulders with flair and feeling. **Girl from UNCLE** is comic-book humour. **Jarrett** is a thriller where the villain (Anthony Quayle) is a comic-book collector. (Sequences where his priceless collection is on view have been known to make comic buffs weep with frustration). Such shows highlight Shear's capacity to handle action and other plastic values. His understanding of pace, rhythm, angle, cutting, etc, place him, if not on the same level as Don Siegel, not far below. On the TV ladder, he is rungs higher than most.

Elliot Silverstein

1960: **Naked City**/*Bullets Cost Too Much, Take and Put.* 1961: **Have Gun-Will Travel**/*The Kid;* **Twilight Zone**/*The Obsolete Man;* **The Defenders**/*Along Came a Spider.* 1962: **Naked City**/*The Night the Saints Lost Their Halos, Landscape with Dead Figures;* **The Defenders**/*Grandma TNT;* **Route 66**/*Layout at Glen Canyon, The Swan Bed.* 1963: **The Defenders**/*The Cruel Hook, The Man Who Saved His Country;* **Twilight Zone**/*Spur of the Moment.* 1964: **Arrest and Trial**/*He Ran for His Life.*

CAT BALLOU established Silverstein as a small-screen figure to follow, if not to get excited about. Logically he would have 'made it' after its success, but quirky, ill-realised films like THE HAPPENING followed and projects slowly dried up. THE CAR is the only recent film to come along for him, and TV does not seem to have welcomed him back (as it did Jack Smight and Tom Gries when they both took to cover after feature fiascos). However, Silverstein spent the early '60s among the most successful and creatively rewarding series. *Grandma TNT,* with Lillian Gish in a rare TV part as a sprightly problem for **The Defenders,** *The Man Who Saved His Country,* from a fine script by Albert Ruben, and *He Runs for His Life* with George Segal at his most vulnerable, suggest that this period was Silverstein's happiest, and most consistently satisfying.

Alexander Singer

1964: **Profiles in Courage**/*The Andrew Johnson Story;* **The Fugitive**/*Runner in the Dark.* 1965: **The Fugitive**/*The Old Man Picked a Lemon, Everybody Gets Hit in the Mouth Sometime, Trial by Fire;* **Lost in Space**/*The Derelict.* 1966: **Mission Impossible**/*The Seal;* **Bob Hope Chrysler Theatre: Enigma**/*A Song Called Revenge;* **The Fugitive**/*Not with a Whimper;* **Hawk**/*Legacy for a Lousy Future.* 1968: **Lancer**/*Foldy;* **The Monkees**/*Monkees a la Modé, Monkee Mayor, 99 Pound Weakling, Art for Monkees' Sake, Everywhere a Sheik Sheik, Monkees Watch Their Feet.* 1969: **Name of the Game**/*The Suntan Mob;* **Mission Impossible**/*Heir Apparent, The Exchange, The Freeze.* 1971: **Alias Smith and Jones**/*How to Rob a Bank in One Hard Lesson, Everything Else You Can Steal, The McCreedy Bust: Going Going Gone.* 1972: **Ghost Story—Circle of Fear**/*Earth, Air, Fire and Water;* **Alias Smith and Jones**/*The Long Chase, High Lonesome Country, The McCreedy Feud, McGuffin, The Biggest Game in the West.* 1973: **Kojak**/*Web of Death;* **Jigsaw**/*Girl on the Run* (co-dir); **Ironside**/*Murder by One;* **Shaft**/*The Kidnapping.* 1974: **The Magician**/*The Illusion of the Stainless Steel Lady;* **Police Woman**/*Above and Beyond, The Killer Cowboys;* **Lucas Tanner**/*Collision.* 1975: **The 1st 36 Hours of Dr Durant;** **Police Woman**/*Flowers of Evil;* **Gibbsville**/*Afternoon Waltz;* **Joe Forrester**/*The Witness, No Probable Cause;* **The Time Travellers.** 1976: **Million Dollar Ripoff.** 1977: **Quincy**/*Touch of Death;* **Rockford Files**/*Forced Retirement;* **Logan's Run**/*The Collectors.*

Having been stills photographer on Kubrick's KILLER'S KISS, Singer began his own directorial career with A COLD WIND IN AUGUST, the highly acclaimed May-December love drama. Singer's sympathy for the older woman in a relationship and his affinity with the desolate urban vistas which acted as a visual simile for her bleak future, led observers to predict big things from him. Perhaps unwisely (after the fascinating PSYCHE '59) he allowed himself to vulgarise the same plot for LOVE HAS MANY FACES. Lana Turner was incapable of getting close to the intensity of Lola Albright's performance in the earlier film, while the sumptuous settings of Acapulco had none of the symbolic reverberations they were supposed to convey. Along with the undistinguished Almeria western CAPTAIN APACHE and GLASS HOUSES (unseen in Britain) that is Singer's movie career to date. Maybe he now regrets introducing Kubrick to James B. Harris—who went on to become The Kube's producer on THE KILLING, PATHS OF GLORY and LOLITA.

It is not our purpose to over-emphasise the distinction between film and

TV. Quite the reverse, in fact. It would be virtually impossible to make COLD WIND IN AUGUST as a movie in the highly competitive '70s, except as a skinflick. If it was any guide to Singer's real interests and ambitions, its intimacy and small scale suggest that he is temperamentally more attuned to TV. Singer should have no regrets for his work is of consistently high quality.

His actual style is as compellingly elegant as Paul Wendkos's, although his concern and sympathy for character make his overall texture warmer and more vital. When emotions erupt, the style mirrors the passion, still meticulous, but expressively reinforcing the drama, sucking the viewer into the appropriate level of care, involvement and excitement. Singer's New York background and almost innate street sense make him ideally suited for torrid crime shows and *Legacy for a Lousy Future* remains in the mind a decade after its first transmission as the best example of Burt Reynolds's **Hawk** series, a masterly orchestration of urban melancholia. *The Kidnapping,* a **Shaft** segment, similarly fuses desperate actions and delicious action into a canvas of cool chaos. **The Magician**'s *Illusion of the Stainless Steel Lady* is perhaps the best of a short-lived but fascinating series—with another engrossing portrait of a pathetic 'older woman' (here, Nina Foch) fused together with a typically audacious plot. The lighter side of Singer has been best seen in the **Alias Smith and Jones** segments—most memorably *McGuffin,* a fifty minute homage to Hitchcock's legendary device, and the apotheosis of the Roy Huggins patent of convoluted plots and daffy deception. In this lighter vein, and most curiously, Singer had a six-segment connection with **The Monkees**—he being the only really 'established' director to work on the series.

The **Gibbsville** segment *Afternoon Waltz,* though far from successful (the series itself never ever quite defines its real nature) was a surprising reprise, once more, of COLD WIND IN AUGUST, this time with Hope Lange, impossibly married to a much older man, taking a young man to her heart and her bed (the situation heightened—or made even more mawkish—by his going blind). Even so, the delicacy of the treatment, and the final shot as the cameras pull away from the couple, dancing their waltz, reaches a level of sad beauty. Elsewhere we find other authentic Singer sensibilities, and realise that indeed he is able to impose himself very firmly on his material.

Robert Stevens

1955: **Alfred Hitchcock Presents**/*The Older Sister, The Gentleman from America, Our Cook's a Treasure, Premonition, Momentum, You Got to Have Luck.* 1956: **Alfred Hitchcock Presents**/*Place of Shadows, The Perfect Murder, Portrait of Jocelyn, One for the Road, The Glass Eye, Heart of Gold.* 1957: **Alfred Hitchcock Presents**/*The Motive, Miss Bracegirdle Does Her Duty.* 1958: **Alfred Hitchcock Presents**/*Design for Loving, A Man with a Problem, Tea Time, The Canary Sedan, The Waxwork, Don't Interrupt, The Hands of Mr Ottermole.* 1959: **Alfred Hitchcock Presents**/*Appointment at Ebren, Speciality of the House, The Impossible Dream, I'll Take Care of You;* **The**

Twilight Zone/*Where Is Everybody?, Walking Distance;* **Playhouse 90**/*Misalliance;* **Rendezvous**/*Alone.* 1960: **Alfred Hitchcock Presents**/*The Dangerous People, The Greatest Monster of Them All, The Ordeal of Mrs Snow, John Brown's Body, The Manacled.* 1963: **Alfred Hitchcock Hour**/*Goodbye George, The Magic Shop;* **The Great Adventure**/*The President Vanishes.* 1964: **Alfred Hitchcock Hour**/*Consider the Ways;* **For the People**/*The Right to Kill.* 1965: **Alfred Hitchcock Hour**/*The Monkey's Paw—A Retelling;* **The Defenders**/*Only a Child, Unwritten Law;* **Coronet Blue**/*Faces.* 1968: **Journey to the Unknown**/*Miss Belle, Eve.*

Shaw's *Misalliance* in Stevens's list of premonitions, murders, shadows, waxworks, dreams, dangers, ordeals, monsters, magic, and mayhem looks like an aberration—and maybe it is, but in truth this is an incomplete list of credits. Stevens's TV activity comes in a period where research is currently proving difficult. It is more than an accident, however, that Stevens has been engaged with such dark and sinister areas. His Hitchcock work is a virtual history of that show's decade of excellence. Taking *Goodbye George* and, particularly, *The Magic Shop* as typical, Stevens's work here is also a summation of the perpetual excellence achieved within the format. *The Magic Shop*—which only exists for young John Megma; his parents, Leslie Nielsen and Peggy McKay have never been able to find it—and its weird proprietor, David Opatoshu, also defines **The Twilight Zone** of the privileged imagination, as well as that series itself. *Where Is Everybody?* (T.Zs premier segment) is a hallucinatory exercise, with a genuinely creepy ambience; Earl Holliman comes into a town suffering from a *Marie Celeste* problem. The 'logical explanation' does nothing to alleviate the disturbing vibrations already set up. *Walking Distance* is more elegaic, with an almost Celtic feel to it; Gig Young yearns nostalgically to return to the simplicity of his youth, and treats the supernatural in an almost Japanese manner.

Stevens seems to have faded from both big and small screens. His work, however, will doubtless prove to be significant, consistent and important.

Don Taylor (1920-)

1958: **M Squad**/*Man in Hiding, Accusation, Frightened Wife;* **Alfred Hitchcock Presents**/*Invitation to an Accident, Total Loss, Listen Listen, The Right Kind of House, Fatal Figures, The Crocodile Case.* 1959: **M Squad**/*The Hand Made Murder;* **Just Dennis (Dennis the Menace)**/*Mr Wilson's Award, The Christmas Story;* **Tightrope**/*Two Private Eyes.* 1960: **M Squad**/*The Outsider;* **Just Dennis**/*Dennis and the Open House.* 1962: **87th Precinct**/*Idol in the Dust;* **Checkmate**/*The Thrill Seeker, Melody for Murder, The Paper Killer, A Funny Thing Happened on My Way to the Game* (+ co-wr). 1963: **Burke's Law**/*Who Killed What's His Name?, Who Killed Marty Kelso?, Who Killed Andy Zygmunt?, Who Killed My Girl?* 1964: **Burke's Law**/*Who Killed the Surf Broad?, Who Killed Cornelius Gilbert?* 1965: **Amos Burke—Secret Agent**/*Operation Long Shadow.* 1968: **The Name of the Game**/*Lola in Lipstick;* **Something for a Lonely Man.** 1969: **The Man Hunter.** 1970: **Night Gallery**/*They're Tearing Down Tim Riley's Bar;* **Wild Women.** 1971: **Night Gallery**/*The Messiah of Mott Street;* **Heat of Anger**; **Cannon**/*Cain's Mark, Dead Pigeon.* 1975: **Mobile One**/*The Bank Job, The Informant, Life Preserver, Californium 252.* 1976: **Petrocelli**/*Night Games* (pilot).

Between Taylor's baby-faced innocence and earnest intensity as an actor in films such as NAKED CITY, BATTLEGROUND, STALAG 17 and his current career directing features (none of which, including ISLAND OF DOCTOR MOREAU have set the world on fire) lies over twenty years of a largely lightweight TV career. His twin-involvement behind the camera as a writer (short stories, radio dramas, one-act plays as well as teleplays) indicates that he has more to say than many actors-turned-director. His two segments of **Night Gallery,** both from Rod Serling scripts, support this view. They are gentle, emotional explorations of human loss and expectation of a very high quality.

They're Tearing Down Tim Riley's Bar, with a fine performance by William Windom, uses the bar of the title and its imminent destruction as a metaphor for the waste of Windom's life as a minor executive, while *The Messiah of Mott Street* is an unashamedly sentimental, yet powerfully moving, Christmas allegory about the human will to live. Edward G. Robinson, whose performance in SOYLENT GREEN was a standout, excels it here in a similar role as a dying man hanging on desperately to life for the sake of his grandson. In a scene where he fights off The Angel of Death, Taylor's camera adopts a distanced high angle to simply, yet ideally, record the performance. It is reminiscent of a similar scene in Mann's FALL OF THE ROMAN EMPIRE. Taylor's orchestration of the elements at his disposal is masterly and suggests that whilst he is unable to go it alone, when he has collaborators of a high order, he can more than match their talent.

Jud Taylor

1966: **Felony Squad**/*Killer with a Badge;* **Man Called Shenandoah**/*Aces and Kings, End of a Legend, The Riley Brand, Muted Fifes & Muffled Drums;* **Girl from UNCLE**/*Garden of Evil Affair.* 1967: **Dr Kildare**/*With Hellfire & Thunder* (pr), *A Reverence of Life* (pr), *The Bell in the School House* (pr). 1968: **Star Trek**/*The Paradise Syndrome, Wink of an Eye, Let That Be Your Last Battlefield, Mark of Gideon, The Cloud Minders.* 1970: **Weekend of Terror.** 1971: **The Bold Ones: The Doctors/** *Discovery at Fourteen;* **Revenge; The Rookies; Suddenly Single.** 1972: **Say Goodbye Maggie Cole.** 1973: **Hawkins on Murder** (pilot); **Tenafly**/*The Cash and Carry Caper.* 1974: **Search for the Gods; Winterkill.** 1975: **The Disappearance of Flight 412.** 1976: **Tail Gunner Joe; Return to Earth** (+ pr); **Future Cop.**

Taylor has made the transition from small screen actor (he can be seen in, for instance, **Fugitive**/*Glass Tightrope)* to a director of often challenging telefeatures, with such intriguing series segments as *Wink of an Eye,* one of the best of the third-season **Star Treks**. Not surprisingly it is as a director of actors that Taylor has garnered most praise. Shelley Winters in **Revenge,** kidnapping the man she feels is responsible for her husband's death; Susan Hayward, in **Say Goodbye Maggie Cole,** another widow, a research doctor, picking up the strands of life again by returning to general practice; Andy Griffith as a rural police officer in **Winterkill,** trying to find a killer before the national law enforcement agencies are called in; James Stewart in **Hawkins on Murder,** playing a variant on his cunning 'backwoods country lawyer' from ANATOMY OF A MURDER. Most impressive of all perhaps, Cliff Robertson in **Return to Earth,** as Buzz Aldrin on his return from the moon, showing the depression into which he sank as a direct consequence of the Apollo mission.

Clyde Ware

1962: **Great Adventure/**(wr) *The Great Diamond Mountain, A Boy at War.* 1964: **Alfred Hitchcock Hour** (wr) *Final Performance.* 1965: **Gunsmoke** (wr) *Piney, The Photographer.* 1966: **Gunsmoke/**(wr) *The Gold Takers, The Wrong Man* (co-wr), *Saturday Night, Old Friend, The Lure, The Ladies from St Louis.* 1967: **Gunsmoke/**(wr) *Cattle Barons, Major Glory* (co-wr). 1969: **The Quiet Gun** (wr). 1971: **No Drums, No Bugles** (wr/pr/dir). 1972: **The Hatfields and McCoys** (wr/dir). 1973: **Pretty Boy Floyd** (wr/dir).

Surfacing to write, produce and direct in the early '70s after a decade as a writer of predominantly western segments, Ware's is a curiously distinctive talent. **No Drums, No Bugles** tells of Ashley Gatrell (Martin Sheen) who is evidently a legend of the American Civil War, not for his courage in battle, but for his courage in refusing to fight at all. Unable to relate to the war, he holes up for three years in a cave near his West Virginia home. The battles and skirmishes are seen in fragmentary long-shots. Martin Sheen, in what is effectively a one-man show, displays masterly talent. **The Hatfields and McCoys** concerns another kind of legend, that of the feuding families of Kentucky and **Pretty Boy Floyd** (Martin Sheen again, with Kim Darby and Michael Parks) is an exploration of the legendary '20s hood.

Whatever Ware's background may be (one suspects he keeps a jug of moonshine next to the typewriter) his love for and curiosity about American history, its heroes and anti-heroes is as strong as that of John Milius. Where Ware's single-mindedness is far less spectacular, it is equally impressive.

Don Weis (1922-)

1955: **The Little Guy.** 1956: **Warner Brothers Presents/***The Deadly Riddle, Explosion;* **Casablanca/***Killer at Large.* 1957: **The Lonely Wizard.** 1958: **Suspense/***Weapon of Courage.* 1959: **M Squad/***Streets of Fear, Face of Evil;* **Wagon Train/***The Nelson Stack Story.* 1961: **Alfred Hitchcock Presents/***A Secret Life, First Class Honeymoon, The Pearl Necklace, Santa Claus and the 10th Avenue Kid.* 1962: **Alcoa Premiere/***Lollipop Louis;* **Checkmate/***The Cyanide Touch, Hot Wind on a Cold Town.* 1963: **Twilight Zone/***Steel;* **Perry Mason/***The Case of the Floating Stones.* 1964: **Burke's Law/***Who Killed Lenore Wingfield?, Who Killed the Tall One in the Middle?, Who Killed Hamlet?, Who Killed the 11th Best Dressed Woman in the World?, Who Killed Half of Glory Lee?, Who Killed Mr Cartwheel?.* 1965: **Bob Hope Chrysler Theatre/***The Longest 100 Miles;* **Kraft Suspense**

Theatre/*Four into Zero, Nobody Will Ever Know;* **Burke's Law**/*Who Killed Harris Crown?, Who Killed Molly?, Who Killed W.H.O. 1V?, Who Killed Mr X?.* 1966: **The Virginian**/*The Captive;* **Midnight Oil; Batman**/*The Joker Is Wild—Batman gets Riled, Hot off the Griddle—The Cat and the Fiddle.* 1967: **Ironside**/*Dead Man's Tale, The Past Is Prologue, The Fastest Runner, Backfire, The Talker, The Monster of Comus Towers.* 1968: **It Takes a Thief**/*A Very Warm Reception, When Boy Meets Girl, Birds of a Feather, When Thieves Fall In, One Night in Soledad, A Sour Note, The Lay of the Land, The Bill is in Committee, Turnabout, The Artist is for Framing;* **Ironside**/*Up, Down and Even, The Prophecy.* 1969: **It Takes a Thief**/*Hans Across the Border* (2 pts), *A Case of Red Turnips;* **Ironside**/*The Tormentor, Alias Mr Braithwaite, Moonlight Means Money, Little Dog Gone, Five Miles High, A Killing Will Occur, Little Jenny Jessup, Love My Enemy, The Machismo Bag, Return to Fiji, Warrior's Return;* **The Survivors**/pts 4 & 6. 1970: **Ironside**/*The Happy Dreams of Hollow Men, Love Peace Brotherhood and Murder, Noel's Gonna Fly, The Quinquax, The Summer Soldier, The Target;* **Paris 7000**/*The Last Grand Tour.* 1971: **Ironside**/*Contract: Kill Ironside, The Professionals, The Gambling Game, Ring of Prayer, Murder Impromptu, Dear Fran . . . , License to Kill, Unreasonable Facsimile, Death by Numbers.* 1972: **MASH**/(multiples inc) *Sticky Wicket, Cowboy, Major Fred C. Dobbs;* **Ironside**/*The Savage Sentry, Down Two Roads, The Countdown, Buddy Can You Spare a Life?, Deadly Gamesman, Cold Hard Cash, Ollinger's Last Case, The Caller, Last Man in December, A Game of Showdown;* **Now You See It Now You Don't.** 1973: **Ironside**/*Fragile Is the House of Cards, House of Terror, Downhill All the Way, The Hidden Man, Riddle at 24,000 Feet, Come Eleven Come Twelve, Confessions: From a Lady of the Night.* 1974: **Kolchak: The Night Stalker**/*The Vampire, The Werewolf, Fire-Fall, The Trevi Collection;* **MASH**/*Crisis;* **Triple Play**/*Ready Willing and Pamela;* **Ironside**/*The Visiting Fireman, Gross Doublecross, Speak No Evil, The Return of Eleanor Rogers;* **Kingston: Confidential**/*The Rage of Hannibal, Triple Exposure, The Cult, The Bus and a Shamrock.* 1975: **Barbary Coast** *(pilot), Funny Money, Crazy Cats;* **Planet of the Apes**/*Escape from Tomorrow* (pilot); **Starsky and Hutch**/*Lousy Streak.* 1976: **Baretta**/*The Ninja;* **Starsky and Hutch**/*The Psychic, In a Mike, Omaha Tiger, Lady Blue.* 1977: **Hawaii Five-O**/*A Short Walk on the Longshore.*

Movie may have over-reacted to Weis's CRITIC'S CHOICE. Sarris may have under-reacted. He did, however, doubt Weis's talent rather than ignore him altogether. A decade later nobody seems clearer. A study of Weis's extremely prolific TV career, however, makes matters more certain. Early on he won two Directors' Guild Awards (for **The Little Guy** and **The Lonely Wizard**); he kept within the mocking bounds of pastiche and parody (**Burke's Law** with its outrageously alluring titles—*Who Killed* (variously) *The Tall One in the Middle?... The 11th Best Dressed Woman in the World?... Half of Glory Lee?... Mr Cartwheel?* and most intriguingly ... *W.H.O. IV?* First season **Batman,** a bakers dozen **It Takes a Thiefs** (including the awful pun, *Hans Across the Border*), the disguise oriented **Barbary Coast,** all kept Weis on his toes. It is far from easy to maintain the correct tone for shows such as these and still make them compulsive viewing. Yet Weis comes through well. Some of the better **MASH** segments are cherries on top of this particular brand of cake.

But much of Weis's more recent history has been, inexplicably, taken up with a monumentally loyal tenure with the **Ironside** series. Weis contributed fifty-five segments and then accompanied its star, Raymond Burr, onto the **Kingston: Confidential** series. We may presume that the relationship would have continued, had the series not folded. The earliest of the **Ironsides** (Weis directed the first actual segment *Dead Man's Tale)* and *Monster of Comus Towers* in particular, have an elegance and urbane detachment. The series, as a whole, began to pall due to Burr's stolid omnipotence and the sheer monotony of the format. As the series 'grew' internally, to assuage the young support cast's frustrations, Weis's segments in particular, reveal much of interest, on both iconographical and creative levels.

Weis easily blended in with the **Starsky and Hutch** format, *Omaha Tiger* and *Lady Blue* helping to popularise the series as a whole, for they were two of the first season's best segments. *Escape from Tomorrow,* the pilot for **Planet of the Apes** and a TV reworking of the 'original' story is perhaps Weis's best recent credit. The promise of this segment was rarely matched in the series proper, which indicates how remote executives can be from their audience (the series illustrates how far TV fantasy has fallen since the peaks of **Twilight Zone** and **Outer Limits**). Weis's involvement with **Kolchak: The Night Stalker** and occasional encounters with fantasy or Gothic themes in other series suggests too that his interests are as broad as his comedy is capable of being.

Whilst, unlike Singer, Shear, Wendkos, Weis seems to have a more anonymous personality, on a purely 'professional' level, he is one of the most accomplished of all contemporary directors. His work dignifies and helps shape the formulas in which he works.

Paul Wendkos (1922-)

1959: **The Untouchables**/*Mr Moon;* **Tightrope**/*Night of the Gun.* 1960: **Naked City**/*Down the Long Night, A Succession of Heartbeats, The Hot Minerva.* 1961: **Award Theatre**/*Coast to Coast;* **Route 66**/*Don't Count Stars;* **Detectives**/*untitled segment, Recoil* (released theatrically in Europe). 1963: **Dick Powell Theatre**/*Luxury Liner.* 1964: **Burke's Law**/*Who Killed Rosie Sunset?;* **I Spy**/*Three Hours on a Sunday Night, Turkish Delight, Lori;* **Slattery's People**/*Question: 'Do the Ignorant Sleep in Pure White Beds?'* 1965: **The Trials of O'Brien**/*The Blue Steel Suite;* **Big Valley**/*Heritage, The Young Marauders.* 1966: **The FBI**/*Cave In, Vendetta.* 1967: **The Invaders**/*The Leeches, Vikor, Nightmare, Doomsday Minus One, Storm, Moonshot;* **I Spy**/*Sparrowhawk.* 1968: **The Invaders**/*The Believers, The Lifeseekers.* 1969: **Fear No Evil**; **Hawaii Five-O** (pilot). 1970: **Travis Logan M.D.**; **Crisis** (pilot); **Brotherhood of the Bell.** 1971: **A Little Game; The Tattered Web; The Death of Innocence; Honor Thy Father.** 1972: **Six Characters in Search of an Author; Footsteps; Haunts of the Very Rich; The Delphi Bureau; The Family Rico; Strangers in 7A.** 1973: **Terror on the Beach.** 1974: **Harry O**/*The Admiral's Lady, Mortal Sin, Shadows at Noon; Underground Man.* 1975: **The Legend of Lizzie Borden; Death among Friends; Medical Story**/*The God Syndrome, Test Case, Million Dollar Baby, Up Against the World* (2 pts). 1977: **The Death of Ritchie; Good Against Evil; Secrets; 79 Park Avenue** (6 pts).

Graduating from the University of Pennsylvania, Wendkos began his film career making documentaries for the State Department. One of these—DARK INTERLUDE—won eight major awards, and doubtless helped him move into a feature career while its subject matter—the rehabilitation of the blind—suggests that the dark preoccupations of his later work were already present. THE

BURGLAR, a memorably confusing David Goodis thriller, is shot with the documentarist's love of the poetry of real places—but FACE OF A FUGITIVE is far more typical of the angular, formal style he was to favour. These two films, plus THE CASE AGAINST BROOKLYN, caught the fancy of young auteurists of the early '60s, who looked forward, with relish, to more of the same. They have been disappointed. But to follow his work on the small screen is a revelation, for Wendkos's TV work is, perhaps, the most impressively 'personal' of all directors.

In his best work, there is a clinical detachment from his characters, which prevents any easy transference from the viewer. His analytic view intensifies the feeling that we are watching insects under a microscope. Some of the insects run bewildered from the various physical and psychological hounds on their trail, whilst others do the pursuing—implacable and imperious. Wendkos's framing of a cold world is usually meticulously correct, frustratingly proper. It conveys a Langian sense of fate, against which individuals are powerless.

The airline passengers in **Haunts of the Very Rich** are led by the ubiquitous Lloyd Bridges. They find, to their horror, that they are actually in a ripoff of OUTWARD BOUND and are, in fact, all dead. The Hell/Limbo they occupy is made more chilling (and the clichés are defused) by the cool stance which Wendkos takes. In **Terror on the Beach,** Dennis Weaver and his family are spending a quiet Sunday in the sun. It explodes into violence with the arrival of a bike gang whose only interest is to humiliate and destroy their middle-class sensibilities. The gang have no reasons which make any sense of their actions.

The boy in **The Death of Ritchie** is hopelessly trapped in his drug addiction; his father (Ben Gazzara) is so busy that he is oblivious of the looming tragedy until it is too late. **The Strangers in 7A** are a gang of thieves whose lowering presence and physical threat spell danger to Andy Griffith and Ida Lupino as the apartment house caretakers. The most obvious, and clearest extension of this facet of Wendkos's world is his adaptation of Pirandello's **Six Characters in Search of an Author.**

Another consistent preoccupation is more conventional—the world of crime. From **The Untouchables,** through **Detectives, The FBI, Honor Thy Father, The Family Rico** etc, Wendkos has charted the life and times of the pursued and the pursuers. Surprisingly, for a director involved with action pictures, he understands the women who move in the predominantly men's world with which he deals: the 'promiscuous' wife, Susan Blakely, married to the star of **Invaders,** Roy Thinnes, in **Secrets,** the unsuccessful but fascinating **The Legend of Lizzie Borden** and the physical and emotional problems of a group of young medical students in *Up Against the World.* Recently, Wendkos has fused this feminine-orientation with the world of organised crime in **79 Park Avenue.** While this is an extremely disappointing show, seen from an auteurist perspective, for it is pure pulp and aimed by Wendkos (who functions as producer as well) at the big audience, it indicates that although he has allowed his style to be subjugated to commercial realities, thematically, at least, it is still consistent.

2/I Also Do The Catering

George Hamilton gave his wicked parody of Italian directors ('I 'ave written the film, I am of course directing it, I am producer, I am also star, I am composing the music, I 'ave designed the costumes—and I also do the catering') in a Granada TV documentary on the filming of Carl Foreman's THE VICTORS. The auteur on TV is in a real sense *not* the director (he often isn't in the cinema)—he is the creator-producer, the writer-producer, the producer-director, or any and all combinations of the four roles. This section comprises those 'hyphenates' who most deserve attention.

Irwin Allen (1916-)

1964: **Voyage to the Bottom of the Sea** (Cr pr) + *Eleven Days to Zero* (wr/dir). 1966: **The Time Tunnel** (cr pr) + *Rendezvous with Yesterday* (dir). 1968: **Land of the Giants** (Cr pr) + *The Crash* (dir). 1970: **Adventures of the Queen** (pr);**Swiss Family Robinson** (pr). 1971: **The City beneath the Sea** (wr/pr/dir).

Allen's work for television has been almost purely in the fantasy vein. He practically monopolised the genre on the home screen during the mid-Sixties. He was creator executive producer on all his shows; **Lost in Space** was the only one whose pilot Allen didn't helm. **Voyage to the Bottom of the Sea** was inspired, quite obviously, by Allen's 1962 feature, and utilised most of its props and effects-footage. Allen is a strictly a showman, but a showman who knows his market. His series were among the most expensively made running at the time, and, commerically, they paid off. All were successful and popular with the juvenile market; **Voyage** and **Lost in Space** ran for almost four years each. **Time Tunnel** was the only Allen show to fail (by his commerical standards), despite early favourable reviews in the trade press.

Both *Rendezvous with Yesterday* and *The Crash* served merely as situation setters, and although Allen-directed, first season episodes of **Voyage** were quite tame compared to the outrageous segments that the show later adopted. It may be unfortunate that Irwin Allen's work for TV (namely, **Lost in Space**) is best remembered among genre critics for 'what *not* to do with science fiction on TV'. Having practically created the disaster movie, single handed, and with sci-fi a big deal at last, Allen may well return to TV and marry his lush production values with material more deserving of them.

Stephen J Cannell (1941-)

1969: **It Takes a Thief** (wr) multiples. 1970: **Adam 12** (wr): *Post Time;* **Ironside** (wr): *Riddle in Room Six, This Could Blow Your Mind.* 1971: **Adam 12**/(wr) *The Ferret, Pickup, The Search, The Radical, The Princess and the Pig, Mary Hong Loves Tommy Chen, Back Up to 20, The Wednesday Warrior.* 1972: **Adam 12** (wr) *Badge Heavy, The Late Baby, The Surprise, Clear with a Civilian* (2 pts); **Madigan** (wr) multiples; **Chase** (series cr); **Jigsaw**/*Kiss the Dream Goodbye.* 1973: **Columbo** (wr) *Double Exposure;* **Toma** (series pr + wr) multiples. 1974: **Rockford Files** (series pr + wr) pilot *The Kirkoff Case, The Countess, In Pursuit of Carole Thorne, Profits and Loss* (2 pts), *This Case is Closed, Portrait of Elizabeth.* 1975: **Baretta** (series cr + wr) *He'll Never See Daylight;* **Rockford Files** (series pr + wr) *Foul on the First Play, The Aaron Ironwood School of Success, Tall Woman in Red Wagon, Chicken Little Is a Little Chicken, The Reincarnation of Angie, Feeding Frenzy, Drought at Indianhead River, 2 into 5.56 Won't Go, The Real Easy Red Dog, Sleight of Hand, The No-Cut Contract;* **City of Angels**/*The November Plan* (wr). 1976: **Baa Baa Black Sheep** (series pr + wr) *Bat Three Out of Five;* **Rockford Files**/*Just Another Polish Wedding* (wr); **Richie Brockleman** (series exec. pr + co-wr) *The Missing 24 Hours;* **Scott Free** (co-exec pr). 1977: **Black Sheep Squadron** (series exec pr + wr) *Forbidden Fruit.*

If Roy Huggins is King of light entertainment, Cannell must be the heir apparent. In his ten year career he has risen from a humble scribe to the executive producer, mainly through his connection with first, Jack Webb (**Adam 12, Chase**), then the Huggins empire (**Toma, Rockford Files, Baretta, City of Angels**), before striking out on his own with **Richie Brockleman** and **Black Sheep Squadron.**

Since 1973 and **Chase,** which he created, he has been right at the heart of the creative/decision making processes of all the series with which he has been connected. He has displayed an apparently inexhaustible invention in ringing the changes on the formulas. When **Toma** star, Tony Musante, tired of the successful show and refused to continue in the fictionalised adventures of a real-life 'master of the disguise' cop, Cannell 'created' **Baretta** in its image, along with a format allowing for the bizarre as well as the sentimental. **Rockford Files** has claimed his major attention, and he is clearly one of the prime reasons for the series's appeal. Whatever the attractions of tougher segments (like *Crack Back* and, in particular, *Hammer of C Block),* Cannell's ability to write convoluted plots in the Chandler manner, at the same time concentrating on human foible rather than darker evils, gives the series the flavour of a tangy summer drink rather than a shot of rye in a sleazy bar. Cannell seems to keep on getting better. *Just Another Polish Wedding* is a *tour-de-force,* suggesting that if Cannell were having less fun, he could become an American Tom Stoppard. A scene with Lou Gossett and Isaac Hayes trying to talk their way out of a Nazi-bar is one of the funniest in recent years, but also carries a sudden blast of chill air which is all the more sinister for its comic content.

William Conrad (1920-)

1957-1959: **Bat Masterson**/multiples. 1960: **Klondike** (series pr + dir) multiples. 1961: **Naked City**/*The Day the Island Almost Sank, A Kettle of Precious Fish, Bridge Party;* **Route 66**/*First Class Mouliak.* 1962: **Gunsmoke**/*Panacea Sikes;* **True**/*The Amateurs, Open Season, O.S.I., Escape* (2 pts), *Security Risk, Pattern for Espionage, Black Robed Ghost, Ordeal.* 1963: **77 Sunset Strip** (series pr) + *Five* (5 pts), *Never to have Loved;* **Temple Houston**/*Billy Hart;* **True**/*Heydrich* (2 pts), *Commando, Harris vs Castro, The Last Day, The Handmade Private, Mile-Long Shot to Kill, The Wrong Nickel, Defendant: Clarence Darrow, Firebug, The Moonshiners, The Tenth Mona Lisa.* 1964: **77 Sunset Strip** (series pr); **Temple Houston**/*Ten Rounds for Baby, A Slight Case of Larceny, The Gun That Swept the West, The Town That Trespassed.* 1968: **Gunsmoke**/*Captain Sligo.* 1970: **The Name of the Game**/*The Skin Game.*

Conrad played a part in the 'golden age' of radio broadcasting, as the original Matt Dillon in the **Gunsmoke** radio series before turning to acting in Siodmak's THE KILLERS, BODY AND SOUL, and SORRY, WRONG NUMBER. He began directing with **Bat Masterson** which led to producing and directing the **Klondike** series, in 1960. Conrad's first substantial period of directing came with Jack Webb's **True** anthology series, a curious variation of the old **You Are There** show. One of the more interesting segments was *Mile-Long Shot to Kill,* which featured the invention of a super-long-range rifle during the American Civil War. Uncharacteristically, the emphasis was directed to the victim who, in an exciting scene, is silently hit by a bullet. Conrad also appeared in front of the cameras for the Webb-directed *Circle of Death* whilst working on the series. **True** was the beginning of Conrad's association with Jack Webb; while Webb was head of Warner Brothers' television division and executive producer on **77 Sunset Strip,** he brought in Conrad as producer-director for the show's final season ('63-'64).

The five-part, five-hour *Five* became one of the most lavish in the series due to this collaboration. The five-parter contained an impressive-for-TV line-up of 24 guest stars and took the plot away from its usual Hollywood locale and halfway around the world; the somewhat unusually structured teleplay was penned by Harry Essex, the long-time movie writer whose best work is, perhaps, KANSAS CITY CONFIDENTIAL.

Since the early sixties, however, Conrad has stuck mainly to acting on TV, taking time out to produce/direct features (TWO ON A GUILLOTINE, MY BLOOD RUNS COLD, COVENANT WITH DEATH, etc). Between appearing in the **Cannon** pilot and the series's premiere, Conrad got together again with Webb for the latter's **O'Hara-U.S. Treasury** pilot. Conrad's **Cannon** series is, however, a big disappointment in all departments—slow and pedantic.

Gene L Coon

1958: **Wagon Train** (wr) *The Mary Ellen Thomas Story.* 1959: **Wagon Train** (wr) *The Colonel Harris*

Story, The Benjamin Burns Story (co-wr), *The Joshua Gilliam Story* (adaptation only), *The Amos Gibbon Story.* 1960: **Cimarron City** (wr) *The People;* **Wagon Train** (wr) *The Albert Farnsworth Story, The Jose Morales Story* (co-wr). 1962: **Rawhide** (wr) *Incident of the Dog Paces.* 1963: **The Virginian** (wr/pr) *The Showdown.* 1964: **Kraft Suspense Theatre**/*The War and Eric Kurtz* (st only); **The Killers** (wr only). 1965: **Laredo** (wr) *The Golden Trail* (co-wr with Eloise Coon), *The Calico Kid.* 1966: **Star Trek** (series pr +) *Arena* (co-wr), *Space Seed* (co-wr), *A Taste of Armageddon* (co-wr); **The FBI**/*Flight to Harbin* (co-wr). 1967: **Star Trek** (series pr + wr) *The Devil in the Dark, Errand of Mercy, Who Mourns for Adonis?* (co-wr), *The Apple* (co-wr), *Metamorphosis, A Piece of the Action* (co-wr). 1968: **Star Trek** (wr) *Bread and Circuses;* **It Takes a Thief** (series pr + wr) *A Spot of Trouble, A Sour Note, Turnabout, The Galloping Skin Game.* 1969: **It Takes a Thief** (series pr). 1970: **Men from Shiloh**/*Flight from Memory* (co-wr), *The Regimental Line.* 1972: **Kung Fu** (wr) *Chains.* 1973: **The Questor Tapes** (co-wr).

Teleastes known Coon best for his writer/producer involvement with the first two seasons of **Star Trek,** for although the series was very much the brainchild of Gene Roddenberry, getting it on to the screen was a team effort. Given that there are few high spots in Roddenberry's subsequent career, it is clear that Coon's experience, first with Universal features, then with such marathon TV series as **Wagon Train,** played a major part in the creative success of the series. (Indeed it was sold to the networks as **A Wagon Train to the Stars).**

Star Trek's story ideas, characters and conflicts had to aim for uniqueness each week. Coon's literate and thought provoking ways with genre material (he learnt on Jack Arnold's Universal westerns) made it possible for him both to treat the show's concept seriously, and to make an action-adventure format consider and analyse human affairs and morality. He is endowed with a prime asset for TV—speed! When Janos Prohaska, **Star Trek**'s make-up expert, appeared one day in Coon's office wearing a newly created monster outfit, Coon was quick to have a script for it—*in four days.* The segment in question became *Devil in the Dark,* one of the best of the first season's output. But his best known writer credit is for **The Killers,** which Don Siegel directed.

In his producer's hat, Coon was responsible for altering Harlan Ellison's script for *City on the Edge of Forever,* which most people consider the best of all **Star Treks**, and won Ellison the Hugo award even though he disowned the 'aborted' work. Thus Coon, as all writer/producers do, trod a difficult path, with the dreaded 'compromise' and made for equilibrium between his 'creative' nature and his 'business sense'.

By the third season of **Star Trek,** Coon, Roddenberry and the story editor D. C. Fontana were no longer connected with the series in a day-to-day sense; their departure shows. Coon went on to **It Takes a Thief** for two years (where he was reunited with Jack Arnold) and his professionalism with genre material again brought forth engaging entertainments. There has been no similar close involvement with any other series and Coon's later credits are primarily as a writer only. However **The Questor Tapes** is a collaborative teleplay with Gene Roddenberry, a story of an android searching for his 'creator'; it was planned as a pilot for a series. As directed by Richard Colla, it is one of Coon's best non-western pieces.

Dan Curtis

1966: **Dark Shadows** (pr). 1967: **Dark Shadows** (pr); **The Strange Case of Dr Jekyll and Mr Hyde** (pr). 1968-1971: **Dark Shadows** (pr). 1972: **The Night Stalker** (pr). 1973: **The Night Strangler** (pr + dir); **The Norliss Tapes** (pr + dir); **The Picture of Dorian Gray** (pr + dir). 1974: **Scream of the Wolf** (pr + dir); **Melvin Purvis, G-Man** (pr + dir); **Dracula** (pr + dir). 1975: **Trilogy of Terror** (dir).

Dan Curtis has become closely associated with the Television of the *fantastique* over the past decade, from producing Gothic soap-opera to directing fantasy tele-features. A one-time sales executive for NBC and MCA, Curtis started producing NBC's day-time **Dark Shadows** soap-opera in 1966. When the Gothic romance serial started slipping in the great ratings struggle, which was soon after its premiere, Curtis introduced a new character into the show, Barnabas Collins (played by Jonathan Frid), and the serial sky-rocketed to the top. The show was unique in that it was the first day-time serial ever to switch to a peculiar blend of horror and score with the viewers on that bizarre level. **Dark Shadows** ran for over five years, and notched up over one thousand episodes.

However, Curtis's biggest success to date (in terms of critical acclaim and viewer-popularity) has been the ABC Movie-of-the-Week **The Night Stalker.** Scripted by Richard Matheson, from 'an unpublished novel' by Jeff Rice (THE KOLCHAK PAPERS) Curtis was assigned to the project by ABC-TV, as producer. **The Night Stalker** remains on record as one of the most perfectly balanced and expertly staged tele-features. Suitably drenched in atmosphere, it is a furiously-paced production, superbly designed for Television.

Although most praise lavished on **The Night Stalker** goes to director John Llewellyn Moxey and writer Matheson, Curtis became sufficiently involved with the theme to produce, and direct, a follow-up, **The Night Strangler.** The blend of a modern-day vampire stalking glittery Las Vegas (in **The Night Stalker**), opposed only by an over-the-hill reporter-hero, signified its successful composition by creating an all-time high in the Nielsen-ratings—over 75,000,000 viewers tuned-into the movie. With this formula in mind, Curtis attempted to repeat the success with his **The Night Strangler,** also scripted by Matheson, but the production turned out to be merely a re-staging of familiar events. Although hero-star Darren McGavin was intoxicated with the 'modern-day horrors' format enough to launch his own series (**Kolchak: The Night Stalker**), Curtis went his own way and arrived at **The Norliss Tapes,** now under the Dan Curtis Productions banner.

The Norliss Tapes aimed at the same **Kolchak: The Night Stalker**

landscape, but failed at the starting-post. The tele-movie, penned by William F. Nolan, was also intended as a series-pilot, with a wooden Roy Thinnes playing a McGavin/Kolchak character.

Curtis's **Dracula,** headlining Jack Palance, was a strange affair. Not so much by way of eerie or unusual, but strange in the way that its director-producer Curtis did not seem to know what to make of Matheson's teleplay—even Matheson's work, here, appears somewhat unsure of itself. The most notable areas of Dan Curtis's TV work have been the ones where he has received the most expert collaboration. As a producer working with talents like Matheson and Moxey, Curtis is able to handle the material efficiently—but if left to direct the material himself, he loses all sense of theme and character motivation, rushing out fast plots and violent action at the expense of coherent film-making.

David Friedkin (1939-)

(In collaboration with Mort Fine). 1962: **The Dick Powell Theatre**/*The Price of Tomatoes;* **The Virginian**/*Woman from White Wing* (wr only); **The Executioners** (wr/pr/dir). 1963: **The Virginian**/*The Man Who Couldn't Die* (dir only), *The Man from the Sea* (wr only), *Strangers at Sundown* (wr/dir). 1964: **Alfred Hitchcock Hour**/*Change of Address* (+pr), *Thou Still Unravished Bride* (wr/pr). 1965: **Alfred Hitchcock Hour**/*The McGregor Affair* (+ pr), *Crimson Witness* (+ pr), *The Monkey's Paw—A Retelling* (wr/pr). 1965/1967: **I Spy** (series pr) + *Three Hours on a Sunday Night* (wr), *A Cup of Kindness* (wr), *Lori* (wr), *None Take Away Three* (co-wr), *Sophia* (wr), *Bet Me A Dollar* (wr), *Mainly on the Plains* (wr), *Tatia* (dir only), *Laya* (wr), *Happy Birthday Everybody* (wr), *The Spy Business* (wr). (As solo director). 1971: **River of Gold.** 1973: **Ironside**/*Double Edged Corner Close to the Heart.* 1974: **Ironside**/*Far Sides of the Fence, Act of Vengeance.* 1975: **Doctor's Hospital**/*Sleepless with Pale Eyes, Knives of Chance;* **Hawaii Five-O**/*A Sentence to Steal.* 1977: **Switch**/*Quicker than the Eye.*

The Team of Mort Fine and David Friedkin wrote and produced together, and Friedkin directed. (In our entry, above, 'wr/pr' should read in the plural, 'dir' in the singular.) By 1971 the team had split up and Friedkin followed a solo directing career, Fine a solo writing career; neither of them produced.

As a team, they were responsible for one of the classic series, **I Spy.** Just as Gene Coon held the reins for Wagonmaster Roddenberry, so Friedkin and Fine functioned for **I Spy**'s Sheldon Leonard. The teamwork of Robert Culp and Bill Cosby is a direct result of the teamwork of the writers/producers. While an 'entertainment', the two actors' intelligence and awareness brought an edge of subversion to the series. Producers and actors never lost their hold on the superficial escapism inherent in the format. Friedkin was no stranger to this kind of approach, for his work on *The Price of Tomatoes* won him an Emmy. There were highs and lows as with any series of course, but **I Spy** had more of the former and less of the latter than most.

What we have seen of Friedkin's solo 70's work indicates that the breakup of the team should have been avoided, and that **I Spy** will remain Friedkin's (and Fine's) main achievement.

Bruce Geller (1931-1978)

1951: **Jimmy Hughes, Rookie Cop** (wr) multiples; **Rocky King: Detective** (wr) multiples; **Flash Gordon** (wr) multiples. 1952-1956: **Kaiser Aluminum Hour** (wr) multiples; **Dupont Show/**(wr) multiples. 1957: **Have Gun-Will Travel** (wr): *Duel at Florence;* **Zane Grey Theatre** (wr) multiples. 1958: **Shirley Temple Storybook** (wr) multiples; **Have Gun-Will Travel** (wr) *The Scorched Feather.* 1959: **The Rifleman** (co-wr) *The Money Gun.* 1960: **The Westerner** (wr) *Brown, The Courting of Libby, Hand on the Gun, The Painting.* 1961/1962: **Dick Powell Theatre** (wr: multiples + co-wr/co-pr) *The Losers.* 1963: **Dr Kildare** (wr) multiples. 1964/1965: **Rawhide** (series pr). 1966/1973: **Mission Impossible** (series cr/wr/pr). 1967/1975: **Mannix** (series cr/pr). 1975: **Bronk** (series pr). 1976: **Savage Bees** (wr/dir/pr). 1978: **Mother, Jugs and Speed** (pr).

The mind boggles at **Jimmy Hughes Rookie Cop** and **Rocky King, Detective**—but that's the sort of thing with which a 20 year old writer had to content himself in the pioneer days of TV. There are those who would have it that **Mission Impossible** and **Mannix** are testament to how little the medium has moved, but that is another argument. Geller's career—untimely cut short by his death in a private plane crash—is evidence of how much can actually be achieved in the medium. His involvement with Westerns took in the classic **Have Gun-Will Travel** series, reached a high water mark with **The Westerner** (all Geller's scripts were written in collaboration with and directed by Sam Peckinpah—a relationship which continued with *The Losers*). They remained at that level with **Rawhide,** Geller collaborating this time with Bernard Kowalski in the producer's chair; between them they revitalised the series—so much so that their contracts were abruptly cancelled in favour of a return to the original format. Perhaps this experience frightened Geller—for his remaining work is resolutely escapist and remarkably successful (eight seasons of **Mission Impossible,** nine seasons of **Mannix**). By then, Geller had become more producer than writer, more business man than artist.

The Savage Bees was an extraordinarily silly project for him to write, direct and produce. If he yearned for artistic self-expression there must have been something else.

His final project was most untypical in being second hand—a TV rip off of the feature **Mother, Jugs and Speed.** It is a further indication that Geller's drive and enthusiasm were drying up.

The best of what he left is very good indeed, peaks of genre TV which current talents are desperately trying to emulate. If his peaks were more often slick than meaningful, it was merely a sign of the times.

Douglas Heyes (1923-)

1956: **Circus Boy** (assoc pr), *Corky and the Circus Doctor* (+ co-wr), *The Little Fugitive* (+ wr); **Adventures of Rin-Tin-Tin**/*Yo-O Rinty!* (+wr), *Scotchman's Gold, Attack on Fort Apache, Rinty Finds a Bone, Forward Ho!* (+wr); **77th Bengal Lancers** (multiples). 1957: **Cheyenne**/*Top Hand, The Last Comanchero;* **Conflict**/*Execution Night, The Velvet Cage;* **Colt .45**/*Judgement Day, A Time to Die;* **Maverick**/*The Long Hunt, The Quick and the Dead, Diamond in the Rough.* 1958: **77 Sunset Strip**/*Lovely Lady Pity Me;* **Maverick**/*Escape to Tampico, Alias Bart Maverick, Two Tickets to Ten Strike, Two Beggars on Horseback, Plunder of Paradise.* 1959: **Maverick**/*Savage Johnny and Jenny Hill;* **Laramie**/*The Star Trail* (+ wr); **Riverboat**/*Payment in Full;* **The Twilight Zone**/*And When the Sky Was Opened, Elegy;* **Cimarron City**/*The Blood Line* (+wr). 1960: **The Twilight Zone**/*The Chaser, The After Hours, Nervous Man in a Four Dollar Room, The Howling Man, The Eye of the Beholder, Dust, The Invaders;* **Thriller**/*The Purple Room* (+ wr), *The Hungry Glass* (+wr). 1961: **Thriller**/*The Premature Burial;* **Alfred Hitchcock Presents**/*The Kiss-Off* (+wr); **Desilu Playhouse**/*The Hard Road* (+co-wr), *Six Guns for Donegan.* 1962: **Checkmate**/*The Murder Game* (+wr). 1963: **The Outlaws**/*Rape of Red Sky* (+wr); **The Richard Boone Show**/*Where Do You Hide an Egg?;* **Bob Hope Chrysler Theatre**/*Seven Miles of Bad Road.* 1964: **Kraft Suspense Theatre: Crisis**/*The Trains of Silence.* 1969: **The Bold Ones**/*A Game of Chance;* **The Lonely Profession** (+ wr). 1970: **Four-in-One: McCloud**/*Who Says You Can't Make Friends in New York City?* (+ wr); **Four-in-One: Night Gallery**/*The Dead Man* (+wr). 1971: **Alias Smith and Jones**/*Never Trust an Honest Man;* **Powderkeg** (+ wr). 1972: **McCloud**/*The Million Dollar Roundup* (+ wr). 1975: **Switch**/*The Late Show Murder.* 1976: **Best Sellers:The Captains and the Kings** (7 pts; +wr); **City of Angels**/*A Lonely Way to Die* (+ wr).

One of the most productive of the small-screen toilers, Douglas Heyes has been travelling a goodly time through the burrows of TV production. His early western series, mainly Warner Brothers material, were fairly lively packages, full of the rapid action so necessary to all the shows that were busy jockeying for position during the great TV-western stampede. Although Heyes had his scripts supplied when he was turning out the **Cheyennes, Mavericks, Colt .45**s, etc, he proved himself to be an efficient director during this chaotic period. He later supplied his own scripts for his segments of **Laramie, Cimarron City, The Outlaws,** etc.

During the early Sixties, Heyes took a sharp swing into the realm of suspense and fantasy, writing and directing for Rod Serling **(Twilight Zone),** Hubbell Robinson **(Thriller),** and for Hitchcock's half-hour anthology series.

The Lonely Profession, also written by Heyes, stands above most of his TV work as an exceptionally constructed and carefully handled tele-feature—initially telecast via the NBC World Premiere slot. Heyes also wrote, as well as directed, the tele-movie, **Powderkeg,** a pilot for an unsold series called **The Big Wheels.** Universal's **Four-in-One** premiered the **McCloud** series with Heyes's competently packaged *Who Says You Can't Make Friends in New York City?* Heyes has never reached a top-grade position in TV, despite his incredible productivity in both the writing and directing departments. His big-screen BEAU GESTE remake was badly received, perhaps because there were certain traces in the picture to suggest that it may have been originally slated for TV production.

Nat Hiken

Somebody should put up a statue of Hiken—for he was the Shakespeare of TV comedy writer/producers, the brains behind that enduring masterpiece, **The Phil Silvers/Sgt Bilko Show/You'll Never Get Rich** (nobody ever seemed to know what to call it).

He majored in journalism at the University of Wisconsin, but became involved with radio. He joined with Jack Lescoulie in an AM show on a Los Angeles station. THE GROUCH CLUB, where listeners wrote in about thei irritations, became a hit and in 1937 was taken over by a national network.

Hiken joined Warner Brothers scripting short subjects in 1939. He then met Fred Allen, the legendary comedian who revolutionised radio comedy; Allen hired Hiken to write for him. In 1949 Hiken left Allen, to develop a radio show for Milton Berle which ran for two years.

Hiken moved to TV and wrote and produced **The Jack Carson Show** and, for three years, **The Martha Raye Show.** CBS then teamed him with Phil Silvers, to see what he could do to create a vehicle for the comedian. 'We knew we would have to be different' Hiken later recalled 'We watched television. Ninety percent of the situation comedies took place in bright, chintzy, modern living rooms. This pointed the way for us. Our show would take place in a typical Army barracks declared obsolete after World War I, but still home to the majority of our armed forces. We then watched the characters who manoeuvered through the living room. They were mostly young couples—loveable, honest, upstanding. That left us with only one choice for Phil. He had to be a finagler, a "gold-brick" and a charlatan. In other words—Sgt Bilko was born'.

The Jack Carson and Martha Raye, **Car 54 Where Are You?** (Hiken's post-Bilko series) came and went, but **Bilko** has become virtually immortal. The shows hardly date at all, and their speed, invention, ensemble playing and brilliant humour mark them as comedy masterpieces. Reading the scripts (some were printed in paperback form years ago) is an education for any would-be comedy writer. The achievement is the greater because the series lasted so long. To be sure, Hiken had collaborators; Neil Simon reportedly served an apprenticeship at Fort Baxter and some of the funniest segments were written by the late Harvey Orkin. But Bilko, Colonel Hall, Doberman, Fender, Riting ('ooh, ooh, ooh') are 'humours' of which Ben Jonson would have been proud.

Alfred Hitchcock (1899-)

1955: **Alfred Hitchcock Presents**/*Breakdown, Revenge, The Case of Mr Pelham.* 1956: **Alfred Hitchcock Presents**/*Back for Christmas, Wet Saturday, Mr Blanchard's Secret.* 1957: **Alfred**

Hitchcock Presents/*One More Mile to Go, The Perfect Crime;* **Suspicion**/*Four O'Clock.* 1958: **Alfred Hitchcock Presents**/*Lamb to the Slaughter, Dip in the Pool, Poison.* 1959: **Alfred Hitchcock Presents**/*Banquo's Chair, Arthur, The Crystal Trench.* 1960: **Ford Star Time**/*Incident at a Corner;* **Alfred Hitchcock Presents**/*Mrs Bixby and the Colonel's Coat.* 1961: **Alfred Hitchcock Presents**/*The Horseplayer, Bang! You're Dead!.* 1962: **Alfred Hitchcock Hour**/*I Saw the Whole Thing.*

If John Brahm's TV work is 'charcoal sketches', Hitchcock's is the kind of anecdotes a slightly sinister uncle would tell around a blazing Christmas hearth. Whilst it is 'minor' Hitchcock, it is characteristic of academics to ignore twenty works by one of the century's most distinctive artists.

One of his 25 minute segments, would have been an ideal place for his favourite non-filmed sequence—the automobile plant where the car is being assembled while we watch. As the vehicle reaches the end of the conveyor belt, somebody opens the newly fitted door and a corpse falls out.

Certainly, *Four O'Clock* is a graphic demonstration of the Hitchcock surprise vs suspense dictum. Surprise is where the bomb goes off when nobody knew it was there. Suspense is when the audience knows it is there but the characters do not. Here, E. G. Marshall plants a bomb in the basement to kill his wife Nancy Kelly—only to have hoodlums burst in to burgle the house and tie him up in the basement next to the bomb.

Here the wicked humour is prevalent. *Revenge* has Ralph Meeker killing the man his wife, Vera Miles, says attacked her—only to discover later that she is demented and claims that scores of men have attacked her. *Lamb to the Slaughter* (scripted by Roald Dahl from his own story) concerns Barbara Bel Geddes who clubs her husband to death with a frozen leg of lamb, which she then cooks and serves to the investigating police who are searching for the murder weapon even as they eat it.

Strong and clear Hitchcock motifs abound *(The Case of Mr Pelham* where a man's sinister duplicate actually takes over the original's life). Joseph Cotten *(Breakdown),* John Williams *(Back Before Christmas, Banquo's Chair* and *Wet Saturday),* Claude Rains *(The Horseplayer)* and other familiar character players appear, all shot by John C. Russell, the lighting cameraman of PSYCHO.

Hitchcock's main TV achievement was to keep an excellent anthology series on the air for a decade whilst employing some of the finest talent in the process. But his own work for the small screen cannot be ignored.

Roy Huggins (1914-)

1955: **Cheyenne** (1st year series producer). 1956: **Conflict** (series prod). 1957: **Colt .45**/pilot (pr); **Maverick**/pilot (pr; series creator, exec pr, wr, 2 seasons). 1958: **77 Sunset Strip**/pilot (pr). 1959: **Doc Holliday**/pilot (pr). 1962: **The Fugitive** (series creator). 1963: **The Virginian** (series exec pr). 1964: **Kraft Suspense Theatre** (series exec pr). 1966: **Enigma**/*Don't Wait for Tomorrow* (exec pr + story); **Pursuit** (pilot) (exec pr);**Run for your Life** (series exec pr). 1967: **The Outsider** (pr). 1968: **The Outsider** (series creator, exec pr). 1969: **Only One Left Before Tomorrow** (pr); **How to Steal an Airplane** (exec pr). 1970: **The Bold Ones: The Lawyers** (series exec pr). 1971: **Alias Smith and Jones**/pilot (series exec pr + stories); **Any Second Now** (exec pr); **Sam Hill: Who Killed the Mysterious Mr Foster?** (exec pr); **Do You Take This Stranger** (exec pr). 1972: **Profane Comedy** (exec pr + wr); **Cool Million** (series exec pr). 1973: **The Story of Pretty Boy Floyd** (exec pr); **Toma** (series exec pr); **The Young Country** (pr, dir, wr); **Drive Hard, Drive Fast** (exec pr + story). 1974: **Target Risk** (exec pr). 1975: **Baretta** (series exec pr); **This Is the West That Was** (exec pr); **The Rockford Files** (series exec pr); **City of Angels** (series exec pr). 1976: **The Invasion of Johnson County** (pr); **Hazard's People** (exec pr). 1977: **The Courier: The 3,000 Mile Chase** (co-pr + story); **Best Sellers: Wheels** (pr; 10 pts). 1978: **Glory and the Lightning** (exec pr); **The Last Convertible** (exec pr).

For nearly 25 years, Huggins has remained unassailable in his fortress as the most consistent and prolific TV creator. As writer, producer and production executive he has created and/or supervised some of the medium's most enduring popular and artistic successes.

A pre-TV career as a mystery writer (numerous stories, three novels—*The Double Take, Too Late for Tears, Lovely Lady Pity Me)* led to a contract with Columbia Pictures. A handful of undistinguished scripts resulted in one remarkable Randolph Scott feature which Huggins wrote and directed, HANGMAN'S KNOT (1954). Western buffs have always praised this highly, but it is still virtually unseen. It remains Huggins's one-off theatrical feature, for the following year, he took the important step into TV, accepting an offer to join Warner Bros. as a producer. In this capacity, he was in charge of the first year of **Cheyenne,** the only series in the company's initial TV output to survive. Huggins also produced the pilots of **Colt .45** (overall a negligible series which was kept running by default rather than enthusiasm) and **77 Sunset Strip**—which became an instantly fashionable show, capitalising on its Hollywood locale, and the chemistry of its leading actors (Ed 'Kookie' Byrnes captured the emergent teenage audience).

It was Huggins's next series in 1957 which first revealed his true personality—**Maverick.** He created the show, wrote many segments and produced all of them for the first two years. It made James Garner a star (as **Cheyenne** had done for Clint Walker), won Huggins an Emmy, ran until 1962 and remains a landmark of 'pure' TV.

In late 1960 he produced a feature at Warners A FEVER IN THE BLOOD, before joining 20th Century Fox TV as vice-president in charge of production, but this seems to have been a less rewarding occupation for in the summer of 1962 he joined Universal TV as a vice-president and production executive (though **The Fugitive,** which he created in the same year, turned up for Quinn Martin Productions) and has remained there ever since—confirming its reputation for loyalty and continuity of personnel.

Huggins's executive position has been instrumental in making the studio the most active of all in the production of telefilms and series. He has continued to contribute in a creative sense. **The Maverick** style of humour and the narratives that are rife with labyrinthine confusion (the essence of the mystery stories which first prompted Huggins to write) animate **Alias Smith and Jones** (over 40 segments came from stories by Huggins and were, who knows, stolen from his **Maverick** days). **The Young Country** found him directing for the first time since HANGMAN'S KNOT; **This Is the West That Was** and **The Invasion of Johnson Country** and of course **The Rockford Files,** which reunited him with James Garner were all Huggins. **Cool Million, Toma, City of Angels** and **Baretta** are series which he personally originated, through his 'Public Arts' company. Latterly he has helped lead Universal's move into larger-scale mini-series, although **Wheels,** his one **Best Sellers** to appear to date, could not lick the problems these extended dramatic pieces cause (it featured his wife, the Republic leading lady, Adele Mara). One suspects that if anybody can find a solution, it will be Huggins, for his understanding of the medium is second to none.

A major career article would be able to elucidate the personal side of Huggins as a visionary and bring out the details of his broader contributions to the medium, as well as his encouragement of younger talents (which must include his three sons under whose combined names he pseudonymously writes as John Thomas James). All we can do here is list the achievements, which, in the field of genre entertainment, are unparalleled in TV.

Richard Irving

1955: **Soldiers of Fortune**/*The Runaway King, Aloha Means Goodbye, Run Till You Die.* 1962: **Checkmate**/*A Matter of Conscience.* 1963: **Arrest and Trial**/*Run Little Man Run.* 1965: **Laredo**/(series co-exec pr). 1966: **Breakout; Prescription: Murder** (+ pr). 1968: **Istanbul Express.** 1969: **The Name of the Game**/*Love-In at Ground Zero* (+pr). 1970: **The Name of the Game** (series exec pr); **San Francisco International Airport** (series exec pr). 1971: **Ransom for a Dead Man; Columbo** (pilot); **Cutter.** 1973: **The Six Million Dollar Man**/pilot (+ pr). 1974: **Roman Grey: The Art of Crime** (+ exec pr). 1977: **Best Sellers: Seventh Avenue**/pts 1 & 2 (+pr); **Exo Man; Whatever Happened to the Class of '65?**/*The Class Hustler* (+ series exec pr).

As producer-director, Irving has been in at the start on two popular recent successes (**Columbo** and **Six Million Dollar Man**) and presided over the production of **Name of the Game,** which always tried to be topical and relevant.

Prescription: Murder introduced **Columbo** back in 1966—but he had to wait another five years for the 'official' pilot, **Ransom for a Dead Man,** and then the subsequent series. Irving was producer/director of both—yet curiously neither, considering the popularity of the series, is a memorable landmark.

Irving likes people, lots of them, but he doesn't want them to do anything. **Ransom for a Dead Man** has countless people milling about, all appearing busy in insignificant departments. There are only three important characters in the story, but Irving seems to make the most intimate of exchanges a bustling crowd scene. His direction, also, seems as cloudy and ill-defined as his overall position and relevance to TV.

Kenneth Johnson

1973: **Adam 12**/*Training Division* (dir). 1975: **The Bionic Woman** (series cr/pr/wr) multiples. 1976: **The Bionic Woman** (series pr + wr) *Black Magic, Sister Jaime.* 1977: **The Bionic Woman** (series pr) + *Doomsday is Tomorrow* (wr/dir—2 pts); **The Incredible Hulk** (series cr/pr) + pilot (wr/dir), *Death in the Family* (wr).

It may seem odd to the casual observer of bionic banalities, but talent will out. When Johnson, **Bionic Woman**'s creator, picked up the megaphone on *Doomsday is Tomorrow* he revealed a breath-of-fresh-air flair in directing his own surprisingly 'liberal' script. It pits Ms Wagner against an incredibly sophisticated computer, programmed to blackmail the world into 'lasting peace'. Aware that the series could be more than merely kiddie capers, further investigation revealed that side by side with the action were 'good ideas' about the multi-national, multi-racial world which, in her non-bionic role as a teacher, the heroine gently but firmly reinforces. In his role as creator/writer/producer, Johnson succeeded in delivering as much escapism to satisfy the audience (especially the female members who had been starved of identification-figures) whilst supplying food for thought and consideration which were light-years beyond the Saturday-morning serials—the previous generation's equivalent of such TV shows. It must be said, however, that they are just as resolutely right wing in their attitudes.

The Incredible Hulk pilot was likewise fashioned by Johnson into a visually elegant morality tale, which actually became moving and beautiful. The second pilot *(Death in the Family)* written and produced by Johnson but directed by Alan J. Levi was a plummet to formula cliché, for which Johnson must share the blame. But he has done enough to indicate that he should be watched, very closely, in the future.

Gene R. Kearney

1971: **Night Gallery**/*House-With Ghost* (wr/dir), *Silent Snow Secret Snow* (wr/dir). 1972: **Charlie Chan: Happiness is a Warm Clue** (wr). 1975: **Kojak** (wr) *A House of Prayer A Den of Thieves, Long Way from Times Square.* 1976: **Kojak** (wr) *Out of the Shadows.* 1977: **Kojak** (series pr) + *Once More from Birdland* (wr/pr), *Summer of '69* (wr/dir/pr).

Silent Snow, Secret Snow is a gently haunting **Night Gallery,** *Long Way from Times Square* yanks **Kojak** out of New York and into a whimsical mid-West made all the more quirky by Ernest Pintoff's direction. *Out of the Shadows* and *Once More from Birdland* are two painful and passionate urban nightmares, the former a sympathetic case history of paranoia, given an edgy panache by Jeannot Szwarc, the latter an elegaic 'setting the past to rights' story which makes an understanding use of a jazz milieu. All of them mark Kearney as one of the most committed of contemporary genre writers. He reveals more of an earnestness to communicate his ideas than he does a conventional technical proficiency. That is another plus. One suspects that he will always be a writer, and that he will tend to veer towards production rather than direction. The feel for humanity which he has already exhibited will hopefully interlace with shows as accommodating as **Kojak.** Kearney avoids the more blatantly exploitative series with which too many of his contemporaries are happy to hedge their bets. It seems that an original voice is surely on the point of breaking.

Roland Kibbee (1914-)

1954/1958: (wr: multiples) **The Ford Show, Ford Star Time, The Bob Cummings Show.** 1959: **The Deputy** (series cr/pr + wr: multiples). 1962: **The Virginian** (wr: multiples). 1963: **Alfred Hitchcock Hour**/*Diagnosis: Danger* (wr). 1967: **Midnight Oil** (wr/pr). 1968: **It Takes a Thief** (series cr + co-wr) *A Thief Is A Thief.* 1972: **Madigan** (series pr) + *The Midtown Beat* (co-wr); **Columbo** (series pr). 1973: **McCoy** (series cr/pr + wr) *The Big Ripoff;* **Brock's Last Case** (pr). 1975: **The Family Hovak** (series co-exec pr). 1977: **A.E.S. Hudson Street** (pilot) (wr/pr).

'Believe half of what you see' says Burt Lancaster, swinging from the rigging and flashing that shark-like grin, 'and nothing that you hear', at the start of THE CRIMSON PIRATE. In a paranoiac age they are words to live by. The film is like Kibbee's career in that it never quite gets where it ought to be going. Apart from his other associations with Lancaster (TEN TALL MEN, VERA CRUZ, THE DEVIL'S DISCIPLE, VALDEZ IS COMING, MIDNIGHT MAN) his work seems largely abortive for a man who worked on Nat Hiken's GROUCH CLUB and wrote radio shows for Fred Allen and Groucho Marx. (Plus A NIGHT IN CASABLANCA).

Kibbee seems to have toyed with TV, using it when convenient, rather than making a serious career out of it. He created, produced and wrote **The Deputy,** but this was self-consciously 'Non-western' for the author of VERA CRUZ. **It Takes a Thief** was more in the pastiche vein of CRIMSON PIRATE, but Kibbee was content to leave after creating it and co-writing the first segment. **McCoy** with Tony Curtis did not run long enough to establish a pattern or style. Somewhere in the early credits **(The Bob Cummings Show** in particular) there may be something worth talking about, but the later ones offer purely functional production jobs. Had he taken TV more seriously, he might have established himself as a Huggins, Hiken or Webb. As it is, he may be running his life on THE CRIMSON PIRATE dictum, adding '. . . and nothing that you write.'

Jack Laird

1957: **M Squad** (co-wr): *The Palace Guard;* **The Third Man** (wr): *The Indispensible Man.* 1958: **Have Gun-Will Travel**/*The High Graders* (co-wr). 1959: **Bronco** (wr) *The Last Resort.* 1960: **Bronco** (wr) *Legacy of Twisted Creek;* **Brothers Brannagan** (wr) *Death Insurance, Border Town.* 1961: **Have Gun-Will Travel** (wr) *Shadow of a Man, The Fatal Flaw, Lazarus, Justice in Hell, Silent Death Secret Death.* 1962: **Ben Casey** (series assoc pr). 1964: **The Hanged Man** (co-wr). 1965: **Alfred Hitchcock Hour**/*Something with Claws* (pr). 1966: **Bob Hope Chrysler Theatre**/*Code Name: Heraclitus* (pr); **Shadow Over Elveron** (pr); **See How They Run** (pr), **How I Spent My Summer Vacation** (pr). 1969: **Trial Run** (pr). 1970: **Hauser's Memory** (pr); **Act of Piracy** (pr); **Four-in-One: Night Gallery** (pr). 1971: **The Bold Ones: The Protectors** (series exec. pr); **Night Gallery** (series pr) + *The Late Mr Paddington* (wr), *Miss Lovecraft Sent Me* (wr), *Satisfaction Guaranteed* (wr), *The Merciful* (wr), *With Apologies to Mr Hyde* (wr), *Professor Peabody's Last Lecture* (wr), *A Matter of Semantics* (dir), *An Act of Chivalry* (wr/dir), *A Midnight Visit to the Blood Bank* (wr), *A Question of Fear* (dir), *Stop Killing Me* (wr), *Pickman's Model* (dir), *Room for One Less* (wr), *I'll Never Leave You-Ever* (wr), *Quoth the Raven* (wr), *How to Cure the Common Vampire* (wr/dir). 1972: **Charlie Chan: Happiness is a Warm Clue** (pr). 1973: **Kojak** (supervising pr/wr) *Requiem for a Cop.* 1974/1975: **Kojak** (supervising pr + wr: multiples). 1975: **One of our Own** (wr/pr); **Doctor's Hospital** (series pr). 1976: **Kojak** (sup pr + wr) *Monkey on a String, A Grave Too Soon;* **Perilous Voyage** (pr). 1977: **What Really Happened to the Class of '65**/*The Class Crusader* (pr), *The Class Athlete* (pr); **Kojak** (supervising pr); **The Dark Secret of Harvest Home** (5 pts).

Born in Bombay, Laird was a child actor in silent films and enrolled in a dramatic workshop in New York after Air Force service. He screen tested in Hollywood and got a series of movie and TV roles, but began writing. Once the scripts began to sell he abandoned Thespe to others. He has writing credits on over 80 TV shows—the earliest, we presume, being predominantly westerns. He made the break into production with the **Ben Casey** series. The medical connection surfaced again later with **One of Our Own** and the series which it inspired, **Doctor's Hospital.**

Night Gallery and **Kojak** are his two main series involvements. He has kept the cover off his typewriter and contributed scripts to both. They are mainly comedy snappers in **Night Gallery** and rarely personally attuned to the concept of fear. His **Kojak** offerings are similarly below the best standards achieved by others.

The two series, overall, however, have stamped themselves on the public consciousness and are uncommonly consistent in choice of talent and level of ambition. As such, they tacitly explain a producer's function, and reveal that Laird has become one of the best.

Glen A Larson

1968: **It Takes a Thief** (wr) *Birds of a Feather, Get Me to the Revolution on Time* (co-wr). 1969: **It Takes a Thief** (wr) *Hans Across the Border* (2 pts), *Guess Who's Coming to Rio* (+pr), *Cat's Paw* (co-wr +pr). 1970: **Four-in-One: McCloud/***The Stage Is All the World* (pr); **Virginian** (series pr +wr) *To be a Man, The Concrete Corral* (co-wr + pr), *With Love Bullets and Valentines;* **Alias Smith and Jones** (series cr + pr + wr) *The Great Shell Game, The Fifth Victim.* 1971: **Alias Smith and Jones** (pr +wr) *The Day They Hanged Kid Curry, Dreadful Sorry Clementine* (co-wr), *Bad Night in Big Butte.* 1972: **McCloud** (exec pr +wr) *The Barefoot Stewardess Caper* (co-wr), *The New Mexican Connection..* 1973: **Six Million Dollar Man/***Wine, Women and War.* 1974: **McCloud/***This Must Be the Alamo* (wr/pr); **Get Christie Love/***The Deadly Sport.* 1975: **Switch** (pilot series cr +exec pr) + *Death Heist* (dir); **McCloud/***The Day New York Turned Blue, Our Man in the Harem* (co-wr), *Return to the Alamo;* **Get Christie Love/***I'm Your New Neighbour.* 1976: **McCloud/***Night of the Shark Meets Dracula* (wr); **Benny + Barney: Las Vegas Under Cover** (wr + exec pr). 1977: **The Hardy Boys & Nancy Drew Mysteries** (exec pr) + *Mystery of the Haunted House, The Secret at Bronson's Grave* (+ wr). 1978: **Galactica** (co-exec pr + wr: pilot); **Evening in Byzantium** (exec pr + co-wr); **Buck Rogers** (co-pr + co-wr).

The puns and parodies in Larson's script titles *(Hans Across the Border, The Stage Is All the World, The Barefoot Stewardess, Our Man in the Harem,* etc.) suggest an enthusiastic talent, but one content to take what is to hand rather than invest dangerously in original ideas. Equally, the series with which he has been connected are either not his own **(It Takes a Thief)** or are direct steals from obvious sources (**McCloud** was inspired by COOGAN'S BLUFF and **Alias Smith and Jones** was a TV BUTCH CASSIDY AND THE SUNDANCE KID, **Switch,** a son of **It Takes a Thief,** with Robert Wagner a common denominator to both). His latest venture, in collaboration with Leslie Stevens, is Universal's leap into the STAR WARS, trend, and owes more than a nod to **Star Trek,** while **Buck Rogers** is an expensive way to cover your bets.

But if Larson has yet to be original, he has been prolific and delightfully professional. **Alias Smith and Jones**—though owing a large debt to the Roy Huggins **Maverick** style of humour, bluff and deception—no doubt taught Larson a great deal. Whilst we wait for a more individual signature from Larson, we will doubtless continue to be impressed by his apparently unerring choice of which banks to rob and the way to escape with the loot.

Arnold Laven (1922-)

1957: **Wagon Train/***The Dora Gray Story.* 1958: **The Rifleman** (series co-pr + dir) *The Sharpshooter, Home Ranch, The Brother-in-Law, The Young Englishman.* 1959: **The Rifleman/***The Retired Gun, The Photographer, The Woman, The Sheridan Story.* 1960: **Law of the Plainsman** (series exec pr + dir: multiples). 1964: **Alfred Hitchcock Hour/***The Return of Verge Likens.* 1965/1968: **The Big Valley** (series co-pr + dir) *The Odyssey of Jubal Tanner, Hazard, The Midas*

Man. 1971: **Marcus Welby MD**/*Portrait of Debbie;* **Alias Smith and Jones**/*Which Way to the OK Corral?;* **Rex Harrison Presents Short Stories of Love**/*Kiss Me Again Stranger;* **Gunsmoke**/*Shadler.* 1972: **Ghost Story**/*Cry of the Cat.* 1973: **Griff**/*Elephant in a Cage.* 1974: **Ironside**/*Terror on Grant Avenue;* **Police Woman**/*Bondage;* **Six Million Dollar Man**/*Lost Love.* 1975: **Baretta**/*Nobody in a Nothing Place;* **Mobile One**/*The Middle Man;* **Six Million Dollar Man**/*The Winning Smile;* **The Secrets of Isis**/*Spots of the Leopard, The Sound of Silence, Rockhound's Roost, The Shoe-Off, Girl Driver, Scuba Duba.* 1976: **Delvecchio**/*Licensed to Kill, Hot Spell, APB Santa Claus, Cancelled Contract.* 1977: **Switch**/*Two on the Run;* **Dog and Cat**/*Yesterday's Woman.*

Jules Levy (producer, script supervisor), Arthur Gardner (producer) and Arnold Laven (director), teamed up in 1951 and made a handful of interesting B thrillers (WITHOUT WARNING, VICE SQUAD, DOWN THREE DARK STREETS). Laven independently made a bid for more respectable fortune with THE RACK—an early Paul Newman vehicle—and ANNA LUCASTA—with Eartha Kitt, Sammy Davis Jr and an all black cast---before the three men came together again at Four-Star TV. Their first success was **Rifleman** (a spinoff of a segment made for **Zane Grey Theatre,** written by Sam Peckinpah) followed by the Robert Taylor series **Detectives, Law of the Plainsman** (a short-lived curio with Michael Ansara as a Harvard educated Apache who becomes a US Marshall in the New Mexico of the 1880s) and **Big Valley,** a matriarchal **Bonanza** with Barbara Stanwyck as Lorne Greene, and an early role for Lee **(Six Million Dollar Man)** Majors.

A high standard was maintained throughout these series, which had such directors as Joseph H Lewis, Paul Wendkos, Michael Ritchie, Sutton Roley, Tom Gries and Arthur Hiller working on them, along with Laven.

Further features followed in the '60s, and then the team broke up. Laven followed a solo career as a director. Most enthusiasts know his work best through THE GLORY GUYS, which extended the relationship with Peckinpah; Laven shot the script which Peckinpah was unable to finance after the disaster of MAJOR DUNDEE. While the film's many Peckinpahesque flavours seem stillborn and under-achieved, Laven's contribution is measured unfairly. Had nobody known anything about Peckinpah, cultists would have naturally praised Laven and not the writer. It would have been hailed as one of the most interesting '60s westerns. Laven's cameras track and crane delightfully, and while there is admittedly little of the visual understanding that makes movement meaningful, the attempt to convey the feeling of the period and the rawness of life, harks back to the early '50s (WITHOUT WARNING with its insane blonde killer, VICE SQUAD and its day in the life of a police officer, DOWN THREE DARK STREETS neatly juggling three separate storylines). It attempts to use reality and get behind it to where the observers lurk.

Since the Levy-Gardner-Laven breakup, Laven has been little more than a journeyman, and his involvement with such series as **Secrets of Isis** with its kidvid slant indicates that he has lost a lot of his enthusiasm and energy. Scattered in the police and crime shows, however, are enough individual felicities to make him an important contributor to series TV.

Richard Levinson and William Link

1962: **Alfred Hitchcock Hour**/*Day of Reckoning* (wr only), *Dear Uncle George* (co-wr + st), *Captive Audience* (wr); **The Third Man**/*Diamond in the Rough* (wr). 1964: **Burke's Law**/*Who Killed Everybody?* (wr), *Who Killed Merlin the Great?, Who Killed Mother Goose?;* **Fugitive**/*Tiger Left Tiger Right.* 1966: **Prescription Murder** (wr only). 1968: **Name of the Game**/*The Taker* (wr/pr), *Incident in Berlin* (wr only). 1969: **Mannix** (cr). 1970: **My Sweet Charlie** (wr/pr Emmy Award). 1971: **Columbo** (cr + exec pr + wr: multiples); **Sam Hill: Who Killed the Mysterious Mr Foster?** (wr/pr). 1972: **That Certain Summer** (wr/pr); **Savage** (exec pr + wr). 1973: **Partners in Crime** (exec pr). 1974: **The Gun** (wr/pr); **Ellery Queen** (wr/pr). 1975: **Tenafly** (cr + exec pr series, wr: pilot); **Ellery Queen** (wr/pr). 1977: **The Storyteller** (wr/pr).

The two L's met during their undergraduate days at the University of Pennsylvania's Wharton School of Business—which is, may be, where aspirant writers should go, rather than creative writing classes. This team has become extremely successful writer/producers. Slipping with easy facility from the formal rigours of **Alfred Hitchcock** segments, to the rarely more than clever **Burke's Law,** to the chase and character confrontations of **The Fugitive,** Levinson and Link were a team producers could rely upon to deliver just about any goods with style and imagination. To be fast, prolific, dependable and have ideas on top is a bonus in the TV vortex. It was natural for such a team to take over a part of the asylum.

Since the late '60s they have functioned as writer/producers, and their present eminence is, in part, due to their persistence with **Columbo.** Having introduced the character of an apparently bumbling detective in **Prescription Murder,** they resuscitated him in **Ransom for a Dead Man**—and this time the project clicked, into the 'Mystery Movie' slot along with **MacMillan and Wife, McCloud, Banacek** and other feature length rotating detective shows.

The **Columbo** concept was initially striking. In the majority of detective stories, 'whodunnit? is the question, but in **Columbo,** an elaborate murder will be committed up front. The grubby Peter Falk will arrive on the scene and the cat and mouse game that ensues between the detective and the known (to the audience) murderer becomes the basis for each segment. At its best, this is ideal formula TV; it won the team an Emmy for the splendid *Death Takes a Hand* segment, directed by Bernard Kowalski and starring Robert Culp. Encouraged by **Columbo**'s success, Levinson and Link subsequently resurrected **Ellery Queen** (which, unusually, had been a series before), but there is little magic in such properties which start as novels and are then transferred to the screen. Levinson and Link should have known that **Columbo** was already the closest TV has ever come to capturing the flavour and fascination of the crime novel.

The team's other Emmy—for **My Sweet Charlie**—reflects the other side of their work, a concern for more 'human' issues that genre affairs can only reflect tangentally. **That Certain Summer** extended development by dealing with the hitherto taboo TV subject of homosexuality; Scott Jacoby discovers that his father, Hal Holbrook, has Martin Sheen as a lover; agony and confusion result. With Lamont Johnson again directing, it was stylish and moving. **The Gun** was much more elliptical, a 'seriously aware' WINCHESTER '73 with a built-in suspense factor. All those in whose lives the gun becomes a temporary part, never get to fire it (including the young executive who is breaking down under the threat of being himself fired, and stands on a busy corner, pointing the weapon at passers by, mentally shooting but merely pulling the trigger). At the end, the gun, destined to be pulped with other weapons hauled in by the police department, gets a reprieve, and escapes destruction by being taken home by one of the workmen. It is found by his very young son, who examines it eagerly, curiously. The camera—pans away—there is an awfully long pause, and the only shot we hear fades into the final titles. Guns are designed to be fired.

Savage is a blend of detective story and social thriller, with Martin Landau as a TV journalist who is offered a compromising photograph of a supreme court candidate by a young woman who shortly afterwards is found dead in mysterious circumstances. Steven Spielberg's direction and Edward Abroms's editing have a field day. Both obscure and surpass the obvious paranoiac undertones. **The Storyteller** keeps up the L + L tradition of working with directors who shortly afterwards get the big screen breaks. (Robert Markowitz has repeated the pattern.) Their connections with the world of Levinson and Link would seem to have more than just a coincidental value.

Gene Levitt

1965/1967: **Combat** (series pr + wr). 1968: **The Outsider** (series pr + wr). 1969: **Run a Crooked Mile** (wr/dir). 1970: **Alias Smith and Jones** (pilot + wr), *The McCready Bust;* **The Bold Ones: The Lawyers**/*Point of Honour;* **The 48 Hour Mile.** 1971: *Any Second Now* (wr/pr/dir). 1972: **Cool Million** (pilot (dir only), *Search for a Lovely Girl* (wr/pr/dir). 1973: **Tenafly**/*Man Running;* **The Deadly Tide** (pr/dir); **Barnaby Jones** (series pr). 1974: **The Phantom of Hollywood** (wr/dir).

With a grounding as a reporter in Chicago, Levitt became a writer of radio mysteries, **The Whistler,** and 102 consecutive weeks of **Adventures of Philip Marlowe**. Early TV credits have eluded us, but he turns up as a producer for the first time on **Combat**, the best and most 'responsible' war series. His first writing/directing credit is **Run a Crooked Mile**, an unbelievably absurd would-be sophisticated thriller. Things get better with the **Alias Smith and Jones** pilot, and **The Forty Eight Hour Mile,** an unusual private-eye adventure with the ubiquitous (and always excellent) Darren McGavin. **Cool Million** was back to sophisticated adventure formulas, but **The Deadly Tide** was an exciting and unusual caper-cum-chase thriller, with the beautiful (but, here, deadly) Susan Dey, and a gang of hoods featuring the always weird and wonderful Don Stroud.

Phil Silvers played an untypical role as a derelict, and Levitt (producing and directing a script by Ben Masselink) looked like he was off and rolling.

But **The Phantom of Hollywood** took him back to the style-less inanity of **Run a Crooked Mile.** It was a monumentally ludicrous PHANTOM OF THE OPERA reprise which seems to have been made solely to record the destruction of the MGM backlot. Shots of the place being levelled by bulldozers were sadistic cruelty to those who loved the movies.

We reserve judgement on Levitt. As writer/director/producer he sometimes has trouble remembering which hat he is wearing at any given time.

James E. Moser

1954/1956: **Medic** (cr + pr + wr: multiples). 1961/1966: **Ben Casey** (cr + pr + wr: multiples). 1965: **Slattery's People** (exec. pr + wr).

A key figure in the development of 'concerned' and 'aware' TV drama. Moser gave up his plans for the priesthood to attend university in San Francisco and subsequently to become a newspaper man for Associated Press. This street training was invaluable when, he helped develop the format for Jack Webb for the radio version of **Dragnet** in 1949. Altogether he wrote 70 scripts for the series, leaving in 1951 to concentrate on developing a show which, in 1954, became **Medic**. By this time **Dragnet** and **Gunsmoke** had both transferred from radio to TV, and **Medic** made up the trilogy of raw reactive, emotional series which, alongside the celebrated anthology series (**Playhouse 90**, etc.) made up TV's first truly 'golden age'.

Subsequently, Moser was creator/writer/producer for **Ben Casey,** and the less successful and only dimly remembered **Slattery's People**, which amazingly was able to dramatize the workings of the legislature with hardly any concessions to so-called 'popular taste', at least for its first season. It was shuffled around the schedules, never really finding its real audience, until a mixture of poor ratings and the addition of more conventional elements (a regular girl friend) took it from the tube.

While it lasted, it was a lesson, as were Moser's other shows, in how to hit the highest common factor. Perhaps because his employers only require the lowest common denominator, Moser has done little since.

John Newland (c.1916-)

1952-1957: **Robert Montgomery Presents** (multiples). 1959: **One Step Beyond** (dir entire 1st season). 1960: **One Step Beyond** (dir second season). 1961: **One Step Beyond** (dir third eason); **Thriller**/*Pigeons from Hell, The Return of Andrew Bentley, Portrait Without a Face;* **endezvous**/*The Wonderful Ice Cream Suit, Blow Out.* 1962: **Thriller**/*Man of Mystery;* **The efenders**/*Invisible Badge;* **Alcoa Premiere**/*Mr Easy;* **Naked City**/*Strike a Statue.* 1963: **Route 6**/*There I Am—There I Always Am.* 1964: **The Man from UNCLE**/*The Double Affair.* 1965: **Dr ildare**/*Rome Will Never Leave You, An Exchange of Gifts, No Mother to Guide Them.* 1966: **The lan Who Never Was**/*Minus One—Equals One.* 1967: **Star Trek**/*Errand of Mercy.* 1969: **The urvivors**/*Chapter 8.* 1971: **Rod Serling's Night Gallery**/*There Aren't Any More MacBanes; rawlspace;* **The Deadly Hunt.** 1972: **The Sixth Sense**/*And Scream by the Light of the Moon, the loon, Through a Flame Darkly, Dear John, We're Going to Scare You to Death.* 1973: **Don't Be fraid of the Dark.** 1974: **Police Woman**/*Shark;* **Harry O**/*For the Love of Money, Second Sight, ound of Trumpets, Double Jeopardy.* 1975: **Switch**/*Ain't Nobody Here Named Barney, Round Up e Usual Suspects;* **The Family Holvak**/*First Love* (2 pts). 1978: **Overboard: A Further Step eyond.**

ohn Newland had been a successful actor for many years prior to becoming ıvolved with **One Step Beyond** as series director. He had acted, often directing lso, in the **Robert Montgomery Presents** anthology series before joining roducer Collier Young and creator-associate producer Merwin Gerard on **lcoa Presents One Step Beyond** (the series's title was shortened to simply **)ne Step Beyond** when it went into syndication, the title that has since stuck). lewland's direction on the show was only significant in that he did manage to ıaintain a consistent standard of presenting psychic phenomena as seriously nd realistically as possible. His **Thriller** segments, somewhat in the same vein, evive memories of shadowy worlds and Gothic suspense; the *Pigeons from lell* segment, adapted from a Robert E. Howard story, remains as one of the ıost truly frightening journeys into small-screen fantasy. **The Man from JNCLE** is also a pleasant reminder of the innocent spy-action programmers of ıe mid-1960s; *The Double Affair* also turned up on the big-screen as THE SPY ITH MY FACE, in 1966. Following the trend of clandestine spy and war drama eries, **The Man Who Never Was** (loosely patterned after the 1956 feature film) as an even stranger mish-mash of events, with the anonymous hero freely abotaging the East Germans. Question: in the final wrap-up segment, before ıe series finally went off the air, was the hero allowed to stop being who it was ıat he wasn't?

Night Gallery's *There Aren't Any More MacBanes* appeared to have ıore going for it than most similar Lovecraftian themes employed on the show. lewland successfully stirred the sense of 'something lurking on the threshold' in is **Night Gallery** and **Sixth Sense** segments, finally weaving them all into the lefeature **Don't Be Afraid of the Dark**. Unfortunately, the initial eerie quality ıat Newland sets up is rapidly dissipated in the final build-up, when Kim Darby nd Barbara Anderson are attacked by strange little imp-like creatures, and the amera darts about trying to focus in on the bizarre activities from the point f view both of the attackers and the victims. Newland's work, overall, has an ıteresting inclination toward the supernatural/supernormal; when allowed, he can deliver the goods. But, for reasons that suggest a lack of complete control, h promises more than he is able to supply.

Gene Roddenberry

1952: **Chevron Theatre**/*The Secret Defense of 117* (wr). 1954: **Mr District Attorney** (w multiples). 1955: **Highway Patrol** (wr multiples). 1956: **Four Star Playhouse** (wr multiples **Kaiser Aluminium Hour** (wr multiples). 1958: **West Point** (wr mulitples); **Have Gun-Will Travel** (w multiples). 1959: **Have Gun-Will Travel** (wr multiples). 1960: **Whiplash** (wr multiples). 196 **Dr Kildare** (wr multiples). 1962: **Naked City** (wr multiples); **True**/*V-Victor* (co-wr). 1963: **Th Lieutenant** (cr-pr). 1966: **Star Trek** (cr-pr) *Charlie X* (co-wr), *The Menagerie* (2 pts; wr). 196 **Star Trek** (exec pr). 1968: **Star Trek** (exec pr) *A Private Little War* (wr), *The Omega Glory* (w 1969: **Star Trek** (exec pr) *Assignment: Earth* (co-wr), *The Savage Curtain* (co-wr). 1973: **Genesis** (wr + pr); **The Questor Tapes** (exec pr st + co-wr). 1977: **Spectre** (co-wr + pr).

Star Trek is Roddenberry's **The Untouchables**. He will always be associate with it, as will Quinn Martin with the latter. Whatever these men were doin before seems, to many observers, unimportant—only their later work i considered comparable. Roddenberry, like the majority of TV producers, entere the medium as a writer, contributing to both anthologies (**Four Star Playhouse Kaiser Aluminum Hour**, etc.) and regular series (**Highway Patrol, Hav Gun-Will Travel**, etc.).

Roddenberry has still to overcome his greatest success, **Star Trek**. Comin in at a time when both America and American TV were going through somewhat shaky period, **Star Trek** breathed new life and hope into the medium Its incredible success is solely due to the creative genius of Gene Roddenberry He was, at last, able to offer a series that the networks were convinced woul never survive (after all, **Lost in Space** was barely breaking even)—a seriou science fiction series, with continuing characters, aimed at a mature, adul audience. He carefully prepared his scripts, utilised such accomplished genr writers as John D. F. Black, Richard Matheson, Robert Bloch, Theodor Sturgeon, Norman Spinrad, etc., to present the best possible stories and ofte worked on the scripts himself during shooting. Two of his most able assistants Gene Coon and Dorothy Fontana, also helped supply the quality that emerge from the series. Harlan Ellison created *The City on the Edge of Foreve* segment, one of **Star Trek's** supreme achievements, and picked up the covete Hugo award. Any merit awards to **Star Trek**, and its creator, are justly deserved Be it a product of its times or simply that rare spark of brilliance, Roddenberr was there when it happened.

The series, has, since its initial airing, expanded into an awesome giant, an industry unto itself. The phenomenon appears to have had a serious side-effect on Roddenberry's aims, because he seems to have devoted a decade to trying for a new 'Star Trek' with various feature/pilots, nearly all in the science fiction genre. The *Assignment: Earth* segment of **Star Trek**, directed by Marc Daniels, was originally intended as a pilot for another series, but failed. Like Ahab chasing his whale, Roddenberry pursues the elusive series that will, hopefully, once again put him on top. **Genesis II, Planet Earth** and **The Questor Tapes** have all been tentative springboards for a new Roddenberry series; **Genesis II** was a disappointing offering but was remade the following year as **Planet Earth. The Questor Tapes,** another un-sold pilot, was an undetermined mixture of **The Fugitive** and Eando Binder's Adam Link stories.

Roddenberry is still working at it. His most recent venture is **Spectre**, a moody demon-hunting exercise filmed in England, and directed by Clive Donner. It remains to be seen if 'The Great Bird of the Galaxy' still has the zest and zing that made **Star Trek** a classic in the medium over a decade ago.

Meta Rosenberg

1971: **Nichols** (series exec pr). 1974: **Rockford Files** (series exec pr +) *In Pursuit of Elizabeth* (dir). 1976: **Rockford Files** (exec pr +) *Rattler's Class of '63, There's One in Every Port* (dir), *Quickie Nirvana* (dir), *The Queen of Peru* (dir); **Scott Free** (co-exec pr). 1977: **Rockford Files** (exec pr). 1978: **The New Maverick** (exec pr).

An assistant to William Dozier when he was head of Paramount's story department in 1943, Ms Rosenberg seems to have been one of the few people whom Raymond Chandler remembered with any degree of affection from his self-destructive time as a screen poet. She subsequently became an agent and businesswoman—one of whose clients was James Garner.

In 1963, following the success of **Maverick**, Garner and Rosenberg formed Cherokee Productions, to guarantee the actor more than a mere salary for his work, but it was not until 1971 that the company had any meaning to TV. Then with Garner's movie career in the doldrums, he returned to Warner Bros. with **Nichols**, and Meta Rosenberg as executive producer.

With the creation of **Rockford Files**, and functioning still as executive producer, she has become more evidently active, directing five segments of the series; *In Pursuit of Elizabeth*, in particular, is a haunting and evocative episode. It is happy duty to welcome her in the thin list of *femme*-directors and to pay her full due for her part in the formulation of the Cherokee projects.

Jimmy Sangster (1925-)

1958: [GB] **Armchair Theatre**/*I Can Destroy the Sun.* [US] 1971: **A Taste of Evil.** 1972: **Ghost Story** (co-st con + wr) *The Concrete Captain, Doorway to Death, Spare Parts* (co-wr), *The Phantom of Herald Square* (co-wr); **Banacek** (st con). 1973: **McCloud** (st con) *A Cowboy in Paradise* (aka *Hawaiian Hula Murder*); **Faraday & Co**/*A Wheelbarrow Full of Trouble* (co-wr); **Scream Pretty Peggy** (co-wr). 1974: **Kolchak: The Night Stalker**/*Horror in the Heights* (wr); **Ironside**/*The Visiting Fireman* (wr), *Raise the Devil* (2 pts co-wr). 1975: **Cannon**/*Victim* (wr); **Movin' On** (series pr + st con + wr) *The Big Wheel.* 1976: **Most Wanted** (series pr + st con); **Wonder Woman** (wr) *The Feminum Mystique* (2 pts), *Wonder Woman in Hollywood.* 1977: **Young Dan'l Boone** (series pr + wr + dir: multiples).

Raymond Durgnat had a deliciously wacky dream (which he happily recounted in *A Mirror for England*) 'that I was touring the script crypt at Bray. The light of the full moon poured in through the Gothic windows, and producer Anthony Hinds stared in horror at his hands, as they grew hairy and twitched—another script idea was taking them over, and he was turning into one or another of his dreaded alter egos, John Elder or Henry Younger*. Young Baron Sangsterstein was there, cackling hideously and with fiendish cunning was sewing together bits of scenarios from the old Universal book . . .'

The 'Young Baron' finally fled such inevitable type-casting as Hammer Films Prince of Panic (and the lack of other movie opportunities in England) at the beginning of the 70's, but it took a while to augment the reputation in Hollywood. **Taste of Evil** is yet another reworking of Sangster's 'who's-driving-me-mad?' model (which itself owes a lot to PSYCHO), while **Scream Pretty Peggy** is more of the same, with John Moxey and Gordon Hessler respectively calling the shots; the old magic (however corney it was becoming) worked again. **Ghost Story** was a more interesting assignment—*The Phantom of Herald Square* (with a pre-Hutch David Soul, and moody direction by James H. Brown) reached misty mysticism levels. But Sangster was becoming involved in the more interesting reaches of mainstream series, and (having produced and directed for Hammer in England) was soon taking more and more production responsibility. His work with **Movin' On** — an engaging 'buddie' series with Frank Converse and Claude Akins—are gems of pace, invention, style, and humour. His 'own' full show, **Young Dan'l Boone**, was as far as you can get from Bray script crypt—but it bombed in the hyper-nervous fall of 1977, along with **Lucan, Logan's Run, Fantastic Journey** and a myriad other 'family hour' shows. Sangster will always swim with the tide—and continue to be a fascinating talent to watch grow and expand.

*Henry Younger is, in fact, the alter ego of Michael Carreras.

Rod Serling (1924-1975)

1954: **Kraft Television Theatre**/*You Be the Bad Guy* (wr); **US Steel Hour** (wr multiples); **Studio One** (wr multiples); **Elgin Hour** (wr multiples); **Fireside Theatre** (wr multiples). 1955: **Kraft Television Theatre**/*Patterns* (wr); **Center Stage** (wr multiples); **Lux Video Theatre** (wr multiples); **Suspense** (wr multiples). 1956: **Playhouse 90**/*Requiem for a Heavyweight* (wr); **Danger** (wr multiples); **G.E. Theatre** (wr multiples); **Armstrong Circle Theatre** (wr multiples). 1957: **Climax** (wr multiples). 1958: **Playhouse 90**/*Forbidden Area* (wr); **Desilu Playhouse** (wr multiples). 1959: **The Twilight Zone** (cr + pr + wr: multiples). 1960: **The Twilight Zone** (wr multiples). 1961: **The Twilight Zone** (wr multiples). 1962: **The Twilight Zone** (wr multiples). 1963: **The Twilight Zone** (wr multiples); **The Visitor**/*Those Who Wait* (wr). 1964: **The Twilight Zone** (wr multiples). 1965: **The Loner** (wr multiples). 1966: **The Doomsday Flight** (wr). 1969: **Night Gallery** (pilot + wr). 1970: **Four-in-One: Night Gallery** (cr) *The Last Laurel* (wr), *They're Tearing Down Tim Riley's Bar* (wr), *The House* (wr), *Certain Shadows on the Wall* (wr), *Clean Kills and Other Trophies* (wr), *Make Me Laugh* (wr), *Pamela's Voice* (wr), *Lone Survivor* (wr), *The Doll* (wr), *The Little Black Bag* (wr), *The Nature of the Enemy* (wr). 1971: **Rod Serling's Night Gallery** (wr multiples). 1972: **Rod Serling's Night Gallery**; (wr multiples). 1975: **The Time Travellers**.

Possibly one of the most prolific and talented TV authors of the 1950s and '60s, Rod Serling was highly respected in critical circles as a serious dramatist who explored and spot-lighted controversial topics and issues. He was constantly battling with networks and TV sponsors over subject matter deemed too 'dangerous' for national telecasting, especially following the recent McCarthyist paranoia. Serling's TV-writing career brought him a total of six Emmys (of which three were for his **Twilight Zone** series) and the Peabody Award. However, Serling had to fight for these prizes all along the way. Sponsors and their agencies, at the time, almost had a strangle-hold on TV scripts, demanding changes and censoring themes. Serling arrived with the wave of 'new' TV writers during the early-to-mid Fifties, authors such as Reginald Rose, David Davidson, and Paddy Chayefsky. Chayefsky, more than any other writer of the time, was instrumental in opening the gates to the anthology writers with his landmark teleplay, *Marty*. The impressive *Patterns* and *Requiem for a Heavyweight* were among Serling's landmark contributions to the medium (he also wrote the screenplay for *Patterns*, in '56).

However, it is for **The Twilight Zone** that Serling is most fondly remembered, having created, produced, written and hosted the show. The series came on the air in October, 1959, as the first serious, adult-market fantasy series, set in an anthology format. Serling, himself, wrote a total of 84 scripts for the show, and hired the fertile minds of talents such as Richard Matheson, Charles Beaumont and George Clayton Johnson to supply the rest. Many directors served their early TV apprenticeship on the show (Jack Smight, Elliot Silverstein, etc.), alongside the more expert ranks of John Brahm, Robert Florey, Richard Bare, etc. For five seasons **The Twilight Zone** presented extraordinary stories in a highly-polished fashion.

During the Sixties, Serling penned the screenplay for his REQUIEM FOR A HEAVYWEIGHT, along with SEVEN DAYS IN MAY, ASSAULT ON A QUEEN, and completed the first draft for PLANET OF THE APES. The **Night Gallery** period was one of his unhappiest, and left Serling in a hateful state of mind towards Universal. He created and packaged the show, which was sold to NBC solely on his reputation which went back to **Twilight Zone**. With CBS countering **Night Gallery** with their **Mannix** actioner, Universal executives increased their demands and wanted the series more rapidly paced. Despite Serling's opposition, Universal got their way and he was left with little more than a bare contractual commitment (merely playing host on the series). However, two of his scripts, *They're Tearing Down Tim Riley's Bar* and *The Messiah of Mott Street*, were nominated for Emmys, which must have assured Serling that his writing skill, at least, had not been totally shackled by Universal.

Serling's writing strongly reflects his perceptive view of ordinary people who try to eke out an existence in a harsh, if not turbulent, world. It may not be *what* he sees but, more importantly, the *way* he sees it that has built Rod Serling into a major creative talent.

Leonard B. Stern

1955/1956: **The Sgt Bilko Show** (co-wr: multiples). 1965: **Run Buddy Run** (series cr exec pr + dir *pilot);* **Get Smart** (series exec pr + *Ship of Spies*—co-wr). 1969: **The Governor and J.J.** (series exec pr + wr) *There Goes the Judge, Cat on a Hot Tin Mansion.* 1971: **Once Upon a Dead Man** (cr + dir). 1972: **The Snoop Sisters** (exec pr + dir). 1974: **MacMillan and Wife** (series exec pr). 1976: **Holmes and Yoyo** (exec pr +) *Funny Money* (wr/dir), *Dental Dynamite* (dir). 1977: **Lanigan's Rabbi** (series exec pr +) *Corpse of the Year* (dir); **Operation Petticoat** (series exec pr); **Rosetti and Ryan** (exec pr series). 1978: **Windows, Doors + Keyholes** (exec pr/dir/co-wr).

Run Buddy Run (a short-lived mixture of NORTH BY NORTHWEST and THE FUGITIVE played as parody) and the wonderfully silly **Get Smart** (created by Mel Brooks and Buck Henry) were in the 30 minute sit com tradition, but Stern branched out in the '70s into more elaborate capers. The most successful of these was **MacMillan and Wife**. One of the first really feature-length series, the format of domestic comedy and detection initially worked well. The extra length allowed time for digressions of character idiosyncracies and of joking—long the sole-privilege of cinema. Susan Saint James (a young veteran of many Universal series) finally got the showcase her talents had long warranted, while Rock Hudson effortlessly slipped back in time to his Mr. Doris Day persona (charming enough, but an absurdity when portraying the police commissioner of San Francisco).

Lanigan's Rabbi should have been an equally successful series—but perhaps religious pussyfooting flattened the basic idea. **Snoop Sisters** (Helen Hayes and Mildred Natwick as ancient thriller writers-cum-detectives), **Holmes and Yoyo** (the cop and the robot) were good ideas with nowhere to go. So lately Stern has reincarnated the Blake Edwards feature into an **Operation Petticoat** series—shades here of **Sgt. Bilko** again, and a foolproof format.

Stern's sure comic touch, unostentatious direction (usually of the series pilots) and lively response to genuinely superb comedy performers (Don Adams, Art Carney, Ms Saint James *et al*) keep alive both Hollywood and vaudeville traditions. They maintain a gentle flow of wit, parody and invention that never reaches great heights but are seldom inane, crude or repetitive.

Leslie Stevens (1924-)

Writer: 1956: **Four Star Playhouse**/*The Award;* **Producers Showcase**/*Bloomer Girl.* 1957: **Kraft Theatre**/*The Duel;* **Playhouse 90**/*Charley's Aunt, Invitation to a Gunfighter.* 1958: **Playhouse 90**/*Portrait of a Murderer, The Violent Heart, Rumors of Evening.* 1959: **Playhouse 90/The Second Man.** 1962: **Stoney Burke** (cr, pr, dir). 1963: **The Outer Limits** (cr, exec pr) *The Galaxy Being* (+ wr), *The Borderland* (+ wr), *Controlled Experiment* (+ wr). 1964: **The Outer Limits/** *Production and Decay of Strange Particles* (+wr). 1966: **I Love a Mystery** (+wr); **Something for a Lonely Man.** 1967: **The Virginian** (exec pr fifth season) *The Modoc Kid* (co-wr), *To Be a Man, Lady of the House* (wr). 1968: **The Name of the Game** (pr) *Collector's Edition* (+ co-wr), *The Black Answer* (+wr), *Shine On, Shine On, Jesse Gil;* **It Takes a Thief**/*A Thief Is a Thief Is a Thief* (+co-wr), *A Very Warm Reception* (wr), *It Takes One to Know One* (+wr), *Where Thieves Fall In* (wr +pr). 1970: **The Men from Shiloh** (exec pr, Doug McClure segments) *The Best Man* (wr), *Lady at the Bar* (wr +pr), *Follow the Leader* (wr + pr); **Four-in-One: McCloud** (exec pr). 1972: **Search** (exec pr) *The Murrow Disappearance* (wr), *One of Our Probes is Missing* (wr), *Short Circuit* (wr), *Numbers for Death* (wr). 1975: **The Invisible Man** (pr) *Eyes Only* (wr), *Power Play* (wr). 1976: **Gemini Man** (pilot: wr + pr) *Escape Hatch* (wr + pr); **Stonestreet: Who Killed the Centerfold Model?** (exec pr + wr). 1978: **Galactica** (series co-cr, co-pr).

When Stevens was ten, he got a penny a line allowance from his father (Vice Admiral Leslie C. Stevens, then American attaché in London) for memorising Shakespeare. Today, provoked by a proper bet, Stevens can still recall the Bard flawlessly. This art for money's sake training stains his work and will not wash off. His TV work has been—with due exception—more geared to manna than the muse.

Admirers of the man behind THE LEFT HANDED GUN, THE WARLORD, PRIVATE PROPERTY and especially (perhaps because so few of us love it) HERO'S ISLAND feel that he should spend his time on more challenging stuff than **Invisible Man** (and its lookalike replacement **Gemini Man**), **Virginian** and **Men from Shiloh**.

For Stevens's best TV is early in his career; his scripts, his series **Stoney**

Burke and especially **Outer Limits**, a science-fiction anthology series for the late-night adult audience. The inclusion of a 'Thing' in each segment was an obvious sign of conforming to the pressures of the commercial market. Because the stories and production were of such a high standard the alien never dominated but merely motivated the events. Leslie Stevens's name hangs in the Tele-Fantastique Hall of Fame alongside the other notables, such as Rod Serling and Gene Roddenberry. However, before he could really settle into the series, Stevens had to vacate his chair and hand it over to partner Joseph Stefano, who went on to inject his own dye into the ball that Stevens had started rolling. The show is often credited purely to Stefano but, in effect, it was essentially Stevens's floor that Stefano was polishing.

Since then, **The Name of the Game** has seen Stevens's best work (*The Black Answer* being a brave confrontation of racial issues), for **Search** was almost exclusively formula-bound. **Galactica** may return to the heights of **Outer Limits**—but admirers wish that Stevens would rediscover the creative forces that fuelled his most satisfying achievements.

Jerry Thorpe

1959/1962: **The Untouchables** (exec pr). 1969: **Dial: Hot Line, Company of Killers.** 1970: **Lock Stock and Barrel.** 1971: **Hawaii Five-O**/*3,000 Crooked Miles to Honolulu;* **Crosscurrent** (aka *The Cable Car Murder).* 1972: **Kung Fu** (series pr + dir: pilot) *King of the Mountain, Dark Angel, Blood Brother, An Eye for an Eye.* 1973: **Kung Fu** (series exec pr + dir) *The Well, The Chalice.* 1974: **Harry O** (series exec pr + dir) *Smile Jenny You're Dead* (+ pr), *Gertrude, Guardian at the Gates, Ballinger's Choice, Elegy for a Cop;* **Kung Fu** (series exec pr + dir) *My Brother My Executioner.* 1975: **Harry O** (series exec pr + dir) *Anatomy of a Frame, The Mysterious Case of Lester and Mr Fong;* **Antonio and the Mayor.** 1976: **Lester** (pilot: pr/dir); **I Want to Keep My Baby.** 1977: **Yesterday's Child.** 1978: **A Purely Legal Matter** (+ co-pr).

A production involvement with **The Untouchables** got Thorpe off to an important start in TV; although he appears not to have directed any of the series. His features, particularly DAY OF THE EVIL GUN alerted enthusiasts to a talented 'new' name, though his TV work did not at first fare well. **Dial Hot Line** (the pilot for the **Matt Lincoln** series) came under attack by bodies as diverse as a national conference of telephone counseling services and Harlan Ellison (who described Thorpe's work as 'needlessly artsy-craftsy in the Richard Lester vein'. Ellison felt the script 'tense and well-written', but that the show, and the series to follow, might indeed do harm to the credibility of real-life hotlines). Whether cautioned or not by these reactions, thrillers (**Company of Killers** and the particularly good **Cross Current**) and a western (**Lock, Stock and Barrel**) followed. And then Thorpe became the creative equivalent of a superstar with the **Kung Fu** series. He won an Emmy for his *An Eye for an Eye.*

Though obviously stealing a march on the Bruce Lee trend, the series had enough of its own individuality. Its popularity was equalled by its excellence. The 'artsy-craftsy' direction now made perfect sense, and the interconnection in time between the West (more venal than it had appeared on the small screen since the early days of **Gunsmoke**) and the milieu of the Shaolin temple, where Caine (David Carradine) learned the discipline and the art of Kung Fu, was a stylistic breakthrough. The technical developments in cinematography that TV had studiously avoided were here utilised to the full. It joined the slow motion action, long takes and telegraphed flashbacks in a kaleidoscope technique and brought TV out of its visual dark age.

Thorpe's next series, **Harry O**, was an attempt to create a private-eye with a more than passing resemblance to a human being. As played by David Janssen, whose mannered loner-in-pain persona had been ill-served since **The Fugitive**, the series promised much, especially as the pilot *Smile Jenny You're Dead*, written by Howard Rodman, was a splendid mixture of homage to the '40s and contemporary angst, directed by Thorpe with great style. But a detective with a bad back who also couldn't drive a car in spite of its Chandler flavour was a no-no. The freshness of the approach became leaden when he was given wheels and a more conventional set of problems. Even so, the style was not entirely lost—and the series maintained a high degree of interest and credibility. As with **Kung Fu** (whose final year overlapped **Harry O**'s first), Thorpe remained in overall, executive control, directing a handful of segments each season, including *The Mysterious Case of Lester and Mr Fong*, with its charming '40s style throwbacks, Lester the adolescent crime-spotter and Mr Fong the criminologist sage, who featured in the abortive **Lester** series.

Lately, Thorpe has stayed clear of genre, action and formal experiments, in favour of apparently untypical projects. **Antonio and the Mayor**, again from a script by Howard Rodman, is Mexican whimsy in the 20s, an 'artless' tale of village life and the rivalry between a young boy and the mayor. **I Want to Keep My Baby** is a slice of 'social awareness' involving a 15 year old girl (a startling performance by Mariel Hemingway) who becomes pregnant, while **Yesterday's Child** has overtones of the past in more than just its narrative; is the 17 year old girl really the little child who was kidnapped and never seen again by rich mother Shirley Jones and grandmother Geraldine Fitzgerald? All of these projects carry a human charge, while the 'artsy-craftsy' direction matures and mellows. Thorpe has come a long way from **The Untouchables**—and he can go further.

Charles Marquis Warren

1955/1957: **Gunsmoke** (cr + exec pr + wr + dir: multiples). 1958/1960: **Rawhide** (cr + exec pr + wr + dir: multiples). 1961: **Gunslinger** (cr + exec pr). 1962: **The Virginian** (cr + exec pr). 1966: **Iron Horse** (exec pr + wr) *The Bridge at 40 Mile.*

ONLY THE VALIANT, STREETS OF LAREDO, SPRINGFIELD RIFLE are among Warren's best western script credits. He wrote and directed the fascinating, downbeat, sometimes savage, LITTLE BIG HORN, HELLGATE, ARROWHEAD, TROOPER HOOK and others which are a writer's films needing another director. They are imbued with a stylistically clumsy fervour which is curious and attractive.

If any of Warren's personally directed TV work has as much interest, it was way back in the 50's, when **Gunsmoke** was a dirty, overpoweringly raw show. Warren produced and directed the first thirty-nine segments, the majority of which were adapted from radio scripts of the show (it is unclear whether Warren was involved in the earlier incarnation, but as he is listed as **Gunsmoke**'s 'creator', we assume he was. He claims credit as the 'creator' of the **Virginian** too—which Owen Wister would challenge). Sam Peckinpah adapted Warren's two final segments, *The Queue* and *Yorky*, but an original Peckinpah was turned down—and in time became the pilot for **Rifleman.**

Warren's involvement in TV has become increasingly that of executive producer. **Gunslinger, The Virginian** and **Iron Horse** no doubt gained from Warren's western affinities, but there is little of him in them, more's the pity!

Jack Webb (1920-   )

1951 + 1956: **Dragnet** (cr, pr/dir/star). 1958: **The D.A.'s Man** (series pr). 1959: **Pete Kelly's Blues** (series wr). 1962: **True** (series pr + dir) *Circle of Death, Code Name: Christopher* (2 pts). 1963: **True** (series pr + dir) *Little Richard.* 1967: **Dragnet 1967** (pr + dir + star). 1968: **Dragnet 1968** (series pr + dir + star); **Adam 12** (series exec pr). 1969: **Dragnet 1969** (pr + dir +star); **Adam 12** (series exec pr); **The D.A.** (series pr + dir) *Murder One.* 1970: **Dragnet 1970** (series pr + dir + star); **Adam 12** (series exec pr). 1971: **Emergency** (pilot pr + dir series exec pr);**O'Hara—US Treasury** (pilot: pr + dir) *Operation: Cobra;* **The D.A.** (series pr); **Adam 12** (series pr). 1972: **Adam 12** (series exec pr); **Emergency** (series exec pr). 1973: **Chase** (pilot: pr + dir) (series exec pr); **Emergency** (series exec pr); **Adam 12** (series exec pr). 1974: **Emergency**/*905-Witch* (dir); **The Rangers** (series pr); **Adam 12** (series pr + dir) *Clinic on 18th Street.* 1975: **Mobile One** (series exec pr); **Emergency** (series exec pr). 1977: **Project UFO** (series exec pr).

Just as MAGNIFICENT AMBERSONS was first adapted by Welles for his Mercury Theatre of the Air, so too did **Dragnet**'s staccato brass introduction and Webb's throaty 'This is the city—Los Angeles, California' first hit the audience via radio in 1949. It became an enormous success and won all manner of awards. When the transition was made to TV, **Dragnet** was to become one of the high-water marks of '50s television. Its unique identity and integrity made it a masterpiece of form and style; its bleak, uncompromising view of L.A. and life within the city had the anguish of Bergman on a visual level, of dehumanised nightmare on the verbal. Webb, as creator, actor, producer, director could not have achieved success without the writers, but even so the concept and the execution was his and the entire work remains a masterpiece, but a most unusual one—hundreds of separate pieces of work. Thus, a TV masterpiece.

Webb attempted to revive the series in 1967 and it ran for three years, but by then the once revolutionary style seemed a parody of Stan Freberg's marvellous take-offs (as in *The Interrogation*, written by Preston Wood). On the other hand, the stark, emotionless behaviourism of *The Shooting*, written by David Vowell, indicated that if allied to the right material (based on watching rather than listening) Webb's vision still had power and frightening value.

Webb was naturally tempted into movies; **Dragnet** became a feature and the following year another radio show was made into a movie, PETE KELLY'S BLUES. This is a film one can love and remember with almost total recall. '-30-', with its bold-for-the-cinema but conventional-for-TV style (set entirely in a newspaper office, spanning the events of one night, intercutting the personal lives of the staff with the news stories as they develop, never strayed from the building. Our attention was hooked to the dramas in the outside world, solely through the reactions and emotions of the staff) and impassive vision builds into a beautiful and moving portrait of human nature, the antithesis of the cold world of **Dragnet**. The final line can invoke tears in a not-normally sentimental viewer. Thus Webb is either *super*-sentimental or a marvellously astute director.

Webb's recent activities have been devoted almost solely to production. Following the journalistic, professional, in-the-streets, as-it-happens, day-in-the-life style which his Mark VII company favour, series such as **Emergency** have been rolling through the developing tanks.

Without Webb's guiding hand, these formula shows can appear shapeless, cliché, banal, almost unwittingly extolling the All-American virtues for which today's generation has been led to feel little sympathy. Allied to Webb's right-wing attitudes, these shows have made an enemy of those people who should be able to see more clearly but cannot.

A major study of Webb's career and achievements is long overdue, not just because of his influence (both personal and stylistic) but because of his continual attempts to look beyond the conventions for his inspiration. Robert Mitchum's stated fondness for THE LAST TIME I SAW ARCHIE can't *simply* be because it was shot on a location Mitchum had never before visited. Perhaps those who root for Mitchum might look at ARCHIE — and then at Webb.

3/Made It Ma, Top of the World!

When Cagney defiantly yells that immortal line in WHITE HEAT, it is microseconds before the chemical plant blows up and he is scattered all over the city.

It is, to say the least, ironic.

No irony is intended here, however, in what is as close as we get to a 'Pantheon' listing.

These are the directors who, in conventional terms, have 'made it', have 'graduated' from small to big screen.

We only hope we all get a chance to see—or re-see—at least a portion of the best works listed here.

It *is* a mad world, my masters, otherwise . . . . . .

Robert Altman (1925-)

1955: **The Millionaire** (multiples). 1956: **Alfred Hitchcock Presents**/*The Young One, Together.* 1957: **Whirlybirds**/*The Midnight Show, A Matter of Trust, Guilty of Old Age, Christmas in June.* 1958: **Whirlybirds**/*Till Death Do Us Part, Time Limit, Experiment X-74, The Big Lie, The Perfect Crime, The Unknown Soldier, Two of a Kind, In Ways Mysterious, The Black Maria, The Sitting Duck.* 1959: **Hawaiian Eye**/*Three Tickets to Lani;* **Lawman**/*The Robbery.* 1960: **Surfside 6**/*Thieves Among Honor;* **Sugarfoot**/*Apollo with a Gun, The Highbinder;* **Bronco**/*The Mustangers;* **Roaring Twenties**/*The Prairie Flower, Brother's Keeper, White Carnation, Dance Marathon;* **Maverick**/*Bolt from the Blue.* 1961: **Roaring Twenties**/*Two a Day, Right off the Boat* (2 pts), *Royal Tour, Standing Room Only;* **Hawaiian Eye**/*Touch of Larceny;* **M Squad**/*Lovers' Lane Killing;* **Desilu Mystery Theatre**/*Death of a Dream;* **Route 66**/*Some of the People Some of the Time;* **Bus Stop**/*County General, The Covering Darkness, The Door Without a Key, Summer Lightning, The Pursuit of Evil.* 1962: **The Gallant Men** *(pilot);* **The Long Hot Summer** *(pilot).* 1963: **Kraft Suspense Theatre**/*The Long, Lost Life of Edward Smalley;* **Combat** (multiples). 1964: **Kraft Suspense Theatre**/*Once Upon a Savage Night* (aka *Nightmare in Chicago);* **Bonanza** (multiples).

It is appropriate that Altman should pop up at the opening of the section. The existence of nearly fifty signed pieces of work which are virtually unknown, and, if discussed at all, occupy only a footling footnote or pedantic parenthesis, calls into question the whole rationale of what passes as academic criticism. Quite simply, we ask, how can more than thirty hours of film made by one of the most unique of modern directors be ignored in this way?

It may be unlikely that, say, *Thieves Without Honor* shares anything but a word in common with THIEVES LIKE US, that **Hawaiian Eye** has any clear affinities with THE LONG GOODBYE, or that any of the **Roaring 20s** segments do with Chicago what Altman did with NASHVILLE —but this is not the point. The unique personality and attitude to genre which Altman has subsequently exhibited make any of the above works worthy of attention in its own right.

Can the man who so cruelly, yet breathtakingly, punctures the myth of Buffalo Bill Cody really take **Sugarfoot, Bronco** or **Maverick** as seriously as his employers would reasonably expect? Did he indulge his acerbic streak of humour? Is there some meaningful connection between Brewster, the hero of **Sugarfoot** and Brewster McCloud?.

Altman's apparently late blossoming has always been a puzzle to his admirers. Plainly, the solution to the puzzle lies in some, maybe all, of the titles listed above, and therefore in some kind of Altman tele-festival (which would, incidentally, be a useful miniature retrospective of a golden TV age).

Reports which surface periodically about *Once Upon a Savage Night (Nightmare in Chicago)* indicate that at least *one* bizarre delight is in store.

John Badham

1970: **Night Gallery**/*The Boy Who Predicted Earthquakes;* **The Bold Ones: The Senator**/*Someday They'll Elect a President.* 1971: **The Sixth Sense**/*Lady Lady Take My Life;* **Sarge**/*A Push over the Edge, A Terminal Case of Vengeance;* **Night Gallery**/*Camera Obscura, Green Fingers, The Girl with the Hungry Eyes, You Can Come up Now Mrs Millikan;* **The Bold Ones: The Senator**/*A Single Blow of a Sword;* **The Bold Ones: The Doctors**/*A Threatened Species.* 1972: **The Sixth Sense**/*Witch Witch Burning Bright;* **Owen Marshall Counselor at Law**/*An Often and Familiar Ghost;* **Night Gallery**/*The Doll of Death;* **Cool Million**/*Assault on Gavaloni;* **The Bold Ones: The Doctors**/*Is This Operation Necessary?, A Nation of Human Pincushions, End Theme.* 1973: **Isn't It Shocking?, Cannon**/*The Seventh Grave;* **Rex Harrison Presents Short Stories of Love**/*Epicac;* **Sunshine**/*Sweet Misery.* 1974: **The Gun; The Godchild; Reflections of Murder.** 1975: **The Impatient Heart.** 1976: **The Keegans.**

Having followed his first feature (the well-reviewed but little-seen THE BINGO LONG TRAVELLING ALL STARS AND MOTOR KINGS) with the jackpot-hitting SATURDAY NIGHT FEVER, Badham has presumably earned the right to choose or originate projects. It is interesting to speculate about what they might be, for many people are confused about FEVER. Undeniably exciting and on the button, its coarse view of human relationships, while arguably 'true to life', leaves a lot to be desired in a director. An uneasiness of form also suggests that the rigidity of TV formats may take some while to forget.

His TV work seems to split almost equally between Gothic fantasy (**Night Gallery, Sixth Sense**), prestigious series-drama and movies of the week. **The Bold Ones** was an overall title for four revolving series—**The Senator, The Doctors, The Lawyers, The Protectors**—each with a different set of producers but, generally speaking, a common pool of talent—most of it from the first division. Badham was considered temperamentally and artistically suited to this kind of serious show, and his six segments featured scripts by Robert Collins (*A*

Nation of Pincushions) and Jerrold Freedman (*A Single Blow of a Sword*). The series never played in the U.K. and seems to be the last, elaborate gasp of that literate, liberal tradition first codified in **Naked City, Defenders** etc., which the ratings-race has made a more and more endangered species as the 70s have progressed.

If **The Bold Ones** needs (re)appraisal in the light of Badham's recent activities, his movies of the week will obviously reveal more of his talent and nature. Certainly the interest in 'ethnic' matters (Black baseball teams in the 30s, the Bronx disco scene) revealed in the two features is already evident in **Isn't it Shocking?**, a bizarre comedy-thriller set in a small New England town where somebody is murdering the community's senior citizens; **The Gun** is a kind of modern WINCHESTER '73 which follows a weapon from the assembly line through its possession by such characters as a Spanish car-wash worker; **The Impatient Heart** deals with the life of a social-worker (Carrie Snodgrass) and in **The Keegans**, New York Irish family ties are the underpinning for another in-the-streets thriller. The exception that may prove the rule is **The Godchild**, a remake of Ford's THREE GODFATHERS, with Jack Palance, Jack Warden and Jose Perez as the eponymous heroes.

Those seeking clues to Badham's character and a clearer indication of whether he will become a distinctive directorial personality will plainly find it instructive to sift through what appears to be an impressively coherent body of work while awaiting the further biggies. They will undoubtedly follow.

Richard A. Colla (1938-)

1966: **The Legend of Jesse James**/*Wee Benjamin Bates* (+ co-wr); **Gunsmoke**/*The Moonstone*. 1968: **The Virginian**/*The Storm Gate;* **Ironside**/*Due Process of Law, Desperate Encounter, Price Tag: Death.* 1969: **McCloud** (pilot) *Who Killed Miss USA?, The Whole World is Watching.* 1970: **The Other Man.** 1971: **Ironside**/*The Priest Killer;* **Sarge**/*The Badge or the Cross* (+ exec pr). 1972: **Tenafly** (pilot). 1973: **The Questor Tapes; The Tribe.** 1974: **Live Again, Die Again.** 1975: **The UFO Incident.**

Colla seems as much a child of cinema as Steven Spielberg, and their careers have similar parallels, Spielberg making feature length 8mm home movies, Colla directing short films and eventually winning awards at the Venice Film Festival in 1964 and Monte Carlo in 1965. He produced children's records, edited and directed documentaries and commercials, even acted in **The Days of our Lives** daytime TV series before getting into the medium as a director. He co-wrote and directed *Wee Benjamin Bates*, a truly unusual segment of Don Siegel's production **Legend of Jesse James**, and *the Moonstone* for **Gunsmoke**, before landing himself a Universal contract a year before Spielberg.

Whatever the niceties of his initial series segments, the **McCloud** pilot certainly emphasised the promise of *Wee Benjamin Bates*, if only on a stylistic level. For here, he may have invented the long-lens, long-take style singlehanded. This technique can irritate some people as much as Sidney Furie's singleminded pursuit of a Griffithian purity of image, but is really only a modern equivalent of the dream of the total fusion of eye and mind taken to excess by Hitchcock's ROPE.

Colla was all set for the bigtime with SOMETIMES A GREAT NOTION, but an unspecified fight with star Paul Newman resulted in Colla being fired and the star picking up the fallen megaphone. But FUZZ followed and one suspects that it is only a matter of time before Colla's talent is more widely recognised.

As things stand, **The Other Man** has been criticised for 'over indulgence', **Sarge** for its 'melodrama'. **Tenafly**, however, attempts to bring a sense of the real rhythms of life to a suspense framework. **The Tribe** is a rare foray into Stone Age drama and the highly regarded **U.F.O. Incident** (where James Earl Jones has a close encounter three years before Spielberg) suggest that Colla is attempting to remake the form of things, find new narrative styles suitable to the more curious and open '70s audience.

Richard Donner

1961: **Have Gun-Will Travel**/*Odds for Big Red, The Piano, Drop of Blood, Blind Circle.* 1962: **Route 66**/*A Bridge across Five Days;* **Have Gun-Will Travel**/*Cream of the Jest.* 1963: **The Twilight Zone**/*Nightmare at 20,000 Feet, From Agnes-with Love;* **Sam Benedict**/*Not Even the Gulls Shall Weep, The Boiling Point, Accomplice, Some Fires Die Slowly.* 1964: **The Twilight Zone**/*The Jeopardy Room, The Brain Centre at Whipple's, Come Wander with Me;* **Perry Mason**/*The Case of the Missing Button, The Case of the Tragic Trophy, The Case of the Gambling Lady;* **The Man from UNCLE**/*The Iowa Scuba Affair, The Terbuf Affair, The Quadripartite Affair.* 1965: **Get Smart**/*Our Man in Leotards.* 1966: **The Fugitive**/*Wife Killer, In a Plain Paper Wrapper;* **The FBI**/*The Spy Master;* **Bob Hope Chrysler Theatre/Enigma**: *The Eighth Day;* **Gilligan's Island**/*President Gilligan, Home Sweet Hut;* **It's About Time** sr. 1967: **Felony Squad**/*The Death of a Dream, A Penny Game a Two Bit Murder, A Date with Terror.* 1968: **Jericho**/*Upbeat and Underground.* 1972: **World Premiere/ Hernandez: Houston P.D.**/*The Night Crawler;* **Ghost Story**/*The Concrete Captain;* **Cannon**/*Death Is a Double Cross, Flight Plan, Memo from a Dead Man.* 1973: **Cannon**/*He Who Digs a Grave;* **Kojak**/*One for the Morgue.* 1974: **The Streets of San Francisco**/*A String of Puppets;* **Kojak**/*Best War in Town, Wall Street Gunslinger;* **Petrocelli**/*Death in High Places;* **World Premiere/ Lucas Tanner, Sara T., Portrait of a Teenage Alcoholic, Sons and Daughters**/*The Runner, Lucille's Problem;* **Senior Year**. 1975: **Bronk** (pilot), premiere segment; **Shadow in the Street.**

Donner must be privately blessing his luck. After nearly two decades in TV, and with such critical and financial movie failures as TWINKY and SALT AND PEPPER as blots on his shield, THE OMEN dumbfounded everyone in becoming a box-office champ and Donner landed the coveted SUPERMAN chore. While, arguably, special-effects excellence is the bedrock in both cases, Donner's long apprenticeship in series TV makes him able to punch over the narrative with force and vigor.

If he truly has a voice, a style, a point of view, the cans need to be unearthed from network vaults and syndication company warehouses. There is a certain amount of fantasy—**Twilight Zone** (including the classic *Nightmare at 20,000 Feet* by Richard Matheson, where William Shatner sees a 'Demon' on the wing of his plane. . .), *The Concrete Captain* written by the dean of the 'Who's driving Me Mad?' school of shockers, Jimmy Sangster. Mainly, through, Donner has been prowling the mean streets, with **Sam Benedict** in the 60s, **Kojak** and **Bronk** in the 70s and latterly looking in on melodramatically-damaged lives—often young ones (**Sara T.**, teenage alcoholic; the mid-50s high-school kids, in **Senior Year**, and the various **Sons and Daughters**), revealing a healthy and welcome penchant for all-location shooting (*The Night Crawler* in Houston, **Lucas Tanner** in Missouri).

While it is unlikely that any but fantasy buffs are going to rush to the vaults for Donner material it is just possible that Donner—less 'artist' than 'artisan'—has left behind a consistently interesting body of work.

Blake Edwards

1958: **Peter Gunn** (series cr + dir: multiples). 1959: **Richard Diamond** (series cr). 1960: **Mr Lucky** (series cr) 1961: **Dante's Inferno** (series cr). 1962: **Dick Powell Theatre**/*The Boston Terrier* (wr/dir).

Edwards was born in Tulsa, Oklahoma but educated at Beverly Hills High School. Whether it is legitimate to draw any conclusions from these basic facts, the feeling constantly generated in Edwards's work is that of the social outcast aspiring to a position he had not been born to expect; his TV work exists on the level of snob fantasy. **Peter Gunn** (Craig Stevens), finger popping private eye, keeps his cool while chaos erupts around him. He is a Brooks Brothers hero, rich enough not to care who is paying him, and well enough connected to take no stick from the law. Edwards's humour was never far away, irrespective of who actually activated its individual segments (*Come Fill the Cup*, for example, anticipates DAYS OF WINE AND ROSES). The show gained an extra level of sleekness because of it and because of Henry Mancini's jazz score. It became a unique property, one of, if not *the*, first TV ikon to challenge received ideas of what TV could or should do.

Richard Diamond (David Janssen) was, more or less, a second cousin to **Peter Gunn**. The gimmick of a sexy switchboard operator whose legs are all we ever see of her may have been derived from the radio origins of the series. **Mr Lucky** and **Dante's Inferno** sank without trace, compared to the success of

Gunn and **Diamond**, but make up a homogeneous quartet. *The Boston Terrier*, with Robert Vaughan as a rich Boston dilettante whose hobby is criminology ('60's Philo Vance) might have made up a quintet had the segment become a series. Certainly it was more of the same—cheeky humour with a touch of the bizarre, and offered a relatively cold view of the world which is Edwards's dramatic complement to his concept of comedy.

James Frawley

1966: **The Monkees**/*Royal Flush, Monkee See Monkee Die, Your Friendly Neighborhood Kidnappers, Success Story, Monkees in a Ghost Town, Monkees á la Carte, One Man Shy, Dance Monkee Dance, Too Many Girls, Son of Gypsy, Monkees in the Ring, Captain Crocodile, Monkees Chow Mein.* 1967: **The Monkees**/*Monkee Mother, Monkees on the Line, A Nice Place to Visit, The Picture Frame, Double Barrelled Shotgun Wedding, Monkees Marooned, The Card Carrying Red Shoes, Hitting the High Seas, Monkees in Texas, Fairy Tale, The Monstrous Monkee Mash, The Devil and Peter Tork, Monkees Race Again, Some Like It Lukewarm.* 1974: **Paper Moon**/*The Imposter, Who Is MP Sellers?, Visions of Las Vegas, Day Off* (co-dir). 1977: **Columbo**/*Try and Catch Me, Make Me A Perfect Murder.*

The Monkees, a series which seemed at the time to be rather desperately trying to capitalise on the success of The Beatles gave 'purists' a nasty taste because the group itself was as cunningly manufactured as the show itself. Of the four members of the group, only Michael Nesmith had an independent life as a singer, and seems to have spent the last decade endeavouring to convince a post-Monkees world that he is a fine exponent of modern country-rock.

But the series—whose pilot was co-written by Paul Mazursky—proved to be a most unlikely jumping-off point for at least three significant careers—Bob (then Robert), Rafelson, Bert (then Berton) Schneider and James Frawley, who won the 1967 Emmy for comedy directing on the show. Since then, he has had an uneasy time, in establishing precisely what kind of talent he has, and indeed finding contexts in which to use it.

CHRISTIAN LIQUORICE STORE is an expensive post-Monkees home movie (featuring such people as Monte Hellman and family among the cast), but KID BLUE with its wholly engaging, anti-heroic yet positively upbeat and quirky view of the turn-of-the-century West is one of the few successful recent westerns owing nothing to Peckinpah and everything to the unique vision of its creators. THE BIG BUS, while not as satisfying as one would have hoped, managed to be a unique enough comedy without doffing any caps to Mel Brooks.

The commerical success of THE BIG BUS probably means that Frawley will henceforth use TV, if at all, only as a way to pay the rent. **Paper Moon** was little more than a life-line at a bleak time in his career, but the **Columbo** segments are surely a different matter and are of more than passing interest.

Overall therefore, Frawley's is a comic vision, and one with an underlying love and affection for his characters which is a welcome throwback to older comedy styles in this age of almost perverted cynicism. It is one of the most refreshing and committed 'visions' that we have at the moment, and should therefore be sought out with anticipation, whether it surfaces in the future on large or small screen.

William Friedkin (1939-)

1964: **The Alfred Hitchcock Hour**/*Thou Still Unravished Bride.*

Our research has, of necessity, been restricted but, this solitary segment came as a surprise to us, believing as we did that Friedkin's TV career was composed entirely of documentaries. There may be other early 60s fiction work from Friedkin awaiting discovery, which may prove to be extremely interesting, for Friedkin's set-piece style seems a unique and lonely one. If it was being honed on series such as **Alfred Hitchcock Hour** they would be fascinating to see, especially in the light of such monsters as THE EXORCIST.

Sidney J. Furie (1933-)

1959: **Hudson Bay** (multiples).

Furie made it into the money with LADY SINGS THE BLUES, although he was on the *bête noire* rankings of most critics with his willful style on IPCRESS FILE and THE APALOOSA. The critics have a point, but Furie is a resolute original and it is hard not to have a soft spot for his attempts to redefine the visual horizons of the modern screen. Whether such early Canadian work as **Hudson Bay** (and perhaps, other local TV drama which we have not been able to positively identify) reveals an emergent visual consciousness, or merely a young director still learning somebody else's craft, is still uncertain. His ventures in popular TV—notably as the creator of **Petrocelli**—make his interests in this sphere clearer.

James Goldstone (1931-)

1958: **Court of Last Resort** (dir multiples + story editor); **Highway Patrol** (dir multiples); **Harbor Command** (dir multiples). 1959: **Tombstone Territory** (dir multiples); **Sea Hunt** (dir multiples). 1960: **Route 66** (dir multiples). 1961: **Dr. Kildare** (dir multiples). 1962: **It's a Man's World** (dir multiples); **The Eleventh Hour** (dir multiples); **Dennis The Menace**/*The Fifty-Thousandth Customer.* 1963: **The Lieutenant** (dir multiples); **The Outer Limits**/*The Sixth Finger.* 1964: **The**

Fugitive/*Cry Uncle, Tiger Left Tiger Right, Devil's Carnival;* **The Outer Limits**/*The Inheritors* (2 pts); **Voyage to the Bottom of the Sea**/*The Price of Doom, Mutiny, Doomsday;* **The Man from UNCLE**/*The Brain Killer Affair;* **Rawhide**/*The Retreat.* 1965: **Amos Burke–Secret Agent**/*Nightmare in the Sun;* **Voyage to the Bottom of the Sea**/*The Human Computer, The Exile;* **Perry Mason**/*The Case of the Duplicate Case.* 1966: **Star Trek**/*Where No Man Has Gone Before* (pilot), *What Are Little Girls Made Of?;* **Iron Horse**/*Scalplock* (pilot), *The Rails Run West;* **Bob Hope Chrysler Theatre/Enigma:** *Code Name: Heraclitus* (2 pts). 1967: **World Premiere/Ironside** (pilot); **Ironside**/*The Beginning of a Difference.* 1969: **The Bold Ones: The Senator; Premiere/Shadow Over Elveron**/*A Clear and Present Danger.* 1974: **Cry Panic; Dr Max; Things in Their Season.** 1975: **Eric; Journey from Darkness.**

Goldstone is a classic example of 'How to succeed in movies by trying extremely hard'. Beginning as a film editor, he joined TV as a story editor on **Court of Last Resort**, and began directing on that show—twenty years ago. He moved on to ZIV-TV, directing archetypal series like **Sea Hunt, Highway Patrol** and **Tombstone Territory**—which memory suggests had a gritty realism and a desire to tell things like they are/were (but a fondness for these series may simply be base nostalgia). Goldstone yelled 'action' on thirty-six segments in eighteen months, and then began to freelance.

After upmarket series like **Route 66, The Lieutenant** and **The Fugitive** one would have thought he would have gone the way of a Pollack or Rydell, but instead the mid-60s found him in what, at first sight, appears to be a private silly-season, on **Man from UNCLE, Voyage to the Bottom of the Sea** etc. He may have a preference for this kind of fantasy, but in all likelihood these assignments are a result of a strange numbing terror which often strikes technicians and actors—the fear of being out of work and the concomitant acceptance of any and every job.

This of course does not happen to 'artists'—who are used to being unemployed—and it may explain the confusion which critics feel about Goldstone's later, and therefore more accessible work. For he resolutely plugged away, becoming part of Universal TV and finally broke through into what the overground consider to be bigger and better things—pilots and movies of the week—before finally moving into Universal features (A MAN CALLED GANNON, his first and a remake of MAN WITHOUT A STAR which began life as a TV movie).

So, is Goldstone a technician along the lines of a Robert Wise, who may get bemused by a SWASHBUCKLER but respond to the challenges of a classical thriller like ROLLERCOASTER? Or do films such as RED SKY AT MORNING and THE GANG THAT COULDN'T SHOOT STRAIGHT (which have a goodly collection of admirers) more accurately define an artist in search of a subject?

His two **Star Treks** offer a possible clue. *Where No Man Has Gone Before* is a key segment, being the series's *second* pilot (the first having failed to 'sell') and the touchstone by which network chiefs decided to give the series the green light. Goldstone had already worked with creator/producer Gene

Roddenberry on the latter's **Lieutenant**; from a script by Samuel Peeples (an avid movie-buff and a regular contributor to such infuriatingly indispensable magazines as *Films in Review*). Goldstone fleshed out the characters and delineated the world of the starship 'Enterprise' and its modus operandi. His basic seriousness of purpose and intelligence thus gave the embryonic **Star Trek** a vital quality which was to make visible Roddenberry's ultimate ambitions for the series, while the narrative (involving a 2001-like transformation of an officer into an awesome celestial 'divinity') ideally demonstrated the intellectual and physical pretensions of the series.

Goldstone would seem to have been a most important creative cog in this process—and in later years he was to perform the same 'trick' with other series pilots (**Iron Horse**—which he co-created—**Ironside, The Senator**). But his second **Star Trek** is another matter altogether. *What Are Little Girls Made Of?* seems both badly untypical of the series and almost banal in its presentation of a female android story.

Plainly therefore, given good material and tractable actors, Goldstone can be inspired. Although he remains something of an enigma, his TV years offer a good example of how to grapple with formats and formulas and still achieve consistently high standards. A closer search for an answer to the enigma (in **Outer Limits, Lieutenant, Fugitive** and the later pilots and tele-features) is a fascinating one for teleastes.

Tom Gries (1922-1977)

1959: **Richard Diamond**/*The Pay Off.* 1960: **The Westerner**/*Line Camp.* 1961: **The Detectives**/*See No Evil.* 1962: **Route 66**/*Give the Old Cat a Tender Mouse.* 1963: **East Side, West Side**/*Who Do You Kill?;* **Checkmate**/*An Assassin Arrives, Andante;* **Route 66**/*Only by Cunning Glimpses.* 1964: **The Defenders**/*Survival;* **Bob Hope Chrysler Theatre**/*The War and Eric Kurtz;* **Kraft Suspense Theatre**/*Kill No More;* **The Reporter**/*Rachel's Mother, A Time to Be Silent* (pr), *Extension Seven* (+ co-wr & pr). 1965: **For the People**/*Between Candor and Shame;* **I Spy**/*The Trouble with Temple;* **Trials of O'Brien**/*Charlie's Got All the Luck;* **A Man Called Shenandoah**/*Run and Hide, An Unfamiliar Tune.* 1966: **Rat Patrol** (series' cr); **Kraft Suspense Theatre: Crisis**/*The Safe House;* **Batman**/*A Riddle a Day Keeps the Riddler Away—When the Rat's Away the Mice Will Play, Fine Finny Fiends—Batman Makes the Scene;* **The Monroes**/*Night of the Wolf, The Hunter.* 1967: **Mission Impossible**/*Wheels.* 1971: **Earth II.** 1972: **The Glass House; Journey Through Rosebud.** 1973: **The Connection; Call to Danger; Lady Ice.** 1974: **The Healers; The Migrants; QB VII.** 1975: **Helter Skelter.**

Gries first came to critical prominence with WILL PENNY, his first dramatic feature in 1968. A deglamorised western in the modern, Peckinpah-prompted tradition, it is perhaps significant that the film actually began life as *Line Camp,* a segment in Peckinpah's **Westerner** series. But Gries was never to garner the critical vote as comprehensively again (although he came close with NUMBER ONE, again with Charlton Heston, the story of an ageing pro-footballer). His later big screen projects have all disappointed critics although THE GREATEST, his last film got grudgingly qualified praise—perhaps because Gries was dead by the time it was released.

It is too early to say whether Gries's total oeuvre is indeed a shapeless mass of contradictions (which is the current view on the subject)—or whether he has yet to find a chronicler sympathetic enough to his frenzied world to make it comprehensible. TV is obviously an important element of his work, for he drifted from small to big screen and back again continually; his feature films—the known quantities so to speak—effectively represent less than a quarter of his career. The two media are, in Gries's work, one. And while **Richard Diamond** or **Mission Impossible** may not exactly reveal burning genius, the best of his series segments and the tele-features he made from 1972 must be taken into full account when attempting to put him in perspective.

If we take WILL PENNY as some sort of signpost to Gries's preferences and intentions, then we should look for a realist, semi-documentary style with which he is attempting to communicate the physical and emotional 'truth'. His initial series work is awash with the social-realist values of the early 60s—**The Defenders, For the People, The Reporter** (a series which he produced) and he won the Emmy for directing *Who Do You Kill?*, a segment of the George C. Scott social worker series.

Of the three 1973 thrillers, **The Connection**—with the admirable Charles Durning and Zohra Lampert—wonderfully captures the down-to-the-wire despair of the debt-ridden loser, while **Journey Through Rosebud** is a downbeat view of contemporary American Indian problems, filmed in South Dakota. **QB VII** is a six hours of TV roaming through four countries and layers of flashbacks knitted together by Anthony Hopkins's central performance. (The two part show won a number of Emmys—including the music award for Jerry Goldsmith—but Gries was pipped by George Cukor for **Love among the Ruins**). If **QB VII** is a TV landmark, certainly in scale and ambition. Truman Capote's **The Glass House** may be Gries's most extraordinary small screen film, being both rousing Big House slammerdrammer and a savage attack on the penal system, making excellent use of BLACKBOARD JUNGLE's Vic Morrow, THE KILLERS's Clu Gulager and MASH's Alan Alda.

Helter Skelter—the harrowing account of the Manson murders—still reverberates, but the cutdown theatrical release version is no real guide to the initial TV impact, or indeed the creative impulses that inspired it. It was castigated for its repellant and irresponsible gratuiousness—and Gries has indeed often been accused of meretriciousness. Did he simply not know when he was going too far—or is there an almost Hitchcockian manipulation of the audience at work, a refusal simply to be 'intelligent', an attempt to make those physical and emotional 'truths' more than merely explicable—to make them live, however ambiguously and dangerously?

THE GREATEST, Gries's last feature, looks like a stab at the ultimate in 'realism'—using the real Muhammed Ali in a dramatisation of his extraordinary life, interwoven with actuality fight footage. Even though the attempt doesn't work, it is, somehow, a fitting last film to an uneven, but always bold and challenging career.

Gordon Hessler

1960/1962: **Alfred Hitchcock Presents, Alfred Hitchcock Hour** (story editor). 1961: **Alfred Hitchcock Presents**/*Final Arrangements* (dir). 1963: **Alfred Hitchcock Hour** (as assoc pr only) *Goodbye George, Beyond the Sea of Death, Kill or Cure, Terror at Northfield, A Nice Touch, The Magic Shop, You'll be the Death of Me, Murder Case, The Dividing Wall, The Ordeal of Mrs Snow, Behind the Locked Door, Starring the Defense, Three Wives Too Many, How to Get Rid of Your Wife, An Out for Oscar, Dear Uncle George, Run for Doom, The Lonely Hours.* 1964: **Alfred Hitchcock Hour** (as assoc pr only) *Final Escape, Anyone for Murder?, The Evil of Adelaide Winters, Night Caller, The Gentleman Caller.* As pr: *Final Performance, See the Monkey Dance, Misadventure, Ten Minutes from Now, The Second Verdict.* 1965: **Alfred Hitchcock Hour**/as pr only: *Wally the Beard, The Trap, The World's Oldest Motive, The Photographer and the Undertaker, Off Season.* 1966: **Run for Your Life** (as pr only) *Strangers at the Door, The Savage Machines* (+ dir) *multiples;* **Convoy** (series pr); **Bob Hope Chrysler Theatre: Enigma**/*Blind Man's Buff* (pr/dir). 1973: **Scream, Pretty Peggy.** 1974: **Skyway to Death; Hitchhike!; Betrayal; Blue Knight**/*Cop Killer, Madman on a Chain;* **Lucas Tanner**/*A Matter of Love, Instant Replay;* **Cry in the Wilderness; Kolchak; The Night Stalker**/*The Spanish Moss Murders;* **Kung Fu**/*multiples.* 1975: **Amy Prentiss**/*Profile in Evil;* **Kung Fu**/*Ambush;* **Switch**/*The Old Diamond Game;* **Sara**/*The Sod House Woman, The Man from Leadville.* 1976: **Hawaii Five-O**/*Man on Fire, To Kill a Mind;* **Spencers' Pilots**/*The Explosives.*

A producer phoned then-Columbia executive David Niven jr. after SINBAD'S GOLDEN VOYAGE to check on the director. The Executive verdict was—'You can't do better than Hessler.' This book would steadfastly echo that opinion, yet would be totally biased for, wearing a screenwriter's hat, author Wicking has worked with Hessler on many projects. Hessler has rarely had a suitable framework in which to release his talent; budgets, schedules and the reality of less-than-luxurious production circumstances have limited and circumscribed his ambitions.

Hessler's background was in documentaries, then from 1960 to 1965 he was key cog in the **Alfred Hitchcock** TV wheel—moving from story editor to associate producer and producer. (Curiously, the one directorial credit we have traced from this stint comes from the early period of 1961.) He went on to other Universal series with the demise of the **Hitchcock** show, then left for European feature film-making. Although many ambitious projects were discussed and planned, the five years with murder, mayhem and malevolence proved to be a double-edged sword—for substantially all that resulted from the European sojourn, were the American International/Edgar Allen Poe/Vincent Price projects, EMBASSY, SINBAD and MEDUSA. Critical attention had been alerted, but the films did little to boost his career. And with genre cinema contracting and TV escalating proportionately, Hessler was lured back to the Coast and part two of a small screen career.

Scream Pretty Peggy (Bette Davis in a self-derivative Jimmy Sangster thriller), **Skyway to Death** (mini-disaster on an aerial tramway), **Hitchhike!** (murderer hitches ride from Cloris Leachman), **Cry of the Wilderness** (George Kennedy in lonely panic believing he has contracted rabies), **The Spanish Moss Murders** (Kolchak the Night Stalker vs a swamp creature in another Sangster script), all capitalise on the dark worlds of inner fear and outer menace for which Hessler had been typecast, and are all enriched by the documentary-realist strain (the 'restless, probing cameras') which has always been a way of seeing. The segments of **Blue Knight, Amy Prentiss, Lucas Tanner** and **Sara** have never surfaced in England.

Ambush is a poor **Kung Fu**, made in the series's dying days (and from a script by Norman Katkov, executive story consultant which, presumably, prohibited any monkeying). It is interesting only because of the opportunity to see Rhonda Fleming and for the curiosity value of guest-star John Carradine, teaming with son David. *To Kill a Mind* has directorial niceties and a guest spot from heavily-disguised Mel Ferrer (Hessler's producer on EMBASSY), but a silly plot. *The Explosives* is the best of the Hessler series-segments, with suspense again to the fore (WAGES OF FEAR—type jeopardy) and some exhilarating flying sequences which remind us that Hessler is himself a pilot.

Personal feelings cannot be pushed aside totally, but 'you can't do better than Hessler', is not entirely subjective. He deserves, and is supremely capable of handling much better material than he has been offered. Hopefully, it is only a matter of time.

Arthur Hiller (1923-   )

1956: **Matinee Theatre** (dir multiples); **Climax** (dir multiples). 1957: **Perry Mason**/*The Case of the Desperate Daughter;* **Playhouse 90** (dir multiples). 1958: **Alfred Hitchcock Presents**/*Flight to the East, Disappearing Trick, The Festive Season, Post Mortem, The Jokester, And the Desert Shall Blossom;* **Perry Mason**/*The Case of the Fancy Figures;* **The Rifleman**/*The Apprentice Sheriff;* **Wagon Train**/*The Jasper Cato Story.* 1959: **Alfred Hitchcock Presents**/*Not the Running Type;* **Perry Mason**/*The Case of the Bartered Bikini;* **Gunsmoke** (dir multiples). 1960: **Thriller**/*The Twisted Image, Child's Play;* **Alfred Hitchcock Presents**/*Woman's Help, The Baby Blue Expression, One Grave Too Many, Make My Deathbed, The Doubtful Doctor;* **Perry Mason**/*The Case of the Ominous Outcast.* 1961: **Route 66**/*The Strengthening Angels, Blue Murder, Trap at Cordova, Fly Away Home* (2 pts), *The Clover Throne, Welcome to Amity, The Newborn;* **Naked City**/*Murder Is a Face I Know, Ooftus Gooftus, Which Is Joseph Creeley?, A Wednesday Night Story;* **Detectives**/*Back Seat Driver.* 1962: **Naked City**/*The Fingers of Henri Tourelle;* **Dick Powell Theatre** (dir multiples);

Route 66/*A Month of Sundays, Blues for the Left Foot, Once to Every Man, Go Read the River;* **I'm Dickens . . . He's Fenster**/*Nurse Dickens;* **Empire**/*The Day the Empire Stood Still.* 1963: **Ben Casey** (dir multiples). 1964: **The Addams Family**/*The Addams Family Goes to School.*

Another expatriate Canadian seeking fame and fortune over the border, Hiller certainly found them with LOVE STORY (which, reportedly, has been so successful that the director need never work for money alone again . . .) But critical approval has been harder to come by and when it has—THE OUT OF TOWNERS and THE HOSPITAL—the writers (Neil Simon and Paddy Chayefsky) have taken the main credit, a rare event in a director oriented world.

Hiller's teleography also includes unidentified anthology drama in the **Matinee Theatre, Playhouse 90** and **Climax** series, but there is an interesting dichotomy between the work above and that for the big screen. With the exception of TOBRUK and THE HOSPITAL, Hiller's films are 'soft'—love stories, comedies, whimsies where the TV work is 'hard'—crime and punishment in various guises. Which then are the 'assignments', which the 'personal works'? Hiller's earliest films smack of being attempts to crack the market, to keep on working until the break comes and LOVE STORY was, commercially, obviously worth waiting for. OUT OF TOWNERS, his first really interesting picture, almost loses the comedy element entirely as painful desperation takes over, while THE HOSPITAL with its grotesque black humour indicates that when Hiller can fuse the two strands of his respective careers, sparks start to fly.

Those early **Hitchcocks**, **Thrillers** and **Naked Citys** could prove to be quite important in terms of 'the real' Arthur Hiller. Those who say there isn't one need to consider them before writing him off.

Peter Hyams (1943-)

1972: **The Rolling Man; Goodnight My Love.**

Starting in TV on the CBS news staff in New York, Hyams became an anchor man and made a documentary in Vietnam in 1966. Such a background is a technological equivalent of Sam Fuller's beginnings as a tabloid journalist; Hyams similarly became a screenwriter, leaving CBS in 1970. By 1972 he was directing, and both his TV films date from that year.

Rolling Man seems reminiscent of Jean Renoir's THE SOUTHERNER, a small-town tale of the vicissitudes in the life of Dennis Weaver, while **Goodnight My Love** teams Richard Boone and Mickey Dunn as an unlikely team of private eyes who become involved in a MALTESE FALCON parody (an homage Hyams tricked up in his later feature, PEEPER).

It would seem that Hyams can be inspired by both the world around him and by the inner world of the imagination and while both films are flawed, it is distressing that they have also been ignored.

Even though Hyams is doing more than OK right now (CAPRICORN ONE, HANOVER STREET) he is receiving no attention from the critics. They will probably feel no embarrassment when they rise to his work.

Jerry Jameson

1972: **Search**/*Goddess of Destruction.* 1973: **Ironside**/*The Helping Hand, Friend or Foe.* 1974: **McCloud**/*The 42nd Street Cavalry;* **Six Million Dollar Man**/*Pilot Error, Doomsday and Counting, Run Steve Run;* **The Elevator; Heatwave; Terror on the 40th Floor.** 1975: **The Secret Night Caller; The Deadly Tower; Hawaii Five-O**/*The Defector;* **The Lives of Jenny Dolan.** 1976: **World Premiere/ The Invasion of Johnson County.**

Whether AIRPORT 76 can really be called 'making it', it is unlikely that Jameson will fail to capitalise on its success. It would appear to be a logical extension of his TV work, where he was already unofficial King of the Crisis Movie—from the small beginnings of **The Elevator** (people trapped along with an escaping thief—shades of Louis Malle) through **Heatwave**, rising to full-scale inferno with **Terror on the 40th Floor** and the coda of **The Deadly Tower** (a TARGETS sniper). Series segment titles hint at an obsession with the holocaust (*Goddess of Destruction, Doomsday and Counting*) while **The Secret Night Caller** dealt with the personal and social crisis of Robert Reed and his 'need' to make obscene phone calls.

Elsewhere there are the inevitable series segments, a low-budget feature, THE BAT PEOPLE, and what may be one of the best recent Roy Huggins projects, **The Invasion of Johnson County**. Whilst, with few exceptions, Jameson's is an unoriginal career, the flair and intensity with which it has been carried out make it one to consider and, in time, soberly appraise.

Lamont Johnson

1958: **Peter Gunn**/*multiples;* **Have Gun-Will Travel**/*The Teacher, Gun Shy, The Five Books of Owen Deaver, The Silver Queen, Silver Convoy, Deliver the Body, A Sense of Justice, Young Gun, The Lady.* 1959: **Five Fingers**/*The Assassin, Moment of Truth.* 1960: **Naked City**/*The Human Trap, Killer with a Kiss;* **Five Fingers/Thin Ice.** 1961: **Twilight Zone**/*The Shelter, Five Characters in Search of an Exit, Nothing in the Dark, One More Pallbearer;* **Rifleman**/*Escort for a Killer.* 1962: **Twilight Zone**/*Kick the Can, Four O'Clock, Hocus Pocus and Frisby;* **Sam Benedict**/*Split Week at San Quentin, Nothing Equals Nothing.* 1963: **Twilight Zone**/*Passage on the Lady Anne;* **The Richard Boone Show**/*Statement of Fact* (pilot), *Don't Call Me Dirty Names, Big Mitch, The Mafia Man;* **The Great Adventure**/*Teeth of the Lion.* 1964: **The Defenders**/*The Sixth Alarm;* **Profiles in Courage** (pilot) *The Oscar W Underwood Story, The Thomas Hart Benton Story;* **Slattery's People**/*Question: What Is Truth?, Question: Whatever Happened to Ezra?, Question: What is Honor What is Truth?.*

1965: **The Trials of O'Brien**/*What Can Go Wrong?;* **Slattery's People**/*Question: How Impregnable Is a Magic Tower?, Question: Where Vanished the Tragic Piper?, Question: Why the Lonely Why the Misbegotten?* 1967: **Cimarron Strip**/*The Roarer.* 1968: **Premiere**/*The Search;* **Call to Danger** (*pilot* unsold); **The Name of the Game**/ *Witness* (aka *The Monster).* 1969: **Deadlock.** 1970: **My Sweet Charlie.** 1972; **Hollywood TV Theatre/Birdbath; That Certain Summer.** 1975: **The Execution of Private Slovik.** 1976: **Fear on Trial.**

Johnson is a former actor (indeed he was thesping as late as 1967 in a **Gunsmoke** segment, *Prodigal,* no doubt as a favour/joke) and with TV as a closeup medium, Johnson's understanding and handling of his actors has taken him a long way. But there is more than just a parade of good performances in his work—there is the concomitant feeling for character, a basic humanism, the quiet affirmation of moral precepts, a feeling for theme, a spirit crusading against injustices large and small, an unusually austere visual style in the frantic world of the zoom lens. There is the sense, too, of a deep interest in America itself (**Profiles in Courage, The Great Adventure, Fear on Trial**) and its institutions (politics: **Slattery's People,** the law: **Defenders, Trials of O'Brien, Deadlock.** The military: **Execution of Private Slovik**).

As many directors have obviously mined similar veins, it would be easy to dismiss such conclusions as coincidence. But there is such an absence of frivolity in the Johnson list (the presence of **Have Gun-Will Travel** and **Cimarron Strip** cause an involuntary moment of shock. Johnson and *westerns?*) that one assumes that here is a career where a rare degree of choice was exercised. **Have Gun-Will Travel** was, after all, a Richard Boone show. Johnson played a key role in **The Richard Boone Show** itself, and his **Cimarron Strip** guest-starred Boone. That makes fourteen separate segments, around nine hours of Johnson/Boone—a somewhat rare continuous-collaboration for TV.

The feeling for people, their emotional lives and their intimate relations to the dramas which involve them, are ultimately what interests Johnson most. The couple in *Teeth of the Lion*—Earl Holliman and Collin Wilcox, battling the elements and, ultimately, locusts (courtesy of Shell's RIVAL WORLD documentary) are made as emotionally real as the apparently melodramatic pair in **My Sweet Charlie**—Al Freeman jr and Patty Duke, he an on-the-run Black lawyer; she a disinherited and pregnant Southern girl—the desolate ranch location of the first equating with the out-of-season resort in the second, the fusing of character and place, each resolution seemingly true and correctly moving.

The Execution of Private Slovik, the harrowingly logical, tragically inevitable story of an almost pathological loser (Martin Sheen) is probably Johnson's most powerful TV achievement, its success a result of the dovetailing of Sheen's performance with Johnson's remorselessly 'undramatic' style, which simply makes the drama more unbearable. **Fear on Trial**—a belated attempt by TV to come to terms with its own guilt about the blacklist—runs it close, and the conclusion (apparent triumph for William Devane, resigned awareness that nothing has really changed, by lawyer George C. Scott) carries its own implacable, emotionally disturbing, charge.

Johnson's break from TV was fine for him, professionally, and in the order of things richly deserved. But his talent is greatly missed on the small screen—and if a revival of his best series segments seems, in retrospect, a visit to the caged animals, at least Johnson makes us understand why they snarl.

Burt Kennedy (1923-   )

1962: **Lawman**/*The Long Gun* (+wr), *Sunday* (+wr), *The Wanted Man* (+wr), Cort; **The Virginian**/*The Woman from White Wing* (+co-wr); **Combat** (multiples wr/pr/dir). 1973: **Shootout in a One Dog Town** (+wr). 1974: **All the Kind Strangers; Sidekicks.** 1976: **How the West Was Won**/*pt1 - 3* (co-dir). 1977: **Best Sellers/The Rhineman Exchange; Big Hawaii (Danger in Paradise)**/ *Yesterdays.* 1978: **Kate Bliss and the Ticker Tape Kid.**

After his scripts for some of the finest late-50s westerns (in particular the marvellous Boetticher's like SEVEN MEN FROM NOW, RIDE LONESOME etc.), Kennedy became a director with THE CANADIANS. Realising he hadn't a clue how to do it, Kennedy took TV assignments to 'learn the trade'.

He moved out again and proved he had indeed learned—with MAIL ORDER BRIDE, THE ROUNDERS and WELCOME TO HARD TIMES. But then something bad happened. The worst a Kennedy character could say about another was 'you've gone gentle. . . .'—and that is what happened to Kennedy. SUPPORT YOUR LOCAL SHERIFF and THE WAR WAGON showed off the best of Kennedy's laconic humour, but where had the irony, the pain, the loneliness of the Boetticher westerns gone?

The slide continues, with the genre western dying out on both large and small screens and Kennedy trying hard to keep them alive, but unable to align his best instincts with any radical shift of direction to make his work rise above genre-parody or, worse, self-parody.

Since 1973, Kennedy has again tied up in the TV corral, with infinitely more success. **Shootout in a One Dog Town**—reuniting him with producer Richard E. Lyons—*seemed* to find Kennedy in an upswing, for here again was the best of his humour and the return of darker feelings. **Sidekicks** could also be a success, a remake of THE SKIN GAME!, with Larry Hagman in the James Garner part and, curiously, Lou Gossett playing his original role, (a pilot, perhaps, for an abortive series), source material ideal for Kennedy.

The currently-shooting **Kate Bliss and the Ticker Tape Kid** may continue to keep Kennedy successfully ducking and weaving, which is all to the good, for he is an original and we need him around—yet he owes it to himself as much as to his admirers to toughen up and stay in shape. We won't take less, so fine are his best achievements. Stay tuned.

Andrew V. McLaglen (1920)

1956: **Gunsmoke**/*Legal Revenge, Poor Pearl, Pucket's New Year, Wrong Man;* **The Lineup** (dir multiples); **Perry Mason**/*The Case of the Deadly Double, The Case of the Empty Tin;* **Have Gun-Will Travel**/*3 Bells to Perdido, The Outlaw, The Great Mojave Chase, Winchester Quarantine, A Matter of Ethics, The Bride, Strange Vendetta, High Wire, Show of Force, The Long Night, The Colonel and the Lady, No Visitors, The Englishman, The Yuma Treasure, Helen of Abajinian;* 1958: **Have Gun-Will Travel**/*Ella West, The Reasonable Man, The High Graders, The Last Laugh, The Bostonian, The Singer, Bitter Wine, The O'Hare Story, Birds of a Feather, Killer's Widow, The Prizefight Story, Three Sons, The Return of Dr Thackeray, 24 Hours at Northfork, The Statue of San Sebastian, In an Evil Time, The Man Who Wouldn't Talk, The Hanging of Roy Carter, Duel at Florence;* **Perry Mason**/*The Case of the Gilded Lily, The Case of the Terrified Typist, The Case of the Shattered Dream.* 1959: **Rawhide**/*Incident of the Shambling Man;* **Have Gun-Will Travel**/*The Protégé, The Road to Wickenberg, The Solid Gold Patrol, Something to Live For, The Moor's Revenge, The Wager, The Taffeta Mayor, Juliet, Hunt the Man Down, The Scorched Feather, Return of the Lady, The Return of Roy Carter.* 1960: **Have Gun-Will Travel**/*Love and a Bad Woman, Never Help the Devil, The Twins, Love's Young Dream, A Head of Hair, The Tender Gun, Fogbound, The Legacy.* 1961: **Gunsmoke**/*Old Dan, Harpe's Blood, Indian Ford, Long Long Trail;* **Gunslinger**/ *Buried People, Appointment in Cascabel, Rampage, The Recruit, Road of the Dead, The Diehards, Johnny Sergeant, The Death of Yellow Singer;* **Have Gun-Will Travel**/*Shadow of a Man, Long Way Home, The Fatal Flaw, The Siege, My Brother's Keeper, Bearbait, The Road, The Uneasy Grave, Soledad Crossing, The Vigil, The Revenger, The Race, Ben Jalisco, The Brothers, A Knight to Remember;* **Rawhide**/*Deserter's Patrol.* 1962: **Gunsmoke**/*The Summons, The Dreamers, The Prisoner, Quint Asper Comes Home, Jenny, Abe Blocker, Us Haggens, Phoebe Strunk, False Front, The Renegades, The Trappers;* **Have Gun-Will Travel**/*Mark of Cain, The Hunt, The Man Who Struck Moonshine, Silent Death–Secret Death, Hobson's Choice, The Coming of the Tiger, The Invasion, Pandora's Box, Jonah and the Trout, The Fifth Bullet, A Place for Abel Hix, Bird of Time, The Predators, Shootout at Hogtooth.* 1963: **Gunsmoke**/*Lover Boy, The Odyssey of Jubal Tanner, Quint-cident, Two of a Kind, The Quest for Asa Janin;* **Have Gun-Will Travel**/*Brotherhood, Penelope, The Treasure, The Burning Tree, Caravan, The Eve of St Elmo;* **The Lieutenant** (dir multiples). 1964: **Gunsmoke**/*Chicken, Crooked Mile, Bank Baby;* **The Virginian**/*Smile of a Dragon.* 1973: **Banacek**/*The $3 Million Piracy, Rocket to Oblivion.* 1974: **Log of the Black Pearl; Hec Ramsey**/*Scar Tissue.* 1976: **The Fantastic Journey**/*Vortex* (pilot); **Banjo Crockett.** 1977: **Murder at the World Series.**

Born, as it were, to the purple (or the green?), as the son of Victor and a virtual godson of both Johns, Ford and Wayne, it was probably inevitable that should McLaglen desire a movie career, it would be achieved. Naturally, had he been a complete idiot, he might have had to settle for being a producer (such being the Ford view of such animals, though the Wayne offspring would no doubt, disagree.), but as it was, he worked his way up through the ranks (ten years an assistant director, including many Wayne-Batjac pictures such as BLOOD ALLEY). He made a very respectable first-feature as a director, GUN THE MAN DOWN with another 'clan' discovery, James Arness—but both had already cut their teeth with **Gunsmoke**. Arness was to spend an extraordinary twenty years with the series, but McLaglen became identified with **Have Gun-Will Travel**—turning segments out with blinding rapidity. This show is something of a legend (its title was soon assimilated into the vernacular), while the other early features purveyed by McLaglen are such forgotten fare as FRECKLES and LITTLE

SHEPHERD OF KINGDOM COME.

Everything changed in 1963 when McLaglen directed MCLINTOCK, and for the next decade he guided—or was led by—Wayne through the more mechanical of the star's September songs. In recent years, McLaglen, like Burt Kennedy, has suffered from the decline of the western—and TV has supplemented the movie career. But lazy segments of **Banacek** (*Rocket to Oblivion*), and a flaccid **Fantastic Journey** pilot indicate that the director is merely going through the paces.

Shenandoah, the most Fordian of his features, is also, perhaps, his most personal—dealing with the breakup of a family during the civil war. Where so many film-makers enter a gold twilight, it would seem that McLaglen instead looks back on a dawn of early promise, and thus the **Have Gun-Will Travel** segments are likely to be his most affecting and exciting TV work. (One of them, incidentally, starred his father, as did his **Rawhide,** *Incident of the Shambling Man.*)

Sam Peckinpah (1925-)

(From 1956 to 1958, Peckinpah wrote the following segments): **Gunsmoke**/*The Queue, Yorky, Cootes, How to Die for Nothing, The Guitar, The Roundup, Legal Revenge, Poor Pearl D, How to Kill a Woman, Dirt;* **Broken Arrow**/*The Teacher;* **Have Gun-Will Travel**/*The Singer* (co-wr Ken Kolb); **Trackdown**/*The Town;* **Blood Brother**/*The Transfer;* **Tombstone Territory**/*The Johnny Ringo Story;* **Man without a Gun**/*The Kidder;* **Zane Grey Theatre**/*The Sharpshooter* (Peckinpah then began to direct). 1958: **Broken Arrow**/*The Knife Fighter;* **Zane Grey Theatre**/*Trouble at Tres Cruces;* **The Rifleman**/*The Marshall* (co-wr), *Home Ranch* (wr only), *The Boarding House* (+ wr), *The; Money Gun* (co-wr), *The Baby Sitter* (+ co-wr). 1959: **Zane Grey Theatre**/*Miss Jenny* (+ co-wr), *Lonesome Road* (+ co-wr). 1960: **Klondike** *(pilot* + co-wr), *Swoger's Mules* (+ co-wr); **The Westerner**/*Jeff* (+ co-wr), *Brown* (+ pr), *The Courting of Libby, Hand on the Gun, The Painting* (+ co-wr), *The Old Man* (+ co-wr), *School Day* (+ co-wr), *Mrs Kennedy* (co-wr only). 1961: **Pony Express**/*The Story of Julesburg* (wr only); **Route 66**/*Mon Petit Chow.* 1962: **Dick Powell Theatre**/*Pericles on 34th Street* (+ co-wr), *The Losers* (+ co-wr). 1966: **ABC Stage 67**/*Noon Wine* (+ wr); **Bob Hope Theatre**/*That Lady Is My Wife.*

Q: 'Who was the most instrumental in helping you become the character you are?'

A: 'My father, my grandfather, my brother, my ex-wife and a 75 year-old Nevada prostitute who told me the story of her first love affair for $3.00 and a four-bit bottle of beer. The story became *Jeff*, the first **Westerner** on the air. A lot of people still talk about it' *

Maybe people talk about it, but precious few can ever *see* it. Certainly, no true understanding of Peckinpah can be achieved until his TV work is assimilated

* Interview with Peckinpah in *Cinema*, 1963.

into the critical spectrum. Arguably, he is the most important of all American directors to have graduated in TV for, while his small screen work is obviously notable for its own creative felicities, Peckinpah, rare for a director, was also the initial *creator* of two of the most significant shows with which he was associated—**The Rifleman** and **The Westerner**, in the latter case having total control of the series, courtesy of producer Dick Powell.

Rifleman is the less interesting of the two series, trapped as it is in the 30-minute format of the late '50s. Much of it takes place in interior street sets, and in the central relationship between father, Lucas McCain (Chuck Connors) and son Mark (Johnny Crawford) mawkish family-hour overtones are never overcome. In fact, the series actually 'spun off' from a segment of Dick Powell's **Zane Grey Theatre** which Peckinpah wrote, *The Sharpshooter.* Peckinpah had then been writing TV westerns for two years, that segment being his seventeenth credit. No doubt he jumped at the chance to expand the concerns of that segment into a series format—but probably lacked the klaut to impose his personality strongly. Also, he was concerned over his primary objective, to become a director—an ambition **The Rifleman** instantly fulfilled.

Nevertheless, in the central series concept one can see strong elements of 'pure' Peckinpah, most notably overtones of autobiography, Peckinpah's love and pride in his ancestry. The McCains (the mother, significantly, is dead) come to settle in North Fork, California—the same spot where Peckinpah's own grandfather had 300 head of cattle which he 'starved to death'. The initial segments detailed the arrival, the problems of settling in, the enmity with other local ranchers and the developing sense of inter-relationship, inter-dependency with other members of the community, made up of a cast of irregulars such as Edgar Buchanan as Doc Burrage. Buchanan, of course, essayed the wondrously corrupt, voluptuously seedy Judge Tolliver in RIDE THE HIGH COUNTRY and other members of the Peckinpah stock company first worked with him on this series. Indeed, Warren Oates and James Drury guest in *The Marshal*, Peckinpah's first directorial credit, while R.G. Armstrong, James (then Jim) Coburn and James Westerfield pop up with regularity. The series was produced by the Gardner/Levy/Laven team, with whom Peckinpah was to be associated in his 'wilderness years' following the personal disaster of MAJOR DUNDEE.

Although beyond the initial inception, his contribution to the series as a whole was a minor one, an embryonic Peckinpah can be seen struggling into shape, and the series provided a launching pad to directing.

The Westerner, curiously, began life exactly as **The Rifleman** did—spinning-off from another **Zane Grey Theatre** segment, *Trouble at Tres Cruces.* But Peckinpah was now a writer/director, **Rifleman** was a hot series, and his position in the industry much more powerful. Developments in TV itself were towards longer series segments, a more overt 'maturity'. **Gunsmoke** and **Wagon Train** were now hour-long shows, as too was **Zane Grey Theatre.**

Trouble at Tres Cruces suggested an ideal series, based on the working-life of the cowboy, a subject dear to Peckinpah's heart. Thus **The Westerner** was created with far more care and control than had been possible with **Rifleman.**

The series central character, Dave Blasingame (Brian Keith) was a composite of people Peckinpah knew personally—'Al Petit, a cowboy; Uncle Wes Qualls, a Madera county cattleman; Brian Keith, me and Bill Dillon. Most of the Blasingame character came from Bill's story about himself as a young man . . . who, when incensed or extremely impressed would say " 'Well kiss my sister's black cat's ass!" ' (one of the memorable lines from THE WILD BUNCH. Plainly censorship requirements in TV would never have permitted the line to be uttered there.) The series itself became both homage to the Old West of legend and an exploration of the reality behind that legend. A flavour of the overall concept can be sensed from Peckinpah's loving affection for the *Jeff* segment, and by Tom Gries's WILL PENNY—which in fact started life as *Line Camp,* a **Westerner** segment. The series was critically successful but not apparently popular with audiences and folded after thirteen segments. (Curiously, but characteristically, it was never shown in England.)

Peckinpah spent two more years in TV before beginning phase one of his feature career. *The Losers,* an impressionistic romp-type affair with fatalistic overtones offered another incarnation of Blasingame in Lee Marvin—older now, in a new era of automobiles and civilisation reminiscent of **Ride the High Country**'s changing world, but Peckinpah's Mack Sennett chases, the country-music track (pre-figuring BONNIE & CLYDE) indicated an unease with the form the material had to take, and with the restrictions of TV itself. Peckinpah was fretting, yearning for a larger canvas. *Pericles on 34th Street* seemed at the time a disappointingly verbose Chekhovian-type tragi-comedy, though it may well appear now as a valuable clue to the Peckinpah enigma.

For Peckinpah remains an enigma. The confusion with which he answers questions about THE WILD BUNCH ('I was shocked by the violence', 'You were *supposed* to be'; 'but I was also stimulated by it', 'you were supposed to be') finds a parallel confusion reigning in THE BALLAD OF CABLE HOGUE. Peckinpah can't yet, harmonise the two contradictory sides of his character. But mostly by virtue of the censorship requirements of '50s and '60s TV and the more intimate requirements of its inherent nature as a medium, it is surely likely that this other Peckinpah, the lyric, the elegaic, was much in evidence in his small screen work. Certainly the *titles* of some of the segments—*The Baby Sitter, The Teacher, The Boarding House, Miss Jenny, Lonesome Road, The Courting of Libby, The Old Man, School Day, Mrs. Kennedy*—suggest that a wholly different Peckinpah to the one we know from the features, but a nonetheless unique and characterful one, was at large on the small screen.

Indeed, *Noon Wine,* made after the disaster of MAJOR DUNDEE when it seemed that Peckinpah's bright flame was in danger of being extinguished by an implacable industry, is perhaps one of his finest achievements. From a Katherine Anne Porter short novel, and with a weird mystical aura surrounding its characters and narrative, Peckinpah fashioned a most beautiful and haunting drama. Made largely on tape, not film, Peckinpah showed that it was possible to use video with as much ease, power and meaning as celluloid: he showed how to build sustained performances (Jason Robards, Olivia de Havailland, Per Oscarsson, plus, for cult value, Ben Johnson and L.Q. Jones) and revealed the gentle side of his personality in a totally together manner. After ten years, *Noon Wine* remains in the mind as a masterpiece of mood, and lyric sadness.

One would like to believe that the bulk of Peckinpah's TV work achieved a similar level of understanding and achievement. Certainly, with a degree of creative control equalled only by Hitchcock—and, probably, a greater desire to excel than Hitchcock felt towards *his* TV projects—Peckinpah had more opportunities than most for personal expression. It seems evident that Peckinpah's total oeuvre is sadly ill-appreciated (if not actually misunderstood). Certainly this rich and vital work is never seen and is rarely discussed.

Sydney Pollack (1934-   )

1962: **Alfred Hitchcock Hour**/*The Black Curtain.* 1963: **Ben Casey**/*For the Ladybug . . . One Dozen Roses, Mrs McBrown and the Cloud Watcher.* 1964: **Slattery's People**/*Question: What Became of the White Tortilla?;* **Kraft Suspense Theatre: Crisis**/*Something About Lee Wiley, The Fliers, Two Is the Number, The Name of the Game;* **Bob Hope Chrysler Theatre: Enigma**/*The Game.*

Pollack began his career as an actor, studying with Sanford Meisner at New York's Neighborhood Playhouse then appeared on Broadway in such plays as *A Stone for Danny Fisher.* He gravitated naturally to TV and can be seen acting in **Alfred Hitchcock Presents** *Contest for Aaron Gold* (1960) and **Have Gun-Will Travel** *Quiet Night in Town* (1961). He began directing during this period, and having appeared in fifteen **Ben Casey** segments, one might expect his first credits to be on it. (Unfortunately, the **Ben Casey** credits have been resolutely closed to us.) In the space of five years, and with an Emmy for his direction of *The Game,* he had moved out of TV into features, and to what has proved to be a most successful career—in no small part due to his relationship with Robert Redford (in which unkind observers claim to see the director in a subservient rôle to his star). Whatever the truth of this, THE SCALPHUNTERS is a marvellous western, CASTLE KEEP has legions of French fans, THREE DAYS OF THE CONDOR is an excellent paranoid thriller.

His TV work would seem to have revolved around the kind of burning emotional intensity exuded by the **Ben Casey** series—many steps beyond the triple-hankie genre, but with overtones embarassing to critics, who don't like to have to fight back tears of pain or anger. Indeed, THE SLENDER THREAD, Pollack's first feature was brimming over with this trait.

However, Pollack remains one of the sturdiest of TV's graduates from the class of the 60s. It follows that he would never have made the transition without an excellent report card.

Ted Post (1925-)

1952: **Schlitz Playhouse of Stars**/*The Playwright, Mr Thayer.* 1953: **Schlitz Playhouse of Stars**/*Parents' Weekend, Jennie, The Devil's Other Name, The Long Shot, Pursuit, Big Jim's Boy;* **Ford Theatre**/*The Doctor's Downfall;* **Studio One**/multiples. 1954: **Schlitz Playhouse of Stars**/*Papa Goes to the Ball;* **Ford Theatre**/multiples; **Studio One**/multiples. 1956: **Gunsmoke**/*The Roundup, Gone Straight, How to Die for Nothing;* **Zane Grey Theatre**/*The Lariat, Quiet Sunday in San Ardo;* **Fireside Theatre**/*The Mirror.* 1957: **Zane Grey Theatre**/*Silent Thunder;* **Loretta Young Show**/*Emergency;* **Perry Mason**/*pilot.* 1958: **Gunsmoke**/*Dirt;* **Rawhide**/*Incident of the Widowed Dove, Incident of the Town in Terror.* 1959: **Wagon Train**/*The Larry Hanify Story, The Tracy Sadler Story, The Countess Baranoff Story;* **Twilight Zone**/*A World of Difference.* [GB]. **ABC Armchair Summer Theatre**/*You'll Never See Me Again* [USA]. **Rawhide**/*Incident of the Curious Street;* **Richard Diamond**/*Lost Testament.* 1960: **Rawhide**/*Incident in Rojo Canyon, Incident at Paco Tiempo, Incident of the Buffalo Soldier, Incident at the Top of the World, Incident Near the Promised Land, Incident of the Fish Out of Water, Incident of His Brother's Keeper, Incident of the Lost Idol, Incident Before Black Pass;* **Wagon Train**/*The Allison Justis Story;* **Checkmate**/*The Mark of Vengeance, Jungle Castle.* 1961: **Gunsmoke**/*Half Straight, The Widow, Old Yellow Boots, Chesterland;* **Rawhide**/*Incident at Rio Salado;* **Wagon Train**/*The Eleanor Calhane Story, Wagon to Fort Anderson;* **Thriller**/*Papa Benjamin;* **Route 66**/*Sleep on Four Pillows.* 1962: **Gunsmoke**/*Shona, Blind Man's Bluff;* **Rawhide**/*Incident of the Portrait;* **Empire**/*Long Past, Long Remembered;* **The Virginian**/*Throw a Long Rope;* **Thriller**/*The Specialists;* **The Defenders**/*Death Takes the Stand;* **Alcoa/Fred Astaire Theatre**/*Guest in the House.* 1963: **Rawhide**/*Incident of the Travellin' Man, Incident of the Rawhiders, Incident of the Geisha, Incident at Ten Trees, Incident of the Rusty Shotgun, Incident of the Dowery Dundee;* **Twilight Zone**/*Probe 7 Over and Out.* 1964: **Suspense**/*Mike Kenny;* **Twilight Zone**/*Mrs Garrity and the Graves, The Fear;* **Detectives**/*Adopted.* 1970: **Night Slaves; Yuma.** 1971: **Dr Cook's Garden; The Bravos; Do Not Fold, Mutilate or Spindle; Five Desperate Women.** 1972: **Sandcastles.** 1975: **Baretta**/*The Fire Man;* **Columbo**/*A Matter of Honor, A Case of Immunity.* 1976: **Rich Man, Poor Man, Book Two**/pts 12, 14; **Ark 11**/*The Robot, The Flies, The Rule, The Tank, The Lottery, The Drought, The Cryogenic Man, Don Quixote.*

Most of Post's earliest, live TV credits remain to be identified (and are outside the scope of this book). He has become identified with the western, even though his work has taken him through virtually every genre from fantasy (**Twilight Zone**) to soap opera (**Peyton Place**). No distinct personality has yet to be discerned in his work—yet evidently Clint Eastwood is some sort of fan, for of all the **Rawhide** directors that the actor took orders from, it was Post who was chosen to direct Eastwood's first non-spaghetti, American western (HANG 'EM HIGH) and the DIRTY HARRY follow-up, MAGNUM FORCE.

So there may be something of more apparent value than any of us yet know in Post's vast and diverse career.

Bob Rafelson

1960/1964: **Play of the Week** (wrote over thirty adaptations); **Du Pont Show of the Week** (wr assoc pr); **The Witness**/*James J Hines* (co-wr). 1964/1965: **The Wackiest Ship in the Army**/*pilot* (co-pr only); **The Greatest Show on Earth** (pr); **Channing** (pr). 1966: **The Monkees** (series co-pr + dir) *Monkee vs Machine, The Spy Who Came In from the Cool, Don't Look a Gift Horse in the Mouth.* 1967: **The Monkees**/*Case of the Missing Monkee, Monkees on Tour* (+ wr), *Monkees in Paris* (+ wr).

With Rafelson having established himself as one of the most unique and fascinating of modern directors with FIVE EASY PIECES, KING OF MARVIN GARDENS and STAY HUNGRY, all one can do is register surprise and rabid curiosity about his unexpectedly extensive TV career—which, his writing credits apart, would appear to be the work of someone else.

Michael Ritchie (1938-)

1965: **Profiles in Courage** (assoc pr); **Big Valley**/*Teacher of Outlaws, Under a Dark Star;* **Dr Kildare**/*From Nigeria with Love* (4 pts). 1966: **Run for Your Life**/*I Am the Late Diana Hays, Hang Down Your Head and Laugh, The Man Who Had No Enemies, A Better World Next Time, Company of Scoundrels;* **World Premiere**/*The Outsider* (aka *The Sound of Anger).* 1967: **Run for Your Life**/*Cry Hard, Cry Fast* (2 pts); **Felony Squad**/*A Walk to Oblivion, Miss Reilly's Revenge;* **Bob Hope Chrysler Theatre: Enigma**/*To Sleep, Perchance to Scream.* 1968: **The Survivors** (pts 1 + 2).

Having first attracted attention by directing the original Harvard production of Arthur Kopit's *Oh Dad, Poor Dad. . .*, Ritchie, like Altman, has developed one of the most distinctive styles of all graduates to the motion picture screen, and it is, therefore, of more than pure academic interest to check back into his 60s TV work and consider these apprentice efforts in the light of DOWNHILL RACER, SMILE, BAD NEWS BEARS et al.

There are pulp shows (**Big Valley, Felony Squad**) rubbing shoulders with more prestigious offerings to which it is reasonable to assume that the director brought a little 'vision'. Certainly the **Run for Your Life** segments remain in the memory for being unusually mature and out-of-the-rut, especially *Hang Down Your Head and Laugh*, co-written by Adrien Joyce (THE SHOOTING, FIVE EASY PIECES) which concerns a weird girl (Kim Darby) discovered in the middle of dust-covered nowhere in outsize cowboy boots and with a battered guitar. Her lightning shifts of behaviour, from the disarmingly sweet to the highly alarming, her enigmatic character, are the backbone to the segment.

Stuart Rosenberg (1928-)

1957: **Decoy**/*Dressed for a Kill.* 1959: **Alfred Hitchcock Presents**/*Road Hog, Dead Weight,* **Richard Diamond**/*The Merry-Go-Round Case;* **The Untouchables**/*The Seventh Vote;* **The Twilight Zone**/*I Shot an Arrow into the Air.* 1960: **Hong Kong**/untitled segment; **The Untouchables**/*Underworld Bank;* **Alfred Hitchcock Presents**/*The Man with Two Faces.* 1961: **The Untouchables**/*The Tommy Karpeles Story, Death for Sale, Tunnel of Horrors* (+ pr), *The Ginnie Littlesmith Story;* **The Defenders**/*The Hickory Indian.* 1962: **Naked City**/*Robin Hood and Clarence Darrow, They Went Out with Bow and Arrow;* **The Untouchables**/*The Chess Game;* **The Defenders**/*The Voices of Death, The Avengers, The Hour Before Doomsday, The Bigamist.* 1963: **The Richard Boone Show**/*The Fling;* **The Twilight Zone**/*Mute He's Alive;* **Espionage**/*The Incurable One, Covenant with Death, The Weakling, The Whistling Shrimp;* **The Defenders**/*The Heathen, The Weeping Baboon, The Empty Heart, Blacklist, The Madman* (2 pts), *The Noose, The Trial of 22;* **The Nurses**/*No Score;* **Bob Hope Chrysler Theatre**/*The Candidate, The Meal Ticket.* 1964: **The Defenders**/*Drink Like a Lady, Die Laughing, May Day! May Day!, The Man Who, Comeback, The Siege;* **Bob Hope Chrysler Theatre**/*The Game with Glass Pieces, Runaway Bay;* **The Reporter**/*Superstar;* **Rawhide**/*The Gray Rock Hotel.* 1965: **For The People**/*. . . The Killing of One Human Being . . ., The Influence of Fear, Dangerous to the Public Peace and Safety, A Competent Witness;* **Bob Hope Chrysler Theatre**/*Memorandum for a Spy* (2 pts); **Enigma**/*Escape into Jeopardy, Back to Back, The Enemy on the Beach, A Small Rebellion;* **Run for Your Life**/*In Search of April;* **Trials of O'Brien**/*A Gaggle of Girls, Over Defense Is Out, Notes on a Spanish Prisoner, The Ten-Foot Six-Inch Pole.* 1966: **Run for Your Life**/*Don't Count on Tomorrow, Strangers at the Door;* **Bob Hope Chrysler Theatre: Enigma**/*The Faceless Man;* **Fame Is the Name of the Game.**

Although Rosenberg flirted with movies in the early 60s, (MURDER INC, QUESTION 7), it was as a TV director that he built up the reputation which finally got him assignments such as COOL HAND LUKE, and arguably he was the most consistently excellent director in a period which more and more people now recognise as a 'golden age'.

Like Lamont Johnson, he distained the 'frivolous' and was fortunate that series such as **The Defenders, Twilight Zone, Naked City** and **For the People** were around at the same time, allowing talents like Rosenberg to get to grips with the emotional nitty-gritty of American life in a wholly unique fashion. It has not yet been truly appreciated how broad was the thematic scope open to the more committed writers and directors working for the small screen. In tandem with such scribes as Rod Serling, Reginald Rose, Howard Rodman, Ernest Kinoy, Larry Cohen, David Karp, Robert Thom, David Rayfiel and S. Lee Pogostin, Rosenberg brought his talent to bear on stories which probed into the emotional background of Nazism, patricide, mercy-killing, the blacklist, Hollywood, East-West relations, along with 'traditional' themes and variations on crime and murder. While, in most cases, these were fitted into series segment formats and on the one hand suffer from an inevitable superficiality, on the other such formats were almost a genre of their own, within which it was possible to play around as successfully as any admired auteur could 'transform from within' westerns or 'film-noirs'.

Rosenberg did just that, with unerring success for at least six years; it is a real tragedy that work like this is not more widely accessible. Rosenberg's work is rarely didactic, gaining its force and emotional involvement from his superb use of actors and his understanding of what to do (and what *not* to do) with the intimate confines of the TV screen.

His features have so far been ambitious but, ultimately, uneven and uneasy. To appreciate just how good Rosenberg is, it is necessary to look back at a remarkable career which, for no good reason (and for too many bad ones), is as hard to get a glimpse of as the inside of Fort Knox.

Mark Rydell (1934-)

1964: **The Reporter**/*Lost Lady Blues;* **I Spy**/*Danny Was a Million Laughs.* 1965: **Wild Wild West**/*Night of the Whirring Death;* **Slattery's People**/*Question: How Do You Catch a Cool Bird of Paradise?;* **I Spy**/*Carry Me Back to Old Tsing Tao;* **Gunsmoke**/*Snap Decision, The Mission, Gunfighter R.I.P., The Hanging;* **The Fugitive**/*A Clean and Quiet Town.*

Afficionados might, ironically, respect Rydell more for his splendidly venal performance in Altman's THE LONG GOODBYE than for his own features. THE FOX was one of Hollywood's first overground grapplings with respectable X rated sexuality, THE REIVERS one of Steve McQueen's periodic attempts to break out of his successful but emotionally crippling mould—but neither took Rydell to unanimous critical favour or financial independence. The later CINDERELLA LIBERTY seems to have come in a very poor second to author Darryl Poinicsan's THE LAST DETAIL, while his career overall has yet to really take off as his friend Sydney Pollack's has (they both studied acting at the Neighbourhood Theatre and formed a company, Sanford Productions, named presumably for Sanford Meisner, the theatre's *eminence grise*).

But there is a feeling that Rydell could, like Michael Ritchie, be more in favour of personal expression than professional advancement, and is willing to play his own rules. Memories of his TV work suggest that he brought both a laconic sense of humour and a feeling for the transience of human affairs to the series on which he worked, and that—even if they allowed for little personal expression (which is debatable)—they should be sought out as among the best of series TV.

Richard Sarafian

1960: **Hawaiian Eye**/*The Last Samurai;* **Maverick**/*The Forbidden City;* **The Roaring 20s**/*Blondes Prefer Gentlemen.* 1961: **Lawman**/*The Persecuted, The Threat, The Break-In, Cold Fear, Trapped,*

The Four, The Stalker, Porphyria's Lover, The Trojan Horse, The Cold One, The Son, Lords of Darkness, Explosion, The Vintage, A Friend of the Family, Tarnished Badge, Change of Venue, The Barber, Clootey Hutter, The Holdout, The Bride, The Actor; **Cheyenne**/*Legacy of the Lost, Guns of the Lawless;* **Surfside 6**/*Count Seven!* 1962: **The Dakotas**/*A Man Called Ragan* (pilot), *The Chooser of the Slain, Sanctuary at Crystal Springs;* **The Gallant Men**/*Retreat to Concord, The 98 Cent Man, One Moderately Peaceful Sunday, And an End of Evil Things, Fury in a Quiet Village, Signals for an End Run, The Bridge, The Warriors, A Taste of Peace;* **Hawaiian Eye**/*Lalama Lady;* **77 Sunset Strip**/*Terror in a Small Town, The Dark Wood, Our Man in Switzerland.* 1963: **Twilight Zone**/*Living Doll;* **The Great Adventure**/*Six Wagons to the Sea.* 1964: **Slattery's People**/*Question: How Long is the Shadow of a Man?, Question: When Do We Hang the Good Samaritan?, Question: Did He Who Made the Lamb Make Thee?, Question: Who You Takin' to the Main Event Eddie?, Question: Bill Bailey Why Did You Come Home?* 1965: **I Spy**/*Trial by Treehouse, Will the Real Goodguys Please Stand Up?, Lisa, Bet Me a Dollar;* **Dr Kildare**/*The Elusive Dik-Dik;* **Trials of O'Brien**/*Alarums and Excursions;* **The Wild Wild West**/*Night of the Inferno, Night of the 1000 Eyes.* 1966: **Big Valley**/*Winner Lose All;* **Batman**/*Joker Trumps an Ace—Batman Sets the Pace;* **The Girl from UNCLE**/*The Romany Lie Affair.* 1967: **Ironhorse**/ *Consignment Betsy the Boiler;* **Cimarron Strip**/*The Battle of Bloody Stones;* **Gunsmoke**/*Vengeance* (2 pts). 1968: **High Chapparal**/*Shadow on the Land;* **Gunsmoke**/*A Noose for Dobie Price;* **Shadow on the Land.** 1975: **One of Our Own.** 1976: **The African Queen.** 1977: **A Killing Affair.**

While there is more pulp than prestige in Sarafian's teleography, he may prove to have taken over from Altman as the joker in the Warner TV pack. Indeed, Altman directed the pilot to **The Gallant Men** series of which Sarafian made more than half, and which is reputedly one of the most impressive series in the TV war genre. When people remember **Lawman** as one of best western series, they might well be recalling Sarafian's segments, from the fourth and last series. Overall, westerns figure prominently in his career, which with the dearth of new material for that genre's afficionados to explore, might be a useful detour in research, bearing in mind the later MAN IN THE WILDERNESS, MAN CALLED HORSE successes. Even though Sarafian's 'known' work—the features—is highly variable, FRAGMENT OF FEAR and VANISHING POINT certainly do enough to make us feel that, in its own way, Sarafian's TV career might be as important and representative of quality and personal expression as that of Johnson or Rosenberg.

Joseph Sargent

1962: **Lassie**/*multiples;* **Bonanza**/*The Cheating Game;* **Gunsmoke**/*Chester's Indian.* 1963: **The Great Adventure**/*The Special Courage of Captain Pratt;* **Gunsmoke**/*Tell Chester;* **Dundee and the Culhane**/*The Cat in the Bag Brief.* 1964: **Man from UNCLE**/*The Alexander the Greater Affair* (2 pts aka *One Spy Too Many), The Cherry Blossom Affair, The King of Diamonds Affair, The Project Strigas Affair;* **Gunsmoke**/*Double Entry.* 1965: **Man from UNCLE**/*The Never Never Affair.* 1966: **Bob Hope Chrysler Theatre: Enigma**/*Time of Flight;* **Star Trek**/*The Corbomite Manoeuver.* 1967: **Garrison's Gorillas**/*The Big Con* (pilot); **The Invaders**/*Beach Head* (pilot), *The Experiment, The Ivy Curtain, Wall of Crystal.* 1968: **The Sunshine Patriot.** 1969: **The Immortal; It Takes a Thief**/*The Family.* 1970: **Tribes** (aka *The Soldier Who Declared Peace);* **The Man Who Died Twice.** 1971: **Maybe I'll Come Home in the Spring; Longstreet**/pilot; **Man on a String.** 1972: **The Man; Emily and Joe.**

Born in New Jersey and christened Giuseppe Danielle Sargente, Sargent set off on a theatrical career via student productions as actor, singer, pianist and photographer. It was as an actor that he arrived in Hollywood, and it was *Lassie* which first gave him a break as a director (although he had directed stage productions like *All the King's Men*). More successfully (and quickly) than most of his contemporaries he managed to move his career from the formula reaches of **Man from UNCLE** to the professional heights of directing pilots, and up-market movies of the week, before embarking on an extensive feature career. He has certainly 'made it'.

His early formula shows are of a muscular, gutsy style reminiscent of Anthony Mann in his visuals and handling of primal emotion, but it is the later more prestigious shows which cry out for more considered attention. He could make **Sunshine**—a LOVE STORY rip-off with Christina Ranes and Cliff de Young—into a powerful shriek for life, the girl dying of bone cancer refusing to go quietly. In **Tribes,** there is a similar obsessed resolve in Jan-Michael Vincent refusing to be broken by the service when drafted into the Marines. The **Longstreet** pilot showed that he is a master at pure visual suspense. **The Marcus-Nelson Murders** illustrates why he gets hired to make pilots—this one became the great success, **Kojak**.

While other directors made their reputations on the hard hitting series of the early 60s, Sargent was one of the first to successfully utilise the expanding TV horizons which have currently been taken to new limits with miniseries like **Holocaust.** As such, he is one of the first in the twilight zone between movie and TV (indeed his films THE HELL WITH HEROES and THE FORBIN PROJECT actually began life as TV projects—while **Sunshine** and **Tribes** were released as theatrical films in Europe.) and has already done enough for us to feel justified in lobbying for a proper forum through which to discuss his troublesome yet important activities.

Franklin Schaffner (1920-)

1953-1958: **Person to Person; Studio One; Kaiser–Aluminum Hour.** 1954: **Twelve Angry Men.** 1955: **The Caine Mutiny Court Martial.** 1958: **The Velvet Alley; Seven against the Wall; Playhouse 90**/multiples. 1961: **The Defenders**/*The Attack, The Boy Between; Gideon's Follies, Killer Instinct, Reunion with Death, The Tarnished Cross.*

While it is embarassing to have to go to press with such a ludicrously incomplete listing, it is important that the research problems facing tele-historians be made so apparent. We are working miles from the source material, in England. But even the TV museum at UCLA encounters the same stone walls, the same elusive information, the same long corridor of frustration and sheer mystery which seems to be the name of the game. We are merely trying to assemble facts and achieve sense of order out of the consumer industry (TV in the 1950s).

Schaffner stayed around longer than Frankenheimer, Mulligan and Penn—but arguably he is the most successful of the generation's graduates, for THE WAR LORD, PLANET OF THE APES and PATTON are true fusions of cinema, style and idea. While it would be fun to look at a kinescope of **Twelve Angry Men** and compare it to Lumet's version (Schaffner's cast was Franchot Tone, Robert Cummings, Edward Arnold, Walter Abel, Paul Hartman, George Voskovec, John Beal, Lee Philips, Norman Fell, Joseph Sweeney, Bart Burns and Will West), and see whether Schaffner's **Caine Mutiny** (with Lloyd Nolan, Barry Sullivan and Frank Lovejoy) works better than Kramer's movie (Schaffner won the Emmy for it), these may be impossible dreams (kinescopes may not exist). Certainly however it is possible to check out **The Defenders** (for which Schaffner won the 1962 Emmy for 'Outstanding Directorial Achievement'). If the iron curtain of apathy lifts and further research uncovers information about the myriad of other shows for which Schaffner was responsible, we may be in for a treat.

Michael Schultz

1974: **Toma**/*The Madam;* **Rockford Files**/*The Dark and Bloody Ground.* 1975: **Baretta**/*The Half Million Dollar Baby;* **Starsky and Hutch**/*Kill Huggy Bear.* 1976: **Starsky and Hutch**/*Captain Dobie You're Dead.*

Schultz must be quite a freaky character (CAR WASH, WHICH WAY IS UP?, SERGENT PEPPER'S LONELY HEARTS CLUB BAND) but on the evidence of **The Half Million Dollar Baby**, his pre-movie TV work was a speedshooting course. That segment was the most conventional of the first season's initially really oddball output. The two **Starsky and Hutch** outings 'typecast' Schultz by giving him the show's Black support characters to work with, and again *Captain Dobie You're Dead* was stylish and fast-paced, but little of any true Schultz came through. They are recent shows and still turn up regularly in re-runs; for those who don't know them they are worth checking out.

Jack Smight (1926-)

1958: **Alcoa Goodyear Theatre/Eddie.** 1959: **Twilight Zone**/*The Lonely.* 1960: **Twilight Zone**/*The Lateness of the Hour, Night of the Meek, Twenty-Two.* 1961: **Naked City**/*Dead on the Field of Honor;* **Route 66**/*Goodnight Sweet Blues;* **The Defenders**/*The Naked Heiress.* 1962: **Alfred Hitchcock Hour**/*The Paragon, What Really Happened?, The Dark Pool, Salt of the Earth, The Lonely Hours.* 1963: **Arrest and Trial**/*Isn't It a Lovely View?* 1964: **Kraft Suspense Theatre**/*Operation Grief.* 1966: **Kraft Suspense Theatre: Crisis**/*In Darkness Waiting* (2 pts aka *Strategy of Terror* in theatrical release). 1971: **Madigan**/*The London Beat;* **McCloud**/*A Little Plot in Tranquil*

Valley, Somebody's Out to Get Jenny. 1972: **Banacek**/*Detour to Nowhere* (pilot), *Let's Hear it for a Living Legend;* **The Screaming Woman; The Longest Night; Madigan**/*The Midtown Beat.* 1973: **Columbo**/*Dead Weight;* **Double Indemnity; Linda; Partners in Crime** (pilot). 1974: **Frankenstein—the True Story.**

Like Gordon Hessler, Smight has had a two-part TV career and has now 'graduated' a second time. Part one included **Eddie** (An Americanisation of **Sammy**, Ken Hughes's British TV play which Hughes later transformed into the feature THE SMALL WORLD OF SAMMY LEE for producer Frank Godwin), for which Smight and his star Mickey Rooney each won Emmies. There was also a profusion of the prestigious shows of the period—**Route 66, Naked City, The Defenders**—and also an apparent predilection for the sleazy and sordid, the mechanics and motivations of crime and punishment, a fascination for the mental and physical underbelly of American life. (It's pure coincidence, presumably, but there are a string of mournful, similarly-evocative titles in the Smight list—*The Lonely, The Lateness of the Hour, Goodnight Sweet Blues, The Dark Pool, The Lonely Hours, In Darkness Waiting, The Longest Night.*)

All this activity became a diving board into a movie career, which impressively revitalised the private eye genre (HARPER/MOVING TARGET), confirmed a penchant for the off-beat and disenchanted (NO WAY TO TREAT A LADY, THE TRAVELLING EXECUTIONER) and lamentably revealed a typically American desire for 'respectability' (RABBIT, RUN). This last film, an adaptation of John Updike's key 60s novel, seems effectively to have sunk Smight—and TV hovered on the horizon again.

If the early 60s found him shaping his craft, the early 70s found him treading water with less challenging series material (**McCloud, Madigan, Banacek**). But **Frankenstein—the True Story** became the opportunity to start swimming again—a Christopher Isherwood script from the Mary Shelley novel, filmed as a four-hour special; it is a brilliant piece of work. Equally impressive is **The Screaming Woman**, an adaptation of a Ray Bradbury story, with Olivia de Havilland trying to convince those around her that she has come across a woman buried alive in the woods. Her nearest and dearest are convinced that she is mad and the only person she finds to help her is (of course) the would-be murderer. Classic cliché-prone material, but Smight (with a script by Merwyn Gerard) hits no false chords or *déja-vu* and builds true suspense and terror whilst conveying the pain and reality of acts of murder.

The Longest Night, based on a real-life kidnapping case, actually uses a similar story device (the kidnappers bury their victim in a special box whose automatic air supply will run out in one week). Equally unpleasant goings-on motivate the **Double Indemnity** remake (with Richard Crenna, Samantha Eggar and Lee J. Cobb) and **Linda**—indicating that this was a particularly fruitful period for Smight. Overall it would certainly seem that his small dark world has many more perverse delights than his supporters have yet encountered.

Steven Spielberg (1947-)

1969: **Night Gallery**/*pilot* (co-dir). 1970: **Night Gallery**/*Make Me Laugh;* **Four In One: The Psychiatrist/–God Bless the Children**/*Par for the Course, The Private World of Martin Dalton.* 1971: **Columbo**/*Murder by the Book;* **Owen Marshall Counselor at Law**/*Eulogy for a Wide Receiver;* **Duel.** 1972: **Something Evil; Savage.**

It is almost painful having to give '1947' as a birthdate for this phenomenon. Spielberg's immense talent eases the agony of finding that directors, like policemen, are getting younger. His extraordinary rise to fame and influence (plus the brilliant way he has used his success) are well enough known. Why should his TV work which took him to the fringe of his current position, be so resolutely ignored?

Had **Duel** not been released as a theatrical feature in Europe (to garner rave reviews and awards), Spielberg might currently be winning Emmys, or shooting a segment of **Charlie's Angels. Duel** is an excellent example of the critical lunacy regarding TV. In Europe, **Duel** would normally have been shown (if at all) on TV–and it is an any money bet that the critics who 'discovered' it in cinemas would not have come across it or would have ignored it on the box.

One would have hoped that, by now, these same critics would have, at least, been alerted to the creative possibilities in modern American TV (even if—given Sturgeon's Law—they are seldom attained), would be paying more serious attention to the small screen, and would be unearthing Spielberg's other work. Some hopes!

While **The Night Gallery** segments are far from impressive, **Something Evil** is a truly startling piece, with two extraordinary sequences and a climax which, though probably banal on paper ('Mother love' triumphs over 'Demon' possessing a child) is made to work beautifully by the power and conviction of Spielberg and the actress Sandy Dennis. At the same time, it is perfectly in keeping with the emotional preoccupations evident in CLOSE ENCOUNTERS. In theory, horror/occult themes should be perfect TV, if only because we watch in the intimate surroundings of a familiar world and not the distancing darkness of a movie theatre. Like murder, for Hitchcock, horror begins at home. Spielberg proved that brilliantly with **Something Evil**—goose bumps can still form at its memory.

Spielberg certainly knew early on how to manipulate both our emotions and the raw material of his trade—but not on any simple, mechanical level. His interest in, and understanding of, children seems also to have been present early on, in **Something Evil** and also in **God Bless the Children** (although some sources credit this to Jerrold Freedman). It can also be seen in *The Private World of Martin Dalton,* where it is fused with his equal fascination for 'fantasy', the eponymous hero being a 12 year old boy who becomes a major behaviour problem at home and at school, as he slips further and further into the private world of his imagination.

Fantasy apparently infuses *LA 2019*, where Spielberg somehow, reportedly manages to spin the contemporary world of a publishing company into the future. Only **Columbo** and **Owen Marshall** would seem in any way to be 'conventional' for **Savage** though not *fantastique*, is a weird fusion of thriller and a critique/celebration of TV itself, with Spielberg indulging his fascination for technology by running his cameras riot in the TV studio set.

Had Spielberg done nothing else, this TV work would still call out for attention. He has become the 1970s Hitchcock, a director of major importance, and one of the few contemporary talents to have an understanding of 'pure' moviemaking. Consequently, the apathy shown to his early work is nothing short of absurd, a serious indictment of film archives and institutes, as well as those who choose to call themselves critics.

Jeannot Szwarc

1967: **Ironside** (series assoc pr +) *Light at the End of the Journey* (+ co-wr). 1968: **Ironside** (series assoc pr +) *The Macabre Mr Micawber, A Matter of Love and Death* (+ co-wr). 1969: **It Takes a Thief**/*The Great Chess Gambit;* **Marcus Welby MD**/*Dance to No Music.* 1970: **Night Gallery**/*Little Black Bag, The Funeral, Class of '99, A Death in the Family, Satisfaction Guaranteed, The Merciful, With Apologies to Mr Hyde;* **Paris 7000**/*Call Me Lee, Call Me Ellen;* **Alias Smith and Jones**/*The Girl from Wickenberg;* **The Virginian**/*Holocaust;* **Men from Shiloh**/*Experiment at New Life;* **Marcus Welby MD**/*A Spanish Saying I Made Up, A Passion of Torches, Aura to a New Tomorrow.* 1971: **Night Gallery**/*The Big Surprise, The Phantom Farmhouse, Stop Killing Me, A Feast of Blood, Room for One Less, Cool Air, The Waiting Room, The Caterpillar, Midnight Never Ends, The Sins of the Fathers, The Return of the Sorceror, The Ring with the Red Velvet Ropes;* **Sarge**/*A Company of Victims;* **The Man and the City**/*Jennifer.* 1972: **Night Gallery**/*Rare Objects, Whisper, Spectre in Tap Shoes;* **The Devil's Daughter; Night of Terror; The Weekend Nun.** 1973: **Kojak**/*Conspiracy of Fear, Mojo, Dead on his Feet, Queen of the Gypsies, Girl in the River* (co-wr); **Columbo**/*Lovely But Lethal;* **Three Faces of Love**/*The Fortunate Painter;* **Toma**/*The Oberon Contract;* **Six Million Dollar Man**/*Population: Zero;* **A Summer Without Boys; You'll Never See Me Again.** 1974: **Kojak**/*The Chinatown Murders, Acts of Desperate Men;* **Toma**/*Pound of Flesh, The Street, Fifty Percent of Normal.* 1975: **The Rockford Files**/*Two Into 5.56 Won't Go;* **Baretta**/*The Glory Game, On the Road, Double Image;* **Crime Club.** 1976: **Kojak**/*Out of the Shadows, Shield for Murder, A Summer Madness, When You Hear the Beep Drop Dead, Where Do You Go When You Have No Place to Go?;* **Hazard's People; The Rockford Files**/*So Help Me God, New Life Old Dragons;* **Baretta**/*It's Hard But It's Fair;* **Baa Baa Blacksheep**/*New Georgia on my Mind.* 1977: **Code Name: Diamond Head.**

Szwarc is identified by fantasy fans as one of their own, for his numerous **Night Gallery** segments, **The Devil's Daughter**, **Night of Terror** and William Castle's BUG (Szwarc's first feature). It seems he will finally beat his way through to the big time with JAWS 2. Having replaced the original director (John

Hancock), throwing out most of his footage and preparing his own work in the rapid time of four weeks, Szwarc seems to be intent on grasping his opportunity.

While there is undoubtedly a preoccupation with the macabre and the marvellous in his work, this might simply be typecasting, for he seems equally happy on the crime beat—and whatever the niceties of *The Ring with the Red Velvet Ropes, Midnight Never Ends* and the other good **Night Gallerys** *(The Caterpillar* is an extremely effective, and thoroughly nasty little gem) his best work may well be *Shield for Murder,* a feature-length **Kojak** scripted by William P. McGivern (who wrote a 1954 feature with the same title). Though not a 'death of famous men'-type conspiracy piece, the actual case slowly unravelled here is as disturbing as THE PARALLAX VIEW, and quite beautifully strung together, a tense and subversive thriller building to an indictment of capitalist power and its abuse in human, if not political, terms. It also includes a wonderfully moving portrait in aberrant psychology (a terrified girl who has lapsed into madness) which, together with another **Kojak,** *Out of the Shadows,* featuring a 'mad assassin' whose acts are claimed as his own by an 'innocent' person, suggest that Szwarc has an awful lot going for him in terms of character understanding and empathy, to complement his fine sense of tempo and narrative flow.

Fortunately much of his work is recent and currently in syndication. Whether or not JAWS 2 does the commercial trick for him, he is someone to whom one should pay close attention.

4/Elephants' Graveyard

The progression of directors from the small to big screens has its inevitable reverse in older talents who virtually ended their careers in TV. Here then are some venerable names whose TV work deserves to be investigated, some obscure ones who deserve more general recognition, and some more negligible ones whose contributions to TV should nonetheless be acknowledged.

Lewis Allen (1905-)

1955: **20th Century Fox Hour**/*Cavalcade, Christopher Bean, Man on the Ledge.* 1965: **20th Century Fox Hour**/*A Gun in His Hand.* 1957: **Perry Mason**/*The Case of the Haunted Husband.* 1959: **Rifleman**/*The Second Witness.* 1960: **Perry Mason**/*The Case of the Violent Vest.* 1961: **Detectives**/*One Lousy Wednesday, Matt's Woman.* 1962: **Court Martial**/*Shadow of a Man, How Ethical Can You Be?* 1964: **The Rogues**/*Take Me In Paris.* 1965: **Big Valley**/*The Guilt of Matt Bentell;* **Burke's Law**/*Who Killed the Swinger on a Hook?;* **The Rogues**/*The Golden Ocean, The Diamond Studded Pie, The Bartered MacBride, A Daring Step Backward.* 1966: **A Man Called Shenandoah**/*A Long Way Home;* **Mission Impossible**/*The Trial.* 1969: **The Survivors (pts 10, 13)**; **Mission Impossible**/*The Pendulum.* 1970; **Dan August**/*Soldier, Epitaph for a Swinger.* 1973: **Cannon**/*The Island Caper.* 1974: **Little House on the Prairie**/*Doctor's Lady.*

English born, an actor and director on the London stage before taking productions to America, Allen spent two years as a production assistant at Paramount before getting his first feature to direct, THE UNINVITED. Perhaps because of his native sensibility towards misty occultism, this is a minor Gothic classic and one of the few films to treat the world of ghosts with a serious and perceptively ambiguous approach. With its successor, THE UNSEEN and, ten years later, SUDDENLY which frighteningly anticipates the world of Lee Harvey Oswald, these are Allen's best films.

Segments of the lightweight **Rogues** and the largely abortive Anglo-American hybrid **Court Martial** indicate that Allen's TV work seldom reached even the modest heights he had already attained—but *Epitaph For a Swinger* evokes real pain and emotional sadness in **Dan August**'s ordinarily glib world. Good performances and a pleasantly old-fashioned professionalism are most likely to be the sum of the virtues of Allen's other work. He was never a hack, and a suspicion persists that something of greater value lurks, unseen but not uninvited.

George Archainbaud (1890-1959)

1948: **Hopalong Cassidy** (multiples). 1950: **Gene Autry** (multiples); **Range Rider** (multiples). 1951: **Range Rider**/*The Hawk, Bad Medicine, Dead Man's Shoe, Western Fugitive, The Blind Trail,*

The Grand Fleece. 1952: **Range Rider** (multiples). 1953: **Champion the Wonder Horse** (multiples); **Annie Oakley** (multiples). 1956: **Circus Boy**/*Hortense the Hippo, The Gentle Giant, The Pawnee Strip, Lady and the Circus, Joey's Wedding, The Remarkable Ricardo, The Great Gambino's Son.*

The French-born Archainbaud's directorial career began in 1915, and finally flickered to a close somewhere in the mid-50s, after many years of what must have been blinding monotony in coaxing various B western heroes and heroines through their paces. The majority of his TV career was spent with the Gene Autry 'Flying "A" company—the singing cowboy having become one of Hollywood's most successful businessmen. Correctly scanning the future, the Autry empire was filming TV in colour as early as 1950—and thus ensured vastly increased residuals once colour became a force. It also kept the B western traditions alive, if only by rainbow proxy, for a little longer.

Archainbaud was at the heart of this—and while it never ever became even low art, such stuff—along with **Flash Gordon, Superman** *et al*—fuelled young imaginations as much as serials and oaters had ever done on the big screen. He helped inspire a new generation to love crystal beads and cathode tubes. In this unlikely role of cultural midwife we prefer to remember Archainbaud.

Jack Arnold (1916-)

1955: **Science Fiction Theatre**/*No Food for Thought.* 1959: **Rawhide**/*Incident at Jacob's Well.* 1961: **Peter Gunn** (multiples); **Wagon Train** (multiples); **Eleventh Hour** (multiples). 1962: **The Travels of Jamie McPheeters**/*Day of the Misfits.* 1964: **Perry Mason**/*The Case of the Scandalous Sculptor, The Case of the Blonde Bonanza, The Case of the Thermal Thief;* **Rawhide**/*Canliss;* **Gilligan's Island** (series pr) + *Waiting for Watubi, Angel on the Island;* **Kraft Suspense Theatre**/*One Tiger to a Hill;* **Dr Kildare** (multiples). 1966: **Run Buddy Run**/*The Bank Holdup.* 1968: **It Takes a Thief** (series exec pr) + *A Matter of Gray Matter* (2 pts). 1970: **Men from Shiloh**/*Hannah.* 1971: **Alias Smith and Jones**/*Something To Get Hung About.* 1972: **McCloud**/*The Park Avenue Rustlers;* **Alias Smith and Jones**/*The Clementine Ingredient, Bushwhack!, What Happened at the XST?, Which Way to the OK Corral?* 1975: **Ellery Queen**/*The Adventure of the Disappearing Dagger, The Adventure of the Twelth Floor Express.* 1976: **Holmes and Yoyo**/*The Last Phantom, The Thornhill Affair;* **Ellery Queen**/*The Adventure of the Two Faced Woman;* **Nancy Drew Mysteries**/*A Haunting We Will Go;* **McNaughton's Daughter**/*The M.O.M. Principle.* 1977: **Sex and the Married Woman.**

Arnold is beloved of cultists for his Universal westerns and fantasy masterpieces of the early and mid '50's, but his career took a nose dive with the decline of middle-budget picturemaking in the '60s. His most recent film credits are dominated by inferior Bob Hope vehicles and other depressing comedy material. In 1961, an entry on him in *Vingt Ans de Cinèma Amèricain* hoped that he would quickly return to B movies, the realm where his 'invention and virtuosity best flourish'. Well of course B movies are no more—but it seems that in TV Arnold found an equally valid framework.

In 1955 there was a segment of **Science Fiction Theatre** which might be something to rank with INCREDIBLE SHRINKING MAN—for certainly *Canliss*, a **Rawhide** written by Sterling Silliphant, and starring Dean Martin in a back-shooting-gunfighter story-with-a-twist, well stands comparison with NO NAME ON THE BULLET and RED SUNDOWN, which worked their own charms on 'gunmen in town' themes. Thus the **Alias Smith & Jones** segments—especially *Bushwhack!* (written by David Moessinger) are worth hunting down. The detective series contain one pure delight, *The Park Avenue Rustlers*, which was directed with all Arnold's old force and vigour and featured a helicopter chase with some of the most breathtaking stunting seen in movies or TV.

Richard H. Bartlett

1958: **Wagon Train**/*The Sarah Drummond Story, The Daniel Barrister Story* (+ co-pr), *The Dan Hogan Story, The Rutledge Monroe Story, The Sacramento Story.* 1959: **Wagon Train**/*The Tent City Story, The Beauty Jameson Story, The Ruth Marshall Story* (+ co-pr); **Riverboat**/*The Barrier, Tampico Raid;* **Cimarron City**/*To Become a Man* (+ co-pr), *Runaway Train, Medicine Man, The Town Is a Prisoner.* 1960: **Riverboat**/*The Sell Out, The Salvage Pirates, Witness to Evil.* 1961: **77 Sunset Strip**/*The Inverness Cape Caper, Twice Dead, The Lady has the Answers;* **Hawaiian Eye**/*A Taste for Money.*

Bartlett's feature career is in its own way as curious and arcane as Edgar G. Ulmer's. THE SILVER STAR which actually starred Bartlett and his producer Earle Lyon; I'VE LIVED BEFORE, an essay on reincarnation; JOE DAKOTA, SLIM CARTER and MONEY WOMEN AND GUNS, three oddball vehicles for Jock Mahoney. It is a career for only the most devoted cultists perhaps, but one full of strange delights. Bartlett's TV career, which was unfortunately short was, however, sweet.

Laslo Benedek (1907-)

1952/1956: **Four Star Playhouse/Dupont Theatre/Stage 7/Loretta Young Show/Telephone Time** (multiples). 1959: **Perry Mason**/*Case of the Demure Defendant, Case of the Cautious Coquette, Case of the Lonely Heiress, Case of the Fugitive Nurse.* 1960: **Thriller**/*The Ordeal of Dr Cardell;* **Perry Mason**/*Case of the Red Riding Boots, Case of the Barefaced Witness.* 1961: **Rawhide**/*The Peddler;* **The Untouchables** (multiples). 1962: **Naked City**/*The Well-Dressed Termite.* 1963: **Outer Limits**/*The Man with the Power, Tourist Attraction.* 1964: **Fugitive**/*Come Watch Me Die;* **Alfred Hitchcock Hour**/*The Evil of Adelaide Winters, Fraudulent Medium, The Thanatos Palace Hotel;* **Outer Limits**/*Wolf 359;* **Voyage to the Bottom of the Sea**/*Long Live the King, The Buccaneer.* 1966: **Ironhorse**/*Town Full of Fear.* 1967; **Legend of Custer**/*Breakout, Desperate Mission, Spirit Woman, The Raiders.*

There is at least as much genuine interest in Benedek's TV work as in his features, which flattered to deceive (as DEATH OF A SALESMAN and THE WILD ONE did). The early '50s anthology drama, segments of **Outer Limits, Naked City** and **Rawhide** and especially *The Evil of Adelaide Winters*, (with Kim Hunter as a fraudulent medium) and *The Thanatos Palace Hotel,* (from a story by André Maurois with Angie Dickinson) in the **Alfred Hitchcock Hour**, are all worthy of respect.

John Brahm (1893-)

1955: **Medic** (multiples); **Screen Director's Playhouse**/*Laura.* 1956: **General Electric Theatre**/*Last Reunion, For Better For Worse.* 1957: **Studio 57**/*The Secret Darkness;* **Johnny Staccato**/*An Act of Terror;* **Video Theatre** (multiples); **M Squad**/*The Alibi Witness, The Woman from Paris, High School Bride.* 1959: **Cimarron City**/*Child of Fear;* **Alfred Hitchcock Presents**/*A Night with the Boys, Dry Run, Insomnia, Pen Pals, Touche;* **The Deputy**/*Lawman's Blood;* **Riverboat**/*Fort Epitaph;* **Twilight Zone**/*Time Enough at Last, Judgement Night, The Four of Us Are Dying, A Nice Place to Visit.* 1960: **Thriller**/*The Watcher, The Prediction, The Cheaters, The Merriweather File, A Good Imagination;* **Twilight Zone**/*Mr Dingle The Strong, Shadow Play.* 1961: **The Defenders**/*The 100 Lives of Harry Sims, The Search;* **Naked City**/*The Pedigree Sheet;* **Twilight Zone**/*Person or Persons Unknown, Young Man's Fancy.* 1962: **Thriller**/*Dark Legacy, The Remarkable Mrs Hawks, An Attractive Family, Waxworks, A Wig for Mrs Devore, Cousin Tundifer, Flowers of Evil;* **Alfred Hitchcock Presents**/*The Five Forty-Eight, The Throwback, The Hero;* **Alfred Hitchcock Hour**/*Don't Look Behind You;* **The Defenders**/*Storm at Birch Glen;* **Alcoa Premiere**/*The Potentate.* 1963: **Twilight Zone**/*The New Exhibit, You Drive;* **The Virginian**/*The Golden Door;* **Alfred Hitchcock Hour**/*Death and the Joyful Woman;* **Naked City**/*The Rydecker Case;* **Arrest and Trial**/*Call It a Lifetime.* 1964: **Outer Limits**/*zzzzz, The Bellero Shield;* **Twilight Zone**/*Queen of the Nile;* **Alfred Hitchcock Hour**/*Murder Case, The Trap, Final Performance;* **Voyage to the Bottom of the Sea**/*The City Beneath the Sea, Hot Line.* 1965: **Bob Hope Chrysler Theatre**/*Terror Island;* **Dr Kildare**/*Behold the Man* (4 pts), *Something Old, Something New* (2 pts). 1966: **The Man from UNCLE**/*The Waverly Ring Affair;* **The Girl from UNCLE**/*The Horns of the Dilemma Affair, The Montori Device Affair, The Jewels of Topango Affair, The Lethal Eagle Affair;* **Dr Kildare**/*Mercy or Murder?* (4 pts). 1967: **The Man from UNCLE**/*The Napoleon's Tomb Affair, The Maze Affair, The Pieces of Fate Affair;* **The Girl from UNCLE**/*The Double-O-Nothing Affair, The Furnace Flats Affair.*

THE LODGER and HANGOVER SQUARE endeared Brahm to fantasy/Gothic buffs. They are compellingly stylish thrillers in the Lewton mould, dealing with 'human' monsters rather than the supernatural. Their feeling is of that peculiarly English vein of seedy, rather depressing, behind-lace-curtains murder so beloved of Hitchcock. Dominated by the sadly grotesque Laird Cregar, they are an extraordinary duo and overshadow the rest of Brahm's somewhat desultory career—although his remake of BROKEN BLOSSOMS in England, GUEST IN THE HOUSE and the private-eye BRASHER DOUBLOON all contain enough idiosyncracies for Brahm to be considered as one of the most interesting of all those directors who never really established a niche big enough to give him freedom or fame.

Brahm's tenure in TV was more creatively rewarding. Although he described his small screen work as 'charcoal sketches for later, full scale projects' the majority of them are firmly entrenched in that dark world of aberration which characterises the two main features. Undoubtedly the macabre was his metier:— *Döppelgängers,* waxworks, Jack the Ripper, ventriloquists, fogs, eternal life, murder, betrayal, triangle relationships, and the desire for lost youth by ageing women are characters and themes which figure prominently and recur often.

TV may have been a salvation to Brahm. He could indulge his penchants, experiment with light and camerawork at every opportunity, work with such stars as Bette Davis, Franchot Tone, John Cassavetes and Ginger Rogers, and help nurse along the early careers of Lee Marvin, Sally Kellerman, Katherine Ross and Robert Duvall.

David Butler (1894-)

1957: **Wagon Train**/*The Hon Don Charlie Story, The Bill Tawnee Story;* **Leave it to Beaver** (multiples). 1958: **Wagon Train**/*The Dick Richardson Story, The Sally Potter Story, The Bernal Sierra Story* (co-dir). 1959: **77 Sunset Strip**/*The Grandma Caper;* **M Squad**/*Mr Grim's Rabbits;* **The Deputy**/*Powder Keg, Like Father, The Johnny Shanks Story, The Big Four, The Next Bullet, The Wild Wind;* **Wagon Train**/*The Jess MacAbbee Story.* 1960: **The Deputy**/*The Truly Yours, The Choice, The Stand Off, The 'X' Game;* **The Seven Little Foys** (multiples). 1961: **Wagon Train**/*The Jim Bridger Story, The Don Alvarado Story;* **The Deputy**/*The Two Faces of Bob Claxton.* 1962: **Bob Hope Show Special.** 1963: **Twilight Zone**/*The Bard;* **Bob Hope Show Special.**

TV represents the final stages of a career covering just about every Hollywood development. Butler was a stage actor, before acting in silent pictures for Thomas Ince and D. W. Griffith. While still acting, he formed his own production company, hiring John Ford, Tod Browning, Frank Borzage, William K. Howard etc. Butler, himself, began directing in 1927 and carried on doing so for the next forty years.

Silent movies, talkies, colour, Cinemascope, TV all found Butler more than able to cope with their respective challenges, even though his ambitions seldom strayed from the lightweight, the cosy. They say that the job of an executive is simply to survive and from that point of view, Butler's career was a major achievement. When retrospectives of **Wagon Train, M Squad, 77 Sunset Strip** and **The Deputy** (Henry Fonda's first TV assignments) get aired, Butler's segments will be seen to stand up in the same way, not too pushy, not too fancy, but the stuff of a journeyman.

Thomas Carr (1907-)

1950: **Range Rider**/*The Peace Pipe.* 1951: **Wild Bill Hickok**/*Wild Bill Hickok* (pilot), *Rock Springs Rustlers, Indian Pony Express* + other multiples; **The Adventures of Superman**/*Superman on Earth, The Haunted Lighthouse, The Case of the Talkative Dummy, The Mystery of the Broken Statue, The Money Mystery, Rescue, The Secret of Superman, The Deserted Village, Treasure of the Incas, Double Trouble, The Runaway Robot, The Evil Three, Riddle of the Chinese Jade, Czar of the Underworld, Crime Wave.* 1953: **The Adventures of Superman**/*Five Minutes to Doom, The Big Squeeze, The Man Who Could Read Minds, Jet Ace, The Defeat of Superman, Superman in Exile, The Dog Who Knew Superman, Panic in the Sky, The Machine That Could Plot Crimes, Jungle Devil, My Friend Superman, The Golden Vulture, Jimmy Olsen Boy Editor, Lady in Black, Star of Fate, The Whistling Bird, Around the World, Stamp Day for Superman* (A Public Service Programme for US Savings Bonds). 1951: **Trackdown**/*The Marple Brothers, Law in Lampasas, Easton Texas, Self Defense, Alpine Texas, End of an Outlaw, The Witness, The Young Gun, The Horse;* **The Adventures of Superman**/*The Last Knight.* 1958: **Cheyenne**/*Incident at Indian Springs;* **Trackdown**/*The Setup, A Matter of Justice.* 1959: **Wanted Dead or Alive**/multiples; **Laramie**/*Fugitive Road;* **Trackdown**/*The Avenger, The Schoolteacher, The Kid, The Threat, Fear, Gift Horse.* 1960: **Laramie**/*Last Warning, Cemetary Road.* 1961: **Dick Powell Theatre**/*The Geetas Box;* **Stagecoach West**/*El Carniciero, The Orphans;* **Richard Diamond** (multiples). 1962: **Rawhide**/*Incident of El Toro, Incident of the Hunter, Incident of the Four Horsemen, Incident of the Lost Woman, Incident of the Wolvers, Incident of the Querencias, Incident of the Buryin' Man, Incident at Spider Rock;* **Laramie**/*Gun Duel, The Wedding Party.* 1963: **Rawhide**/*Incident of Judgement Day, Incident of the Married Woman, Incident of the Commanchero, Incident of the Black Ace, Incident at Rio Doloroso, Incident at Paradise, Incident at Farragut Pass, Incident of the Prophecy, Incident of the Death Dancer, Incident of the Midnight Cave, Incident of the Red Wind, Incident at Gila Flats, Incident of the Swindler;* **Laramie**/*The Stranger.* 1964: **Rawhide**/*Incident of the Odyssey, Incident at Deadhorse* (2 pts), *Incident of the Peyote Cup.* 1965: **Rawhide**/*Walk Into Terror, Six Weeks at Bent Fork, Brush War at Buford.* 1966: **The Virginian**/*High Stakes, Vengeance Trial;* **A Man Called Shenandoah**/*The Verdict.* 1967: **Felony Squad**/*Flame Out!;* **The Virginian**/*The Gauntlet.*

'I'm going to get into this with both feet, and just as soon as I can. This is the biggest thing that's ever hit the entertainment world so far as those of us who make pictures are concerned'. Thomas Carr was talking of TV at a Director's Guild of America meeting in 1948. The son of movie parents (father William Carr a silent period director, mother Mary Carr the star who broke millions of hearts as the mother in OVER THE HILL TO THE POOR HOUSE and appeared as the Quaker woman in FRIENDLY PERSUASION) Carr's first twenty-five years in the business were as an actor. When he became a director, it was with Republic B westerns and serials. His hopes for TV were probably predicated around the thought that he might advance into more prestigious areas. But **Range Rider** and **Wild Bill Hickok** were followed by two stretches on **The Adventures of Superman**—essentially identical material, and identical conditions of budgetary privation, that permeated the poverty row belt which had claimed Carr on the big screen. Indeed, it was his work on the SUPERMAN serial, in 1948, which earned him the TV **Superman** assignment.

But as the '50s progressed, so did Carr's fortunes. The material, to the outsider, would appear to be no different. But there are giant strides from **Range**

Rider to **Rawhide** and **Trackdown**—as there are from SUNSET TRAIL and Republic B westerns to Carr's excellent Cinemascope features, THE TALL STRANGER and GUNSMOKE IN TUCSON.

In fact, Carr's best work has been done in association with producer Vincent M. Fennelly—for **Trackdown, Wanted Dead or Alive, Rawhide, Stagecoach West,** even **Dick Powell Theatre** and **Richard Diamond** saw Fennelly at the producer's desk. As the range of ambition grew, as juvenile westerns gave way to 'adult' material in the late '50s, so a most conducive creative framework opened out for the men who had served more than their fair share of time with unadulterated hokum.

John English (1903-1969)

1953: **Range Rider**/*Baron of Broken Bow, Gunpoint.* 1955: **Soldiers of Fortune**/*Jungle Search, The Greatest Beast, Pearls off Dandra Head, Escort to Namtok, Cut Charlie In, The Gaboon Viper, Hate at Forty Fathoms, The Lady of Rajmahal, The General, The Vanishing Island, The Last Days of Delores, Lady and the Lion.* 1956: **Zane Grey Theatre**/*Courage Is a Gun, Dangerous Orders.* 1957: **Trackdown**/*Like Father;* **Zane Grey Theatre**/*Fugitive, Three Graves.* 1959: **My Friend Flicka**/*The Golden Promise, Against All Odds.* 1960: **Wagon Train**/*The Nancy Palmer Story;* **Perry Mason**/*The Case of the Torrid Tapestry, The Case of the Jealous Journalist.* 1961: **Checkmate**/*One for the Book, Hour of Execution.* 1962: **Thriller**/*The Innocent Bystanders;* **Checkmate**/*Between Two Guns.* 1963: **The Virginian**/*Killer in Town, Brother Thaddeus, A Distant Fury.* 1965: **Laredo**/*Any Way the Wind Blows.* 1966: **A Man Called Shenandoah**/*The Debt.*

Another of those unsung artisans who worked in the engine room and rarely, if ever, saw the bridge or knew what the captain actually did, but without whom the ship would never have left harbour. Movie buffs know English almost solely because of his marathon stint in company with William Witney directing Republic serials—and usually even then it is Witney who gets the credit. It is a fair judgement, for English has never revealed anything terribly distinctive in his other films for theatrical release. His TV work is different: **Soldiers of Fortune** is a favourite from the author's adolescent years; B movie stuff to be sure, but with the excellent John Russell stalking the screen and three ludicrous slambang fights every segment. In spite of them, it had a tougher, more 'realistic' view of the world than serials or B pictures. English's other smallscreen scribblings have an equal elan.

Robert Florey (1900-)

1952: **Four Star Playhouse**/*Dante's Inferno.* 1953: **Four Star Playhouse**/*The Man in the Box, Sound Off, My Love, No Identity, The Last Voyage;* **A Letter to Loretta** (multiples). 1954: **Four Star**

Playhouse/*My Own Dear Dragon, The Executioner;* **Schlitz Playhouse of Stars** (multiples). 1955: **Disneyland** (multiples); **Four Star Playhouse**/*Night at Lark Cottage, Stuffed Shirt.* 1956: **Wire Service**/multiples; **Jane Wyman Theatre** (multiples); **Zane Grey Theatre**/*Vengeance Canyon.* 1957: **M Squad**/*The Watchdog;* **Wagon Train**/*The Ruth Owens Story, The Les Rand Story;* **Telephone Time** (multiples); **Frank Sinatra Show** (multiples). 1958: **The Texan** (multiples); **Desilu Playhouse** (multiples). 1959: **Markham** (multiples); **Joseph Cotten Theatre** (multiples); **June Allyson Show** (multiples); **Twilight Zone**/*Perchance to Dream.* 1960: **Michael Shayne**/*Murder in Wonderland, A Night with Neva, This Is It Michael Shayne, Call for Michael Shayne, Dolls are Deadly, Shoot the Works, The Poison Pen Club* (all co-dir with Paul Stewart); **Hong Kong** (multiples); **The Barbara Stanwyck Theatre** (multiples). 1961: **Michael Shayne**/*Death Selects a Winner, Murder and the Wanton Bride, The Man with the Cane, Murder Plays Charades* (all co-dir with Paul Stewart); **Adventures in Paradise** (multiples). 1962: **Thriller**/*The Incredible Doctor Markesan;* **Checkmate**/*Face in the Window;* **The Untouchables** (multiples); **Alcoa Premiere** (multiples); **Going My Way** (multiples). 1963: **The Great Adventure**/*The Man Who Stole New York City;* **Dick Powell Theatre** (multiples). 1964: **Twilight Zone**/*The Long Morrow;* **Outer Limits**/*The Moonstone;* **Suspense**/*Repercussion, Fast Break, Midnight Kill, Witness to Condemn, Dara.*

The shadows of MURDERS IN THE RUE MORGUE and THE BEAST WITH FIVE FINGERS loom over Florey's other work. After them, nothing can appear routine. His TV list is jammed with stardom—the various Jane Wyman/Joseph Cotten/Frank Sinatra/June Allyson/Barbara Stanwyck shows; **Four Stars, Schlitz, Alcoa, Desilu Playhouse.** Florey's French charm worked miracles on the egos of the big screen who were forced to accept that their lustre was now lacking. The macabre touch which cineastes associate with Florey is ever present, from the *Dante's Inferno* of 1952 to the **Thriller, Twilight Zone** and **Suspense** segments a decade later—numbering among them *Perchance to Dream*, the late Charles Beaumont's story that makes you want never to sleep again.

Norman Foster (1900-)

1954: **World of Disney**/*Davy Crockett Indian Fighter.* 1955: **World of Disney**/*Davy Crockett Goes to Congress, Davy Crockett at the Alamo, Davy Crockett and the Keelboat Race, Davy Crockett and the River Pirates.* 1957: **Zorro**/*Presenting Senor Zorro* (+wr), *Zorro's Secret Passage, Zorro Rides to the Mission, The Ghost of the Mission, Garcia's Secret Mission, Double Trouble for Zorro, Zorro Luckiest Swordsman Alive, The Fall of Monastario.* 1958: **Zorro**/*The Secret of the Sierra* (+wr), *The New Commandante, The Fox and the Coyote, Adios Senor Magistrado;* **Walt Disney Presents**/*The Nine Lives of Elfego Baca.* 1959: **The Loretta Young Show** (multiples); **Bat Masterson** (multiples). 1966: **The Loner**/*A Little Stroll to the End of the Line, Escort for a Dead Man;* **Batman**/*The Thirteenth Hat–Batman Stands Pat.* 1967: **The Monroes**/*To Break a Colt, Teach the Tigers to Purr, Trapped;* **Legend of Custer**/*War Lance and Sabre, The Raiders.* 1968: **It Takes a Thief**/*The Naked Billionaire.*

The 'Is it a bird, is it a plane?' confusion between movies and TV essentially began with **Davy Crockett**—the two 'features' which set off the coonskincap furore in 1954 were made as half-hour segments of **World of Disney.** Three of them were joined to form DAVY CROCKETT; three more made up DAVY CROCKETT AND THE RIVER PIRATES for world theatrical distribution. Thus Foster's feature credit list already includes TV material. His cockeyed career—from MR. MOTO TO KISS THE BLOOD OFF MY HANDS to BRIGHTY OF THE GRAND CANYON—is repeated in TV. It ended in style—with **Legend of Custer,** both Foster's segments written by Shimon Wincelberg, the David Weisbart production which attempted to tell the 'unvarnished' truth about Custer within a series framework; with **The Loner,** Rod Serling's chip-on-the-shoulder western with Lloyd Bridges; and **The Monroes.** The three of them were, perhaps, the most interesting and courageous attempts to break out of the stultifying **Bonanza** trend which doomed westerns to the level of soap opera.

Tay Garnett (1898-1977)

1957: **Four Star Playhouse** (multiples); **Loretta Young Show** (multiples). 1958: **Wagon Train/***The Kate Parker Story, The Jose Maria Moran Story.* 1959: **Laramie** (multiples); **The Untouchables/***The Jake Lingle Killing, Mexican Stakeout, Star Witness.* 1960: **Wagon Train/***The Candy O'Hara Story;* **The Tall Man** (multiples); **The Deputy** (multiples). 1961: **Gunsmoke/***He Learned About Women, Nina's Revenge;* **Rawhide/***The House of the Hunter, The Captain's Wife;* **Frontier Circus** (multiples); **87th Precinct** (multiples); **The Beachcomber** (multiples); **Naked City/***Debt of Honor.* 1962: **Rawhide/***The Immigrants.* 1963: **Naked City/***Button in the Hay Stack;* **Bonanza/***Bullet for a Bride, Love Me Not.* 1964: **Bonanza/***Once a Doctor, The Pressure Game, Triangle.* 1965: **Death Valley Days** (multiples); **Please Don't Eat the Daisies** (multiples); **The Legend of Jesse James** (multiples); **The Loner** (multiples).

Although the inevitable finally happened in 1977, it seemed for a while that Garnett had found, if not the secret of eternal life, or even the philosopher's stone, then at least a way to hold off 'the fellow in the long nightgown'. He was seventy-five when he worked on his last completed feature, and, at the time of his death, was actively engaged like a tyro French cineaste in compiling a book, made up of questionnaires to directors, about the creative forces and working methods which animate most of the world's brightest film-makers.

Garnett appears to have accepted TV as naturally as he greeted all the changes that affected the business of film making during his long career—concentrating on a wide variety of basically formula shows. The **Untouchables** and **Bonanzas**, unfortunately, show clearly that the raunchy verve of HER MAN had been diminished, the bizarre heroics of BATAAN had been neutered.

Cineastes seem to feel no obligation to backtrack into TV to piece together the gestation of the Altmans and the Spielbergs, admirers of veterans like Garnett (perhaps *especially* Garnett who enlivened many a dead project) do look to their smallscreen for his valid late work, his final statements, his parting shots and graceful codas.

Charles Haas (1913-   )

1959: **77 Sunset Strip**/*Conspiracy of Silence, Out of the Past.* 1960: **The Roaring 20s**/*Judge Seward's Secret, Coney Red Shots;* **77 Sunset Strip**/*Spark of Freedom;* **Maverick**/*The Ice Man;* **Hawaiian Eye**/*Little Blalah, Cut of Ice, Hong Kong Passage;* **The Alaskans**/*Behold the Moon, Ballad of Whitehorse;* **Surfside 6**/*Bride and Seek;* **Perry Mason**/*The Case of the Ill-Fated Faker.* 1962: **Route 66**/*Burning for Burning;* **Alfred Hitchcock Hour**/*Forecast: Low Clouds and Coastal Fog.* 1963: **Burke's Law**/*Who Killed Cynthia Royal?* 1964: **Outer Limits**/*Cold Hands Warm Heart, Cry of Silence.* 1965: **Outer Limits**/*Keeper of the Purple Twilight, The Brain of Colonel Barham.*

Fans of obscure figures should check Haas out, on the strength of two stylish and intelligent Universal westerns—SHOWDOWN IN ABILENE and STAR IN THE DUST. A few more features followed, but Haas was already part of the TV scene and so was lost to the few observers who wished to follow his career, but would not stoop to TV. *Forecast: Low Clouds and Coastal Fog,* one of the moodiest of the **Hitchcock** segments and some distinguished **Outer Limits**—including the legendary *Keeper of the Purple Twilight,* mean that Haas has something of value.

Stuart Heisler (1894-   )

1958: **Lawman**/*Outcast, The Joker, The Intruders, Short Straw, The Outsider, The Gunman, The Captives, The Brand Release, The Chef, Warpath, The Runaway, The Encounter, The Big Hat, The Visitor, The Posse, The Gang, The Souvenir;* **77 Sunset Strip**/*A Nice Social Evening.* 1959: **Lawman**/*The Journey, The Huntress, The Senator, The Return;* **Rawhide**/*Incident of the Day of the Dead.* 1960: **Lawman**/*Yawkey, The Return of Owney O'Reilley, Samson the Great, Blue Boss and Willie Shay;* **Rawhide**/*Incident at Superstition Prairie, Incident of the Captive.* 1961: **Roaring 20s**/*No Exit, Everybody Loves Benny.* 1962: **The Dakotas**/*Return to Dryrock, Red Sky Over Bismarck.* 1963: **The Dakotas**/*Mutiny at Fort Mercy, Trouble at French Creek, Crisis at High Banjo, Fargo, Trial at Grand Forks, Terror at Heart River;* **The Virginian**/*The Evil that Men Do.*

Of all the more distinguished veterans, Heisler's TV work looms like a model of consistency and excellence. It suggests that choice played a far from uncommon role in his credits. As a Warner director, he should have been expected to muck in with **Bourbon Street Beat** or **Surfside 6**, but he kept resolutely to **Lawman** and, in his final year with the company, **The Dakotas.** His **Sunset Strip** and **Roaring 20s** are likely therefore to have been taken on for more personal reasons than contractual necessity.

Lawman (with John Russell again) is just about the finest of the 30-minute westerns of the period. Heisler came in early on the first season's segments helping to shape the style and the show's concerns. Those who know DALLAS, THE BURNING HILLS and THE LONE RANGER will realise that Heisler's affinity with the genre and its thematic and visual needs mean that when fans remember **Lawman** as one of the great series westerns, it's more than likely to be

Heisler's segments that float across the mind.

In subsequent seasons of the show, Bert Glennon, veteran cameraman for Ford and Wellman, did his last work for the screen; Richard Matheson, known almost exclusively for his fantasy work, was contributing such untypical scripts as *Yawkey* and *Samson the Great*: while stars such as Sammy Davis Jr. guested in *Blue Boss and Willie Shay.* Whatever the pressures and limitations of scattergun shooting, this was intelligent and interesting work. Similarly, **The Dakotas**, a more rugged and mature series than **Bronco** or **Sugarfoot**, had nearly half its segments with Heisler at the helm. His tenure there has all the earmarks of being a committed and personal one.

Stopovers with **Rawhide** and **The Virginian** make it likely that other work—and other western work—has evaded our researches. But whether as a representative selection of excellent series TV, or part of the conclusion to an always offbeat and unusual career, Heisler's TV work deserves our praise.

Jesse Hibbs (1906-)

1958: **Wagon Train**/*The Rex Montana Story.* 1959: **Rawhide**/*Incident of the Druid Curse, Incident of the Haunted Hills;* **Wagon Train**/*The River Crossing.* 1960: **Hawaiian Eye**/*The Lady's Not for Travelling, Second Fiddle, Sword of the Samurai;* **The Alaskans**/*Kangaroo Court;* **Bronco**/*Winter Kill.* 1961: **Rawhide**/*The Long Count;* **The Outlaws**/*Shorty;* **Perry Mason**/*The Case of the Crippled Cougar.* 1962: **Laramie**/*The Betrayers, The Dispossessed.* **Perry Mason**/*Case of the Promoter's Pillbox, Case of the Hateful Hero, Case of the Weary Watchdog, Case of the Polka Dot Pony, Case of the Prankish Professor, Case of the Surplus Suitor, Case of the Lawful Lazarus, Case of the Greek Goddess, Case of the Potted Planter.* 1963: **Laramie**/*The Stranger, The Wedding Party;* **Perry Mason**/*Case of the Drowsy Mosquito, Case of the Deadly Verdict, Case of the Reluctant Model, Case of the Bouncing Boomerang, Case of the Capering Camera, Case of the Ice Cold Hands, Case of the Arrogant Arsonist, Case of the Careless Kidnapper.* 1964: **Perry Mason**/*Case of the Sleepy Slayer, Case of the Reckless Rockhound, Case of the Latent Lover, Case of the Ruinous Road, Case of the Golden Venom, Case of the Sad Sicilian, Case of the Deadly Debt, Case of the Grinning Gorilla, Case of the Mischievous Doll.* 1965: **Rawhide**/*Prairie Fire;* **Perry Mason**/*Case of the Laughing Lady, Case of the Runaway Racer, Case of the Candy Queen, Case of the Twelfth Wildcat, Case of the Silent Six, Case of the Golden Girls, Case of the Midnight Howler, Case of the Golfer's Gambit, Case of the Sausalito Sunrise, Case of the Fanciful Frail, Case of the Positive Negative, Case of the Final Fadeout.* 1966: **Wild Wild West**/*Night of the Lord of Limbo;* **The FBI**/*The Tormentors;* **Iron Horse**/*The Pride at the Bottom of the Barrel, Broken Gun.* 1967: **The Invaders**/*The Saucer, The Watchers, Valley of the Shadow.*

Like Charles Haas, Hibbs recommended himself to cultists through RIDE CLEAR OF DIABLO, BLACK HORSE CANYON and other top quality Universal westerns of the '50s. Overall, his career seems more substantial, largely because of his five-year stint on **Perry Mason.** Courtroom capers, however, never seem as entertaining as romps on the range, and it is as a specialist in the western that Hibbs's talent was best employed.

Jerry Hopper (1907-   )

1958: **Wagon Train**/*The Jennifer Churchill Story, The Annie Griffith Story, The Conchita Vasquez Story, The Bernal Sierra Story, The Millie Davis Story, The Mark Hanford Story;* **Cheyenne**/*Counterfeit Gun;* **The Rifleman**/*End of a Young Gun.* 1959: **Wagon Train**/*The Alexander Portlass Story, The Dick Jarvis Story, The Shadrack Bennington Story, The Vincent Eaglewood Story, The Clara Duncan Story, The Vittorio Botticelli Story, The Lita Foladaire Story.* 1960: **Wagon Train**/*The Horace Best Story, The Roger Bigelow Story;* **M Squad**/*Race to Death;* **The Untouchables**/*The Dutch Schultz Story.* 1961: **Perry Mason**/*Case of the Roving River, Case of the Left Handed Liar, Case of the Tarnished Trademark, Case of the Counterfeit Crank.* 1962: **Alfred Hitchcock Hour**/*Day of Reckoning;* **M Squad/Zane Grey Theatre**/*Ballad for a Badman.* 1963: **The Fugitive**/*Ticket to Alaska;* **Have Gun-Will Travel**/*Marshal of Sweetwater, Man in an Hourglass, Trouble at Table Rock, Bob Wire, The Unforgiving Minute, American Primitive.* 1964: **The Fugitive**/*The Homecoming, Terror at High Point, Flight from the Final Demon;* **Burke's Law**/*Who Killed the Card?, Who Killed the Toy Soldier?, Who Killed Wimbledon Hastings?* 1965: **Perry Mason**/*Case of the Scarlet Scandal, Case of the Avenging, Case of the Misguided Model, Case of the Crafty Kidnapper;* **Burke's Law**/*Who Killed the Thirteenth Clown?, Who Killed Nobody Somebody?, Who Killed the Rabbit's Husband?, Who Killed Mr Colby in Ladies Lingerie?;* **Voyage to the Bottom of the Sea**/*The Left-Handed Man;* **Amos Burke–Secret Agent**/*The Man's Man.* 1966: **Voyage to the Bottom of the Sea**/*The Day the World Ended, Day of Evil, The Mermaid;* **The Time Tunnel**/*Devil's Island;* **Man Called Shenandoah**/*The Lost Diablo;* **The Fugitive**/ *Coralee.* 1967: **Voyage to the Bottom of the Sea**/*Doomsday Island, Deadly Cloud, Sealed Orders, Fatal Cargo, Time Lock, Terror, The Deadly Amphibians, The Terrible Leprechaun.* 1968: **Voyage to the Bottom of the Sea**/*Manbeast, Attack!* 1969: **It Takes a Thief**/*Catspaw.*

There was more energy than style in Hopper's features—he had something to show but couldn't show it. A rough-around-the-edges look, however, when transposed to the often conventionally framed and lit TV image can become an asset.

The western shows which proliferated in the '50s were an inevitable haven for people like Hopper, but he was making it into a more varied and challenging league with **Alfred Hitchcock Hour** and **The Fugitive** when he became seduced by the superficial sophistication of **Burke's Law.** Then he dropped his guard, for suddenly he slipped and fell into the clutches of Irwin Allen and **Voyage to the Bottom of the Sea.** Although it was much loved by its kidvid audience and boasted relatively high budgets and super FX, a self-regarding director with any remaining ambition would not spend long earning a living on it. Significantly, Hopper faded from the screen shortly afterwards, his energy, perhaps, finally spent.

But while it lasted, he beefed up formulas and brought a distinctive touch to even minor affairs. Overall, his TV work was an honourable segue from big to small screen.

Paul Landres (1912-   )

1955: **Topper** (multiples). 1956: **Wyatt Earp** (multiples). 1957: **Blondie** (multiples). 1958:

Colt .45/*Impasse;* **The Rifleman** (multiples); **Man with a Camera** (multiples). 1959: **Bonanza** (multiples); **The Detectives** (multiples); **Law of the Plainsman** (multiples). 1960: **Maverick**/*The Devil's Necklace* (2 pts; aka *To Kill a Brigadier), Substitute Gun, Benefit of the Doubt;* **The Brothers Brannagan**/*Overexposed, The Model Murder, A Very Special Woman, Advantage: Death;* **Hawaiian Eye**/*Stan City, The Meeting on Molokai, Blackmail in Satin.* 1961: **Bronco**/*Trail of Hatred, A Sure Thing;* **Lawman**/*Jailbreak;* **Cheyenne**/*Cross Purpose, Winchester Quarantine, Retaliation;* **Surfside 6**/*The Green Beret, Elegy for a Bookkeeper, Masquerade, The Quarterback;* **Hawaiian Eye**/*Maid in America, Jefferson Chu, The Queen from Karen County.* 1962: **Bronco**/*Until Kingdom Come, Moment of Doubt, A Town that Lived and Died;* **Cheyenne**/*Indian Gold, The Quick and the Deadly, Wanted for the Murder of Cheyenne Bodie;* **77 Sunset Strip**/*The Catspaw Caper, The Reluctant Spy, The Tarnished Idol, Falling Stars, The Heartbreak Caper, The Man Who Wasn't There, Crashout, Six Feet Under.* 1963: **The Dakotas**/*Thunder in Pleasant Valley, Requiem at Dancer's Hill.* 1964: **Flipper**/*Flipper and the Horse Thieves, Flipper's Odyssey* (2 pts), *Slingshot, Gift Dolphin.* 1966: **Daktari** (multiples). 1968: **The Outcasts** (multiples). 1971: **O'Hara–US Treasury**/*Operation: Moonshine.*

A former film editor, Landres graduated to feature and TV direction in the '50s, turning out some interesting second-feature fantasy pictures (THE VAMPIRE etc.) while FRONTIER GUN and OREGON PASSAGE nudged *Vingt Ans de Cinèma Amèricain* to dub him 'one of the sure hopes of future westerns.' His TV work in the genre, in particular **Wyatt Earp** and the Warner series, saw the hopes realised but **Flipper** and **Daktari** surely dashed them.

Sidney Lanfield (1900-)

1956: **Jane Wyman Theatre** (50 segments). 1957: **Wagon Train**/*The Jean Lebec Story, The Emily Rossiter Story, The Julie Gage Story, The Jesse Cowan Story, A Man Called Horse.* 1958: **M Squad**/*The Double Face;* **General Electric Theatre** (multiples). 1959: **Cimarron City**/*Have Sword–Will Duel;* **Riverboat**/*Forbidden Island.* 1960: **The Deputy**/*Marked for Bounty, The Last Gunfight, Chain of Action;* **M Squad**/*Terror of Dark Street, Robber's Roost, Decoy in White.* 1961: **The Deputy**/*The Lucifer Urge, The Silent Gun, The Hidden Motive, Lady with a Mission, Palace of Chance, Trail of Darkness.* 1962: **Alcoa Premiere** (multiples); **McHales Navy** (60 segments). 1963: **Checkmate**/*Don't Believe a Word She Says;* **Bachelor Father** (20 segments). 1964: **No Time for Sergeants**/*Do Me a Favour and Don't Do Me Any, Spirit of '75;* **Burke's Law**/*Who Killed 711?*

Lanfield had no really distinctive personality, but was adept enough to bring off some good Bob Hope vehicles in the '40s (SORROWFUL JONES being amongst the best). He was a house director somewhere down the line from **Mitchell Leisen**.

His TV work is heavily weighted in favour of comedy, but he was considered grand enough to take care of fifty **Jane Wyman Theatre** segments. He helped, along with John Ford, John Brahm, Tay Garnett and other 'prestigious' big screen directors, to get **Wagon Train** off to an important start, and was a regular on the Henry Fonda **Deputy** series. He didn't have dirty enough finger nails to bring any bite to westerns. Sixty **McHale's Navys** and twenty **Bachelor**

Fathers could not shape up to one top-rate Hollywood feature comedy. For Lanfield, TV was indeed an Elephants' Graveyard.

Philip Leacock (1917-   )

1961: **Route 66**/*Ten Drops of Water, Three Sides, Legacy for Lucia.* 1963: **The Great Adventure**/*The Pirate and the Patriot, The Night Raiders, Kentucky's Bloody Ground, Rodger Young.* 1964: **Alfred Hitchcock Hour**/*Bed of Roses;* **The Defenders**/*Hero of the People, Conflict of Interests;* **Rawhide**/*Piney, El Hombre Bravo;* **Gunsmoke** (series pr). 1965: **Danger Man**/*The Colonel's Daughter.* 1966: **Gunsmoke** (series pr). 1969: **Marcus Welby MD**/*Madonna with Knapsack and Flute, Celia, The Pack Rat, The Sisters, The Thieves, The Devil's Outpost, Jake MacGraw, Roots of Fear;* **Paris 7000**/*No Place to Hide.* 1970: **Men from Shiloh**/*With Love, Bullets and Valentines;* **The Most Deadly Game**/*Little David* (pilot); **Mod Squad**/*A Bummer for R.J., Color of Laughter–Color of Tears;* **Gunsmoke**/*The Witness, Ma Colter, Noon Day Devil;* **Marcus Welby MD**/*To Carry the Sun in a Golden Cup.* 1971: **When Michael Calls; The Birdmen; Gumsmoke**/*New Doctor in Town;* **Bonanza**/*A Time to Die;* **Mod Squad**/*Outside Position, Essay on Getting Involved.* 1972: **Baffled, The Daughters of Joshua Cabe; Cannon**/*Bad Cats and Sudden Death;* **The FBI**/*A Game of Chess;* **Search**/*One of our Probes is Missing;* **Key West.** 1973: **Dying Room Only; The Great Man's Whiskers; The FBI**/*Sweet Evil;* **The Waltons**/*The Minstrel.* 1975: **Hawaii Five-O** (series pr) *Hollywood* (+ dir) *Wooden Model of a Rat, A Killer Grown Wings.* 1976: **Hawaii Five-O**/*Oldest Profession–Latest Price, The Last of the Great Paperhangers.* 1977: **Wild and Woolly; The Waltons**/*The Milestone, The Volunteer.*

Nobody knew what to make of Leacock and his career as a director in England in the 1950s. Was he unusually sensitive to the minds of children (THE KIDNAPPERS, ESCAPADE, THE SPANISH GARDNER, INNOCENT SINNERS) or did his rare understanding of social patterns, as revealed fully in REACH FOR GLORY and (unsuccessfully) in the American LET NO MAN WRITE MY EPITAPH, indicate that the sensitivity was an excuse, a device to hide from reality? Raymond Durgnat describes REACH FOR GLORY as having 'another kind of impressiveness, that of everyday experience suddenly clarified by unexpected patterns.'

In retrospect, one can see that Leacock lacked a cultural climate in England which allowed for head-on confrontations with the 'unexpected patterns', an ambience in which his sensitivity could be channelled to more mature themes and subjects. If only the English genre film allowed scenes such as that in WHITE HEAT where James Cagney climbs onto his mother's lap and cries. Imagine Jack Hawkins doing that, or Dirk Bogarde, or even Stanley Baker!

Retreating, possibly in despair, from the creative confusions and anomalies of English cinema, Leacock has busied himself with American telefilm since 1961. He has, one might say, submerged himself in it, **Route 66** and **The Great Adventure** gradually gave way to **Mod Squad** and **Cannon.** Leacock apparently lost what were once virtues in the competitive jungle of Hollywood.

On the way he has become involved in the production scene, producing **Gunsmoke** and **Hawaii Five-O.** Telefilms he has directed, like **Birdmen** and **Key West,** are, by his original standards, exceptionally poor. But **Dying Room Only,** from a script by Richard Matheson, restores the balance.

An investigation into the second phase of his career seems to yield little of value. It should be seriously undertaken, however, if only by English cineastes bemused by the vagaries of their native cinema. Leacock was once one of its brightest talents, and it is hard to believe it was the light that failed.

Mitchell Leisen (1898-)

1958: **Shirley Temple's Story Book** (multiples). 1959: **The Twilight Zone**/*The Sixteen-Millimeter Shrine, Escape Clause;* **Adventures in Paradise** (multiples); **Markham** (multiples). 1960: **The Twilight Zone**/*People Are Alike All Over;* **Thriller**/*Worse Than Murder, Girl with a Secret;* **Wagon Train**/*The Patience Miller Story, The Prairie Story.* 1961: **Follow the Sun** (multiples); **Empire** (multiples). 1966: **The Girl from UNCLE**/*The Danish Blue Affair.* 1967: **The Girl from UNCLE**/*The Double Gratz Affair, The Petit Prix Affair.*

With the exception of **Shirley Temple's Story Book** and **The Girl from UNCLE,** it would seem that little in Leisen's TV career has any of the spirit and style to be found in his Paramount light comedies and love stories which his admirers are still struggling to make better known.

His *People Are Alike All Over* is one of the best early **Twilight Zones. Markham** reunited him with Ray Milland and reputedly gave both the star and the director a free hand. It is hard to believe that someone as resolutely stylish as Leisen would have thrown in the towel when faced with the demanding strictures of TV. And he didn't. When somebody, at last, talks a Film Theatre into a Leisen retrospective, maybe it will include the best examples of the final phase of his consistently creative career.

Joseph H. Lewis (1900-)

1958: **Rifleman**/*Duel of Honour, The Safe Guard.* 1959: **Rifleman**/*Panic.* 1960: **Detectives**/*The Hiding Place;* **Rifleman**/*Closer than a Brother.* 1964: **Gunsmoke**/*One Killer on Ice.* 1965: **Big Valley**/*Boots with My Father's Name, Night of the Wolf;* **Branded** *(pilot).* 1966: **Man Called Shenandoah**/*Incident at Dry Creek, The Death of Matthew Eldridge, Plunder;* **Big Valley**/*The Man from Nowhere.*

Any cineaste newly alerted to the strange delights of GUN CRAZY, THE BIG COMBO, A LAWLESS STREET *et al* would, if reading Sarris, assume that Lewis stopped working in 1958. But he carried on conjuring up weird niceties for at least another eight years—as teleastes know. Our list is incomplete and more segments of **Rifleman, Detectives** and **Big Valley** are likely, along with other Four Star Productions (**Zane Grey Theatre, Lloyd Bridges Show, Law of the Plainsman**). Lewis's TV work picks up where his big screen work leaves off. *One Killer on Ice,* with John Drew Barrymore, has certain tangental affinities with GUN CRAZY and is a strange episode of **Gunsmoke**. Best of all are two **Big Valleys**—*Boots with My Father's Name* dealing with the hidden past of Barbara Stanwyck's dead husband which she endeavours to track down in a deserted mining town on the eve of a celebration honouring his memory; and *Night of the Wolf,* with Peter Breck faced with imminent death (through anthrax) and endeavouring to re-examine his life and attitudes. Both characters (especially an insane Breck, frothing at the mouth and crawling helplessly around a bemused town) and theme—the attempt in the present to re-make the past—have very clear echoes of A LAWLESS STREET and SEVENTH CAVALRY and are, in all respects, very worthy companions to the more widely known films, as well as being most unique personal series segments.

It is hard not to believe that Lewis's eight 'missing' years do not include more intriguing work—and this should be speedily hunted down and added to his small, but triumphantly distinctive canon.

Arthur Lubin (1901-)

1958: **Maverick**/*Duel at Sundown, Maverick Springs.* 1959: **Maverick**/*Royal Four Flush, Cats of Paradise, The Marquesa, Maverick and Juliet, Guatemala City, A Flock of Trouble, Greenbacks Unlimited, The Misfortune Teller;* **Cheyenne**/*Outcast of Cripple Creek;* **77 Sunset Strip**/*The Widow Wouldn't Weep, Mr Paradise, The Clay Pigeon;* **The Deputy**/*Proof of Guilt.* 1960: **Bronco**/*Game at the Beacon Club.* 1961: **Bonanza** (multiples). 1963: **Mister Ed** (pr/dir entire series).

Although most of Lubin's movie career passed justifiably unnoticed, there were odd highs dotted about—the Claude Rains PHANTOM OF THE OPERA, STAR OF INDIA a curious Cornell Wilde costume caper, FOOTSTEPS IN THE FOG, a moody GASLIGHT variation with Stewart Granger and Jean Simmons. Mainly though, Lubin dealt with comedy—Abbott and Costello, Maria Montez and one film a year from 1949-1955 featuring Donald O'Connor and FRANCIS THE TALKING MULE.

His TV work follows the same pattern. His **Mavericks** are the highs—in those segments featuring Henry Fonda. Comedy began to dominate his TV career, particularly when it was realised that talking quadrupeds had not yet been seen on the small screen. Thus 'Francis' became 'Mr. Ed', a talking horse, with Alan Young a fair imitation of Donald O'Connor, and Lubin produced and directed the entire series. Who said the studio system was over?

Lewis Milestone (1895-　　)

1958: **Have Gun-Will Travel**/*The Girl from Piccadilly, Hey Boy's Revenge.* 1964: **Arrest and Trial**/*An Echo of Conscience.*

Milestone was busy—and presumably well paid—on OCEANS 11 and MUTINY ON THE BOUNTY through the early 60's and had no need for, nor interest in, TV. His TV work is sparse: **Have Gun-Will Travel** represents a reunion with Richard Boone, probably undertaken for reasons of friendship. *Girl from Piccadilly* the 23rd segment of **Have Gun-Will Travel** to be telecast was the first not to be directed by Andrew V. McLaglen, and represents a change of style but not of concept. *An Echo of Conscience* was, however, a purely conventional **Arrest and Trial** and perhaps its very title made the director of ALL QUIET ON THE WESTERN FRONT decide to stay home, where, as Ring Lardner put it, 'You don't have to say nuthin when there's nuthin to say.'

Joseph H. Newman (1909-　　)

1962: **Alfred Hitchcock Hour**/*Dear Uncle George.* 1963: **Alfred Hitchcock Hour**/*Three Wives Too Many, Death of a Cop, Body in the Barn;* **Twilight Zone**/*In Praise of Pip, The Last Night of a Jockey, Black Leather Jackets.* 1964: **Alfred Hitchcock Hour**/*The Beast in View, The Gentleman Caller, See the Monkey Dance, Misadventure;* **Twilight Zone**/*Bewitchin' Pool.* 1965: **Alfred Hitchcock Hour**/*An Unlocked Window, The Second Wife;* **Big Valley**/*The Way to Kill a Killer.*

Newman's sparse TV credits are all extremely interesting; the minor but constantly rewarding virtues of 711 OCEAN DRIVE, OUTCASTS OF POKER FLAT and A THUNDER OF DRUMS were equalled by the majority of the **Alfred Hitchcock** shows. The latter were a curiously symmetrical way to bring to a close the career which began with CRIME DOES NOT PAY MGM shorts.

Death of a Cop by Leigh Brackett (who helped create two very different Philip Marlowes for Howard Hawks and Robert Altman); *See the Monkey Dance*, from a novel by the excellent Margaret Miller; *The Gentlemen Caller*, written by James Bridges; *The Second Wife*, written by Robert Bloch; *An Unlocked Window*, from a novel by Ethel Lina White (who wrote *The Wheel Spins* which formed the basis for THE LADY VANISHES)—the material Newman was working with provided a remarkably sure foundation. In addition, the ace black and white cameraman Stanley Cortez lit *An Unlocked Window*, helping to give a visual sheen to this treasure of aberration.

Gerd Oswald (1916-   )

1955: **20th Century Fox Presents**/*The Ox-Bow Incident.* 1958: **Perry Mason**/*The Case of the Purple Woman, The Case of the Jaded Joker, The Case of the Lost Last Act;* **Ford Theatre** (multiples). 1960: **General Electric Hour** (multiples); **Playhouse 90** (multiples). 1962: **Adventures in Paradise**/*Isle of Eden;* **Rawhide** (multiples). 1963: **The Fugitive** (multiples); **Outer Limits**/*O.B.I.T., Corpus Earthling, It Crawled out of the Woodwork, The Mice, Don't Open Till Doomsday, The Invisibles, The Bellero Shield, Speciman Unknown, Fun and Games.* 1964: **Daniel Boone** (multiples); **Bonanza**/*Five Sundowns to Sunup, The Spotlight, The Deadliest Game;* **Temple Houston**/*Toll the Bell Slowly.* 1965: **The Legend of Jesse James**/*The Pursuers;* **Voyage to the Bottom of the Sea**/*Hail to the Chief;* **Outer Limits**/*The Special One, The Chameleon, The Forms of Things Unknown, Soldier, Expanding Human, The Duplicate Man, The Premonition.* 1966: **Star Trek**/*The Conscience of the King;* **Bonanza**/*Destiny's Child, The Oath, The Unwritten Commandment;* **Blue Light** (multiples); **Shane** (multiples). 1967: **Star Trek**/*The Alternative Factor;* **Gentle Ben**/*Take a Giant Step, Greener Pastures, The Haunted Castle, The Great Mailboat Robbery, Mark of the Arrow, The Prey, Busman's Holiday.* 1968: **Felony Squad**/*Time of Trial;* **Gentle Ben**/*Moma Jolie, Fire in the Glades, Survival in the Swamp, Ol' Joe's Gotta Go, The Wall That Tom and Mark Built, The Intruders, Starr of Green Bay!* 1969: **It Takes a Thief** (multiples). 1970: **Nichols** (multiples).

Oswald's career, from the obvious highs of **Outer Limits** to the apparent lows of **Gentle Ben** seems as confusingly unsatisfying as his movie career. However, it is not a big leap from five-to-seven day B movie shooting schedules to TV pressures.

His style ('a fluency of camera movement is controlled by sliding turns and harsh stops befitting a cinema of bitter ambiguity' says Sarris) was likely to suffer more.

Certainly in his two **Star Trek** segments there is a sense of the Oswald personality. The anti-fascist sentiments evident in his features are quite dominant in *Conscience of the King* which is a 'Hamlet'-like trial-within-a-play of a notorious Fascist warlord whose Hitlerian conquests have been over planets, not countries. *The Alternative Factor* builds from mystery to the ultimate threat of holocaust on a Jekyll/Hyde theme. There is an immense magnetic phenomenon fracturing space from end to end and 'creating' the entities Lazarus A and Lazarus B who, once they meet and fuse together, will implode and erase the entire universe. Here we see Oswald's fear and loathing of a 'final solution' symbolised by some Armageddon. Certainly, the feeling of both segments is less 'fantastic' than psychologically tortured. Oswald was no stranger to the game, and his sixteen **Outer Limits** allowed for similar personal involvement. Best—the most famous anyway—of all, is *Soldier,* Harlan Ellison's own adaptation of his short story, a chillingly bleak view of future-war and the dehumanisation of personality. Here again is the Oswald ambiguity: 'did the soldier kill to protect those he had come to care for or did he revert to his instincts? They are questions from the dark pit. There are no answers; these lie in the future. Is it a future in which men are machines born to kill, or is there time for us . . .?' says the closing narration.

Rawhide and **Fugitive** hide other interesting Oswald pieces. He bowed out with a virtually unknown James Garner series, **Nichols**, which is now fast becoming a cult. Sarris lamented critical indifference to Oswald's films. Sadly there is a need to echo him in this respect. No doubt he will be 'discovered' when someone wants to make a name for himself.

Joseph Pevney (1920-)

1958: **Wagon Train**/*The Vivian Carter Story, The Felizia Kingdom Story, The Sister Rita Story, The Saul Bevins Story.* 1959: **Wagon Train**/*The Amos Gibbon Story, The Sam Livingston Story;* **Johnny Staccato** (multiples). 1961: **Alcoa Premiere**/*The Fortress.* 1962: **Alfred Hitchcock Hour**/*Memo from Purgatory, Starring the Defense.* 1963: **Alfred Hitchcock Hour**/*A Nice Touch, The Trunk, Bonfire.* 1964: **Bewitched**/*Your Witch Is Showing;* **Alfred Hitchcock Hour**/*One of the Family.* 1965: **Legend of Jesse James**/*A Field of Wild Flowers;* **The Big Valley**/*The Brawlers;* **The Munsters**/*Love Comes to Mockingbird Heights.* 1966: **The Loner**/*Widow on the Evening Stage;* **Star Trek**/*Arena.* 1967: **Star Trek**/*Return of the Archons, A Taste of Armageddon, The Devil in the Dark, City on the Edge of Forever, Amok Time, The Apple, Catspaw, Journey to Babel, Friday's Child, The Deadly Years, Wolf in the Fold, The Trouble with Tribbles.* 1968: **Star Trek**/*The Immunity Syndrome;* **High Chapparal**/*Tornado Frances, The Promised Land, A Way of Justice, Shadow of the Land, The Last 100 Miles, Once on a Day in Spring.* 1969: **The Virginian**/*A Love to Remember, A King's Ransom, A Flash of Darkness, The Family Man, A Time of Terror, Black Jade;* **Adam 12**/*Hostage, A Sound Like Thunder, Impersonator, The Hero Bank Robbery, Exactly One Hundred Yards.* 1970: **The Name of the Game**/*The Glory Shooter.* 1971: **The Partners**/*Witness for the Execution.* 1972: **Search**/*The Adonis File.* 1973: **My Darling Daughters; Marcus Welby MD**/*Blood Kin.* 1974: **Emergency**/*The Smoke Eater, Surprise, The Firehouse Four, It's How You Play the Game;* **Petrocelli**/*The Golden Cage, Four the Hard Way;* **Marcus Welby MD**/*Out of Control;* **Adam 12**/*Follow Up.* 1975: **Marcus Welby MD**/*How Do You Know What Hurts Me?;* **Mobile One**/*Murder at Fourteen, The Crusade, The Boxer;* **Who Is the Black Dahlia?; Executive Suite**/*A Day Full of Surprises.* 1976: **Emergency**/*The Great Crash Diet, One of These Days;* **Sara**/*The Bright Boy;* **Marcus Welby MD**/*Aspects of Love;* **The Hardy Boys**/*Meet Dracula* (2 pts), *The African Safari.* 1977: **Nancy Drew Mysteries**/*Nancy Drew's Love Match, The Lady of Thursday at Ten;* **Lannigan's Rabbi**/*The Cadaver in the Clutter;* **Kingston: Confidential**/*Eight Columns across the Top, Monolith.*

One of the more interesting of the second-string of Universal feature directors of the '50s, Pevney climbed from programmers to large-scale projects (AWAY ALL BOATS, TWILIGHT FOR THE GODS, MAN OF A THOUSAND FACES) but was always better with the less-pretentious (DESERT LEGION) or the small scale (FEMALE ON THE BEACH and SIX BRIDGES TO CROSS); his best film THE PLUNDERERS, is among his last, made in 1960, when he had already begun to swim with the TV tide. Throughout the last two decades, he has brought the traditional virtues of features to the small screen and his best work is always positive and punchy. His early training as an actor is reflected in his rapport with his performers.

His **Alfred Hitchcock** segments are among his best—particularly *Memo from Purgatory*, adapted by Harlan Ellison from his book 'Memos from . . ., with James Caan playing the author in a biographical memoir of his days on the mean streets. The association later produced one of the finest pieces of genre TV—*The City on the Edge of Forever* for **Star Trek.**

A mentally-loose Dr. McCoy (DeForrest Kelley) leaps into a time warp—and to retrieve him, Kirk (William Shatner) and Spock (Leonard Nimoy) follow—to find themselves on earth in the 1920s. Now, of course, they are 'aliens', possessing, as they do, enormously more sophisticated knowledge than is available to those around them, as well as a knowledge of the 'future'. Kirk becomes attracted to Edith (Joan Collins) who runs a soup kitchen for derelicts of the depression (the milieu allowed for a few barbed remarks about capitalism), but Spock, having lashed up a communications device to help locate McCoy, discovers on the screen, parallel hypothetical futures. In one, Edith becomes a kind of civil-rights leader, and Hitler wins World War 2. In the other, history proceeds as we know it—but Edith dies in a pointless automobile accident, her value to humanity snuffed out. It is within Kirk's power to save her—but in doing so, he would change the course of history. The moral and human problems, along with the fascinating theories of the 'interference' with time (which are common enough in sci-fi writing but are relatively rare on the screen), as well as the superb pace and involvement with the characters, show Ellison (angry at the way his script was 'necessarily', they said, diluted for the sake of formula and censorship) and Pevney, illustrating how potent a vehicle for ideas and myth, genre TV can be.

In all, Pevney did fourteen **Star Treks**; he seems to have been able to excercise choice and control over the scripts on which he worked. Certainly his other entries are of the highest order—*Wolf in the Fold*, a Robert Bloch-written variation on the Jack the Ripper theme; *Catspaw* also by Bloch; *The Devil in the Dark; The Immunity Syndrome* and *A Taste for Armageddon* (where war is waged by computers).

If we add to these superior segments Pevney's western titles, there is an impressive collection of high quality work.

Since 1970 interest has trailed off in Pevney, who seems to have been coasting, tiring perhaps of the rigours of the medium, which has offered him uninteresting series like **Petrocelli** and the monotonous **Emergency**. In both, the format inhibits expression by writer and director alike, rather than providing a framework for it, which is the essence of genre. His projects may pick up: if they do not, and continue to reflect an apparent apathy, they will nevertheless, always be worth a look.

Lesley Selander (1900-   )

1955: **Fury** (multiples). 1957: **Lassie** (multiples). 1959: **Cannonball**/*The Has-Been, The Iron*

Lung, Small Cargo; **Laramie** (multiples). 1960: **The Tall Man** (multiples); **Laramie/***The Invaders, Duel at Alta Mesa.* 1961: **Frontier Circus** (multiples); **Laramie/***Dragon at the Door.* 1962: **Laramie/***Beyond Justice, No Place to Run, Renegade Brand, The Violent Ones.* 1967: **Laramie/** *Last Battleground.*

It seemed that William K. Everson spent more pages of *The Western* discussing Selander than Boetticher, Mann, Daves, and Peckinpah put together. We include Selander here as homage to Bill, and also because Selander probably set more juvenile hearts a'pounding with his Buck Jones, Hopalong Cassidy, Tim Holt, Red Ryder movies than any other series director. His TV is more of the same. The heart, however, didn't pound at a fraction of the pace.

George Sherman (1908-)

1962: **Naked City/***Make It Fifty Dollars and Add Love to Nona.* 1963: **Naked City/***Her Life in Moving Pictures, Beyond This Place, There Be Dragons, Man Without Skin, Dust Devil on a Quiet Street.* 1964: **Mr Broadway/***Bad Little Rich Girl;* **Daniel Boone** (series pr and multiples). 1967: **Gentle Ben** (series pr + dir) *Fish and Chips.* 1975: **Mobile One/***Libel, Not by Accident, The Listening Ear;* **The Family Holvak/***The Wedding, The Devil's Chariot.*

Along with Carr and Witney, Sherman is one of the few ex-B movie directors able to respond to large challenges. His TV work has been primarily as a producer though, curiously, his directing credits are on more upmarket fare than one would have suspected (**Naked City, Route 66**, etc.). Only those familiar with the **Daniel Boone** series will know that Sherman brought the surprising qualities of THE LAST OF THE FAST GUNS and especially HELL BENT FOR LEATHER to his TV productions.

Vincent Sherman (1906-)

1959: **77 Sunset Strip/***The Fifth Stair.* 1969: **Medical Centre** (12 segments). 1970: **The Bold Ones; The Lawyers/***The Crowd Pleaser.* 1971: **Alias Smith and Jones/***Miracle at Santa Marta.* 1975: **Doctor's Hospital/***The Loneliest Night, Come at Last to Love;* **Baretta/***The Blood Bond, Street Edition, Look Back in Terror;* **Westside Medical/***Sticks and Stones;* **Executive Suite.**

Sherman's features never really set the screen on fire, but OLD ACQUAINTANCE, THE UNFAITHFUL, THE ADVENTURES OF DON JUAN, etc. were stuffed with old school Warner virtues. Sherman brought these qualities to his disparate, stop-start TV career. His **Executive Suites** are a lush reminder of traditional filmmaking; Along with an affinity for woman's magazine work, the various medical shows made use of his ability to respond to 'soft' material. At seventy-two, however, Sherman is unlikely to be able to capitalise on the miniseries format which might have been tailor-made for him.

Lee Sholem

1953: **The Adventures of Superman**/*A Night of Terror, The Birthday Letter, The Mind Machine, No Holds Barred, The Stolen Costume, Mystery in Wax, Drums of Death, The Human Bomb, The Ghost Wolf, The Unknown People* (the latter a two part show edited *from* the feature SUPERMAN AND THE MOLE MEN). 1955: **Adventures of Long John Silver**/*Miss Purity's Birthday* (co-dir w/Byron Haskin). 1956: **Cheyenne**/*Backfire.* 1957: **Sheriff of Cochise**/*The Friends, Cain and Abel, Question of Honor, The Great Train Robbery, Father and Son, Manhunt, Wyatt Earp, Helldorado, Grandfather–Grandson;* **Sugarfoot**/*The Bullet and the Cross;* **Colt .45**/*Return to El Paso.* 1958: **Cheyenne**/*The Long Search, White Terror, Ghost of the Cimmarron, Wagon-Tongue North;* **Sugarfoot**/*The Ghost, Devil to Pay, The Extra Hand;* **Bronco**/*Freeze-Out, Baron of Broken Lance;* **Sheriff of Cochise**/*Robbery;* **77 Sunset Strip**/*The Court Martial of Johnny Murdo;* **Lawman**/*The Badge.* 1959: **Cheyenne**/*Trial by Conscience, The Imposter, Blind Spot;* **Bronco**/*The Belle of Silver Flat, Backfire, School for Cowards, Hero of the Town, Red Water North, Quest of the Thirty Dead, Payroll of the Dead, Bodyguard, The Last Resort, The Devil's Spawn;* **Sugarfoot**/*Return to Boothill;* **Colt .45**/*Ghost Town;* **Lawman**/*The Bandit, The Wayfarer.* 1960: **Cheyenne**/*Incident at Dawson Flats, The Return of Mr Grimm;* **Bronco**/*The Human Equation;* **Colt .45**/*The Escape, Showdown at Goldtown, Appointment in Agoura.* 1961: **Maverick**/*A Bullet for the Teacher, Last Wire from Stop Gap, One of Our Trains is Missing, The Money Machine;* **Cheyenne**/*The Beholden, The Greater Glory;* **Colt .45**/*The Trespasser, Bounty List, Dead Aim.*

Known to his Warner contemporaries as 'Roll 'em Sholem' for the speed of his shooting, and because he could shout very loud. 'I never heard a guy scream as loud as Sholem did when he cut a scene. He'd get it all done and yell at the top of his lungs, C-U-T!' remembers Whitney Ellsworth, **Superman** producer. Hard to picture such dynamism on the set of the 200 **This Is the Life**'s that Sholem later directed for the Lutheran church. They brought a modestly enthusiastic career to a curious close.

R. G. Springsteen (1904-   )

1958: **Whirly Birds**/*Wanted–Alive, The Deacon, Rita Ames Is Missing, The Story of Mary Scott, Mr Jinx, File 77, Hot Cargo, Shootout, Man You Kill Me.* 1959: **Gunsmoke**/*Brother Whelp.* 1960: **Rawhide**/*Incident of the Broken Word, Incident near Gloomy River, Incident in the Middle of Nowhere, Incident of the Blackstorms, Incident on the Road to Yesterday;* **Riverboat**/*Fight at New Canal;* **Trackdown**/*Saturday's Child;* **Wagon Train**/*The Jane Hawkins Story.* 1961: **Trackdown**/*The Feud, The Samaritan, The Protector, The Trick, Back to Crawford.* 1965: **Bonanza**/*The Trouble with Jamie, The Last Mission, The Reluctant Rebel;* **Laredo**/*The Land Grabbers, A Matter of Policy.* 1967: **Gentle Ben**/*Jennifer, A Medal for Ben.* 1968: **Gentle Ben**/*Warden in the Bear Pit, A Waste of Honey, Trophy Bear, The Opportunist, The Battle of Birthday Bay.*

Like Selander, Springsteen toiled in the B western vineyards, and those who have the gift to distinguish between such look-alike artisans would give Selander marks for energy, Springsteen marks for sobriety. Indeed, his films are often stolid, sometimes joyless. His TV work—**Rawhide** and **Trackdown** in particular—brought out the best in him. On the big screen this was only evident in COME NEXT SPRING.

Jacques Tourneur (1904-1977)

1956: **Jane Wyman Theatre** (multiples); **General Electric Theatre** (multiples). 1958: **Northwest Passage**/*The Vulture, The Traitor, The Assassin, The Hostage;* **Walter Winchell File** (multiples). 1959: **Northwest Passage**/*The Gunsmith, The Bond Women, The Burning Village;* **The Californians** (multiples); **Bonanza** (multiples). 1960: **The Alaskans**/*The Devil Makers;* **Barbara Stanwyck Theatre** (multiples); **Follow the Sun** (multiples). 1961: **Adventures in Paradise** (multiples); **Twilight Zone**/*Night Calls.*

'I used to like the live shows, ninety minutes of exciting drama. There's an immediacy, an urgency about live shows. The actors are nervous, they're on edge, they give great performances. There's the flow too of theatre in live television, it builds, the actor gives a continuous performance. But now I dislike television very much. I do it to exist, to survive.'

Sad words from 1964, when Tourneur made his last feature in England. Those who admire his work know that the **Northwest Passage** segments (released in theatrical versions in Europe) are barely recognisable as his. They will be undeterred, however, from attempting to track down and view other examples, although a man like Tourneur, who disliked what he was doing,was unlikely to do it very well. And he didn't.

George WaGGner (1894-)

1957: **Colt .45**/*The Magic Box.* 1958: **Cheyenne**/*Gold, Glory & Custer (Prelude), Gold, Glory & Custer (Requiem), The Rebellion;* **Colt .45**/*Arizona Anderson;* **Wagon Train**/*The John Cameron Story, The Cliff Grundy Story;* **77 Sunset Strip**/*The Girl Who Couldn't Remember.* 1959: **Maverick**/*The Sheriff of Duck 'n' Shoot, You Can't Beat the Percentage* (+ wr); **The Alaskans**/*Cheating Cheaters, Million Dollar Kid;* **Cheyenne**/*Day's Pay, The Idol;* **77 Sunset Strip**/*The Canine Caper, Strange Girl in Town, Secret Island, Lovely Alibi, Hong Kong Caper, Honey from the Bee, Only Zeroes Count, Sing Something Simple, The Treehouse Caper, The Widow and the Web, Created He Them, Ten Cents Death.* 1960: **Maverick**/*The Cactus Switch;* **The Alaskans**/*Disaster at Gold Hill;* **The Roaring 20's**/*Burnett's Woman, The Velvet Frame, Bold Edition, The Maestro, Lucky Charm;* **Cheyenne**/*Satonka;* **77 Sunset Strip**/*Condor's Lair, Safari, Return to San Dede Part 1: Capital City, Return to San*

Dede Part 2: Desert Story, Stranger than Fiction, Genesis of Treason, The Silent Caper, Sierra, The Fanatics, The Laurel Canyon Caper, The Widescreen Caper, Double Trouble, The Antwerp Caper, Once Upon a Caper; **Surfside 6**/*According to Our Files.* 1961: **The Roaring 20's**/*War with the Night Hawkers, The Salvation of Killer McFadden;* **77 Sunset Strip**/*The Space Caper, Vamp 'Til Ready, Hot Tamale Caper parts 1 and 2, The Man in the Crowd, The Unremembered, The Bel Air Hermit, Bullets for Santa, Penthouse on Skid Row;* **Hawaiian Eye**/*There'll Be Some Changes Made, Year of Grace.* 1962: **Bronco**/*Destinies West, The Mountain;* **77 Sunset Strip**/*The Pet Shop Caper, Framework for a Badge, The Left Field Caper, The Checkmate Caper, The Night Was Six Years Long, Target Island, Escape to Freedom, Stranger from the Sea.* 1963: **Cheyenne**/*Johnny Brassbuttons.* 1966: **Batman**/*An Egg Grows in Gotham—The Yegg Foes in Gotham, Green Ice-Deep Ice, Pop Goes the Joker—Flop Goes the Joker, The Wail of the Siren.*

WaGGner's tower of Warner Credits is only shaken by the monolith built up by Les Martinson, another durable member of the pack. WaGGner's big-screen work consists mainly of low-budget Universal thrillers: THE CLIMAX, THE COBRA WOMAN, and his most notable picture, THE WOLF MAN. He is also author of many screenplays and, though the crawls didn't often credit him, many collaborative teleplays. When a retrospective of early Warner Brothers TV is launched, and representative episodes are chosen from each of the series, it is unlikely that any of WaGGner's contributions will be among them. With luminaries the shape of Boetticher in **Maverick** and Altman in **Roaring 20s**, there were many able captains on board the Warners ship at that time.

But you don't need a shot of pentathol to admit that episodes like *Burnett's Woman* and the two part *Gold, Glory & Custer* are pleasing and above-average work. *Gold, Glory & Custer* is interesting in that it attempted to bring something of a small screen THEY DIED WITH THEIR BOOTS ON into a series format—but in more ways that one. Part two of the segment, *Requiem*, succeeded in being one of the stock-footage library's greatest triumphs. Poor Raoul Walsh. Sheer quantity prevents most of WaGGner's work from being anything other than routine fare. Quantity sometimes breeds exceptions; but it doesn't in this case.

William Witney (1915-)

1956: **Great Stories of the Century** (multiples); **Dr Fu Manchu** (multiples). 1957: **Frontier Doctor**/*Strangers in Town, Fury of the Big Top.* 1958: **Zorro**/*Welcome to Monteray, Zorro Rides Alone, Horse of Another Color, The Senorita Makes a Choice, Rendezvous at Sundown, The Runaways, The 'Iron' Box.* 1959: **Mike Hammer** (multiples); **Rescue 8** (multiples); **Zorro**/*Senor China Boy;* **Lassie**/*Tartan Queen.* 1960: **The Tall Man** (multiples); **Coronado 9** (multiples). 1961: **Riverboat**/*The Landlubbers, Three Graves, The Face of Courage, Night of the Faceless Men, The Treasure of Hawk Hill;* **Frontier Circus** (multiples); **Wagon Train**/*The Stagecoach Story.* 1962: **Bonanza**/*The Gamble, The Deserter, The Burma Rarity;* **The Virginian**/*The Devil's Children;* **Wells Fargo**/*Winter Storm.* 1963: **Laramie**/*Broken Honor, The Marshals;* **Bonanza**/*Between Heaven and*

Hell, The Saga of Squaw Charlie, The Wild One, The Deadly Ones; **The Virginian**/*Say Goodbye to All That, Man of Violence, A Time Remembered.* 1964: **Daniel Boone** (multiples); **Bonanza**/*The Trap, Lothario Larkin;* **Alfred Hitchcock Hour**/*Final Escape;* **The Virginian**/*Man of the People, A Man Called Kane.* 1965: **Branded**/*McCord's Way;* **The Virginian**/*Old Cowboy;* **Wild Wild West**/*Night of the Deadly Bed, Night of the Sudden Death;* **Bonanza**/*The Lonely Runner.* 1966: **The Virginian**/*Beloved Ourlaw;* **Bonanza**/*Ride the Wind (Two Parts), Horse of a Different Hue;* **Laredo**/*Limit of the Law Larkin, Treasure of San Diablo, The Sound of Terror.* 1967: **Tarzan**/*To Steal the Rising Sun, Rendezvous for Revenge, Blue Stone of Heaven (Two Parts), The Fanatic;* **Hondo**/*. . . and the Singing Wire,..., And the Apache Kid,..., And the Death Drive.* 1968: **High Chaparral**/*The Firing Wall, The Deceivers, Survival, The Stallion;* **The Virginian**/*Incident at Diablo Crossing.* 1973: **The Cowboys** (multiples). 1974: **Kodiak** (multiples).

Witney rivals Henry King's long tenure at Fox with his own twenty year devotion to Republic. Buffs treasure his vast output of serials (mainly co-directed with John English) from THE PAINTED STALLION in 1937 to G-MEN vs THE BLACK DRAGON in 1943, of which the best, ZORRO'S FIGHTING LEGION is a masterpiece of sustained action and lunatic energy. After war service, Witney made one further serial before graduating, if that's the word, to 'B' features, and working with Republic's leading western star Roy Rogers. He was responsible for toughening up the circus image then purveyed by the actor, and injecting what many thought were unacceptable levels of violence into, essentially, children's movies. He continued the treatment with Rex Allen, Rogers's replacement.

With the death of series westerns in 1954, occasioned by burgeoning TV, Witney continued in movies, and in 1954 directed his finest film, the totally undervalued THE OUTCAST. He also directed a flawed but ambitious trek-epic SANTA FE PASSAGE a year later. These films might have established him as a director in the Anthony Mann mould, but instead he continued at Republic, a studio now dying on its feet. A handful of modern thrillers made by Witney were among the last films put out by the studio, before it turned its full attention to the production of TV films. Witney obeyed orders with **Great Stories of the Century** and **The Rex Allen Frontier Doctor** Show. He might have despaired when, fully two decades after ZORRO'S FIGHTING LEGION, he found himself exhorting the murky justicier to ever greater feats of juvenile-oriented bravado, but now with the Walt Disney studios. The promise of THE OUTCAST was, however, finally matched in the 'adult' TV western.

The *Between Heaven and Earth* segment of **Bonanza** was almost a solo turn for Little Joe Cartright (Michael Landon). He attempts to conquer his fear of heights by climbing a mountain and facing his fear head-on. Splendidly written by Ed Adamson, one remembers this as a tour-de-force of what?—'psychological expressionism'? The rite of passage to manhood represented here was paralleled in *The Stallion* for **High Chaparral**: an attempt is made by the youngest member of the group, Billy Blue, (Mark Slade) to capture a wild stallion, which is also the object of a far more ritualised capture attempt by a Mescalero youth. A similar theme motivated *Say Goodbye to All That* for

Virginian, where an over-machoed rancher attempts to 'make a man' out of his son by provoking the ritual gundown with Trampas.

Equally, Witney seems to have liked to yank characters out of the series concept. In **Ride the Wind** (a two part **Bonanza** segment released as a theatrical feature in some parts of the world) Witney virtually ignored the entire **Bonanza** ranch location. Little Joe became a Pony Express rider. In **The Virginian**'s *Man of Violence* Trampas embarks on a long quest away from Shiloh to find the man who killed a close friend. Almost perversely, Witney, in a **Wagon Train** segment, busied himself instead by telling *The Stagecoach Story.* The **Laredo** format, built around the Hawksian rivalry of a quartet of Texas Rangers, allowed for Witney to broaden and coarsen the kind of fake camaraderie which is the essence of **The Virginian** and its like, while the **Hondo** series (based on the John Wayne feature) allowed for the more traditional virtues of cinema westerns to be explored.

In general terms, any segment of a western series directed by Witney was likely to be head and shoulders above the work of his colleagues—although one should perhaps beware of those featuring aged outcasts like *Old Cowboy, Squaw Charlie* and *Lothario Larkin.* Witney, like John Ford, has his blind spots. Even the **Tarzan** segments have the flavour of the west, for the series as a whole was a variation on western themes, Ron Ely's splendid ape man extended the 'justicier' figure which was first hinted at in Sy Weintraub's fine feature productions directed by Robert Day and John Guillermin. Tarzan is, in a sense, a naked Zorro.

Witney seems to be the most vital and engaging of the veteran directors. This is due to the similarity of TV pressures and restrictions to those at Republic. After coping with the delirious excesses of PERILS OF NYOKA, DAREDEVILS OF THE RED CIRCLE, SPY SMASHER, etc., the relative maturity of any TV storyline must have seemed like an encounter on a dark night with Henry James.

His action is what ultimately turns us on, for so much of the TV west consisted of characters who talked about what they were planning to do, only to be talked out of it for the benefit of the family audience. Witney shapes his action like few other directors on TV; he had a predilection for a certain shot that spans the years from ZORRO'S FIGHTING LEGION to *The Stallion.* There will be a sudden explosion of movement as the camera starts to track back, down a road/across a desert/through a forest. But, momentarily, there is nothing else to see in the frame (save the camera-truck tyre marks). Then, either from the left or right of the screen, posses/Indians/cavalry/pony riders/the heroes or the villains come charging into view. It comes from a technician who knows his audience. Witney's energy and enthusiasm in such shots, his apparent fondness for horses (*The Stallion*, the crooked horse races in *Horse of a Different Hue,* the cowboy who defies a court order and becomes an outlaw to recover his black mare in *Lonely Runner*, the killer stallion the heroine tries to tame in *Beloved Outlaw*) and for the characters and emotions of the western breed, somehow enlivened and redefined the essence of the western at a time when it was being undermined. He may only be a chamber-auteur when this small screen work is extensively examined, but his personality and special talents command attention over some more lauded artists who failed on the box.

5/How Do You Get to Carnegie Hall?

'You gotta practice' is the time-honoured answer, and these gentlemen have had nothing, if not practice. Generally speaking, these directors are the most interesting of the solid, workmanlike, purely professional bedrock on which all 'higher' achievement on TV is based. They rarely reach the heights themselves; even more significant, they do not aspire to. The older ones have more than paid their dues. The younger are still practising.

Hy Averback (c.1925-)

1963: **Burke's Law**/*Who Killed Billy Jo?, Who Killed Purity Mather?* 1964: **The Rogues**/*Bless You, C Carter Huntington, The Stafanini Dowry.* 1965: **F Troop** (multiples). 1966: **Man from UNCLE**/*The Round Table Affair;* **Chamber of Horrors** (pilot: released as feature). 1971: **Columbo**/*Suitable for Framing;* **MacMillan and Wife**/*The Face of Murder.* 1972: **McCloud**/*The New Mexican Connection* (co-dir); **MASH**/*The Moose, Requiem for a Lightweight, I Hate a Mystery;* **Columbo**/*A Stitch in Crime.* 1976: **Richie Brockleman: The Missing 24 Hours; City of Angels**/*The Bloodshot Eye.* 1977: **Quark; The Adventures of Freddie.** 1978: **The New Maverick.**

Averback's television is as lightweight in theme and manner as his features. **Burke's Law, The Rogues** and **The Man from UNCLE** were suitable training-grounds for his WHERE WERE YOU WHEN THE LIGHTS WENT OUT? and I LOVE YOU ALICE B. TOKLAS, none of which are either notable or memorable.

An odd variation from Averback's main stream is the curious one-shot, **Chamber of Horrors.** Warners had originally planned, with this pilot, for a **House of Wax** tele-series (based on their 1953 property) but, when things failed to click, they released the finished product directly to the movie-theatres. The **Quark** pilot is an equally odd venture, coming in during a period when many similar projects were lined for execution without a blindfold; but **The New Maverick** — Warner TV's attempt to revitalise the classic fifties series — ought to be director proof.

Richard L. Bare (c.1909-)

1951: **Gangbusters** (pilot). 1953: **Topper** (dir multiples). 1955: **So This Is Hollywood** (pilot); **Cheyenne**/*Julesburg* (pilot), *The Travellers, Mountain Fortress, Border Showdown, The Outlander.* 1956: **Casablanca**/*Siren Song;* **Cheyenne**/*Decision, The Storm Riders, Rendezvous at Red Rock, West of the River, Star in the Dust, Johnny Bravo, The Dark Riders, The Argonauts* (aka *Showdown at Paso Alto), Death Deals the Hand;* **Man Against Crime** (pilot). 1957: **Maverick**/*Hostage, Rope of Cards, The Seventh Hand, Seed of Deception;* **Sugarfoot**/*Price on His Head;* **Cheyenne**/*Born Bad,*

Mustang Trail, The Lone Gun, Devil's Canyon, Town of Fear; **Colt .45**/*Golden Gun;* **Broken Arrow** (dir multiples). 1958: **Lawman**/*The Prisoner, The Jury;* **Maverick**/*High Card Hangs, The Judas Mask, The Thirty-Ninth Star, Holiday at Hollow Rock;* **77 Sunset Strip**/*All Our Yesterdays* (pilot), *Casualty, Iron Curtain Caper, Dark Vengeance;* **Walt Disney Presents** (pilot). 1959: **Maverick**/*The Lass with the Poisonous Air, Trooper Maverick;* **The Twilight Zone**/*Third from the Sun, The Purple Testament;* **Adventures in Paradise** (dir multiples); **Tombstone Territory** (dir multiples). 1960: **The Twilight Zone**/*Nick of Time;* **Donna Reed Show** (dir multiples); **The Islanders** (pilot). 1961: **The Twilight Zone**/*The Prime Mover;* **Donna Reed Show** (dir multiples); **Bus Stop** (dir multiples). 1962: **The Dakotas**/*A Walk through the Badlands;* **The Gallant Men**/*Ol' Buddy;* **The Twilight Zone**/*To Serve Man, The Fugitive.* 1963: **Cheyenne**/*Showdown at Oxbend;* **77 Sunset Strip**/*In Memoriam;* **The Virginian**/*Run Away Home, If You Have Tears;* **Route 66**/*Every Father's Daughter;* **Petticoat Junction** (dir mulitples). 1964: **Kraft Suspense Theatre**/*My Enemy This Town;* **The Twilight Zone**/*What's In the Box?;* **The Virginian**/*The Hour of the Tiger, The Hero, Stopover in a Western Town, The Long Quest.* 1965: **Green Acres** (dir entire season); **Run for Your Life** (dir multiples). 1966: **Green Acres** (dir entire season); **Pruitts of Southampton** (dir multiples). 1967: **Green Acres** (dir entire season). 1968: **Green Acres** (dir entire season). 1969: **Green Acres** (dir entire season). 1970: **Nanny and the Professor** (dir multiples). 1971: **Alias Smith and Jones** (dir multiples). 1973: **Faraday and Co**/*A Wheelbarrow Full of Trouble.*

The TV historian has many more urgent tasks to face before beginning to make sense out of Bare's quarter century of work, none of which springs immediately and unaided, to the mind. Yet there is **Topper**, enshrouded in the fog of nostalgia as one of the most delightful of early '50s comedy series. Bare also made some of the phenomenally successful **Cheyenne;** 11 **Mavericks** (a show which was virtually director-proof) and some outstanding **Twilight Zones**. In short, from 1953 to 1963, Bare was dealing with, and to some degree helped formulate the meaning of 'classic' TV, sometimes as writer/director/producer. A close study of Bare's work during this period ought to concentrate on the Warner years, for it is there that the greatest interest lies.

In the mid-Fifties, when the major Hollywood studios were beginning to see a gleam of sympathetic light shining from their arch-rival—Jack Warner set up a TV production unit under the supervision of son-in law William T. Orr. Warner brought forth a package called **Warner Brothers Presents**, under which three series were shown in rotation: **Casablanca, Cheyenne** and **King's Row**. All three were based on earlier WB properties, with **Cheyenne** (utilising the title of their 1947 Raoul Walsh picture) the least known of the batch. Ironically, it was the **Cheyenne** series that took off with the viewers, making the unknown Clint Walker a hot-item overnight.

Bare put in time on the short-lived **Casablanca** series, but settled down with the **Cheyenne** show and turned out some above-average episodes in the form of *Julesburg* (the series's pilot episode), *The Storm Riders, The Outlander, Rendezvous at Red Rock, Decision,* and *The Travellers,* all of which were released theatrically in Europe.

The 1957-1959 period spawned countless western series on TV, giving Bare an opportunity to work on other Warner shows (**Sugarfoot, Colt .45, Lawman & Maverick**) as well as **Broken Arrow** and **Tombstone Territory**. **Maverick** holds a special position here because Bare spent much time on the show, before finally returning to direct the very last **Cheyenne** segment (*Showdown at Oxbend*). Considering the square-jawed, determined heroes of the regular Warner westerns, **Maverick** acts as a negative force, offering weekly instalments of tongue-in-cheek subversion. Whether Bare saw the **Maverick** series merely as an excursion into irregularity or as a welcome alternative in TV western assignments is not clear, but his episode *Lass with the Poisonous Air* does offer some clues.

Bare picked up the Directors Guild of America Award for his *All Our Yesterdays* segment of **77 Sunset Strip** in 1958, a classic pilot episode that springboarded the WB private-detective series on its six-year run. The occasion also marked the third time that Bare worked with the multi-talented Roy Huggins. It was a creative association that was repeated several times in the following twelve years.

Rod Serling's **Twilight Zone** gave Bare a new territory. He had the good fortune of being able to work from scripts by three of the show's top writers: Richard Matheson, Charles Beaumont, and Serling. Most of Bare's **Twilight Zone** episodes have some form of 'escape' theme, or pattern: *Third from the Sun, Nick of Time,* and *The Fugitive*, especially, have central characters who are trying desperately to avoid an imminent disaster. *Nick of Time* is particularly pleasing, drawing a claustrophobic net around the two central characters whose lives are undergoing a drastic change due to an uncanny fortune-telling machine.

Bare moved on from Warner shows when his old Wagonmaster, Roy Huggins, relinquished his creative role at the studio. Bare followed his trail to 20th Century Fox (**Adventures in Paradise, Bus Stop**) then to Universal (**Virginian, Run for Your Life, Alias Smith and Jones,** etc.), freelancing on a myriad of other series. There is a big jump from the heady days of **Topper** to rustic romps like **Petticoat Junction** and the five years of **Green Acres**, of which Bare directed 168 segments. After that, a decline in Bare's creative ambition might be expected; the middle period **Virginians** see Bare already preparing to be put out to pasture, for all but one, are resolutely 'non-western', and are centred around amorous intrigues and jealousies rather than the more primal emotions of the genre.

A weird feature film in 1973, WICKED, WICKED, which Bare wrote, directed and produced seemed like a spark of creative conscience, an attempt to re-find his once original voice. But it was little more than a despairing cry. Bare must, one feel, stand or fall on the results of that 'classic' decade. Back in 1964, he was only two blocks from Carnegie Hall. Unfortunately, it seems that his silly sit-com season placed him on a cross-town bus, going in the wrong direction.

Allen Baron

1965: **Mister Roberts**/*Splints for a Broken Heart.* 1969: **My World and Welcome to It**/*Monroe the Misogynist.* 1972: **The Sixth Sense**/*Five Women Weeping, I Did Not Mean to Slay Thee.* 1973: **Griff**/*The Last Ballad.* 1974: **Kolchak: The Night Stalker**/*The Ripper, UFO, The Devil's Platform;* **Lucas Tanner**/*Pay the Two Dollars.* 1975: **Switch**/*Kiss of Death, Mistresses, Murder and Millions.* 1976: **Charlie's Angels**/*The Mexican Connection.* 1977: **San Pedro Beach Bums** (multiples); **Charlie's Angels**/*Circus of Terror, Unidentified Flying Angels.*

Baron's work appears to be very much of a tongue-in-cheek endeavor. His comedy shows (**Mister Roberts, My World and Welcome to It**) seem to have cast the die for Baron's later work: **The Sixth Sense**, with Gary Collins immersing himself in ESP stories has implied supernatural overtones; **Griff**, and Lorne Greene's over-the-hill detective provides further outlandish shows—this happens whenever he meets up with companion series player, Buddy Ebsen (**Barnaby Jones**). More pronounced examples of Baron's strange humour appear in **Kolchak: The Night Stalker**, which is funny where it means to be amusing, merely moody when it seems to be creepy. **Switch,** again, is a remarkable team effort by contrasting players, Eddie Albert and Robert Wagner. The TV work of Allen Baron, in effect, operates through a mask of mirth, while lurking under a thin veil of mayhem.

Earl Bellamy (1917-)

1954: **Adventures of Rin-Tin-Tin** (multiples). 1955: **Schlitz Playhouse of Stars** (multiples); **Jungle Jim**/*Jungle Justice.* 1956: **Alfred Hitchcock Presents** (multiples); **The Crusader** (multiples). 1957: **Tales of Wells Fargo** (multiples). 1958: **Wagon Train**/*The Clara Beauchamp Story, The Gable Carswell Story;* **Donna Reed Show** (multiples). 1959: **Desilu Playhouse**/*Murder Is a Private Affair;* **Leave It to Beaver** (multiples). 1960: **M Squad**/*Pitched Battle at Bluebell Acres.* 1961: **Andy Griffith Show** (multiples); **Batchelor Father** (multiples). 1962: **The Virginian**/*The Big Deal, The Judgement;* **Alcoa Premiere** (multiples); **Laramie** (multiples). 1963: **Perry Mason**/*The Case of the Badgered Brother, The Case of the Festive Felon, The Case of the Decadent Dean;* **Arrest and Trial** (multiples); **The Virginian**/*Roar from the Mountain, Portrait of Marie Vallone, A Bride for Lars;* **Rawhide**/*Incident at El Crucero.* 1964: **The Virginian**/*First to Thine Own Self;* **The Munsters**/*Herman the Great, Tin Can Man, All-Star Munster, Herman Munster, Shutter Bug, John Doe Munster;* **Kraft Suspense Theatre: Crisis**/*Jungle of Fear.* 1965: **I Spy**/*Apollo, Turnabout for Traitors, The 7th Captain, Now You See Her, Now You Don't;* **The Virginian**/*We've Lost a Train, Bald Faced Boy.* 1966: **Laredo**/*The Golden Trail, No Bugles One Drum;* **Tarzan**/*Three Faces of Death, The Fire People;* **The Monroes**/*Ride with Terror;* **Iron Horse**/*Big Deal;* **I Spy**/*Tag You're It, Happy Birthday Everybody.* 1971: **The Partners**/*Pen Pals, North Is Now South, They Steel Cars, Don't They?.* 1972: **MASH**/*Cease Fire;* **The Sixth Sense**/*Echo of a Distant Scream.* 1974: **Six Million Dollar Man**/*Taneha.* 1975: **Six Million Dollar Man**/*Outrage in Balinderry;* **Quest**/*The Buffalo Hunters.* 1976: **Starsky and Hutch**/*Little Girl Lost, The Velvet Jungle;* **Stranded; The Secrets of Isis**/*The Hitch-Hikers, The Seeing-Eye Horse.* 1977: **Starsky and Hutch**/*Fatal Charm, Murder Ward.*

Earl Bellamy is one of those directors who is almost forgotten whilst he is still working. Bellamy's career has all the signs of a ship that passes during the night, with no purpose and no destination, and with only the flag of Universal Studios to indicate from where it came. His forgettable features like FLUFFY, GUNPOINT and MUNSTER GO HOME are similar to his TV work. He has walked across the backyards of many series without leaving footprints. **The Virginian** and **Laredo** remain the nearest, perhaps, to what really is Earl Bellamy; the **Virginian** segment called *We've Lost a Train* is an energetic romp, revealing a good sense of humour. It became the pilot for **Laredo** (premiering some 5 months later) which was one of the most successful series from the dogdays of TV westerns; Bellamy can legitimately be credited with helping establish its style. In more recent years, Bellamy has swung between juvenile and almost juvenile material, from **Six Million Dollar Man** to **Secrets of Isis** and **Starsky and Hutch**—still skillfully managing to maintain anonymity. His segments of **Starsky and Hutch**, however, have the same bouncy feel of **Laredo**.

Richard Benedict (c.1920-)

1961: **Lawman**/*The Appointment, Get Out of Town;* **Hawaiian Eye**/*Scene of the Crime, Tusitala, Cricket's Millionaire.* 1965: **Run for Your Life**/*Keep My Share of the World, This Town for Sale, The Savage Machines, Night Train from Chicago;* **The Virginian**/*Dream of Stavros Karns.* 1966: **Hawk**/*The Living End of Sisterbaby, 'H' Is a Dirty Letter;* **Laredo**/*Above the Law;* **Run for Your Life**/*Rendezvous in Tokyo, Three Passengers for the Lusitania, Down with Willy Hatch;* **Iron Horse**/*Right of Way Through Paradise.* 1967: **The Invaders**/*Genesis, The Condemned;* **Get Smart**/*The Apes of Rath;* **Dundee and the Culhane**/*The Vasquez Bride.* 1968: **Mission Impossible**/*The Vault, The Legend;* **Hawaii Five-O**/*Full Fathom Five, Tiger by the Tail, Pray Love Remember, Face of the Dragon, Along Came Joey.* 1969: **Mission Impossible**/*The Bargain;* **Ironside**/*A Bullet for Mark, Beyond a Shadow, One Hour to Kill;* **Marcus Welby MD**/*The Vrahnas Demon, Chemistry of Hope;* **Hawaii Five-O**/*Sweet Terror, All the King's Horses.* 1970: **Four-In-One: Night Gallery**/*Pamela's Voice;* **Four-In-One: San Francisco International Airport**/*We Once Came Home to Paradise, Supersonic Transport;* **Men from Shiloh**/*Follow the Leader;* **Alias Smith and Jones**/*The Great Shell Game, Stagecoach 7;* **The Bold Ones: The Lawyers**/*Trial of a Mafioso, The Search for Leslie Grey;* **The Bold Ones: The Doctors**/*Tender Predator.* 1971: **The Partners**/*The Prisoner of Fender, The Magnificent Perception;* **Alias Smith and Jones**/*The Man Who Broke the Bank at Red Gap;* **Dan August**/*Circle of Lies, The Manufactured Man.* 1972: **Hawaii Five-O**/*Thanks for the Honeymoon, The Listener.* 1974: **Lucas Tanner**/*Shattered.* 1975: **The Waltons**/*The Intruders;* **Medical Story**/*Moonlight Healer;* **The Blue Knight**/*The Creeper.* 1977: **Oregon Trail**/*Return from Death.*

Benedict worked in front of the cameras for nearly two decades before taking a seat behind the lens for TV production; he picked up an Oscar nomination for Best Supporting Actor, in Billy Wilder's ACE IN THE HOLE, along the way. His earliest directorial credits place him on Warner Brother's **Lawman** and **Hawiian Eye** series, where the shadow of the WB shield broke most efforts down into an indistingishable shade a grey.

During the 65-66 period, Benedict emerged like a heady brew for **Run for Your Life**, but before he could bottle this, he flowed away into a rough sea of insignificant skirmishes, bouncing from the frustrating frolics of **The Invaders** to the complex contrivances of **Mission Impossible** to the galloping grins of **Alias Smith and Jones**. There was a period during the early days of **Hawaii Five-O** when it looked as if Benedict might survive intact, but anyone who actively reponds to such cushioned capers as **The Waltons** and **Oregon Trail**, in the way that Benedict does, cannot be saved.

Leon Benson

1955-1956: **West Point** (pr-dir). 1956-1960: **Sea Hunt** (pr-dir). 1960-1962: **Ripcord** (pr-dir). 1962: **Ben Casey** (multiples). 1963: **Flipper** (pr-dir); **Empire**/*Down There the World, Duet for Eight Wheels;* **The Eleventh Hour** (multiples); **The Lieutenant** (multiples). 1964: **The Outer Limits**/*I Robot;* **Arrest and Trial**/*The Best There Is.* 1965: **Kraft Suspense Theatre** (+ pr); **The Virginian**/*Farewell to Honesty, The Awakening, Show Me A Hero, Men with Guns* (+ pr); **Bob Hope Chrysler Theatre**/*Streetcar, Do You Read Me?, Twixt Cup and Lip, The Last Clear Chance, The Long Ravine;* **Laredo**/*Which Way Did They Go?* 1966: **Tarzan** (pr); **Rat Patrol** (multiples); **The Loner**/*The Vespers.* 1967: **Bonanza**/ *Desperate Passage, The Late Ben Cartwright, The 13th Man;* **High Chaparrel**/*Hanging Offence.* 1968: **The Wild Wild West** (multiples). 1969: **High Chaparral**/ *Time of Your Life, A Piece of Land.* 1971: **Owen Marshall, Counselor at Law**/*The Forest and the Trees.* 1972: **Mission Impossible**/ *The Merchant;* **Owen Marshall, Counselor at Law**/*A Question of Degree, Love Child, Sometimes Tough Is Good.* 1973: **Owen Marshall, Counselor at Law**/*Poor Children of Eve, Etude for a Kidnapper, A Foreigner among Us.*

Working his way through various departments at Paramount, Leon Benson eventually found himself running the Story Department at ZIV TV. After spending many years producing and directing multiple episodes of **West Point, Sea Hunt, Ripcord** and **Flipper**, he was put under contract by Universal. For the middle-Sixties, Benson clocked-in on the Universal shows, taking time out only to produce the **Tarzan** series.NBC Productions then hired him, making Benson a staff director for their western shows, **Bonanza** and **High Chaparral**. For most of his career on the small screen, Benson never strayed far from any large flock, and his work appears as little more than a series of studio project numbers. His **Outer Limits** segment marks what may have been his only deviation from an uneventful path.

Abner Biberman (1909-1977)

1957: **Maverick**/*Stampede, The Naked Gallows;* **Colt .45**/*Dead Reckoning.* 1958: **Wagon Train**/*The Bije Wilcox Story, The Ben Courtney Story;* **The Thin Man** (dir multiples). 1959:

Tightrope/*The Frame, Man in the Middle, The Patsy, The Money Fight.* 1960: **Tightrope**/*The Perfect Circle, The Lady, Cold Kill, Appointment in Jericho.* 1961: **Ben Casey** (dir multiples); **Gunsmoke** (dir multiples). 1962: **The Twilight Zone**/*The Dummy;* **Sam Benedict**/*The Bird of Warning, Green Room, Grey Morning, Seventeen Gypsies and a Papa Named Charlie, Read No Evil.* 1963: **77 Sunset Strip**/*Don't Wait for Me, Eighty-Eight Bars, Dead as in 'Dude';* **Temple Houston**/*The Twisted Rope;* **The Outer Limits**/*The Human Factor;* **Twilight Zone**/*Number Twelve Looks Just Like You, The Incredible World of Horace Ford;* **Empire**/*Ride to a Fall, The Convention, Pressure Lock.* 1964: **The Twilight Zone**/*The Masks, I am the Night–Color Me Black;* **Mr Novak** (dir multiples); **12 O'Clock High** (dir multiples). 1965: **Seaway**/*Hot Line, Billy the Kid;* **Trials of O'Brien**/*No Justice for the Judge, A Horse Called Destiny, The Greatest Game* (2 pts; aka *Too Many Thieves);* **Convoy** (dir multiples); **The Fugitive** (dir multiples). 1966: **The Virginian**/*An Echo of Thunder, Trail to Ashley Mountain, Yesterday's Timepiece, The Modoc Kid, Melanie, Nightmare at Fort Killman, A Welcoming Town, Lady of the House;* **Voyage to the Bottom of the Sea**/*The Death Ship;* **Laredo** (dir multiples). 1967: **The Virginian**/*Deadly Past, Star Crossed, To Bear Witness, The Fortress, Johnny Moon, The Barren Ground, The Crooked Path, Jed;* **Run for Your Life** (dir multiples). 1968: **The Virginian**/*Dark Corridor, A Vision of Blindness;* **Ironside**/*The Sacrifice, An Obvious Love of Guilt, Side Pocket, In Search of an Artist;* **Hawaii Five-O**/*Once Upon a Time* (2 pts, co-dir), *Not That Much Different.* 1969: **The Virginian**/*A Woman of Stone;* **Ironside**/*Not with a Whimper but a Bang, Ransom;* **Hawaii Five-O**/*Which Way Did They Go?, Blind Tiger.* 1970: **The Virginian**/*Home to Methusulah;* **Men from Shiloh**/*The Mysterious Mr Tate;* **Ironside**/*The People Against Judge McIntyre;* **The Bold Ones: The Doctors**/*Killer on the Loose.* 1971: **Men from Shiloh**/*The Wolf Track.*

The question could be asked: Just who is Abner Biberman? His directorial credits for the small screen are as diverse as his acting roles. Biberman's mark can be found in almost every popular phase of dramatic television; he was there when the TV Western first began riding the range, (**Maverick**, etc.), when TV fantasy came of age (**Twilight Zone**, etc.), when the social and medical series hit their high points (**Mr. Novak, Ben Casey**, etc.), and when police drama gained greater strength and numbers (**Ironside, Hawaii Five-O**, etc.). However, if there is a true Biberman signature, then it is most likely to be found creeping cautiously among his **Virginian** credits, which span the latter part of his career.

Working on the premises that most actors-turned-directors invade actual TV production on a 'mercenary' basis, Biberman proved to be 'regular army'. His area of work for TV during the late 1960s was, not surprisingly, along the same tracks that he had travelled a decade earlier—only the titles had changed 'to prevent investigation'. Further involvement, a deeper sense of purpose, reveals itself among his **Trials of O'Brien** segments, possibly because he was directing Mrs. Biberman (Joanna Barnes). The two-parter, *The Greatest Game,* is not really bad—but then, it is not really good.

Abner Biberman signed-in during the great 1950s teleseries boom and continued using the same pen for almost two decades without once returning to recharge at the inkwell. It may be comfortable to let this complacent judgement go at that, but his *Number Twelve Looks Just Like You* segment of **Twilight Zone** had flashes of brilliance. Was that Abner Biberman?

Cliff Bole

1974: **Six Million Dollar Man**/*The Bionic Badge.* 1975: **Six Million Dollar Man**/*The Blue Flash.* 1976: **Six Million Dollar Man**/*Big Brother, Danny's Inferno, Vulture of the Andes;* **Emergency**/*Not Available;* **Baretta**/*Under the City.* 1977: **Emergency**/*Family Ties;* **Six Million Dollar Man**/*The Dark Side of the Moon* (2 pts), *Deadly Countdown* (2 pts), *Lost Island;* **Charlie's Angels**/*Hours of Desperation.*

'Gentlemen, we can rebuild him' must be Bole's password, having spent a goodly time over-cranking bionic characters and under-cranking the camera. In as much as Robert Altman couldn't be evaluated solely on the strength of **The Roaring 20's**, Bole cannot be examined and observed purely via the Harve Bennett productions. Bole shows the kind of potential, along with his stable-mate Alan Levi, that can only be understood in a critical light when he steps outside the bionic series and applies his talents to unfamiliar material.

Phil Bondelli

1974: **Six Million Dollar Man**/*Return of the Robot Maker.* 1975: **Get Christie Love!**/*My Son the Murderer;* **Six Million Dollar Man**/*Love Song for Tanya.* 1976: **The Bionic Woman**/*Winning of Eveything;* **Six Million Dollar Man**/*The White Lightning War, The Bionic Boy, The Infiltrators;* **Charlie's Angels**/*Angels in Chains, To Kill an Angel.* 1977: **Six Million Dollar Man**/*To Catch the Eagle, U-509;* **Switch**/*Dangerous Curves.*

Bondelli, like Cliff Bole and Alan Levi, has so far made the area of his contributions the Universal **Six Million Dollar Man** and **The Bionic Woman** series. His TV term reflects more the work of a staff director than a creative artist, though he has his high and low points. For the time being, Bondelli should be observed for his possibilities in a confined sphere rather than his probabilities in the open field.

Michael T. Caffey

1967: **Ironside**/*Message from Beyond.* 1968: **It Takes a Thief**/*Totally by Design, A Matter of Larceny, To Steal a Battleship;* **Garrison's Gorillas**/*Operation Hellfire;* **Hawaii Five-O**/*Once Upon A Time* (2 pts, co-dir). 1969: **It Takes a Thief**/*The Galloping Skin Game;* **The Survivors**/*Chapter 14.* 1970: **Paris 7000**/*Journey to Nowhere;* **Lancer**/*Lamp in the Wilderness.* 1971: **The Bold Ones: The Doctors**/*Moment of Crisis;* **The Devil and Miss Sarah.** 1972: **Search**/*The Packagers.* 1973: **Cannon**/*The Limping Man.* 1974: **Kolchak: The Night Stalker**/*Horror in the Heights;* **The Hanged Man.** 1975: **Bert D'Angelo Superstar**/*Men with No Past.* 1976: **Gemini Man**/*Sam Casey Sam Casey, Targets;* **Serpico**/*Traitor in Our Midst;* **Hardy Boys Mysteries**/*Mystery of the*

Flying Courier, Mystery of the Whispering Walls; **Streets of San Francisco**/*Dead or Alive.* 1976: **Kingston: Confidential**/*Golden Girl.*

Mike Caffey appears to have a weakness for deviating from the general tele-drama path and picking up on oddities and one-shots. **The Survivors, Paris 7000, Search, Kolchak, Bert D'Angelo, Gemini Man**,etc., were all short-run series, failing to make their mark on the ratings. Whether Caffey was foolishly experimenting or merely exploring is a question better left but there are some interesting and valid moments among the débris. *Horror in the Heights*, remains as a fine tribute to the Val Lewton school of implied-horror. Overall, Caffey's TV work seems translucent. There could be more to Caffey than meets the screen, but unless he is given an area in which to work that allows for development, Caffey will be doomed to follow rather than lead.

William F. Claxton

1956: **The Whistler**/*Letters from Aaron Burr, Fatal Freud, Lady in Waiting, The Glass Dime, Stranger in the House, Kind Thought, Roark Island, Sleep My Pretty One, The Jubilee Earring, The Other Hand, A Case for Mr Carrington, An Actor's Life.* 1959: **Twilight Zone**/*The Last Flight.* 1960: **Route 66**/*Sheba.* 1961: **Detectives**/*The Informer;* **Twilight Zone**/*The Jungle;* **Desilu Playhouse**/*Dead on Nine.* 1962: **Thriller**/*The Hollow Watcher;* **Twilight Zone**/*The Little People;* **Bonanza**/*Knight Errant, The Decision, The Hayburner, The Brass Box.* 1963: **Bonanza**/*The Debt, A Dublin Lad, To Kill a Buffalo, The Code, The Companeros.* 1964: **Bonanza**/*A Dime's Worth of Glory, The Underdog, Fire into the Wind, Jonah, The Flapjack Contest, Woman of Fire, The Search.* 1965: **Bonanza**/*All Ye His Saints, The Dilemma, The Emperor Norton, Amigo, Judgement at Red Creek.* 1966: **Bonanza**/*Credit for a Kill, The Prince, A Dream to Dream;* **High Chaparral**/*Destination Tucson—The Arrangement* (2 pts pilot), *Best Man for the Job, Quiet Day in Tucson, Shadows on the Land, The Widow from Red Rock.* 1967: **High Chaparral** (series pr) + *The Covey, For What We Are About to Receive, The Lion Sleeps, Stinky Flanagan, Surtee, A Fella Named Kilroy, No Bugles No Drums, For the Love of Carlos.* 1968/1969: **High Chaparral** (pr + dir multiples). 1974: **Little House on the Prairie**/*Country Girls, The 100 Mile Walk, The Love of Johnny Johnson, School Marm, The Raccoon, The Award, Plague, The Circus Man, Family Quarrel, Survival, Christmas at Plum Creek.* 1975-1976: **Little House on the Prairie** (pr) + *The Race, Little Women, To Live with Fear* (2 pts), *The Wisdom of Solomon, Times of Change.*

After a decade dealing with crime, murder, fantasy and a myriad of dark doings, Claxton appears to have undergone a Moral Rearmament conversion, gradually becoming the prime proponent of the 'family' virtues through long tenures with **Bonanza, High Chaparral** and, latterly, **Little House on the Prairie** where he shares the chores almost equally with the series star and executive producer, Michael Landon. The two met, we assume, on **Bonanza** (Claxton's segment *A Dream to Dream* was written by Landon in an early attempt by the actor to exercise a greater degree of control and creativity). Both men must therefore share similar ambitions. **Little House..,** is a 'western' in look and period, but is rooted more in Americana and in the precepts of moral virtue with which it is associated than in the action genre per se. It is, overall, successful for Claxton's vision of the west, and the people that populated it, but it is little more than a soap-opera.

For the last decade of his career, Claxton has surrounded himself with formats dominated by wealthy (whether financially or spiritually), predominantly-male oriented families, residing in the remotest of regions. The trials and tribulations, the ongoing, uneven relationship between members of the family group appear as essential Claxton components. The group in **Bonanza** is really no different from that in **High Chaparral.** Leif Erickson is simply a lookalike product manufactured from the Lorne Green blueprint, along with the assorted sons and ranch hands. David Dortort, executive producer/creator of both shows, expanded a popular path into a successful highway. Claxton's segments, however, are generally stodgy, and, it must be said, that Landon's own segments of **Little House...** are in every way superior. A degree of ignorance about his overall career seems like a just reward.

Barry Crane

1969: **Mission Impossible**/*The Rebel, Encounter, Nerves, The Connection.* 1970: **Mission Impossible**/*The Fountain, Ultimatum, Double Dead, Double Circle, Gitano, The Catafalque, Flight, The Hostage.* 1972: **Hound of the Baskervilles.** 1973: **The Magician** (pilot, pr only). 1974: **Caribe**/*Vanished, The Survivor, Flowers of Death;* **Harry O**/*Material Witness;* **Streets of San Francisco**/*Target: Red;* **Kung Fu**/*The Vanishing Image, Battle Hymn.* 1975: **Six Million Dollar Man**/*Hocus-Pocus;* **Three for the Road**/*Fear, The Ghost Story, The Care;* **Quest**/*The Last of the Mountain Men.* 1976: **Hawaii Five-O**/*Let Death Do Us Part;* **Fantastic Journey**/*Atlantium;* **The Bionic Woman**/*The Return of Bigfoot* (2 pts), *Black Magic, Kill Oscar* (2 pts); **Six Million Dollar Man**/*Task Force;* **Wonder Woman**/*Fausta the Nazi Wonder Woman, Wonder Woman Meets Baroness von Gunther.* 1977: **The Bionic Woman**/*Jaime's Shield* (2 pts), *The Pyramid, The Bionic Dog* (2 pts), *The Dijon Caper;* **Man from Atlantis**/*Shootout at Lands End.*

Target: Red, Let Death Do Us Part and *Material Witness* are all better-than-average series segments; Crane reveals an affinity for urban action and a sophisticated panache in building jigsaws. His **Mission Impossibles** are where he must have learned to do it, although they predate the abysmal **The Hound of the Baskervilles.**

Most recently, he has been fooling around in the juvenile fantasy leagues and although *Black Magic* with Vincent Price, Hermione Baddeley and Julie Newmar supporting Lindsay Wagner, is an amusing—and occasionally creepy—Gothic homage, it opts for too many easy laughs and not enough genuine *frissons.* His succeeding encounters with **Wonder Woman** and *The Bionic Dog* take fun to excess and are dull.

Shootout at Land's End confirms that the panache is fading; confusion is creeping into areas of faith, hope and clarity: his skill at exposition has gone. Crane revealed positive qualities in his early shows, but he has forgotten how to accentuate them.

Alan Crosland Jr.

1957: **Cheyenne**/*The Empty Gun, The Renegades;* **Colt .45**/*Law West of the Pecos, The Gypsies, Sign in the Sand;* **Maverick**/*Trail West to Fury.* 1958: **Lawman**/*The Lady in Question, Riding Shotgun;* **77 Sunset Strip**/*Not an Enemy in the World.* 1959: **Bronco**/*Prairie Skipper, Shadow of a Man, The Besieged, The Turning Point, Four Guns and a Prayer, Trail to Taos.* 1960: **Alfred Hitchcock Presents**/*The Man Who Found the Money, The Money, I Can Take Care of Myself.* 1961: **Alfred Hitchcock Presents**/*Deathmate, The Hat Box, Keep Me Company, The Kiss Off, Servant Problem, The Gloating Place;* **Bonanza**/*Four Sisters from Boston;* **87th Precinct**/*Occupation: Citizen;* **Alcoa Premiere**/*Of This Time Of This Place.* 1962: **Alfred Hitchcock Hour**/*Night of the Owl, House Guest, Last Seen Wearing Blue Jeans, The Woman Who Wanted to Live;* **Alcoa Premiere**/*Mr Lucifer;* **True**/*Black Market.* 1963: **The Twilight Zone**/*The Old Man in the Cave, The 7th is Made Up of Phantoms, Ring-a-Ding Girl, The Parallel;* **The Great Adventure**/*The Secret.* 1964: **The Outer Limits**/*The Mutant;* **Voyage to the Bottom of the Sea**/*Turn Back the Clock;* **Portrait of an Unknown Man.** 1965: **Mr Broadway**/*Sticks and Stones May Break My Bones;* **The Reporter**/*The Man Behind the Man;* **The Virginian**/*The Outcast;* **Rawhide**/*Escort to Doom;* **Wild Wild West**/*Night of the Torture Chamber.* 1966: **Iron Horse**/*Welcome for the General;* **Tarzan**/*Leopard on the Loose;* **Wild Wild West**/*Night of the Poisonous Posey, Night of the Man Eating House, Night of the Skulls, Night of the Gypsy Peril, Night of the Surreal McCoy, Night of the Deadly Blossom.* 1967: **Hondo**/*Hondo and the Hanging Town;* **Wild Wild West**/*Night of the Assassins, Night Dr Lovelace Died, Night of the Cutthroats, Night of the Headless Woman.* 1968: **Adam 12**/*Log 91, Log 71.* 1969: **Adam 12**/*S.W.A.T, Shoplift, Light Duty, Bottom of the Bottle, Vengeance Airport, Child Stealer.* 1971: **Adam 12**/*The Ferret;* **O'Hara–US Treasury**/*Operation: Crystal Springs, Operation: White Fire;* **The D.A.**/*The People Versus Gayda, The People Versus Swammerdam.* 1972: **O'Hara–US Treasury**/*Operation: Spread, Operation: Mr Felix;* **The Sixth Sense**/*Gallows in the Wind.* 1973: **Emergency**/*Promise, An English Visitor, Alley Cat;* **Chase**/*The Winning Ticket Is the Loser, Right to an Attorney, John Doe Bucks, Hot Beef.* 1974: **Chase**/*The People Parley.* 1975: **Six Million Dollar Man**/*Welcome Home Jaime* (2 pts), *The Secret of Bigfoot, Divided Loyalty.* 1976: **The Bionic Woman**/*Kill Oscar* (pts 1 and 3), *Jaime's Shield* (pt 1), *In this Corner Jaime Sommers, Assault on the Princess, Bionic Beauty;* **Wonder Woman**/*Judgement from Outer Space;* **Six Million Dollar Man**/*Nightmare in the Sky.* 1977: **The Bionic Woman**/*Jaime and the King.*

Son of the famed Crosland senior, notable Old Hollywood director of DON JUAN (1926) and THE JAZZ SINGER (1927), Crosland Jr. has worked his way through 20 years of Television. The years can be broken down into three basic stages: the Warner Brothers period, the Jack Webb period and the Harve Bennett period. His Warners term contains most of the statutory WB material being produced at the time, such as the **Cheyenne, Colt .45, Maverick, Lawman** and **Bronco** westerns. Far more important careers have emerged from this shelf and they, in effect, relegate Crosland's contributions to the level of a contract director. Along the line there was some flirtation with the unusual and the uncanny (**Mr. Lucifer**, written by Alfred Bester, **Alfred Hitchcock Hour, Twilight Zone, The Outer Limits, Voyage to the Bottom of the Sea**). Crosland's second stage was with the Jack Webb/Mark VII shows: **O'Hara—US Treasury, the D.A. Emergency** and **Chase**—all of which are typical Webb products, and deal with the active procedures of various government departments. Webb's stock in trade—action with a hard documentary flavour—generally managed to overshadow any personal styles or motifs of his directors and so it is with Crosland.

Harve Bennett's Bionic series, **Six Million Dollar Man** and **The Bionic Woman**, have taken up most of Crosland's time in recent years and, although nothing particularly notable has come out of them for Crosland, there are two episodes which are so silly that they are almost perfect Bionic fare: *The Secret of Bigfoot* and *Jaime's Shield* (part one). The plot of the former begins in a curious actually intriguing, manner with the Lee Majors character being despatched to unravel the Sasquatch enigma. The segment then flies off on a juvenile tangent laden with alien beings on Earth. The Sasquatch sequences are handled quite well, consider the absurdity of the characters and plot, but the later alien section lacks any form or overall style. Part one of *Jaime's Shield* works well, on its own level, as a crazy piece of unquestioned fantasy. However, it so prolongs the craziness that superwoman Jaime Summers must be regarded by the characters around her as somewhat *weird*. Crosland's TV career represents a series of audacious gulps—which is, however, preferable to the insincerity of delicate sipping.

Marc Daniels

1960: **The Witness**/*Jack 'Legs' Diamond, Dutch Schultz, John Dillinger.* 1961: **Dick Powell Theatre**/*Goodbye Hannah, Ricochet.* 1962: **Dick Powell Theatre**/*The Legend.* 1963: **Burke's Law**/*Who Killed the Paper Dragon?.* 1964: **Man from UNCLE**/*The Finny Foot Affair, The Shark Affair.* 1965: **Dr Kildare**/*The Life Machine* (7 pts); **Man from UNCLE**/*The Secret Sceptre Affair, The Love Affair;* **Slattery's People**/*The Hero.* 1966: **Star Trek**/*The Man Trap, The Naked Time, Menagerie* (new footage), *Court Martial;* **Gunsmoke**/*The Well, Champion of the World, The Favor, The Returning, The Lure.* 1967: **Star Trek**/*Space Seed, Who Mourns for Adonais?, The Changeling, Mirror Mirror, The Doomsday Machine, I Mudd;* **Mission Impossible**/*Elena.* 1968: **Star Trek**/*A Private Little War, By Any Other Name, Assignment: Earth, Spock's Brain;* **Bonanza**/*The Arrival of Eddie;* **It Takes a Thief**/*To Catch a Roaring Lion.* 1969: **Gunsmoke**/*The Well;* **Paris 7000**/*A Time for Lying* (pilot); **The Survivors**/*pt 7;* **Marcus Welby MD**/*Go Get 'Em Tiger, Let Ernest Come Over;* **The Queen and I**/*The No-Cruise Cruise.* 1970: **Men from Shiloh**/*The Price of Hanging;* **Marcus Welby MD**/*The Basic Movement* (2 pts). 1971: **Marcus Welby MD**/*Men Who Care* (pt 1); **Owen Marshal Counselor at Law**/*Men Who Care* (pt 2); **Men from Shiloh**/*Tate: Ramrod;* **Marcus Welby MD**/*Crossmatch, Echo from Another World, Just a Little Courage, This Is Max, Solomon's Choice, Hello Goodbye Hello.* 1972: **Jigsaw**/*The Bradley Affair;* **Owen Marshal: Counselor at Law**/*Requiem for Young Lovers;* **Search**/*Live Men Tell Tales.* 1973: **Cannon**/*Arena of Fear;* **Marcus**

Welby MD/*The Mugging, Friends in High Places, For Service Rendered, The Panic Path;* **Toma**/*Frame Up.* 1974: **Planet Earth; Marcus Welby MD**/*Unindicted Wife, The Time Bomb;* **Kung Fu**/*The Garments of Rage, One Step to Darkness, Barbary House, Flight to Orion, Full Circle.* 1975: **Marcus Welby MD**/*To Live Another Day, Tidal Wave, Prisoner of the Island Cell, An End and a Beginning, The Lie.* 1977: **Man from Atlantis**/*The Death Scouts.*

Nearly 20 years alternating between silliness and sensitivity suggests a director who is good enough to keep on working, who is involved enough to enjoy what he is doing but is without the ambition to carve out a slice of the world he can properly call his own. Back in the '60's, **Burke's Law** alternated with **Dick Powell Theatre, Dr. Kildare** with **Man from UNCLE.** In the mid '70's, **Man from Atlantis** and **Cannon** alternated with **Marcus Welby M.D.** The two strands came together most successfully in Daniels's 14 **Star Treks,** which—along with Joseph Pevney's work—established the series with his high standards of excellence.

Star Trek and a spell on **Gunsmoke** make the late '60's, Daniels's most interesting period. On the strength of them an observer would understandably have reasoned that his career would take off. His cheerful acceptance of a myriad of **Marcus Welby** assignments—though, like the series itself, generally affecting, seems to have doomed him to the role of a latter-day Martinson. His segments are seldom dull, usually painless, occasionally brilliant. Practice alone, however, does not guarantee a seat on the bus, let along a place in the orchestra stalls. Daniels certainly made it—but only into the gallery.

Herschel Daugherty

1955: **Soldiers of Fortune**/*The Elephant Gun, Torch of Olympiad, Malayan Magic, Girls in the Jeep.* 1956: **Alfred Hitchcock Presents**/*The Belfry.* 1957: **Alfred Hitchcock Presents**/*Sylvia, Return of the Hero, Cream of the Jest, Kill with Kindness;* **Wagon Train**/*The Story of Willy Moran.* 1958: **Alfred Hitchcock Presents**/*Little White Flock, The Morning After, The Last Dark Step, A Better Bargain;* **Buckskin**/*Tell Me Leonardo;* **Wagon Train**/*Around the Horn, The Tobias Jones Story, The Liam Fitzmorgan Story, The Sakae Ito Story, The C L Harding Story, The Danny Benedict Story;* **G.E. Theatre**/*One Is a Wanderer.* 1959: **Alfred Hitchcock Presents**/*Graduation Class, The Blessington Method, Coyote Moon, The Cure, The Diamond Necklace;* **Wagon Train**/*The Tom Tuckett Story, The Christine Elliott Story, Wagons Ho!–A Greenhorn's Odyssey, The Albert Farnsworth Story;* **The Deputy**/*Queen Bea.* 1960: **Alfred Hitchcock Presents**/*Summer Shade, The Dusty Drawer;* **Thriller**/*The Poisoner, Hay-Fork and Bill-Hook;* **Wagon Train**/*Weight of Command, The Christopher Hale Story.* 1961: **Thriller**/*Late Date, Parasite Mansion, The Prisoner in the Mirror, The Grim Reaper, The Weird Tailor, God Grante That She Lye Stille, Masquerade, Letter to a Lover, Dialogue with Death.* 1962: **Alcoa Premiere**/*Rules of the Game;* **Thriller**/*The Storm, Till Death Do Us Part, Kill My Love;* **Checkmate**/*Interrupted Honeymoon, Terror from the East, Tight as a Drum.* 1963: **Alfred Hitchcock Hour**/*The Star Juror, A Home Away from Home.* 1964: **For the People**/*With Intent to Interference;* **Mr Broadway**/*Maggie, Queen of the Jungle, The He-She Cheating, Between the Rats and the Finks, Pay Now–Die Later;* **Rawhide**/*The Backshooter, Josh;* **Alfred Hitchcock Hour**/*Nothing Ever Happens in Linvale.* 1965: **Seaway**/*Last Free Man, RX for Murder;* **Dr**

Kildare/*Lullaby for an Indian Summer, Marriage of Convenience, Make Way for Tomorrow.* 1966: **The Time Tunnel**/*Kill Two By Two;* **Girl from UNCLE**/*The Prisoner of Zalimar Affair.* 1967: **Winchester '73; Mission Impossible**/*The Confession;* **Cimarron Strip**/*Big Jessie, Fool's Gold, Whitey;* **Custer**/*To the Death! Massacre;* **The Time Tunnel**/*Town of Terror;* **Star Trek**/*Operation Annihilate.* 1968: **It Takes a Thief**/*A Spot of Trouble;* **Hawaii Five-O**/*Some Day We Shall Be Strangers in Our Own Land, No Blue Skies, Yesterday Died and Tomorrow Won't Be Born, Deathwatch, The Big Kahuna;* **Gunsmoke**/*Johnny Cross, Exodus 21:22.* 1969: **Marcus Welby MD**/*Enid;* **Star Trek**/*The Savage Curtain.* 1970: **Marcus Welby MD**/*Cynthia, Warn the World About Mike, The Windfall.* 1971: **Emergency**/*Botulism.* 1972: **Circle of Fear**/*Dark Vengeance;* **The Victim** (aka *The Storm);* **Cannon**/*Murder for Murder;* **Emergency**/*Nurses Wild;* **Hec Ramsey**/*Mystery of the Green Feather.* 1973: **She Cried Murder; Banacek**/*Horse of a Slightly Different Color.* 1974: **Six Million Dollar Man**/*The Peeping Blonde;* **Paper Moon**/*Gimme That Old Time Relation.* 1975: **Three for the Road**/*Adventure in Los Angeles;* **Petrocelli**/*Once Upon a Victim.*

Herschel Daugherty is essentially a draughtsman of mood and atmosphere, with a penchant for the grim and the morbid. His lengthy association with the Hitchcock shows and **Thriller** are testimony to this inclination. *Kill with Kindness* is a near gruesome rendition of ARSENIC AND OLD LACE, with a murderous brother and sister team (Hume Cronyn & Carmen Matthews) setting up the death of an old vagrant (James Gleason)—the intention being not to 'save' the old feller but to fake an insurance claim. Daugherty allows his characters to question both their method and their consciences, amid an effective atmosphere of gloom and lost causes. William Frye's **Thriller** (at first a regular drama series which later adopted a supernatural theme) offered Daugherty a chance to drench his characters in further confusion of motive and black mood. *Parasite Mansion, Prisoner in the Mirror, The Grim Reaper, God Grante That She Lye Stille, Masquerade* and *The Storm* are all active in the eerie confines of large, shadowy houses. Within this setting, Daugherty fashions direct and indirect hazards, steering the confusions of the captive characters into further flights of panic. Sometimes subtle, sometimes harsh, the suggestions of malevolence are handled with an impressive degree of care for dramatic flow as well as claustrophobic visuals. The best of Herschel Daughterty appears to be cloaked in a world of shadows, blacks and greys but when colour became a dominant factor in TV production, Daugherty lost his way in the light.

Lawrence Doheny

1972: **Adam 12**/*O'Brien's Stand, Hot Spell, Keeping Tabs.* 1973: **Adam 12**/*Venice Division, Rampart Division, Krash, Capture, North Hollywood Division, South West Division.* 1974: **Six Million Dollar Man**/*Straight on Til Morning, Athena One;* **Houston We've Got A Problem; Rockford Files**/*Profit & Cost* (2 pts), *Find Me If You Can, Pastoria Prime Pick, The Great Blue Lake Land Development Company.* 1975: **Doctors Hospital**/*My Cup Runneth Over;* **Rockford Files**/*Chicken Little Is a Little Chicken, The Farnsworth Stratagem, Where's Houston?* 1976: **Rockford**

Files/*Drought at Indian Head River, Joey Blue Eyes, Piece Work;* **Baa Baa Black Sheep**/*Best Three Out of Five, Presumed Dead, War Biz Warrior, Last One for Hutch;* **Charlie's Angels**/*Angels on a String.* 1977: **Blacksheep Squad**/*Divine Wind;* **Switch**/*Fade Out;* **Big Hawaii**/*Candy.*

Dependable rather than dynamic, Doheny has unostentatiously moved through a succession of formula assignments. He has been as good as his material (**Rockford Files**) or better (**Charlie's Angels**), though it is still too soon to say whether the ambition evident in **Houston We've Got a Problem** (a fictionalised behind-the-scenes drama based on the rocky Apollo 13 space shot, with Robert Culp and Clu Gulager in mission control) has since been deadened. Fine segments such as the *Great Blue Lake Land Development Company* suggests that Doheny's work will usually be worth the effort.

Dennis Donnelly

1971: **Adam 12**/*Day Watch.* 1972: **Emergency**/*Trainee, Dinner Date, Syndrome;* **Adam 12**/*AW Drop, Lost and Found, The Chase, The Surprise, Clear with a Civilian, Night Watch, Anatomy of a 415.* 1973: **Emergency**/*Inheritance Tax, Body Language, Insomnia, Heavyweight, The Floor Brigade, Frequency;* **Adam 12**/*Hollywood Division, Taking It Easy, Hartone Division, Van Nuys Division, Northeast Division, Trouble in the Bank, Sky Watch* (2 pts), *Sunburn, The Sweet Smell of . . .* 1974: **Emergency**/*Sky Watch* (pt 1); **Adam 12**/*Pot Shot, Lady Beware, Camp* (2 pts), *Pressure Point.* 1975: **Emergency**/*Communications, The Old Engine Cram, Simple Adjustment, Involvement;* **Adam 12**/*Operation Action, Gus Corbin, Suicide;* **Marcus Welby MD**/*Strike II.* 1976: **Emergency**/*That Time of Year, Loose Ends.* 1977: **Emergency**/*Upward and Onward, Hypochrondri-Cap, Bottom Line;* **Hardy Boys Mysteries**/*Oh Say Can You Sing?;* **Charlie's Angels**/*Angels in the Wings;* **Hawaii Five-O**/*The Silk Trap.*

The possibility of personal expression in a show like Webb's **Emergency** is as possible as *not* hearing a siren screaming in one of its episodes. Splitting the events between **Emergency** and **Adam—12**, both Mark VII productions, Donnelly has probably instigated more carnage on the streets of Los Angeles than Robert Wise achieved with EARTHQUAKE. **Adam 12** hovers somewhere between THE NEW CENTURIONS and **Streets of San Francisco**, and maintains an authentic flavour through its police-procedure events. **Emergency**, however, features cataclysmic events merely as fodder for the later, confusing, para-medic jargon. Subsequently, Donnelly is content to follow a theme rather than create one.

Charles S. Dubin

1962: **The Defenders**/*The Apostle.* 1963: **The Defenders**/*The Captive, The Last Day, Loophole, Who'll Dig His Grave?* 1964: **Mr Broadway**/*Nightingale for Sale.* 1965: **The Virginian**/*The*

Laramie Road, Letter of the Law. 1966: **Crisis**/*Grafitti;* **Hawk**/*Some Devil Whispered in His Ear.* 1967: **The Virginian**/*Ah Sing vs Wyoming, The Reckoning;* **Ironside**/*An Inside Job, Tagged for Murder, Light at the End of the Journey, Memory of an Ice Cream Stick, The Lonely Hostage, All in a Days Work;* **Tarzan**/*Eyes of the Lion.* 1968: **The Virginian**/*The Saddle Warmer, The Mustangers, Death Waits in Medicine Bow, Crime Wave in Buffalo Springs;* **Ironside**/*Perfect Crime, And Be My Love;* **Hawaii Five-O**/*The Ways of Love;* **To Die in Paris** (co-dir). 1969: **The Virginian**/*The Long Ride Home.* 1970: **Hawaii Five-O**/*And a Time to Die . . ., Highest Castle Deepest Grave, Two Doves and Mr Heron.* 1971: **Cannon**/*A Flight of Hawks;* **Owen Marshall, Counselor at Law**/*Make No Mistake;* **The Man and the City**/*Pipe Me a Loving Tune;* **Hawaii Five-O**/*Death Is a Company Policy, Vashon–The Son, The Father, The Patriarch* (3 pts), *The Diamond That Nobody Stole;* **Murder Once Removed.** 1972: **Circle of Fear**/*Spare Parts;* **Cool Million**/*The $1,000,000 Rubber Check;* **Banyon**/*The Clay Clarinet, A Date with Death;* **Cannon**/*Hard Rock Roller Coaster, Hear No Evil, Prisoners;* **Kung Fu**/*The Praying Mantis Kills, Superstition, The Third Man.* 1973: **Murdock's Gang** (pilot); **Kojak**/*Cop in a Cage, Knockover, Before the Devil Knows, Deliver Us Some Evil;* **Hawaii Five-O**/*Draw Me a Killer, The Finishing Touch, Anybody Can Build a Bomb, Try to Die on Time, 30,000 Rooms and I Have the Key.* 1974: **Ironside**/*What's New with Mark;* **Lucas Tanner**/*Why Not a Happy Ending?, One to One;* **Sons and Daughters**/*The Pregnancy, The Locket;* **Toma**/*Joey the Creep;* **Kojak**/*Hush Now, Don't You Die;* **Death in Space; Hawaii Five-O**/*Hawaiian Nightmare, I'll Kill 'Em Again, Welcome to our Branch Office, Presenting in the Center Ring Murder.* 1975: **Hawaii Five-O**/*Target? The Lady, The Case Against McGarrett, Loose Ends Get Hit, Love Thy Neighbour: Take His Wife.* 1976: **Kojak**/*Kojak's Days* (2 pts), *The Pride and the Princess, Black Thorn;* **Ellery Queen**/*The Adventure of the Lover's Leap;* **Executive Suite** (pilot: co-dir). 1977: **Kojak**/*The Captain's Brother's Wife;* **Charlie's Angels**/*Angels in Paradise;* **The Wilds of Ten Thousand Islands.**

Crime drama is the core of Charles Dubin's TV activity; he has a particular emphasis on the concrete jungle, sidewalks-of-the-city variety. His heroes operate mainly out of the large, over-populated cities: **The Defenders, Hawk, Toma, Kojak,** etc., in New York; **Ironside** in San Francisco; **Cannon, Charlie's Angels,** etc., in Los Angeles; even **Hawaii Five-O** in Honolulu. Dubin's crime/cop shows are very much from the hard-grain **Naked City, 87th Precinct, M Squad** vein of TV drama, maintaining the hard-hitting, ruthless ingredients. After some fifteen years of wailing sirens, Dubin can now rest his case on the exceptional *Kojak's Days* two-parter—one of the best segments in the series, and one of the best examples of the small-screen genre. Charles Dubin has taken a long time trying to get to Carnegie Hall, through countless mobsters, armed robberies, and sleezy characters. If he fails to make it soon the place may well be cordoned-off by police.

Rick Edelstein

1975: **Marcus Welby MD**/*Four Plus Hot.* 1977: **Starsky and Hutch** (story editor), *I Love You Rosey Malone, A Body Worth Guarding* (+ wr).

Edelstein was shipped in, it appears, when the networks slammed down the violence in shows like **Starsky and Hutch**, reducing them to the level of sugar-coated soap-operas. The *I Love You Rosey Malone* segment is a suitable example of this slushiness; The two heroes get weepy and mushy when one of them can't walk into the sunset with a gangster's daughter. This shouldn't really reflect on Edelstein's capabilities—but his natural pasture does seem to be in the direction of something like **As the World Turns**—long running day-time soap-opera.

Harry Falk

1969: **Mr Deeds Goes to Town**/*The Education of Longfellow Deeds, Sparkling Spring, Touching Is Believing, The Marriage Saver, Tricks of the Trade, Tarnished Armor;* **Three's A Crowd**. 1970: **Owen Marshall, Counselor at Law**/*Eight Cents Worth of Protection;* **The Tim Conway Show**/*Gone Is My Co-Pilot, All of Our Aircraft Is Missing, The Boys in the Bandwagon, A Star Is Airborne.* 1971: **Alias Smith and Jones**/*The Posse That Wouldn't Quit;* **Owen Marshall, Counselor at Law**/*Shadow of a Name, Burden of Proof, Shine the Light on Me, Victim in Shadows.* 1972: **Hawaii Five-O**/*The Jinn Who Clears the Way;* **Owen Marshall, Counselor at Law**/*Murder in the Abstract, Libel Is a Dirty Word, Who Saw Him Die?, Words of Summer, Five Will Get You Six;* **McCloud**/*The Barefoot Stewardess Caper.* 1973: **Caribe**/*The Patriots;* **Owen Marshall, Counselor at Law**/*Final Semester, The Prowler.* 1974: **MacMillan and Wife**/*Guilt by Association, The Game of Survival;* **Men of the Dragon; Owen Marshall, Counselor at Law**/*Desertion of Keith Ryder;* **The Streets of San Francisco**/*Mask of Death, Jacob's Boy.* 1975: **MacMillan and Wife**/*Aftershock;* **The Abduction of St Anne; The Streets of San Francisco**/*The Glass Dart Board, Runaway, Requiem for Murder, The Honorable Profession;* **Harry O**/*One for the Road, The Acolyte;* **Cannon**/*Killer on the Hill;* **Bert D'Angelo Superstar**/*The Brown Horse Connection, The Book of Fear, What Kind of Cop Are You?* 1976: **Whatever Happened to the Class of '65?**/*Everybody's Girl, The Class Athlete;* **Tales of the Unexpected**/*Devil Pack;* **The Streets of San Francisco**/*The Drop;* **Rich Man, Poor Man: Book II**/pts 5 & 7. 1977: **Rosetti and Ryan**/*Ms Bluebeard.*

Harry Falk's TV career reflects a slow-but-sure move from lightweight programme material, through semi-social middle-ground series, to the tough, heavyweight areas of the mid-1970's. *The Posse That Wouldn't Quit* (via **Alias Smith and Jones**) connects directly back to the inspirational source of BUTCH CASSIDY AND THE SUNDANCE KID, with an episode emulating the *superposse* sequence. Nevertheless, the segment remains an interesting variant on the theme and is, perhaps, one of the show's better segments. Falk also appears to have an inclination, an involvement with family feelings during times of trouble, whether paternal or marital. Both *Jacob's Boy* and *The Drop* segments of **Streets of San Francisco** play out the cause and then hover, almost voyeur-like, around the effect.

More recently, Falk has lost himself somewhere among the prime-time programmers, but he's almost sure to re-surface in the vicinity of a YOU ONLY LIVE ONCE theme.

John Florea (1920-   )

1957-1960: **Sea Hunt** (pr-dir). 1962: **Bonanza**/*Any Friend of Walter's, Rich Man Poor Man.* 1963: **Temple Houston**/*The Dark Madonna;* **Bonanza**/*The Saga of Muley Jones, The Roper, Twilight Town.* 1964: **The Virginian**/*The Girl from Yesterday, The 30 Days of Gavin Heath;* **Bonanza**/*A Man to Admire, Old Sheba, Walter and the Outlaws, Invention of a Gunfighter.* 1965: **The Virginian**/*Legend for a Lawman, The Payment;* **Honey West** (multiples). 1966: **Daktari** (multiples). 1967: **Gentle Ben**/*The Green-Eyed Bear, Gator Man, Battle of Wedloe's Woods, Warden for Man and Beast;* **Islands of the Lost** (+ pr); **Cowboy in Africa** (multiples). 1969: **Ironside**/*Programmed for Danger, The Wrong Time The Wrong Place, Dora, No Game for Amateurs.* 1970: **Mission Impossible**/*Elixir;* **Ironside**/*Backfire, Escape, Riddle in Room 6.* 1975: **Barbary Coast**/*The Ballad of Redwing Jail.*

John Florea was a photo-journalist with *Life* magazine for ten years, then, during the early 1950s, associate editor of *Colliers*, before taking up with TV and becoming producer-director of the **Sea Hunt** series. Florea's most interesting work for the small screen *may* well be found somewhere among his western material, the **Bonanzas**, the **Temple Houstons**, and the **Virginians**. Following that phase he slumped into the realm of juvenile programming and Ivan Tors's productions; **Gentle Ben** may be worse than **Daktari**, but **Islands of the Lost** is surely hitting the rock-bottom. **Ironside**, at first, appeared to be a swing in another, more serious, direction, particularly with a side-trip to the complexities of **Mission Impossible**, but the journey was short and Florea was soon back among the silly symphonies.

Kenneth Gilbert

1975: **Cannon**/*House of Cards.* 1976: **Streets of San Francisco**/*One Last Trick.* 1977: **Bionic Woman**/*Motorcycle Boogie.*

Practice has only recently begun for Gilbert, but he deserves inclusion here for *Motorcycle Boogie*, which teams **The Bionic Woman** with Evel Knievel. (It was inevitable that he should guest on such a show, for *he* is the real sensation, being held together with all manner of mechanical marvels if not real bionics). 'Coded tapes' are stolen and bionic Wagner is sent to an Eastern country to recover them—encountering Evel there, but refusing to believe that he is who he really is. Much of the show—dialogue scenes included—takes place on fast moving machines, and to some it is one of the best of the series, if only for the splendid action which Gilbert orchestrates. Slow motion and fast-cutting build up the atmosphere of chase-in-progress, and there is exciting stunt action; in an attempt to jump a broken bridge Evel and Wagner plummet into the water below; the climax occurs when, surrounded by KGB-types and police, Evel takes the one way out to cross the border (a sixty foot wide road with fencing all around). 'You're crazy, only Evel Knievel could do that' screams Ms Wagner—but, of course—and mighty spectacularly—the jump is made. If there is a question mark about Gilbert's handling of any scene not on wheels, maybe it can be put down to Evel's lack of dramatic talent. As Gilbert's other shows are firmly formula (though *One Last Trick* is co-written by Chris Kazan, son of Elia), perhaps we should welcome a talent that is not afraid to just have fun. *Boogie* is probably not a flash in the pan and there should be more refreshing action from forthcoming Gilbert segments.

Robert Gist

1960: **Peter Gunn** (multiples). 1963: **Great Adventure**/*Escape;* **Ben Casey** (multiples); **Empire**/*When the Gods Laugh.* 1967: **Slattery's People**/*Question: What's a Genius Worth This Week?, Question: Remember the Dark Sins of Youth?, Question: How Do You Fall in Love with a Town?, Question: Is Democracy Too Expensive This Year?, Question: What's a Swansong for a Sparrow?* 1965: **Trials of O'Brien**/*Never Bet on Anything That Talks, How Do You Get to Carnegie Hall?;* **Dundee and The Culhane**/*The To Catch a Thief Brief.* 1969: **Hawaii Five-O**/*Singapore File.* 1970: **The Virginian**/*Nightmare.*

STRANGERS ON A TRAIN, THE NAKED AND THE DEAD, AL CAPONE are some of the films Gist acted in from 1949 to 1961. He is, however, a TV research problem. A mere smattering of directorial credits—one of which, *How Do You Get to Carnegie Hall?* plants Gist firmly in this category, although the quality of the work itself should guarantee him a place in the Ballroom. His 1966 feature AN AMERICAN DREAM was mentioned in the Sarris despatches (' . . . can be described with some affection as the worst picture of the year because of the hilarious misalliance of Mailer and Hollywood. Robert Gist's direction lingers films Gist acted in from 1949 to 1961. He is, however, a TV research problem. A conviction deserves another chance with less intransigent material'). Not only has there not been another chance, there has been precious little TV either, and what there is is a far cry from the heady days of **Peter Gunn**, the engaging antics of **Trials of O'Brien**, and the ever excellent **Slattery's People**. We can only conclude that Gist failed to practice enough, and has been forced through circumstances to give up altogether. We could always be wrong!

Alex Grasshoff

1973: **Toma**/*The Bambara Bust, A Funeral for Max Fabian.* 1974: **Movin' On**/*Ransom;* **Kolchak: The Night Stalker**/*The Zombie, Bad Medicine, The Energy Eater;* **The Rockford Files**/*The Dexter*

Crisis, Exit Prentice Carr; **Toma**/*The Friends of Danny Beecher, The Contract on Alex Cordeen.* 1975: **Get Christie Love!**/*For the Family Honor;* **The Rookies** (multiples); **Barbary Coast**/*Arson and Old Lace, The Dawson Marker, The Day Cable Was Hanged, Irish Luck.*

In the capacity of writer/producer/director, Alex Grasshoff has collected three Academy Award nominations (for documentaries), won an Oscar (for YOUNG AMERICANS, in '68), and scored at the 1973 Cannes Film Festival (with FUTURE SHOCK). Grasshoff's TV material has generally been above-average although he is still regarded as an outside runner. Crime drama interests him most; he has devoted the greater part of his time to such police/private-eye material as **Toma, The Rockford Files, Get Christie Love!**, and **The Rookies**. Odd-ball humour seems to surface here, though (particularly with **Rockford Files**), it implies that Grasshoff doesn't take his subject matter too seriously. This lightweight streak can be pleasing in some segments, detrimental in others. His **Kolchak: The Night Stalker** segments are surprisingly routine, in comparison with the general theme of the demons-and-devils format; *Bad Medicine*, in which an evil American Indian spirit turns up in Chicago, is one of Grasshoff's better attempts at creating atmosphere with incredible material. Grasshoff, it seems, has yet to decide whether he should work in semi-serious drama or semi-serious comedy.

Harry Harris

1961: **Gunsmoke**/*Catawomper, Durham Bull, Perce, Miss Kitty, All That, Apprentice Doc;* **Stagecoach West**/*A Place of Still Waters.* 1962: **Gunsmoke**/*The Dealer, Cale, The Boys, The Search, Collie's Free, Call Me Dodie, The Hunger, The Way It Is, Cotter's Girl, The Cousin, Ash.* 1963: **Gunsmoke**/*Old York, Jeb, Kate Heller, Far Places, I Call Him Wonder, Anybody Can Kill a Marshal;* **Naked City**/*Howard Running Bear Is a Turtle;* **Rawhide**/*Incident at Two Graves, Incident at Confidence Creek, Incident of the Wild Deuces, Incident of the Pied Piper;* **1964**: **Gunsmoke**/*The Violators, Doctor's Wife, Take Her She's Cheap, Innocence, Jonah Hutchinson, Help Me Kitty, Deputy Festus, Run Sheep Run.* 1965: **Voyage to the Bottom of the Sea**/*And Five of Us Are Left, Leviathan;* **Lost in Space**/*The Keeper* (2 pts); **A Man Called Shenandoah**/*The Locket, A Special Talent for Killing, Obion–1866;* **The Legend of Jesse James**/*The Man Who.* 1966: **Voyage to the Bottom of the Sea**/*Killers of the Deep, Monster from the Inferno, The Haunted Submarine, The Plant Man;* **Lost in Space**/*His Majesty Smith, All That Glitters, Space Circus, The Deadly Games of Gamma 6;* **The Time Tunnel**/*One Way to the Moon.* 1967: **Voyage to the Bottom of the Sea**/*The Mummy, No Escape from Death, The Deadly Dolls, Journey with Fear, Man of Many Faces;* **Lost in Space**/*Treasure of the Lost Planet;* **The Time Tunnel**/*Merlin the Magician;* **Hondo**/*Hondo and the Sudden Town, Hondo and the Ghost of Ed Dow;* **Mission Impossible**/*The Ransom.* 1968: **Land of the Giants**/*Framed, The Flight Plan, Double-Cross, The Weird World;* **High Chaparral**/*Ebeneezer, The Glory Soldiers.* 1969: **Land of the Giants**/*The Lost Ones, Brainwash, The Bounty Hunter, Deadly Lodestone, Seven Little Indians, Rescue, Sabotage, Shell Game, The Mechanical Man, The Inside Rail, The Unsuspected, Giants, And All That Jazz, Every Boy Needs a Dog;* **High Chaparral**/*Feather of an Eagle, Our Lady of Guadaloupe.* 1970: **Land of the Giants**/*Comeback, Home Sweet Home, Pay the Piper, The Deadly Dart, Doomsday, A Small War, Wild Journey;* **Men from Shiloh**/*Gun Quest, The*

Town Killer, Jenny. 1971: **The D.A.**/*The People Versus Drake, The People Versus Lindsay, The People Versus Walsh, The People Versus Boley.* 1972: **Adam 12**/*Gifts and Long Letters.* 1974: **Kung Fu**/*This Valley of Terror, The Predators, A Lamb to the Slaughter, The Thief of Chendo, The Brothers Caine.* 1975: **The Blue Knight**/*The Pink Dragon;* **Doc Elliot**/*A Man of Importance, The Carrier, A Time to Grow, Survival Story;* **The Waltons**/*The Sermon, The Prophecy, The Search, The Genius, The Estrangement.* 1976: **Gibbsville** (pilot); **Hawaii Five-O**/*Requiem for a Saddle Bronc Rider;* **The Waltons**/*The Burnout* (2 pts), *The Fledgling, The Vigil, The Cloudburst.* 1977: **Man from Atlantis**/*Hawk of Mu;* **The Waltons**/*The Elopement, The Career Girl, The Inferno, The Long Night, The Achievement, The Stray, The First Casualty.*

The Harry Harris and Sobey Martin collections seem almost identical, at least from the '60's on. The frames are the same—only the individual canvasses, on closer inspection, contain a slight variation. Wherever the possibility of comparisons arise—and there are many—it is Martin who comes out ahead in the content and structure department. Both applied themselves to the western during the early 1960s (**Gunsmoke, Rawhide**, etc.), then spent many years daubing Irwin Allen landscapes during the mid-to-late '60s. Martin got in first here, and spent the first-season sharing the **Voyage to the Bottom of the Sea** canvas with John Brahm, Leonard Horn, Alan Crosland, Gerd Oswald, etc., before Harris picked up on the second-season. **Lost in Space** was almost the same, except that Harris came in during the first-season and did his best work for Allen, with the two-part *The Keeper*. Scripted by Barney Slater (a regular **Lost in Space** writer), and featuring a cool, methodical Michael Rennie as the title character, *The Keeper* stands as the Mount Rushmore of **Lost in Space** episodes, the juvenile outlook and antics are broken down to a bare minimum, allowing the cold Rennie character to dominate the story and demand a serious approach. Harris managed to turn this two-parter into the closest example of intelligent s-f that the show achieved. (His later efforts returned and conformed to the regular juvenile requirements.) **Land of the Giants** was a carefully controlled circus of special effects that didn't allow Harris, or even Martin, scope to develop anything other than the routine Allen juvenilia. Harris made a sudden jump into more adult, urban landscapes with Jack Webb's D.A. series—but as if shocked by what he saw on the streets, he quickly retreated, into pastoral portraiture with **The Waltons.**

Leonard Horn (1926-1976)

1956-1958: **Playhouse 90, Studio One** (multiples). 1959: **Alfred Hitchcock Presents**/*True Account.* 1960: **Route 66** (multiples); **The Untouchables** (multiples). 1961: **Follow the Sun** (multiples); **Dr Kildare** (multiples). 1962: **Alfred Hitchcock Hour**/*Tender Poisoner;* **Stoney Burke** (multiples). 1963: **The Defenders**/*Mind Over Murder, The Pillman;* **The Outer Limits**/*The Man Who Was Never Born, The Zanti Misfits;* **The Eleventh Hour** (multiples); **Empire**/*Hidden Asset.* 1964:

The Defenders/*The Objector;* **The Outer Limits**/*Children of Spider Country;* **Voyage to the Bottom of the Sea**/*The Fear Makers, The Mist of Silence, The Sky Is Falling, Submarine Sunk Here, The Magnus Beam;* **The Nurses** (multiples). 1965: **Voyage to the Bottom of the Sea**/*The Condemned, The X Factor, Terror on Dinosaur Island;* **The Farmer's Daughter** (multiples); **Lost in Space**/*Invaders from the Fifth Dimension.* 1966: **Hawk**/*The Shivering Pigeon, Thanks for the Honeymoon;* **The Fugitive**/*With Strings Attached, A Taste of Tomorrow;* **Voyage to the Bottom of the Sea**/*The Death Watch.* 1968: **Ironside**/*Split Second to Our Epitaph* (2 pts); **It Takes a Thief**/*One Illegal Angel, Locked in the Cradle of the Deep, The Packager* (+ pr), *Get Me to the Revolution on Time.* 1969: **Lost Flight; Mission Impossible**/*Operation Rogosh, Zubrovnik's Ghost, The Short Tail Spy, Action! The Reluctant Dragon, Trek, Operation Heart.* 1970: **The Bold Ones: The Lawyers**/*One Lonely Step, Dagger in the Mind.* 1971: **The Hunter.** 1972: **Ironside**/*Five Days in the Death of Sgt Brown;* **Corky; Climb an Angry Mountain.** 1973: **The Snoop Sisters**/*Corpse and Robbers, The Devil Made Me Do It;* **The Bait; Faraday and Co**/*Fire and Ice;* **Hijack.** 1974: **MacMillan and Wife**/*Night Train to LA;* **Police Woman**/*No Place to Hide.* 1975: **The New Original Wonder Woman.**

Leonard Horn was duty officer on much of the best that TV has to offer, yet no personal imprint remains. His involvement with prime-time material for over two decades would lead one to expect some personal expression or preference. Horn's record, however, merely shows a series of potential peaks and dangerous depths that read like a cardiograph register. There is no sense of balance and no common themes to be found in his work. **The Defenders** does not relate to **Voyage to the Bottom of the Sea; The Untouchables** does not parallel **Dr. Kildare.** Television influenced Horn more than Horn influenced television. During the '70s, Horn shifted into a lower gear with female-dominated series (**The Snoop Sisters, MacMillan and Wife, Police Woman** and **The New Original Wonder Woman**), none of which are quality re-run material—with the single possible exception of the Wonder woman telefeature. It is easy to dismiss Horn in favour of directors who have progressed to 'better' things, but it should be remembered that Horn had a hand in almost everything that was good for 20 years.

Alf Kjellin (1920-)

1962: **Alfred Hitchcock Hour**/*A Tangled Web, Beyond the Sea of Death, Kill or Cure, Night Caller, Captive Audience, The 31st of February.* 1963: **Alfred Hitchcock Hour**/*How to Get Rid of Your Wife, The Cadaver.* 1964: **Alfred Hitchcock Hour**/*Where the Woodbine Twineth, Babel, Ten Minutes from Now.* 1965: **I Spy**/*Bridge of Spies, Rome . . . Take Away Three, Get Thee to a Nunnery, A Gift from Alexander;* **Man from UNCLE**/*The See Paris and Die Affair, The Gazebo in the Maze Affair, The Foxes and Hounds Affair;* **Dr Kildare**/*The Sound of a Faraway Hill, Take Care of My Little Girl;* **The Virginian**/*Nobody Said Hello;* **Alfred Hitchcock Hour**/*Completely Foolproof.* 1966: **Man from UNCLE**/*The Bat Cave Affair, The Deadly Quest Affair;* **I Spy**/*Blackout;* **Dr Kildare**/*The Bell in the Schoolhouse;* **Mission Impossible**/*The Bank.* 1967: **Man from UNCLE**/*The J for Judas Affair;* **Girl from UNCLE**/*The Uncle Samurai Affair, The Paradise Lost Affair.* 1968: **Mission Impossible**/*The Condemned, A Game of Chess.* 1970: **Ironside**/*From Hruska with Love.* 1971: **The Sixth Sense**/*I am Not a Part of the Human World;* **The Deadly Dream; Ironside**/*His Fiddlers*

Three; **The Bold Ones: The Doctors**/*Angry Man;* **Hawaii Five-O**/*Bait Once Bait Twice, Goodnight Baby, Time to Die.* 1972: **The Sixth Sense**/*Can a Dead Man Strike from the Grave?, The Man Who Died at Three and Nine* (co-dir); **Hawaii Five-O**/*Ya Don't have to Kill to get Rich but It Helps, Jury of One;* **Gunsmoke**/*Bohannon, Quiet Day in Dodge.* 1973: **The Girls of Huntington House; MacMillan and Wife**/*Freefall to Terror, The Long Way Down;* **Columbo**/*Mind Over Mayhem, Negative Reaction;* **Hawaii Five-O**/*One Big Happy Family, Flash of Color Flash of Death;* **Gunsmoke**/*The Hanging of Newly O'Brien.* 1974: **Six Million Dollar Man**/*Eyewitness to Murder;* **Hawaii Five-O**/*Computer Killer;* **Little House on the Prairie**/*Town Party Country Party.* 1975: **Switch**/*Death by Resurrection;* **The Waltons**/*The Competition, The Emergence, The Loss, The Nurse;* **Joe Forrester**/*Stakeout, Act of Violence, The Best Laid Schemes;* **Police Woman**/*Shadow of Doubt;* **The Quest**/*72 Hours;* **Code R**/*The Invaders;* **Cannon**/*Vengeance;* **The Family Holvak**/*The Long Way Home* (2 pts). 1976: **The Fantastic Journey**/*Child of the Gods;* **Sara**/*A Lady.*

Night Caller is a somewhat suitable label for Kjellin; he is attracted to potential peril and faceless fear. The **Alfred Hitchcock Hour** was a powerhouse of poisonous people; **I Spy, Man from UNCLE** and **Mission Impossible** were loaded with deadly agents and clandestine capers; **The Sixth Sense** was a further nocturnal outing with the unusual. In **The Deadly Dream**, Lloyd Bridges wakes from a nightmare that a strange group of people are after him only to discover that they *really* are. *The Invaders*, in **Code R** arrive as a potentially menacing motorcycle gang and are treated like an advance scout from Hell. Though he tends to cut a path through the deepest part of the forest, Kjellin usually manages to rise above the formal and suggest a thirst and an urgency. There is an increase in adrenalin even when it is unnecessary.

Paul Krasny

1970: **Mission Impossible**/*The Mercenaries, Bag Woman, The Crane, Cable Car* (aka *Train), Break, Imitation, The Fighter, The Killer;* **Hawaii Five-O**/*Force of Waves;* **The D.A.**/*Conspiracy to Kill.* 1972: **The Adventures of Nick Carter.** 1974: **Lucas Tanner**/*Cheers, A Touch of Bribery;* **Big Rose.** 1975: **Mobile One**/*Road Block.* 1976: **Gemini Man**/*Suspect Your Local Police;* **Serpico**/*Danger Zone;* **Joe Panther.** 1977: **Man from Atlantis**/*Imp;* **Quincy**/*Matters of Life and Death, Accomplice to Murder;* **Switch**/*Who Killed Lila Craig?, Dancer;* **Chips** (multiples).

The Adventures of Nick Carter, with its rich 1900s detail, and **Joe Panther**, with its feel for the everyday life and reality of the modern Seminole Indian, suggest that a latent documentarist lurks behind the **Mission Impossible** and **Gemini Mans**. Krasny is more interested in the 'how' than the 'why'. Krasny has to function as best he can in the frenetic world of TV. Moments of trust frequently break through in even the most routine of his work (*Imp*) to make us feel that, at any moment, the 'real' Krasny will reveal himself and take everyone by surprise with a masterpiece.

Harvey S. Laidman

1975: **The Waltons**/*The Wingwalker, The Abdication.* 1976: **The Waltons**/*The Secret, The Test, The House, The Comeback, The Nightwalker, The Rebellion;* **Hawaii Five-O**/*See How She Runs, Tsunami.* 1977: **Kojak**/*Mouse;* **Kingston: Confidential**/*Seed of Corruption.*

Harvey Laidman served time on the domestic trivialities of the sudsy **Waltons** before emerging suddenly into the dark avenues of the wailing-siren shows. Many directors have made the transition, stepping from a soft-hearted genre into a mean-streets locale, and many have rapidly returned to green pastures. **Kojak** does not seem to be a natural advancement from such tissue-paper material as **The Waltons**, which may suggest that Laidman might well revert to handling corn-cob drama.

Richard Lang

1972: **Kung Fu**/*The Soul Is the Warrior.* 1973: **Kung Fu**/*The Assassin, The Brujo, The Salamander, The Soldier, The Gunman, A Dream Within a Dream, In Uncertain Bondage, Crossties, The Arrogant Dragon, The Cenotaph* (2 pts). 1974: **Harry O**/*Eyewitness, Coinage of the Realm, Confetti People, Silent Kill, Street Games, The Last Heir;* **Kung Fu**/*Blood of the Dragon* (2 pts), *Cry of the Night Beast, A Small Beheading.* 1975: **Harry O**/*Portrait of a Murder, Shades, Tender Killing Care, APB Harry Orwell, Reflections, Mr Five and Dime, Past Imperfect, Forbidden City, Ruby, Victim.* 1976: **Tales of the Unexpected**/*The Final Chapter, Mark of Adonis, Force of Evil;* **Charlie's Angels**/*Hellride, Target Angels, Night of the Strangler;* **Most Wanted**/*The Hit Man;* **Streets of San Francisco**/*Monkey is Back.* 1977: **Scorpion** (aka **Shack**); **Fantasy Island.** 1978: **Vegas** (pilot); **The Word** (8 pts).

The thirty-two segments of Jerry Thorpe's **Kung Fu** and **Harry O** series established him as a stylish and elegant talent, with an ability to communicate the pain and isolation of losers and loners in a natural, unsentimental manner. **Charlie's Angels** and **Most Wanted** segments were warning signs which Lang seems to have heeded—for two interesting telefeatures **Scorpion** and **Fantasy Island** and the **Vegas** pilot earned him **The Word**, which was an eight hour miniseries from the Irving Wallace novel. It reunited him with **Harry O**'s David Janssen. Lang had locations in Los Angeles, New York, London, Rome and Amsterdam, 85 shooting days and a total budget of $7,000,000. Such luxury is a graphic illustration of how far TV films have progressed from the original Warner Bros. deal—and indicates Lang's rise on the commercial ladder. If he can keep his cool, concerned style, and rise to the challenge that has defeated other directors, he will have achieved something very major in anyone's terms.

Anton (Tony) M. Leader

1953: **Schlitz Playhouse of Stars**/*The Twelve Year Secret.* 1957: **Playhouse 90** (multiples). 1958: **Sugarfoot**/*Small Hostage.* 1959: **Lawman**/*The Master.* 1960: **The Twilight Zone**/*Long Live Walter Jameson;* **The Brothers Brannagan**/*Tune in for Murder, Mistaken Identity, The Twisted Root, Delayed Payment, Sunday's Jewels, Equinox, Treasure Hunt, Death Is Not Deductable, A View of Murder, Shot in the Dark, The Damaged Dolls, Duet, Murder Fits the Frame.* 1961: **The Twilight Zone**/*The Midnight Sun;* **Rawhide**/*The Black Sheep;* **Father of the Bride**/*The Wedding.* 1962: **Rawhide**/*Abilene.* 1963: **Espionage**/*Castles in Spain.* 1964: **Daniel Boone** (multiples). 1965: **Lost in Space**/*The Reluctant Stowaway, Island in the Sky;* **Rawhide**/*The Calf Woman;* **Laredo**/*Pride of the Rangers;* **The Virginian**/*The Brothers, The Horse Fighter, Morgan Starr, Ride a Cock Horse to Laramie Cross, The Mark of a Man.* 1966: **The Virginian**/*Ride to Delphi;* **I Spy** (multiples). 1967: **The Virginian**/*The Gentle Tamers;* **Ironside**/*The Man Who Believed, Force of Arms, To Kill a Cop, The Challenge* (aka *Eye of the Beholder), Trip to Hashbury;* **Get Smart**/*House of Max* (2 pts); **Tarzan** (multiples). 1968: **Star Trek**/*For the World Is Hollow and I Have Touched the Sky;* **The Virginian**/*Aleen;* **Ironside**/*Shell Game, Sgt Mike.* 1969: **The Virginian**/*Touch of Hands, The Runaway, The Bugler;* **Ironside**/*L'Chayim;* **It Takes a Thief** (multiples). 1970: **The Virginian**/*The Substitute, Rich Man Poor Man;* **Hawaii Five-O**/*The Guamerius Caper, Beautiful Screamer, The Gunrunner.* 1971: **Nichols**/*Man's Best Enemy.*

The West has been Tony Leader's most significant arena for the small screen. His forays into other fields and areas have been unrewarding. William Claxton's West is one of sprawling family ranches; Richard Bare's West is one of wandering adventurers; Leader's West is populated with the basic elements of the genre, sometimes cliché, but mostly essential for the myth. Characters with a definite aim in life populate his films. From the backwoodsmen of **Daniel Boone** to the Rangers of **Laredo,** Leader deals with men who have a purpose in what they do, regardless of method and manner. The **Sugarfoot** character may be as cliché as the **Lawman** character, but he has a slot to fill, and as such, serves a purpose.

Leader's professionals have a definite aim; the drovers in **Rawhide** may take an inordinate time to move their herd along the Sedalia Trail but they still have an objective, and they make it. The cowboys in **The Virginian** are employed to run and maintain the Shiloh ranch and they do it, regardless of the events that otherwise affect their lives. It is no more than justice that the Western Heritage Award was presented to Tony Leader for *The Horse Fighter* ('65) segment of **The Virginian**—clear evidence that his **Virginian** episodes were seen to be amongst the high-rollers of the series. Critics may miss them but the lovers of the West do not.

His spy and cop shows are all essays on team-work; From Steve Dunne and Mark Roberts in **The Brothers Brannagan** to Jack Lord and James MacArthur in **Hawaii Five-O**, from Cosby and Culp in **I Spy** to Wagner and Astaire in **It Takes a Thief**, people run in pairs and interdependency. The need for others to help one to survive under duress is a perennial feature of all Leader's work. There may be a target, but it cannot be reached alone.

Alan J. Levi

1975: **The Bionic Woman**/*A Thing of the Past, Angel of Mercy;* **The Invisible Man**/*Man of Influence, Eyes Only, Barnard Wants Out, The Klae Dynasty, Power Play.* 1976: **The Gemini Man** (pilot) *Smithereens, Minotaur, Night Train to Dallas, Return of the Lion;* **The Bionic Woman**/*The Deadly Missiles, Road to Nashville, Biofeedback, Sister Jaime, Deadly Ringer* (2 pts). 1977: **The Bionic Woman**/*Escape to Love, The African Connection, Once a Thief, The Night Demon, Beyond the Call;* **Six Million Dollar Man**/*Sharks!* (2 pts); **Return of the Incredible Hulk.**

Alan Levi does not appear to have worked with one 'normal' hero/heroine during his Universal TV spell. From the anatomical gadgetry of **Six Million Dollar Man** and its off-shoot, **The Bionic Woman**, to the fading heroes of **The Invisible Man** and, the follow-up, **The Gemini Man**, Levi has had to dodge and duck between the special effects and camera trickery. However, *The Night Demon*, via **The Bionic Woman**, contains some effectively eerie moments, supported convincingly by Jeff Corey and Gary Lockwood, and manages to combine supernatural and scientific effects quite successfully. *Sharks!* opened the fifth season ('77-'78) of the **Six Million Dollar Man** series with some impressive underwater photography, though there is little else to distinguish this formula—two-parter. Alan Levi appears to operate as an efficient component in bringing kiddie-oriented shows to the adult-viewer market.

Jerry London

1969: **Hogan's Heroes**/*The Defector, Get Fit or Go Fight, Standing Room Only, Six Lessons from Madame La Grange.* 1970: **Hogan's Heroes**/*That's No Lady That's My Spy, Klink for the Defense, Cuisine à la Stalag 13, The Big Broadcast, Operation Tiger.* 1971: **Bob Newhart Show**/*You Can't Win Them All.* 1972: **Killdozer.** 1973: **Marcus Welby MD**/*Death Is Only a Side Effect.* 1974: **The Rockford Files**/*Tall Woman in Red Wagon, Just by Accident;* **Marcus Welby MD**/*The Resident, The 266 Days, Last Flight to Babylon;* **Kojak**/*Night of the Piraeus, Nursemaid;* **Six Million Dollar Man**/*Nuclear Alert, Burning Bright;* **Lucas Tanner**/*Look the Other Way.* 1975: **Harry O**/*Mayday, Hostage;* **The Rockford Files**/*The Hammer of C Block, Reincarnation of Angie, Bad Deal in the Valley;* **Switch**/*Stung from Beyond;* **McNaughton's Daughter** (pilot); **Six Million Dollar Man**/*The Wolf Boy, Target in the Sky, Look Alike, The ESP Spy.* 1976: **Hawaii Five-O**/*Ready—Aim, Tour de Force, Killer Abroad;* **The Rockford Files**/*Sticks and Stones May Break Your Bones but Waterbury Will Bury You, The Trees The Bees and T.T. Flowers* (2 pts); **The Quest**/*Portrait of a Gunfighter;* **The Feather & Father Gang**/*The Golden Fleece;* **Delvecchio** (pilot), *The High Price of Justice, The Avenger;* **World of Darkness; City of Angels**/*Say Goodbye to Yesterday;* **Baretta**/*This Ain't My Bag.* 1977: **Cover Girls; Best Sellers: Wheels.**

Like Russ Mayberry, London's career began in sit-coms which is ideal training to bring out the flip humour of **Switch** and **Rockford Files**, and to cope with bionic-characters and their nutty exploits. Thus *Sticks and Stones May Break Young Bones but Waterbury Will Bury You* was a brilliant blend of throwaway, naturalistic comedy (Simon Oakland superb as a down-at-heel private eye who had to supplement his income by working in his brother's shoe store) and paranoia (Waterbury being a Pinkerton-like agency, resorting to dirty tricks to drive out the small operators like **Rockford**). But London's best **Rockford** was the impressive *Hammer of C Block*, with Garner endeavouring to help Isaac Hayes to prove his innocence of the murder of his girlfriend, for which he has just served fifteen years, only to discover that Hayes *did* effectively kill her; she committed suicide because of his constant violence. The segment expertly used Hayes's image and persona, to undermine and expose it, and was an excellent, fully-rounded character study; the jokes and humorous surface slowly eroded, and we were left with the pain of a brutish, but helpless loser. What is he to do at the end? He has lived for revenge, to prove his innocence. Not only has the platform of his life been whipped away, the world has changed, he can only turn back to crime. There are no answers in Gordon Dawson's script, just a mute freeze frame. (In fact, Hayes returned to the series, in the equally excellent, but totally different *Just Another Polish Wedding*).

Killdozer, London's first telefeature, used Theodore Sturgeon's short story to capitalise the success of **Duel**. But the bulldozer does not have the significance of the truck; the island isn't as evocative as the highway and Clint Walker doesn't have Dennis Weaver's shrill vulnerability; London is no Spielberg.

But part one of **Wheels** indicated that at least London's apprenticeship was over and that he could waltz into the ballroom. Overall, however, this **Best Sellers** entry rollercoasted through moods, styles and rhythms. It was both the best of shows and the worst. The one necessary ingredient—a controlling directorial hand was the one missing element. Perhaps no one can lick the kind of material of which **Best Sellers** is made (certainly Paul Wendkos failed with **79 Park Avenue**), for their sheer length is self-defeating. Drama demands selection and allusion: as much is left out as is kept in. In this series, the narrative has none of its own essential dramatic flow. It does not supplement the novel, it supplants it, for *nothing* is left out. Having said that, **Wheels** came closest to working—and some of its individual moments (which had more of the naturalistic comedy which London does so well) made it clear that London is sure to get it right before long.

George McCowan

[CANADA] 1964: **Playdate**/*Salt of the Earth, The Origin of the Species.* 1965: **Seaway**/*The Provocative Mademoiselle, Ghost Ship, The Viking, Abraham's Hand, The 24th Man, A Border Incident, What the Rats Knew, Don't Forget to Wipe the Blood Off* (2 pts), *Wharf Rat.* 1966: **Wojeck**/*The Cold Smile of Friends* (2 pts), *Listen! An Old Man is Speaking.* 1967: **Wojeck**/*Swing Low Sweet Chariot.* [US] **The Invaders**/*Dark Outpost.* 1968: **Felony Squad**/*Let Him Die, The 30-gram Kill.* 1969: **The Monk; Carter's Army; Ballad of Andy Crocker.** 1970: **The Love War; Dan August**/*The Union Forever, Love Is a Nickel Bag, The Titan;* **Love Hate Love; The Over the Hill Gang Rides Again.** 1971: **Face of Fear; If Tomorrow Comes; Travis Logan; Cannon** (pilot), *Blood on the Vine, The Nowhere Man, The Salinas Jackpot, The Predators;* **Run Simon Run; Welcome Home Johnny Bristol.** 1972: **Cannon**/*The Rip-Off, Sky Above Death Below, That Was No Lady;* **Streets of San Francisco**/*The Setup;* **Banacek**/*The Greatest Collection of Them All;* **The Mod Squad**/*The Connection* (pilot); **Search**/*Moment of Madness.* 1973: **Cannon**/*Come Watch Me Die, Murder by the Numbers;* **Streets of San Francisco**/*Chapel of Damned, The Victims.* 1974: **Cannon**/*Death of a Hunter, Triangle of Terror, The Deadly Trial, The Exchange, The Conspirators, Coffin Corner, A Killing in the Family, The Man Who Couldn't Forget, The Sounds of Silence.* 1975: **Cannon**/*Lady on the Run, The Set Up, The Investigator;* **Starsky and Hutch**/*The Hostages;* **Murder on Flight 502**. 1976: **Starsky and Hutch**/*The Committee, Gillian, Murder at Sea, Las Vegas Strangler.* 1977: **Starsky and Hutch**/*Starsky and Hutch on Playboy Island, The Setup* (2 pts); **Charlie's Angels**/*Lady Killer, The Consenting Adults, Bullseye, Angels on Wheels, The Vegas Connection.* 1978: **Charlie's Angels**/*Mother Goose Is Running for His Life, The Jade Trap.*

George McCowan sprang out of Canadian TV into the turmoil of phase-indicated American TV. He had a tele-feature spree during the early Seventies, proving that he was an efficient technician who could handle assignments without causing cardiac arrest in the executive block. In recent years, however McCowan has fallen steadily into that quagmire of 'series-directors', helming multiple episodes of **Cannon, Starsky and Hutch**, and **Charlie's Angels. The Set Up**—a two-part **Starsky and Hutch**—written by Joe Reb Moffly indicated that when he has topgrade material, McCowan will more than rise to the challenge. **The Set Up** was the best of the whole series. Unfortunately, McCowan is all too easily pleased, and his recent stint with **Charlie's Angels** shows how far down the tubes can go.

Don McDougall

1955: **Jungle Jim**/*The Avenger, The Silver Locket, Gift of Evil.* 1957: **Trackdown**/*San Saba Incident, Sweetwater Texas, Look for the Woman.* 1958: **Trackdown**/*The Town, Man and Money, The Reward, The Farrand Story, Right of Way, The Toll Road, The Wedding, The Trail, The Bounty Hunter, The Judge, The Pueblo Kid, The Winter Boys, The Mistake, The Dead, The Jailbreak, The End of the World, The Brothers, The Governor, Killer Takes All, Outlaw's Wife, Chinese Cowboy, A Stone for Benny French, Trapped.* 1959: **Trackdown**/*Enter Tenier Smith, The Deadly Decoy, Three-*

Legged Fox, Guilt, Bad Judgment, Terror, Hard Lines, Stranger in Town, The Vote, The Unwanted, Toss Up, Quiet Night in Porter, Blind Alley. 1960: **Stagecoach West**/*Life Sentence.* 1961: **Stagecoach West**/*Red Sand, Fort Wyatt Crossing, The Big Gun, High Lonesome.* 1962: **Rawhide**/*Incident of the Dogfaces, Incident of the Reluctant Bridegroom, Decision, Incident of the Trail's End, Incident of the Mountain Man, Incident at Crooked Hat;* **Bonanza**/*Song in the Dark, The Saga of Whizzer McGee.* 1963: **Rawhide**/*Incident of the Clown, Incident of the Hostages, Incident at Alkali Sink;* **The Virginian**/*No Tears for Savannah, Siege;* **Bonanza**/*King of the Mountain, The Pure Truth, No Less a Man, The Good Samaritan, A Pink Cloud Comes from Old Cathay, She Walks in Beauty, A Question of Strength, Ponderosa Matador, The First Born.* 1964: **The Virginian**/*Dark Challenge, The Brazos Kid, A Gallows for Sam Horn, Portrait of a Widow, The Drifter, Dark Destiny;* **Bonanza**/*The Hostage, Logan's Treasure, The Ballerina, The Flannel-Mouth Gun.* 1965: **A Man Called Shenandoah**/*The Young Outlaw;* **The Virginian**/*Shadows of the Past, Lost Yesterday, Beyond the Border, Timberland, The Showdown, The Fortunes of Jimmerson Jones.* 1966: **The Virginian**/*The Challenge, The Girl on the Glass Mountain, Jacob Was a Plain Man, The Strange Quest of Claire Bingham, Legacy of Hate, Linda, Without Mercy, Bitter Harvest, The Girl from the Pinto;* **T.H.E. Cat**/*The System.* 1967: **The Virginian**/*Doctor Pat, Felicity's Spring, A Small Taste of Justice, The Hell Wind, Paid in Full, Lady from Witchita, The Masquerade, Bitter Autumn, A Bad Place to Die, With Help from Ulysses;* **Star Trek**/*The Squire of Gothos.* 1968: **The Virginian**/*Silver Image, Fox, Hound and the Widow McCloud, Image of an Outlaw, Nora;* **Ironside**/*Reprise, Why the Tuesday Afternoon Bridge Club Met on Thursday.* 1969: **Lancer**/*The Measure of a Man;* **The Virginian**/*No War for the Warrior;* **Ironside**/*Eye of the Hurricane.* 1970: **The Aquarians; Men from Shiloh**/*The Animal;* **Ironside**/*The Accident, Blackout, A Killing at the Track, Laying on of Hands, Man on the Inside.* 1971: **Mission Impossible**/*Image;* **Ironside**/*In the Line of Duty, If a Body Sees a Body.* 1972: **Ghost Story**/*At the Cradle Foot, Elegy for a Vampire;* **Circle of Fear**/*Graveyard Shift, The Ghost of Potter's Field.* 1973: **The Caper.** 1974: **Kolchak: The Night Stalker**/*Legacy of Terror, The Youth Killer;* **Ironside**/*Run Scared, The Over-The-Hill Blues, The Rolling Y.* 1975: **Barbary Coast**/*Sauce for the Goose, Guns for a Queen;* **The Blue Knight**/*Candy Man;* **Gibbsville**/*Chautauqua Chautauqua Chautauqua.* 1976: **Gemini Man**/*Buffalo Bill Rides Again.* 1977: **The Bionic Woman**/*The Antidote, Max;* **Six Million Dollar Man**/*Just a Matter of Time, Rollback.*

Don McDougall is the director-who-came-to-dinner. Once involved in a series, he sees it through, even working through the entire life-span of the show. **Trackdown, Bonanza, Rawhide** and **The Virginian** all sent out invitations, and McDougall didn't decline. He likes a series to be a *series*—the longer it runs, the better. A decade, or bust, is his motto. To be sure, a series of indefinite length raises considerable formal problems as well as obvious difficulties in maintaining or developing elements of it. McDougall can hold up his end of the bargain in the directing department, but there is usually no demand made on his talent. When McDougall strayed from the established masses and made *Squire of Gothos* for Roddenberry's **Star Trek** in '66, he made the McDougall *non-western* masterpiece. *Squire of Gothos* is actually better than the *entire* third season of the show.

McDougall stayed with the TV Western for almost a decade after the genre began to disintegrate. It is a sign of the dedication and true 'feeling' for the western. McDougall has an almost serious 'seriousness'. What he couldn't do with a few telefeatures we do not know. If he is given his head, he may well push other directors down the ladder. They will then want his.

Bernard McEveety

1958-1961: **Lawman** (asst dir multiples). 1962: **Empire**/*The Tiger Inside, Season of Growth, Seven Days on Rough Street, Burnout.* 1963: **The Virginian**/*The Fatal Journey, It Takes a Big Man, The Invaders, The Mountain of the Sun.* 1964: **The Virginian**/*Black Stallion;* **Rawhide**/*The Race.* 1965: **Laredo**/*Three's Company;* **The Big Valley**/*Forty Rifles, A Time to Kill;* **Branded**/*Very Few Heroes, No Way Out;* **Rawhide**/*The Vasquez Woman.* 1966: **Bonanza**/*The Far Far Better Thing;* **The Big Valley**/*Last Stage to Salt Flats, The Death Merchant.* 1967: **Cimarron Strip**/*The Last Wolf, The Search.* 1968: **Gunsmoke**/*The Hide Cutters, Uncle Finney, The Miracle Man, Lobo, The Twisted Heritage, Reprisal, The Good Samaritans;* **Wild Wild West**/*Night of the Fire and Brimstone, Night of the Pistoleros.* 1969: **Gunsmoke**/*Coreyville, Danny, Ring of Darkness, The Cage, The War Priest, Doctor Herman Schultz MD, Kiowa, Morgan.* 1970: **Step Out of Line; Gunsmoke**/*Sam McTavish MD, Luke, The Gun, McCabe, Sergeant Holly, Tycoon, Jaekel, Pike* (2 pts). 1971: **Killer by Night; Gunsmoke**/*The Bullet* (3 pts), *Tara, One for the Road, The Predators, The Wedding.* 1972: **Gunsmoke**/*Milligan, Jesse.* 1973: **Gunsmoke**/*The Boy and the Sinner, The Widowmaker, The Widow and the Rogue, Lynch Town, Susan Was Evil, The Foundling, The Schoolmarm, A Trail of Bloodshed.* 1974: **Gunsmoke**/*A Town in Chains, Thirty a Month and Found, The Fourth Victim, The Colonel, The Angry Land, Hard Labor, The Busters;* **Banacek**/*Now You See Me—Now You Don't;* **Marcus Welby MD**/*The Outrage.* 1975: **Manhunter**/*To Kill a Tiger;* **Petrocelli**/*A Night of Terror;* **Three for the Road**/*Match Point, The Fugitives.* 1976: **Quest**/*Prairie Woman, Day of Outrage, Welcome to America Jade Snow, The Longest Drive* (2 pts), *Dynasty of Evil, Incident at Drucker's Tavern;* **The Macahans.** 1977: **How the West Was Won** (co-dir).

There are three McEveety brothers (sons of a movie pioneer father, Bernard F. McEveety, who was a unit manager at New York's Edison Studios and later director of melodramas) and thankfully for our purposes one of them (Joseph) is a writer, for Bernard and Vincent's careers so closely parallel each other that they could be, and may be are, twins.

They both began their careers as assistant directors, Bernard in 1953 at Paramount, where he remained for six years, debuting as director on **The Rebel TV** show; westerns have remained his prime field of operations. **Empire** (the modern west), **Virginian, Rawhide, Laredo, Big Valley, Branded, Bonanza, Cimarron Strip, Gunsmoke, Wild Wild West, Quest, The Macahans, How the West Was Won,** are all shows that have hit the trail with McEveety riding point.

The Fatal Journey has the most ancient of B movie plots (hero posing as an escaped convict to nail his girl friend's killer, only to learn that another escapee, who can reveal the fake's identity is due . . .) and *It Takes a Big Man* isn't any more original, 'making a man' out of a wildly spoiled youth. Things develop with *Black Stallion* in which Robert Culp is a drunken ex-vet who trains a killer horse (where was William Witney for this one?). The best McEveety of this period is *Mountain of the Sun* with James Drury guiding three widows into dangerous Yacqui country. The rough-around-the-edges style perfectly suits the trek narrative, and even the familiar backlot locations do not embarrass the conception.

Forty Rifles (Lee Majors's debut segment of **Big Valley**) reprises the 'rebel tamed' theme, and, written by Christopher Knopf is, with *Last Stage to Salt Flats* (a desert survival theme, with Lamont Johnson guest starring) McEveety's better credit at this time. He embarks on a mammoth 48 segments of **Gunsmoke** (we may presume he was happy with the show, and it with him). Clearly, a 'Gunsmokeologist' is needed to chart the astonishing twenty-year history of this series, but McEveety may like to best remember his start for: *Kiowa*, a 'searchers' theme with James Arness searching for a teenage girl captured by Indians; *A Trail of Bloodshed,* more trackdowns, more revenge; two 'outlaws-take-over-the-town' variants *Morgan* and *A Town in Chains* (with Don Stroud down in the cast list); *The Fourth Victory*, random killings panicking the Dodge citizens with Doc next on the list; *Hard Labor*, with Arness sentenced to life imprisonment for shooting a fugitive; and the three-part *The Bullet* possibly the-then longest TV western, built around Arness, who, bushwhacked, is facing death or paralysis if the bullet is not removed from his spine. Equally, however, McEveety may have other, less 'dramatic' favourites, for the majority of his shows eschew such elements and concentrate very much on 'feminine' themes, emotions and problems.

With the decline in western series through the seventies, McEveety turned to a variety of other chores, then grabbed fast to **Quest**, another SEARCHERS inspired project (Tim Matheson and Kurt Russell searching for the Indian-captured sister) but it failed the ratings test. *Welcome to America, Jade Snow* was the best of McEveety's seven segments and showed the merits of the series which were a bustling sense of reality, of 'life nasty, brutish and short' along with its defects which were Tim Matheson and Kurt Russel (no offence to them, but you can't send boys to do a westerner's job).

Vincent McEveety

1959-1963: **The Untouchables** (1st asst dir multiples). 1964: **Bonanza**/*A Knight to Remember;* **Rawhide**/*The Lost Herd, The Photographer, No Dogs or Drovers.* 1965: **Perry Mason**/*The Case of the Careless Kitten, The Case of the Baffling Bug.* 1966: **Star Trek**/*Miri, Dagger of the Mind, Balance of Terror;* **Gunsmoke**/*The Goldtakers, The Jailer, Whispering Tree;* **The Road West**/*This Savage Land* (2 pts; synd title). 1967: **Cimarron Strip**/*The Legend of Jud Starr, Journey to a Hanging, The Greeners;* **Gunsmoke**/*The Prodigal, The Pillagers, The Victim, Nowhere to Run.* 1968: **This Savage Land; Wonderful World of Disney**/*Kit Carson and the Mountain Men* (2 pts); **Gunsmoke**/*Zavala, Abelia, The Money Store, Time of the Jackals, The Mark of Cain, The Intruder;* **Star Trek**/*Patterns of Force, The Omega Glory, Spectre of the Gun.* 1969: **Cutter's Trail; Gunsmoke**/*A Man Called Smith, Charlie Noon, The Judas Gun, The Badge, Albert, Hackett, Chato.* 1970: **Gunsmoke**/*The Noose, Gentry's Law, Mirage, Cleavus, Lavery, Step Out of Life;* **Smoke.** 1971: **Gunsmoke**/*Waste* (2 pts), *Yankton, Alias Festus Haggen.* 1972: **Gunsmoke**/*Talbot.* 1973: **Gunsmoke**/*Women for Sale* (2 pts), Kitty's Love Affair, To Ride a Yellow Horse. 1974: **Wonder Woman; Gunsmoke**/*I Have Promises to Keep;* **The Rockford Files**/*The Big*

Rip-Off; **Kolchak: The Night Stalker**/*The Knightly Murders.* 1975: **Petrocelli**/*A Very Lovely Lady;* **The Last Day.** 1976: **Fantastic Journey**/*A Dream of Conquest, Innocent Prey.* 1977: **Ghost of Cypress Swamp; How the West Was Won** (co-dir). 1978: **The Busters.**

While his brother was at Paramount as a first assistant director, Vincent McEveety worked as second assistant at the Hal Roach studios and Republic before TV assignments for Disney (**Davy Crocket** and **Mickey Mouse Club**). He became a first assistant in 1959 on **The Untouchables**, graduating to associate producer and director. Like brother B., he has worked on many westerns (enthusiasts are fond of his 1968 feature, FIRECREEK) including thirty-four **Gunsmokes** (brother B. beat that by fourteen). The best of these is **Chato**, some kind of first and better run, surely, for Michael Winner's feature CHATO'S LAND. Here Ricardo Montalban plays the hunted Indian, and there are splendid sequences of pursuit and duel, Montalban leaping rocks and chasms, outfoxing those on his trail.

This was written by Paul Edwards, but McEveety's other best segments come from the pen of Jim Byrnes; all have chase and pursuit themes. The two-part *Women for Sale* (Indians capture a group of settlers and travellers and sell them to white slave traders, with Dillon on their tail); another two-parter, *Waste* (Arness delaying his hunt for an outlaw to help a small boy find his mother—a segment featuring Ellen Burstyn), and *Charlie Noon*, (with Arness taking prisoner James Best across the desert, pursued by Comanches). Trivia collectors will find it interesting that director Robert Totten acts in four McEveety segments (*The Noose, Mark of Cain, Gentry's Law, Alias Festus Haggen*) and actually stars in a fifth *Cleavus*. (Lamont Johnson is to be seen in *The Prodigal*).

Those **Gunsmokes** are among the best in the series, McEveety's urgent style is an ideal complement to the themes and variations of the genre.

He was a perfect choice to handle the tensions, the technology and territorial tournaments of **Star Trek**. One of his six segments—*Spectre of the Gun*—actually zips the crew of 'The Enterprise' back in time to the old west. *Dagger of the Mind* (where scientists on a penal planet are experimenting with the minds of the inmates) and *Balance of Terror* are, however, McEveety's best segments.

Overall there has been none of the absolute western specialisation of brother B.V. McEveety's credits are diverse. The one common denominator which links all parts of his career is, sadly, the Disney studio. From his second-assistant days through segments of **Wonderful World of Disney**, to features such as SUPERDAD and THE STRONGEST MAN IN THE WORLD McEveety (and brother Joseph who wrote both of these features and many more for Disney) has been content to coast gently where he might once have taken off. Nevertheless, when a TV western historian comes along to dissect, analyse and elucidate twenty years of small screen oaters, McEveety will be queuing for a place among the top ten talents—along with brother B. of course.

Sobey Martin (1909-)

1954: **Big Town** (dir multiples); **Cavalcade of America** (dir multiples). 1955: **Paris Precinct** (dir multiples); **Public Defender** (dir multiples); **Crusader** (dir multiples); **Millionaire** (dir multiples). 1958: **US Marshal** (dir multiples). 1960: **The Outlaws**/*Return to New March, Ballad for a Badman, Quiet Killer.* 1961: **Rawhide**/*Grandma's Money, Reunion, The Blue Spy, The Gentleman's Gentleman, The Boss's Daughters.* 1962: **Gunsmoke**/*Root Down, The Bad One.* 1964: **Voyage to the Bottom of the Sea**/*The Ghost of Moby Dick, The Invaders.* 1965: **Voyage to the Bottom of the Sea**/*The Creature, Secret of the Loch, The Traitor, Jonah and the Whale, Time Bomb, The Deadliest Game, The Peacemaker, The Silent Saboteurs, Deadly Creature Below, The Sky's On Fire;* **Lost in Space**/*The Hungry Sea, The Raft, The Sky Pirate.* 1966: **Voyage to the Bottom of the Sea**/*The Mechanical Man;* **Lost in Space**/*The War of the Robots, The Space Croppers, A Change of Space;* **The Time Tunnel**/*End of the World, The Last Patrol, Revenge of the Gods, Reign of Terror, Secret Weapon, The Alamo.* 1967: **Lost in Space**/*Visit to a Hostile Planet, The Haunted Lighthouse, Flight into the Future, The Space Creature, Deadliest of the Species, Castles in Space;* **The Time Tunnel**/*Visitors from Beyond the Stars, The Ghost of Nero, Idol of Death, Pirates of Dead Man's Island, Chase Through Time, Attack of the Barbarians, The Kidnappers.* 1968: **Lancer**/*The Prodigal, Jelly, The Wedding;* **Land of the Giants**/*Underground, Terror-Go-Round, Manhunt, The Trap, The Creed, The Golden Cage, On a Clear Night You Can See Earth.* 1969: **Land of the Giants**/*The Night of Thumbeldinbar, Target: Earth, Genius at Work, Return to Inidu, The Chase, Six Hours to Live, Collector's Item, Chamber of Fear, Land of the Lost, Our Man O'Reilly.* 1970: **Land of the Giants**/*The Secret City of Limbo, Panic, The Marionettes, Graveyard of Fools.*

Born in Leipzig, Germany, and educated at the Sorbonne in Paris, Martin was a film editor for MGM between 1936-1942. After U.S. Army service, he began to direct documentaries then joined the infant TV industry with **Your Showtime** in 1948. He won a Best Director Emmy in 1949, and has been a freelance since 1950.

Effectively he has been a sort of TV midwife, yet his career is embarrassingly shy of what today we recognise as the best of the first period. There are no **Playhouse 90s, General Electric Theatres**, etc., instead such shows as **Paris Precinct** and **Millionaire** — a series so anonymous that the remaining records list none of the creative personnel. (It is always possible, if unlikely that Martin directed all 188 segments . . .).

From 1964, he clocked in on time at the Irwin Allen fantasy factory. He remained there for over six years, undaunted by the fact that his job was to take three corners and make a square. Some of his contributions show a sense of flair and movement (*Pirates of Dead Man's Island*, for instance). Most do not, but it is presumably unfair to judge a twenty-year plus career on its tail end.

It would be more than just, if a pioneer such as Martin should prove to have done more than merely blaze trails, and left some important sign-posts along the way.

Leslie H. Martinson

1956: **Cheyenne**/*Quicksand, The Long Winter.* 1957: **Conflict**/*No Man's Road, Pattern for Violence, Passage to Maranga;* **Maverick**/*The Ghost Rider, Stage West, Relic of Fort Tejon, The Jewelled Gun, Rage for Vengeance, Days of Reckoning, Black Fire;* **Sugarfoot**/*Bunch Quitter, Brannigan's Boots, Trail's End, Strange Land, Reluctant Hero;* **Cheyenne**/*Test of Courage, Iron Trail, Dead to Rights, The Gamble, Border Affair, The Conspirators;* **Colt .45**/*Rare Specimen, Split Second, Circle of Fear.* 1958: **Bronco**/*The Long Ride Back* (pilot); **Lawman**/*Wanted, The Oath, Bloodline;* **Maverick**/*Gun Shy, The Belcastle Brand, Shady Deal at Sunny Acres, The Rivals;* **Sugarfoot**/*Brink of Fear, Ring of Sand, Royal Raiders;* **Cheyenne**/*Road to Three Graves;* **Colt .45**/*The Deserters, Decoy, Night of Decision;* **77 Sunset Strip**/*The Bouncing Chip, Vicious Circle, Hit and Run.* 1959: **The Alaskans**/*Golden Fleece;* **Lawman**/*The Young Toughs, The Ring, Red Ransom, Shackled, Lily;* **Maverick**/*The Saga of Waco Williams, The Betrayal, A Tale of Three Cities, The Ghost Soldiers;* **Doc Holliday**/*Birth of a Legend;* **Bourbon Street Beat**/*The Taste of Ashes, Torch Song for a Trumpet, The Inside Man.* 1960: **The Alaskans**/*The Long Pursuit;* **Lawman**/*Firehouse Lil, The Promoter;* **Maverick**/*Hadley's Hunters, The Bundle from Britain, Triple Indemnity;* **The Roaring 20's**/*Champagne Lady?, The Vamp, Mademoiselle from Armentieres, Million Dollar Suit;* **77 Sunset Strip**/*Publicity Brat, The Corsican Caper;* **Bourbon Street Beat**/*Target for Hate, If a Body, Last Exit, Suitable for Framing.* 1961: **Bronco**/*Beginner's Luck;* **Lawman**/*Catalog Woman, Owny O'Reilly Esquire;* **The Roaring 20's**/*Asparagus Tipps, You Can't Fight City Hall;* **77 Sunset Strip**/*The Parallel Caper;* **Hawaiian Eye**/*Man in a Rage, The Big Dealer, Swan Song for a Hero.* 1962: **The Gallant Men**/*One Puka Puka;* **Room for One More**/*The Anniversary* (pilot), *A New Twist, Little Schoolhouse in the Red, Greeks Bearing Gifts;* **77 Sunset Strip**/*Adventure in San Dede, Reunion at Balboa, Shadow on Your Shoulder.* 1963: **Temple Houston**/*The Case for William Gotch, Fracas at Kiowa Flats, The Last Full Moon.* 1964: **Temple Houston**/*Miss Catherine, Do Unto Others Then Gallop, Thunder Gap;* **No Time for Sergeants**/*Blue's Wild Yonder, Bloodhounds are Thicker Than Water, Bully for Ben, Will Gets a Right Hand Man, Have No Uniform–Will Travel, The Velvet Wriggle.* 1965: **Mister Roberts**/*Captain My–Captain?;* **Run for Your Life**/*Someone Who Makes Me Feel Beautiful, Never Pick Up a Stranger, Where Mystery Begins;* **No Time for Sergeants**/*Too Many Stockdales, How Now Brown Cow, It Shouldn't Happen to a Sergeant, The Sergeant's Kimono, Andy Meets His Match, The Day Blue Blew, Stockdale General Nuisance, A Hatful of Muscles, Where There's a Way There's a Will Stockdale, The Case of the Revolving Witness.* 1966: **Batman**/*The Penguin Goes Straight–Not Yet He Ain't.* 1969: **The Challengers; Mission Impossible**/*The Invasion, Trapped, Stone Pillow, The Question, The Deal, The Western, Two Thousand.* 1970: **The Bold Ones: The Doctors**/*A Matter of Priorities;* **Alias Smith and Jones**/*The Girl in Boxcar Number 3.* 1971: **How to Steal an Airplane; Charlie Chan: Happiness is a Warm Clue; Ironside**/*Joss Stick and Wedding Bells, Good Samaritan, No Motive for Murder.* 1972: **Ghost Story**/*Half a Death.* 1973: **Six Million Dollar Man**/*Day of the Robot, Survival of the Fittest.* 1974: **Cannon**/*Daddy's Little Girl.* 1975: **Six Million Dollar Man**/*The Bionic Criminal;* **Code R**/*A Federal Case.* 1976: **Most Wanted**/*Ms Murder.*

There is a segment of **Lawman** entitled *The Old Warhorse* which Martinson did not direct. A pity, for he surely deserves a big bag of oats and a luxuriant pasture for having toiled so long in, what would appear to be, a largely unrewarding career.

Martinson directed segments in almost every Warner TV show that appeared during the late '50s and early '60s, and spent nearly a decade drifting between them. His place has always been somewhere *down* the line; only on three occasions does Martinson actually head the line-up. Martinson came in on **Cheyenne** and **77 Sunset Strip** after Richard Bare had set the series rolling, and on **Maverick** shortly after Budd Boetticher had directed the initial episodes. Martinson's chance finally came in late 1958 with *The Long Ride Back*, which premiered the **Bronco** series which was part of the Warner Brothers' strategy against Clint Walker, the actor, following constant demands over the **Cheyenne** show. In 1959 came the intriguing one-off, the **Doc Holliday** pilot, called *Birth of a Legend.* The segment was produced by the indomitable Roy Huggins, a veritable powerhouse of small-screen ingenuity, and starred Adam West (some seven years before his famed **Batman** capers) as Doc Holliday. Sadly, there seems to be no trace of this pilot-episode in either public reference or contemporary telecast listings, and it may well be another contribution to that ever-widening limbo-land of 'lost' Television. It is especially sad as it seems to be the last great Martinson effort on tele-film before his somewhat plodding exercises on established themes and forms.

If Leslie Martinson has a style to define, then that style is exclusive to 1950's filmed TV. As such, it cannot readily be adapted to late '60s and '70s TV production. He may well be a medium director without a medium. Martinson, like so many others of his period is one of those workmen whose work for TV will be dismissed in ignorance by film theorists. The 'intellectual' army of TV historians and critics will form ranks and blindly despatch him to an area beyond snobbish concern. Like many big screen directors of earlier periods, his unyielding energy to stay the distance suggests someone of character. His best may not be 'the' best; his vision may not be startling, but it is well expressed and worthy of closer study.

Russ Mayberry

1967: **Bewitched**/*The No-Charm Charm;* **The Monkees**/*Monkees in Manhattan, Monkees in the Movies.* 1968: **The Flying Nun**/*With Friends Like Him Who Needs . . .?* 1969: **Marcus Welby MD**/*The Soft Phrase of Peace.* 1970: **Marcus Welby MD**/*Elegy for a Mad Dog, False Spring, The Highest Mountain* (2 pts); **The Virginian**/*To Be a Man;* **Four-In-One**: **McCloud**/*The Stage is All the World, A Walk in the Dark, Our Man in Paris.* 1971: **Alias Smith and Jones**/*Night of the Red Dog;* **McCloud**/*Fifth Man in a String Quartet, Encounter with Aries.* 1972: **Search**/*The Murrow Disappearance, The Gold Machine, Let Us Prey, Honeymoon to Kill, Suffer My Child;* **Ironside**/*All About Andrea, The Ghost of the Dancing Doll, An Honorable Man;* **A Very Missing Person**; **McCloud**/*The New Mexican Connection* (co-dir). 1973: **Ironside**/*In the Events of the Night, The Armageddon Song, A Death in Academe;* **Marcus Welby MD**/*No Charity for the McAllisters;* **Six Million Dollar Man**/*Wine, Women and War, The Solid Gold Kidnapping.* 1974: **Ironside**/*Raise the Devil* (2 pts), *Trial of Terror, Set Up: Danger;* **The Rockford Files**/*The Counter, Charlie Harris at Large;* **Kojak**/*Slay Ride, Two-Four-Six for Two-Hundred;* **McCloud**/*Lady on the Run;* **Fer-De-Lance**. 1975: **Baretta**/*The Secret of Terry Lake;* **Harry O**/*Book of Charges, Exercise in Fatality, Death Certificate, Group Terror;* **Six Million Dollar Man**/*Steve Austin Fugitive;* **Fools, Females and Fun**/*What About That One?* (co-dir). 1976: **Baa Baa Black Sheep**/*pilot, The Cat's Whiskers;*

Stonestreet: **Who Killed the Gatefold Model?**; **Kojak**/*A Need to Know, The Godson;* **Martinelli**: **Outside Man**; **The Rockford Files**/*The Oracle, Feeding Frenzy, Gulfe City Wildcat.* 1977: **The Rockford Files**/*Hotel of Fear;* **The Courier**: **The 3,000 Mile Chase**; **Kojak**/*Chain of Custody, I Could Kill My Wife's Lawyer;* **Best Sellers**: **Seventh Avenue** (pt 3); **The Snatching of Little Freddie**. 1978: **Kaz** (pilot).

Orignally billed as 'Russell I.B. Mayberry', he soon settled for the simpler 'Russ' and a TV career which, after a smattering of comedy, appears to have been mainly devoted to the mean streets of the Universal crime beat. Even here, comedy is not far away. It is this side of Mayberry's character that has made him a choice for many segments of the Roy Huggins/Stephen J Cannell shows (**Rockford Files, Baa Baa Black Sheep**). Although Mayberry's crime beat covers most of his recent TV work, his side-trips to the Bionic bureau also have their value and interest. The *Wine, Women and War* segment comes out as being one of the better utilisations of the science-fantasy **Six Million Dollar Man** theme. Mayberry fashions all the story's pulp/comic elements into an excellent panorama of special-effects and large-scale action, making the episode an enjoyable and acceptable excursion into the *fantastique.*

A further area of evaluation, regarding Mayberry's TV, can be found in the **Seventh Avenue** miniseries. Among the other styles and influences on it one can detect Mayberry's; the third part is actually his. It is, perhaps, the best segment in a sprawling story that tries to succeed on too many different levels.

Gerald Mayer (1919-)

1954: **Ford Theatre**/*The Mason-Dixon Line.* 1955-1956: **The Millionaire** (multiples: + pr). 1960: **Thriller**/*The Fatal Impulse, Man in a Cage.* 1961: **Adventures in Paradise**/*Somewhere South of Suva, Castaways, The Siege of Troy;* **Have Gun-Will Travel**/*The Last Judgement.* 1962: **Ben Casey** (multiples). 1963: **Bob Hope Chrysler Theatre** (multiples); **The Defenders**/*All the Silent Voices.* 1964: **Doctors and Nurses** (multiples + assoc pr); **Profiles in Courage**/*Edmund Ross.* 1965: **Slattery's People**/*Question: Does Nero Still at the Ringside Sit?, Question: What's New in Timbuctoo?;* **Peyton Place** (multiples). 1966: **The Virginian**/*Sue Ann;* **Voyage to the Bottom of the Sea**/*Deadly Waters, The Lost Bomb;* **Slattery's People**/*Color Him Red.* 1967: **The Fugitive**/*The Last Oasis;* **Voyage to the Bottom of the Sea**/*The Heat Monster;* **The Invaders**/*Task Force;* **Cimarron Strip**/*The Blue Moon Train.* 1968: **Garrison's Gorillas**/*48 Hours to Doomsday;* **Judd for the Defense** (multiples). 1969: **Mannix**/*Return to Summer Grove;* **Mission Impossible** (multiples). 1971: **O'Hara–US Treasury**/*Operation: Big Store;* **Dan August**/*The Worst Crime;* **Nichols**/*The Marrying Fool.* 1973: **Police Surgeon** (series pr) *Equal Right to Die.* 1975: **Westside Medical**/*The Witch of Four West.* 1976: **Six Million Dollar Man**/*A Bionic Christmas Carol.* 1977: **Quincy**/*The Hero Syndrome;* **Logan's Run**/*Fear Factor.*

Gerald Mayer entered TV after directing some negligible big-screen features during the 1950s. He had been involved with TV earlier, but it wasn't until the beginning of the '60s, with **Thriller, Adventures in Paradise, Have Gun-Will**

Travel, etc., that Mayer really began directing for television. Mayer worked on some of the best of the period; he was also associate producer on the **Doctors and Nurses** series (this show being a tail-end product of the acclaimed **The Nurses** series, itself inspired by Herbert Brodkin's earlier success. **The Defenders**). Mayer has travelled through many interesting TV areas, usually with a curious inclination toward legal/social dramas; **The Defenders** (lawyers), **Slattery's People** (state legislator), **Judd for the Defence** (lawyers, again), **Quincy** (medical examiner), etc. are all his field. Gerald Mayer's TV is a controlled, almost sedate, world and examines the way that people and society interact. The medical dramas (**Police Surgeon** and **Westside Medical**) also utilise this inter-relation of professional people working for the common people. *The Witch of Four West*, as a suitable example, takes the whole human-arena a step further by promoting a head-on clash between modern medicine and ritualistic self-healing, in the confines of the title hospital; the premise of the episode could be quite absurd, but Mayer handles it in a way that provokes thought rather than laughter—harking back to the old **Defenders** days of human reactions and values. The struggle for human values is, perhaps, Mayer's concern, and his perception of this area makes his TV work more *affecting* than *effective*.

Don Medford

1954: **Kraft Television Theatre; G.E. Theatre; US Steel Hour; Climax!** (multiples). 1955: **Alfred Hitchcock Presents**/*Triggers in Leash.* 1957: **Decoy** (multiples). 1958: **M Squad**/*More Deadly.* 1959: **M Squad**/*Ten Minutes to Doomsday, The Fire Makers;* **The Detectives**/*The Bait.* 1960: **The Twilight Zone**/*A Passage for Trumpet, The Man in the Bottle.* 1961: **Dick Powell Theatre**/*Tomorrow the Man;* **The Twilight Zone**/*The Mirror, Deaths-Head Revisited.* 1962: **The Detectives**/*The Trap;* **Dick Powell Theatre** (multiples); **Sam Benedict**/*Life is a Lie Love is a Cheat, Hear the Mellow Wedding Bells.* 1963: **Dr Kildare**/*A Hundred Million Tomorrows;* **The Twilight Zone**/*Death Ship;* **The Eleventh Hour** (multiples). 1964: **The Man from UNCLE** (multiples); **Suspense**/*Christopher Bell, Donald Roberts, The Savage;* **12 O'Clock High** (multiples). 1965: **The FBI**/*The Giant Killer, The Hijackers, The Insolents, Flight to Harbin.* 1966: **The Fugitive**/*Death Is the Door Prize.* 1967: **Cimarron Strip**/*The Battleground;* **The Fugitive**/*The Judgement* (2 pts); **The Invaders**/*Condition: Red, Summit Meeting* (2 pts); **The FBI**/*The Executioners* (2 pts). 1968: **The FBI**/*The Divided Man, An Elephant is Like a Rope, Courage of a Conviction, The Problem of the Honorable Wife;* **Lancer**/*Warburton's Edge.* 1969: **The FBI**/*A Mouthful of Dust, The Chameleon;* **Incident in San Francisco.** 1971: **Cannon**/*Fool's Gold;* **Streets of San Francisco**/*A Wrongful Death, The 24 Karat Plague.* 1975: **Baretta**/*The 5½ Pound Junkie, The Copelli Oath, Keep Your Eye on the Sparrow;* **City of Angels**/*The November Plan* (pilot; 3 pts). 1976: **Baretta**/*Don't Kill the Sparrows, The Reunion* (+ story), *Playin' Police, The Sky is Falling;* **Most Wanted** (pilot), *The Sky Killer, The Wolf Pack Killer, The Dutchman.* 1977: **Baretta**/*Who Can Make the Sun Shine?, All That Shatters, Hot Horse, I'll Take You to Lunch, Big Bad Charlie, Think Mink, The Runaways.*

Don Medford is something of a back-stage technician, working on above-average material yet never receiving acknowledgement or praise. Medford was a staff-director with the then-underdog network, ABC-TV,during the 1950-53 period. By the mid-fifties he broke loose into freelance directing and supplied many segments for the popular anthology shows running through the 1950s. There is a long hard strain of detective-actioners running through Medford's credits, beginning in the hard-boiled milieu of **Decoy, M Squad, The Detectives,** etc., and continuing through to the streets of **Baretta, City of Angels,** and **Most Wanted.** Medford may never attain a permanent place in the ivory halls of big-screen picture-making, due to his persistent anonymity. He is a craftsman aware of his limitations who knows where his pasture lies. His features, THE HUNTING PARTY and THE ORGANISATION, both have an edge that is not sharp enough for the cinema, but could fit well into TV slots. Medford belongs to the structure and rhythm of Television production; his theatrical features seem to have an air of the mid-Sixties Kulik TV circus. In both cases he can seem characterless.

However, most small-screen afficionados will give full credit to Don Medford for his *The Judgment* two-parter, climaxing **The Fugitive** series. Although the second part seemed to have allusions to the finale of a William Witney chapter-play, *The Judgement* remains in memory as a most polished denouement and shows that there may be more to offer.

Medford's work for the cinema may not shake cathedral bells, but the distributors keep offering up his TV work to the big-screens: the two-part *The Executioners* segment of **The FBI** turned up in Euro-theatres as COSA NOSTRA, AN ARCH ENEMY OF THE FBI, and the **City of Angels** pilot was released as a feature, retaining the title THE NOVEMBER PLAN, partly featuring the private eye, partly concerned with contemporary American paranoia, involved at plot level with a para-military operation for a *coup d'etat* in the United States. Whether the screening of a made-for-TV product in movie theatres is something of a veiled compliment to television, or merely a mis-use of media can be argued. THE NOVEMBER PLAN lacked the necessary production values for the cinema. Despite his anonymity, however, Medford may go down in records as a big screen director, simply by working for Television.

Irving J. Moore

1959: **Tightrope**/*The Neon Wheel, Broken Rope, Three to Make Ready, The Model and the Mob, The Brave Pigeon, The Park Avenue Story.* 1960: **Lawman**/*The Promise;* **Maverick**/*The Bold Fenian Men, Dodge City or Bust;* **Roaring 20's**/*The Twelfth Hour;* **77 Sunset Strip**/*The Duncan Shrine, The Affairs of Adam Gallante, The Hamlet Caper, The Positive Negative;* **Tightrope**/*The Chinese Pendant, Achilles and His Heels, Gangster's Daughter, The Penthouse Story, Borderline, A Matter of Money.* 1961: **Lawman**/*No Contest, By the Book;* **Maverick**/*Flood's Folly, The Maverick Report,*

Epitaph for a Gambler, Dade City Dodge, The Golden Fleecing; **Roaring 20's**/*Scandal Sheet* (aka *Party Girl), Among the Missing;* **Hawaiian Eye**/*Somewhere There's Music.* 1962: **Surfside 6**/*Country Gentleman, Double Image;* **Hawaiian Eye**/*Caves of Pele;* **77 Sunset Strip**/*Leap My Lovely, The Floating Man.* 1963: **Bonanza**/*Journey Remembered;* **Temple Houston**/*Enough Rope, Sam's Boy;* **Perry Mason**/*The Case of the Bountiful Beauty, The Case of the Devious Delinquent, The Case of the Wednesday Woman, The Case of the Woeful Widower, The Case of the Garrulous Go-Between.* 1964: **Perry Mason**/*The Case of the Illicit Illusion, The Case of the Tandem Target.* 1965: **Wild Wild West**/*Night of the Grand Emir, Night the Dragon Screamed;* **Hogan's Heroes**/*Look at the Pretty Snowflakes.* 1966: **Gunsmoke**/*Stage Stop, Noose of Gold, The Ladies from St Louis;* **Wild Wild West**/*Night of the Golden Cobra, Night of the Raven, Night of the Watery Death, Night of the Ready Made Corpse, Night of the Tattering Tontine, Night of the Vicious Valentine, Night of the Deadly Bubble, Night of the Bogus Bandits.* 1967: **Lost in Space**/*A Day at the Zoo;* **Gunsmoke**/*Wonder, Baker's Dozen, Buffalo Man;* **Wild Wild West**/*Night of the Bubbling Death, Night of the Jack of Diamonds, Night of the Montezuma Hoardes, Night of the Circus of Death, Night of the Deathmaker.* 1968: **Lost in Space**/*Space Beauty;* **Gunsmoke**/*The Night Riders;* **Wild Wild West**/*Night of the Big Blackmail, Night of the Doomsday Formula, Night of the Juggernaut, Night of the Avaricious Actuary, Night of the Janus, Night of the Plague.* 1969: **Hawaii Five-O**/*Leopard on the Rock.* 1971: **Gunsmoke**/*Lijah, No Tomorrow.* 1972: **Gunsmoke**/*Sarah, Eleven Dollars, Arizona Midnight.* 1973: **Gunsmoke**/*A Child Between, Like Old Times.* 1974: **Korg 70,000 BC** (multiples co-dir wr: Chris Nyby). 1975: **Quest**/*The Seminole Negro Indian Scouts.* 1976: **Fantastic Journey**/*Beyond the Mountain;* **Petrocelli**/*Edge of Evil, Mirror Mirror on the Wall, The Sleep of Reason, A Lonely Victim, The Outsiders.* 1977: **Bigfoot and Wildboy**; **Logan's Run**/*Carousel, Capture.*

Law and Lawmen are Irving Moore's most favoured images. Moore has promoted the private investigations of **Tightrope, 77 Sunset Strip, Hawaiian Eye** and **Surfside 6,** the direct law-enforcement of **Lawman, Gunsmoke** and **Hawaii Five-O,** and the courtroom justice of **Temple Houston, Perry Mason** and **Petrocelli. The Roaring 20's** and **Bonanza** also orbit somewhere around this central theme, maintaining the Irving Moore right-v-wrong signature. The only exception to Moore's pattern during this period was **Maverick,** which unloaded on him a couple of itinerant mischief-seekers. Moore's code is such that had he directed **The Fugitive** he would have made David Janssen give himself up. **Hogan's Heroes** may have been an early, almost forgivable mistake, but there is no reprieve for Moore over **Lost in Space.** More recently, his badge-carrying brigade have given way to the jarring juvenilia of **Korg 70,000 B.C., Fantastic Journey** and **Logan's Run.** There is little hope for Irving Moore unless the small-screen again pulsates with crime dramas and crime-fighters.

Hollingsworth Morse

1958: **Zorro**/*The Gay Caballero, Tornado Is Missing, Zorro Versus Cupid, The Legend of Zorro, Spark of Revenge, The Missing Feather, Please Believe Me, The Brooch;* **The Line-Up** (multiples); **The Gray Ghost**/*Problem of Command, The Humanitarian, Eye for an Eye, Point of Honor, Christmas Carol, Charity, The Missing Colonel, Jimmy, Conscript, The Escape, Renegade Rangers.* 1959: **Zorro**/*The*

Hound of the Sierras, Manhunt, Man from Spain, Treasure for the King, Exposing the Tyrant, Zorro Takes a Dare, An Affair of Honor, Invitation to Death, The Captain Regrets, Masquerade for Murder, Long Live the Governor, Finders Keepers; **The Gray Ghost**/*Russell of the Times, Ulysses S Grant, The Trial, Taps for a Hero, The Master Spy, The Bribe, The Long Way Home, Manhunt, The Hero, Secret and Urgent, Strange Bedfellows, The Picnic;* **Riverboat**/*The Quick Noose, The Long Trail, Hang the Men High.* 1963: **Laramie**/*Badge of Evil.* 1964: **No Time for Sergeants**/*Will Goes to Washington, The $100,000 Canteen.* 1968: **Adam 12**/*Log 131, Log 101, Log 11, Log 111, Log 32, Log 62, Log 122, Log 152, Log 172.* 1970: **Men from Shiloh**/*Flight from Memory, The Regimental Line.* 1971: **Emergency**/*Brushfire;* **The D.A.**/*The People Versus Saydo, The People Versus Whitehead;* **Adam 12**/*Tyrant.* 1972: **Wonderful World of Disney**/*Justin Morgan Had a Horse* (2 pts). 1973: **Marcus Welby MD**/*Endless Moment, A Question of Fault;* **Adam 12**/*Routine Patrol.* 1974: **Marcus Welby MD**/*Dark Fury* (2 pts), *Jake's Okay, No Gods in Sight, Hell is Upstairs;* **Adam 12**/*Credit Risk, Suspect No 1, Something Worth Dying For* (2 pts), *Victim of the Crime.* 1975: **Marcus Welby MD**/*Killer of Dreams, Go Ahead and Cry, The Medea Factor;* **Adam 12**/*Dana Hall;* **The Secrets of Isis**/*Light of Mystery Mountain, Fool's Dare, Lucky, To Find a Friend, The Outsider, Funny Gal, Dreams of Flight, No Drums No Trumpets.* 1976: **The Secrets of Isis**/*The Cheerleaders, The Class Clown, Year of the Dragons;* **Ark II**/*The Wild Boy, Omega, The Slaves, The Balloon, The Mind Group, Robin Hood.* 1977: **Oregon Trail**/*The Trappers' Rendezvous.*

The directorial personality of Hollingsworth Morse remains as shadowy as the characters he first directed on TV. Spending a couple of terms on the **Zorro** and **The Gray Ghost** series, Morse contributed to various series but stayed the longest with Mark VII's **Adam-12**. This police-drama series was probably his last adult-market/prime-time series, for he has since taken up with the Saturday-morning-type 'kiddie' shows; such negligible material as **Secrets of Isis** and **Ark II**. Morse's credits are long on segments but short on exceptions—proving, perhaps, that *capability* is not necessarily a consequence of *durability*.

James Neilson (1918-)

1956: **Father Knows Best**/*Bud Takes Up the Dance.* 1957: **Suspicion**/*Rainy Day;* **Alfred Hitchcock Presents**/*Reward to Finder, A Man Greatly Beloved, The Orderly World of Mr Appleby.* 1958: **Cimarron City**/*A Respectable Girl;* **M Squad**/*Shot in the Dark;* **Wagon Train**/*The Kitty Angel Story, The Last Man;* **Alfred Hitchcock Presents**/*Help Wanted, The Legacy.* 1959: **Wagon Train**/*The Martha Barham Story.* 1960: **Adventures in Paradise**/*Passage to Tua;* **Have Gun-Will Travel**/*An International Affair.* 1961: **Adventures in Paradise**/*The Color of Venom, There is an Island.* 1962: **World of Disney**/*The Scarecrow of Romney March* (3 pts). 1966: **Adventures in Paradise**/*Beached.* 1964: **Batman**/*The Clock King's Crazy Chimes–The Clock King Gets Crowned;* **The Fugitive**/*10,000 Pieces of Silver.* 1967: **Return of the Gunfighter**. 1969: **The Virginian**/*You Can Lead a Horse to Water.* 1970: **Paris 7000**/*Task Force Lockner;* **Ironside**/*Lesson in Terror, This Could Blow Your Mind.* 1971: **O'Hara–US Treasury**/ *Operation: Death Watch;* **Ironside**/*Class of '57.* 1972: **Ghost Story**/*Death's Head;* **O'Hara–US Treasury**/*Operation: Smoke Screen, Operation: Hot Shot.*

James Neilson suggests a director with schizophrenic ambitions; his theatrical features reflect a kindly Dr. Jekyll who cheerfully handles Disney fodder

(SUMMER MAGIC, THE MOONSPINNERS, BULLWHIP GRIFFIN, etc), while his Mr. Hyde character reveals a passion and tears grimly through the murder, mayhem and madness of **Alfred Hitchcock Presents, M Squad, Ironside, O'Hara—U.S. Treasury**, and **Ghost Story**. Neilson's TV-westerns (**Wagon Train, Have Gun—Will Travel, The Virginian**) exude a similar colouring of malevolence, which reaches a peak in his **Return of the Gunfighter.** Occasionally, the two natures blend and the results emerge either as diluted segments or *The Scarecrow of Romney Marsh* (aka DR. SYN ALIAS THE SCARECROW) and **Batman.** The uncertainty which occurs from operating on two conflicting paths renders Neilson an ineffectual force in television. Trapped between stuff for the kiddies and tough stuff for the adults, he vacillates and produces programmes which are too weak for the youngsters and too strong for the grown-ups.

Sigmund Neufeld Jr.

1975: **Kojak**/*Close Cover Before Killing;* **Invisible Man**/*The Fine Art of Diplomacy, Go Directly to Jail, Sight Unseen.* 1976: **Baretta**/*Soldier in the Jungle;* **Kojak**/*The Frame;* **Serpico**/*Prime Evil.* 1977: **Switch**/*Three for the Money, The Four Horsemen, The Snitch, Downshift, Go for Broke, Lady of the Deep.*

Neufeld Sr. was the producer of a flock of unbelievably bad B westerns (his are the only ones on record where shots of the stuntmen landing on mattresses after a fall are left in the release prints). If Jr. had anxieties about matching his father's achievements, they were presumably solely ones relating to the amounts of coin those pictures earned. Nevertheless, from a creative point of view he is out in front. Graduating from the **Kojak** cutting rooms to the director's chair, his series segments are punchy and vigorous and show signs of his training in their crisp setups. Having served in the packing department, he merely moved on to the shop floor. Whether he has his eyes on a management seat, or aspirations to set up his own shop, time alone will tell.

Christian Nyby

1953: **Schlitz Playhouse of Stars**/*Lucky Thirteen.* 1957: **Zane Grey Theatre**/*The Village of Fear, There Were Four.* 1958: **Wagon Train**/*The Steele Family Story, The Jenny Tannen Story.* 1959: **Wagon Train**/*The Luke Grant Story.* 1962: **Rawhide**/*Incident at Cactus Wells, Incident of the Prodigal Son, Incident at Sugar Creek, Incident at Quivira, Incident of the Gallows Tree, Incident of the Pale Rider;* **The Twilight Zone**/*Showdown with Rance McGrew;* **Bonanza**/*The Jury, The Actress, The Beginning, Gallagher's Sons.* 1963: **Rawhide**/*Incident of White Eyes, Incident of Iron Bull;* **Perry Mason**/*The Case of the Malicious Mariner, The Case of the Shapely Shadow.* 1964: **Gunsmoke**/

Hammerhead, Nightmare at Northoak; **Rawhide**/*Incident of the Wanderer, Incident at Zebulon, Incident at Hourglass, Incident of the Banker, Incident of the Gilded Goddess, Incident at Seven Fingers;* **Bonanza**/*Thanks for Everything Friend, The Scapegoat, Napoleon's Children.* 1965: **Legend of Jesse James**/*Put Me in Touch with Jesse;* **I Spy**/*Cops and Robbers, The Lotus Eater.* 1966: **Legend of Jesse James**/*Vendetta;* **I Spy**/*Laya;* **The FBI**/*The Defector* (2 pts), *The Bomb that Walked Like a Man, Quantico, Pound of Flesh, The Forests of the Night, How to Murder an Iron Horse, The Animal, The Sacrifice.* 1967: **Custer**/*Blazing Arrows;* **I Spy**/*Anyplace I Hang Myself Is Home, The Spy Business, Jelly Hoskins' American Dream, Legacy, The Rivals.* 1969: **Lancer**/*The Heart of Pony Alice, The Devil's Blessing.* 1969: **Lancer**/*The Lorelei.* 1971: **Emergency** (pilot), *Cook's Tour.* 1972: **Emergency**/*Peace Pipe, Fuzz Lady, School Days, Crash, Publicity Hound, Dilemma, Problem;* **The Partners**/*Requiem for a Godfather.* 1973: **Chase**/*The Dealer-Wheelers, Gang War, One for You Two for Me.* 1974: **Korg 70,000 BC** (multiples co-dir wr: Irving Moore); **Kojak**/*Elegy in an Asphalt Graveyard, A Killing in the Second House;* **Six Million Dollar Man**/*Stranger in Broken Fork.* 1975: **Six Million Dollar Man**/*The Deadly Test.* 1976: **Emergency**/*An Ounce of Prevention;* **The Rockford Files**/*The Trouble with Warren.* 1977: **Kingston: Confidential**/*Shadow Game.*

Those critics who exhume THE THING almost every year as an excuse to lay more palm leaves at the feet of Howard Hawks and dismiss Nyby as an accident of geography are the same faction who regard filmed Television as nothing more than a forest of insignificant, unlabelled trees. It has been said that the limitations of TV do not allow a director full scope to exhibit any style of meaning— but the same was said of Hollywood cinema for years. Nyby may appear, in general, to fail as an effective technician on the big screen, but his efforts in other areas have some value. Nyby spent over a decade directing western series for TV (**Wagon Train, Rawhide, Bonanza, Gunsmoke, Legend of Jesse James, Custer,** and **Lancer**). They reveal an area of Nyby craftsmanship unknown outside TV.

Christian I. Nyby II

1971: **Ironside**/*Find a Victim, Bubble Bubble Toil and Murder.* 1972: **Emergency**/*Musical Mania, Boot, Honest.* 1973: **Chase**/*A Bit of Class;* **Emergency**/*How Green Was My Thumb, Inferno, The Hard Hours, The Promotion, Zero, The Old Engine, Rip-Off, The Professor;* **Adam 12**/*Football Division, West Valley Division, Hot Shot.* 1974: **Six Million Dollar Man**/*The Pioneers, Act of Piracy, The Deadly Replay;* **Emergency**/*Nagging Suspicion, The Bash, Prestidigitation, The Mouse;* **Adam 12**/*Point of View, L.A. International, G.T.A.;* **The Rangers.** 1975: **Emergency**/*The Girl on the Balance Beam, The Stewardess, On Camera, TeeVee, Above and Beyond Nearly.* 1976: **Emergency**/*The Game* (+ wr), *Captain Hook, Welcome to Santa Rosa County;* **Six Million Dollar Man**/*The Thunderbird Connection.* 1977: **Emergency**/*Limelight;* **The Hardy Boys**/*Sole Survivor.*

Christian Nyby II is something of a mystery, in that his TV career is as bare of interesting areas as his father's is varied. Formerly an assistant director, his TV career reflects a hard struggle through mainly routine shows; **Six Million Dollar Man** may be the only exception to this bland route. There is further confusion by way of TV credits producing a 'Christian Nyby III' (credited for the tele-feature **Pine Canyon is Burning**, in '76). If there is Nyby III, then there may also be a Nyby IV, and so on *ad-infinitum.*

Michael O'Herlihy (1929-)

1961: **Bronco**/*The Cousin from Atlanta;* **Maverick**/*Three Queens Full, The Art Lovers, Poker Face;* **77 Sunset Strip**/*Designing Eye, The Missing Daddy Caper, The Down Under Caper, The Lovely American;* **Hawaiian Eye**/*The Manchu Formula.* 1962: **Profiles in Courage**/*The Richard T Ely Story.* 1963: **The Richard Boone Show**/*A Tough Man to Kill.* 1964: **Gunsmoke**/*Big Man Big Target, Blue Heaven;* **Rawhide**/*A Man Called Mushy, Damon's Road* (2 pts), *The Meeting, Mrs Harmon.* 1966: **Crisis**/*The Gun.* 1967: **Star Trek**/*Tomorrow Is Yesterday.* 1968: **Mission Impossible**/*The Emerald, The Town, The Legacy.* 1969: **It Takes a Thief**/*The Baranoff Timetable;* **Hawaii Five-O**/*Forty Feet High and It Kills! The Devil and Mr Frog, Run Johnny Run.* 1970:**Hawaii Five-O**/*The Second Shot, The Ransom, The Reunion, The Double Wall, Paniolo, F.O.B. Honolulu* (2 pts). 1971: **Cannon**/*The Torch, Bitter Legion;* **Hawaii Five-O**/*No Bottles No Cans No People, Wednesday—Ladies Free, . . . And I Want Some Candy and a Gun That Shoots, Air Cargo—Dial for Murder, Is This Any Way to Run a Paradise, While You're at it Bring in the Moon, Cloth of Gold, Follow the White Brick Road.* 1972: **MASH**/*To Market to Market;* **Deadly Harvest**; **Hawaii Five-O**/*Fools Die Twice, Will the Real Mr Winkler Please Die, Here Today Gone Tonight;* **Streets of San Francisco**/*Shattered Image;* 1973: **Hawaii Five-O**/*Charter for Death, The Sunday Torch, Murder is a Taxing Affair, Why Wait Till Uncle Kevin Dies?, Murder with a Golden Touch, Nightmare 'n Blue.* 1974: **Sons and Daughters**/*The Rejection, Anita's Reputation;* **Gunsmoke**/*The Tarnished Badge.* 1975: **Joe Forrester**/*Deadly Weekend;* **Medical Story**/*Woman in White;* **Quest**/*The Freight Train Rescue.* 1976: **Kiss Me Kill Me**; **The Young Pioneers**; **Hawaii Five-O**/*Nine Dragons.* 1977: **Man from Atlantis**/*Man O'War;* **Logan's Run**/*Future Past.*

Michael O'Herlihy took a few turns at directing theatrical features (THE FIGHTING PRINCE OF DONEGAL, THE ONE AND ONLY GENUINE ORIGINAL FAMILY BAND, etc.) but was always retreating to the more controllable landscape of TV. His career, despite the features is uncomfortably uneven, almost suggesting that O'Herlihy has yet to find a firm footing where he can breathe whilst standing on one foot. Hop-scotching his way through western, private-eye, s-f, spy and police genres may well imply that O'Herlihy is still waiting for a suitable genre to come along. However, as there are few suitable genres, he strung along with **Hawaii Five-O** for over 7 years.

John Peyser (1916-)

1950-1954: **I Remember Mama; Studio One; Danger; Suspense; Man Behind the Badge** (multiples). 1955: **Casablanca**/*The Return, The Obsession, Who Holds Tomorrow, Hand of Fate.* 1956: **Casablanca**/*Fortune's Child* (aka *Shadow on the Land), Fateful Night, Dead-*

lock. 1957: **M Squad**/*Family Portrait;* **Frank Sinatra Show** (multiples). 1959: **US Border Patrol**/*Crime Wave at Coral Gables, The Deadly Fool, Lapse of Time, Terror on the Gold Coast.* 1960: **The Untouchables**/*The Otto Frick Story, Little Egypt, The Waxey Gordon Story.* 1961: **Westinghouse Summer Theatre** (multiples). 1962: **Combat** (multiples); **Naked City**/*Idylls of a Running Back.* 1963: **True**/*Nitro;* **The Virginian**/*Ride a Dark Trail.* 1964: **The Man from UNCLE**/*The Dove Affair, The Green Opal Affair.* 1965: **Amos Burke–Secret Agent**/*The Wildest Raid of All, The Chain of Death Raid, The Do or Die Raid, The Last Harbour Raid* (3 pts). 1968: **Garrison's Gorillas**/*Thieves' Holiday.* 1969: **Four Rode Out; Honeymoon with a Stranger.** 1975: **Switch**/*The Cold War Con, Through the Past Deadly, The Walking Bomb, Come Die with Me, The Case of the Purloined Case, Girl on the Golden Strip, Death Squad.* 1976: **Baa Baa Black Sheep**/*High Jinx, Meatball Circus;* **Delvecchio**/*Thicker Than Water, My Brother's Keeper.* 1977: **Switch** (series pr), *Heritage of Death, Portraits of Death, The Argonaut Special, Legend of the Macunas* (2 pts).

John Peyser's most interesting TV work is in the gritty areas of crime and conflict. **M Squad, The Untouchables** and **Naked City** all revel in the dark world of victims and death, a grey landscape of tormentors and tormented, hunters and hunted. He had further opportunities to explore conflict in the wartime-based shows; Peyser was given almost free-rein with the 'freedom'-fighters: **Combat** (G.I. dogfaces), **Rat Patrol** (desert group), **Garrison's Gorillas** (saboteurs), **Baa Baa Black Sheep** (fighter squadron). The short-lived **Rat Patrol** series (shot in Spain) seemed to be a Peyser favourite—the three-part *The Last Harbour Raid* (scripted by Richard Landau from Peyser's story) was later re-edited into a theatrical-release feature, MASSACRE HARBOR. Peyser's more recent commitment to TV has been with the con capers of **Switch,** a show with its roots hidden somewhere in the **It Takes a Thief** sphere. For a director who has given so much conflict to the small-screen, this battle-weary veteran has found a peaceful grotto for relaxation.

Michael Preece

1976: **Sara**/*The Child Bride;* **Streets of San Francisco**/*Trail of Terror.* 1977: **Bionic Woman**/*Fembots in Las Vegas* (2 pts), *Brainwash;* **Dog and Cat**/*The Only Way to Fly, Dead Dog and Cat.*

A handful of formula series segments is all there is to judge Preece on at the moment, but his **Dog and Cats** (Lou Antonio and Kim Basinger as a veteran cop and his beautiful rookie partner in a short-lived series created by Walter Hill) had a youthful elan. *The Only Way to Fly* had a fine, extended chase format with Preece, his camera team and stunt crew, cooking up splendid action. If Preece gets up to nothing else, we can at least be guaranteed some wild and woolly moments for the future.

Allen Reisner

[LIVE TV] 1948-1958: **Studio One; Suspense; Pulitzer Playhouse; Danger; Climax; Playhouse 90** (dir multiples). 1959: **The Twilight Zone/***Mr Denton on Doomsday;* **Desilu Playhouse/***Chez Rouge.* 1960: **Rawhide/***Incident of the Boomerang;* **The Untouchables** (multiples). 1961: **Ben Casey** (dir multiples); **Route 66** (dir multiples). 1962: **Empire/***Sixty-Five Miles Is a Long Long Way.* 1965: **I Spy/***Always Say Goodbye;* **Slattery's People/***A Sitting Duck Named Slattery.* 1966: **Felony Squad/***The Nights of the Shark* (2 pts), *The Desperate Silence, Target!* 1967: **High Chaparral/***The Filibusteros;* **Mannix** (dir multiples). 1968: **It Takes a Thief/***The Funeral is on Mundy;* **Lancer/***The Lawman, The Buscaderos;* **Ironside/***Rundown on a Bum Rap, Puzzle Lock.* 1969: **Lancer/***The Gifts, The Kid, Little Darling of the Sierras, Goodbye, Lizzie, The Lions and the Lambs, Black Angel, Blue Skies for Willie Sharp.* 1970: **Four-In-One: Night Gallery/***The Nature of the Enemy;* **Four-In-One: San Francisco International Airport/***Crisis.* 1971: **Cannon/***Call Unicorn, Country Blues, Treasure of San Ignacio, To Kill a Guinea Pig;* **O'Hara–US Treasury/***Operation: Bandera, Operation: Bribery;* **Owen Marshal, Counselor at Law/***The Baby Sitter;* **Rod Serling's Night Gallery/***Brenda.* 1972: **Kung Fu/***Nine Lives.* 1973: **Kojak/***Death is Not a Passing Grade.* 1974: **Kojak/***Loser Takes All;* **Movin' On/***The Big On.* 1975: **Cannon/***Man in the Middle;* **City of Angels/***The Palm Springs Answer.* 1976: **Best Sellers: Captains and the Kings** (pts 4, 5 & 6); **Hawaii Five-O/***Man in a Steel Frame;* **Streets of San Francisco/***Castle of Fear.*

One-time Broadway actor, Allen Reisner has travelled through some twenty-five years of Television like a good wine, directing with vigour and retaining a strong flavour and a good nose. For most of the 1950s he worked on 'live' shows, sharing some of TV's best years alongside the Frankenheimers, Schaffners, Mulligans, and Roy Hills. Most of this material is now gone, forever, representing almost a lost decade of a director's career. His TV-film career has made its way through some of the best during the '60s and '70s: **The Untouchables, Ben Casey, I Spy, High Chaparral, Kung Fu, Kojak. Captains and the Kings** was, perhaps, not among the best of the **Best Sellers** miniseries, but it did have a certain polish, a particular charm that allowed the dullest of story-lines to lend itself out to pleasing visuals.

Cannon, from the Quinn Martin chamber, has been criticised for sluggishness in a genre that daren't be sluggish; **Kojak,** from the Abbey Mann chamber, was initially acclaimed for its earthiness, its down-to-the-street-on-feet quality. Reisner has tasted both, obviously preferring the almost-action of **Cannon** to the over-action of **Kojak.** It may prove interesting to place Reisner's **Felony Squad** segments against **Kojak** (re police drama), and his **Mannix** segments against **Cannon** (re private-eye drama).

Don Richardson

1957: **Mama** (multiples). 1959: **Play of the Week/***The World of Sholom Aleichem.* 1960: **Play of the Week/***Don Juan in Hell.* 1961: **The Defenders/***The Treadmill.* 1962: **The Defenders/***The*

Incredible Silence, The Brother Killers, The Savage Intent. 1963: **Sam Benedict**/*Image of a Toad;* **The Defenders**/*Taste of Vengeance, The Crowd Pleaser.* 1965: **Lost in Space**/*Ghost in Space;* **The Virginian**/*Ring of Silence, Jennifer, A Little Learnin'.* 1966: **Lost in Space**/*The Challenge, Lost Civilisation, Follow the Leader, Wild Adventure, The Forbidden World, The Android Machine, The Thief of Outer Space, The Dream Monster, The Golden Man, The Questing Beast.* 1967: **Lost in Space**/*Mutiny in Space, Rocket to Earth, Cave of the Wizards, Revolt of the Androids, Trip Through the Robot, The Astral Traveller, A Visit to Hades, Kidnapped in Space, Hunter's Moon, The Space Destructors;* **Custer**/*Gauntlet.* 1968: **Lost in Space**/*Collision of the Planets, Two Weeks in Space, Princess of Space, The Flaming Planet, The Great Vegetable Rebellion;* **Lancer**/*The Last Train for Charlie Poe, The Black McGloins, Angel Day and Her Sunshine Girls, The Knot, Man Without a Gun.* 1969: **Lancer**/*Child of Rock and Sunlight, Dream of Falcons;* **High Chaparral**/*The Legacy.* 1974: **Emergency**/*Daisy's Pick, Quicker Than the Eye.*

Don Richardson appeared to be sailing merrily along through the pleasantly creative waters of **The Defenders** and **Sam Benedict** when he suddenly hit the Irwin Allen rapids and plummeted deep into **Lost in Space**. Drifting in the Allen whirpool for almost three years, Richardson finally made his way back to *terra-firma* via the footholds of **Custer** and **Lancer**, though they, too, were none too steady. For a director to journey from the Jewish theatre of *The World of Sholom Aleichem* to the juvenile theatre of *The Great Vegetable Rebellion* prompts the historian to go back and look for traces of insanity in Richardson's credits. Moving from the sluggish family saga of **Lancer** onto the restless family saga of **High Chaparral** may be natural, though unrewarding, but turing to the extravaganza of carnage with the noisy **Emergency**, rules out all salvation from the guillotine of bad judgement. To lose one foothold is unfortunate. To lose both seems like carelessness.

Seymour Robbie

1955-1962: **Studio One; Omnibus; Play of the Week; The Honeymooners; Dupont Show of the Week** (multiples). 1962: **Room for One More**/*Two Many Parents.* 1963: **The Eleventh Hour** (multiples). 1966: **Felony Squad**/*Hit and Run Run Run;* **F Troop** (multiples). 1967: **Lost in** *and Why Won't She Stay Dead?;* **Mister Roberts**/*Love at 78 RPM, +*=c/o The Torpedoes, The Reluctant Draggin', The World's Greatest Loser, The Reluctant Mutiny;* **Honey West** multiples). 1966: **Felony Squad**/*Hit and Run Run Run;* **F Troop** (multiples). 1967: **Lost in Space**/*The Mechanical Men;* **The FBI** (multiples); **Bewitched**/*I Confess.* 1968: **Hawaii Five-O**/*By the Numbers, Uptight, Six Kilos;* **The Name of the Game**/*The Revolutionary.* 1969: **Mission Impossible**/*Decoy;* **It Takes a Thief**/*Rock-Bye Bye Baby;* **The Virginian**/*Journey to Scathelock, The Power Seekers.* 1970: **The Name of the Game**/*All the Familiar Faces;* **Mod Squad** (multiples); **The Virginian**/*The Gift.* 1971: **High Chaparral** (multiples); **Sarge**/*John Michael O'Flaherty Presents the Eleven O'Clock War, Quick Silver.* 1972: **Mannix** (multiples); **Streets of San Francisco**/*Deadline.* 1973: **Cannon**/*A Deadly Quiet Town, Stone Cold Dead, A Well-Remembered Terror;* **Streets of San Francisco**/*The Runaways, The Stamp of Death, No Badge for Benjy, Winter-kill.* 1974: **Streets of San Francisco**/*Solitaire, One Chance to Live;* **Cannon**/*The Core That Kills;* **Kolchak: The Night Stalker**/*The Sentry;* **Kojak**/*A Very Deadly Game, You Can't Tell a Hurt Man How to Holler.* 1975: **Ellery Queen**/*The Adventure of the Pharaoh's Curse, The Adventure of the Sunday Punch, The Adventure of Veronica's Veils, The Adventure of Colonel Niven's Memoirs, The Adventure* *of the Tyrant of Tin Pan Alley.* 1976: **The Feather and Father Gang**/*Two Star Killer, Sun Sand and Death, The Judas Bug.* 1977: **Big Hawaii**/*The Sun Children;* **What Really Happened to the Class of '65**/*The Girl Who Always Said No.* 1978:**Wonder Woman**/*The Bermuda Triangle Crisis.*

One of the most handsomely-mounted series of recent years was Levinson and Link's **Ellery Queen**, a show so well-made and ornately constructed that it seemed tailored for a short run. It fell to the absurdity of the ratings guillotine. Robbie directed five segments of that one excellent season and they are in keeping with the standards of the show—each being better than the other. Whether this was an exception in Robbie's long and prolific career, or the norm for a man trained in **Studio One** drama, is a question easier to ask than to answer.

Charles Rondeau

1961: **The Roaring 20's**/*Nobody's Millions, Pinky Goes to College, Kitty Goes West;* **77 Sunset Strip**/*Ghost of a Memory;* **Surfside 6**/*Race Against Time, Deadly Male, Spinout at Sebring;* **Adventures in Paradise**/*The Violent Journey* (+ wr); **Hawaiian Eye**/*The Moon of Mindanao, The Doctor's Lady, Pill in the Box, Kill a Grey Fox, Broken Thread, RX Cricket, Location Shooting, Nightmare in Paradise, A Scent of Whales, Four Cornered Triangle.* 1962: **The Gallant Men**/*And Cain Cried Out, Lesson for a Lover, Some Tears Fall Dry, Robertino, A Place to Die, To Hold Up a Mirror, Boast Not of Tomorrow, Dogs of War, The Leathernecks, The Crucible, Tommy;* **Room for One More**/*Danger—Man at Work;* **77 Sunset Strip**/*The Long Shot Caper.* 1963: **77 Sunset Strip**/*The Odds on Odette, Flight 307;* **Bonanza**/*Calamity Over the Comstock;* **Temple Houston**/*The Law and Big Annie.* 1964: **Perry Mason**/*The Case of the Fatal Fetish;* **Rawhide**/*A Time for Waiting;* **No Time for Sergeants**/*Will's Misfortune Cookie, The Living End, My Fair Andy, O Kropnik My Kropnik, Two for the Show, Stockdale's Island, Stockdale's Millions.* 1965: **No Time for Sergeants**/*Stockdale in the Stockade, Whortleberry Roots for Everybody, Target Stockdale;* **Laredo**/*A Prince of a Ranger, Oh! Careless Love.* 1966: **Wild Wild West**/*Night of the Tatter, Night of the Colonel's Ghost, Night of the Wolf;* **Batman**/*The Curse of Tut–The Pharaoh's in a Rut, Death in Slow Motion–The Riddler's False Notion;* **F Troop**/*Corporal Agarn's Farewell to the Troops, The Girl from Philadelphia;* **Gunsmoke**/*Mad Dog.* 1967: **Mission Impossible**/*The Psychic, Odds on Evil;* **Felony Squad**/*The Death Bag;* **Cimarron Strip**/*The Beast That Walks Like a Man, Killer with a Knife;* **Iron Horse**/*Steel Chain to a Music Box.* 1968: **Voyage to the Bottom of the Sea**/*Nightmare, Secret of the Deep, The Death Clock;* **Wild Wild West**/*Night of the Sabatini Death.* 1971: **Mission Impossible**/*The Missile.* 1973: **Kojak**/*18 Hours of Fear.* 1975: **Baretta**/*Sharper Than a Serpent's Tooth.* 1976: **Gemini Man**/*Run Sam Run.*

Rondeau is another emigré from the Warnerland of the early '60s. His work for WB is as forgettable as Richard Bare's is memorable, and his later non-Warner material suffers in the shadows of more able talents. From the hick humour of **No Time for Sergeants** to the painful puns of **Batman**, there really isn't much to distinguish Rondeau from other land-term TV toilers. His worst must be the last season segments of **Voyage to the Bottom of the Sea**—his best must be *Killer with a Knife*, an Harlan Ellison script with Jack the Ripper loose on Cimarron Strip.

Oscar Rudolph

1956: **Navy Log**/*Operation Three-In-One, Captain's Choice.* 1957: **Navy Log**/*Little More Than a Brother, Man Alone, Incident at Formosa, A Guy Called Mickey.* 1959: **Richard Diamond**/*The Homicide Habit, Picture of Fear, The Big Score.* 1960: **Tightrope**/*The Horse Runs High, The Long Odds, First Time Out, Big Business.* 1964: **My Favourite Martian**/*That Little Old Matchmaker Martin, Raffles No 2, Martin and the Eternal Triangle, If You Can't Lick 'Em.* 1966: **Batman**/*The Greatest Mother of Them All: Ma Parker, Hizzoner the Penguin–Dizzoner the Penguin, Come Back Shame–It's the Way You Play the Game.* 1967: **Batman**/*The Contaminated Cowl–Mad Hatter Runs Afoul, Zodiac Crimes–Joker's Hardtimes–Penguin Declines, That Darn Catwoman–Scat Catwoman, The Joker's Last Laugh–The Joker's Epitaph, A Piece of the Action–Batman's Satisfaction, Black Widow Strikes Again–Caught in the Spider's Den, Ice Spy–The Duo Defy, Enter Batgirl Exit Penguin, The Ogg and I–How to Hatch a Dinosaur, Surf's Up!–Joker's Under!, The Londinium Larcenies–The Foggiest Notion–The Bloody Tower, The Ogg Couple, Funny Feline Felonies–The Joke's on Catwoman.* 1968: **Batman**/*Nora Clavicle and Her Ladies' Crime Club, Penguin's Clean Sweep, The Great Escape–The Great Train Robbery.*

Oscar Rudolph's greatest contribution to TV must be his spell in William Dozier's **Batman** show, during the mid-sixties. Rudolph really became active with the series during the third (and last) season, where he shared the directing chores with Sam Strangis. This last season, after being given a reprieve by ABC-TV, didn't survive the decreasing ratings, and the comic-action format of the early episodes soon lapsed into a tired formula, as did Oscar Rudolph.

Robert Scheerer

1971: **The Bold Ones: The Doctors**/*Broken Melody;* **The Man and the City**/*Diagnosis: Corruption.* 1972: **Poor Devil.** 1973: **Ironside**/*Two Hundred Large.* 1974: **Lucas Tanner**/*Those Who Cannot–Teach, Requiem for a Son;* **Kolchak: The Night Stalker**/*The Primal Scream;* **Target Risk.** 1975: **The Blue Knight**/*A Fashionable Connection.* 1976: **Hawaii Five-O**/*Target–A Cop.*

Man and the City and **Poor Devil** suffered from curious, if not bizarre, casting: Anthony Quinn as a battling mayor in **Man and the City** did not endear anyone to City Hall and its politics; and Sammy Davis Jr., playing an apprentice devil out to earn his horns, in the failed **Poor Devil** pilot, comes across like a cabaret-artist in search of a suitable night club. **Target Risk, The Blue Knight** and **Hawaii Five-O**, however, just managed to redeem Scheerer as a TV director of substance. It might well be a developing talent.

Ralph Senensky

1963: **Arrest and Trial**/*My Name is Martin Burnham;* **Twilight Zone**/*Printer's Devil.* 1964: **The**

FBI/*The Plunderers, Special Delivery.* 1965: **The Fugitive**/*An Apple a Day, When the Wind Blows;* **Slattery's People**/*Question: What Can You Do with a Wounded Tiger?;* **Kraft Suspense Theatre**/*The Jack Is High, The Easter Breach.* 1966: **Dr Kildare**/*A Journey to Sunrise;* **I Spy**/*This Guy Smith;* **Mission Impossible**/*The Train;* **Wild Wild West**/*Night of the Big Blast;* **Big Valley**/*By Fires Unseen.* 1967: **High Chaparral**/*The Terrorist;* **Star Trek**/*This Side of Paradise, Metamorphasis, Obsession, Return to Tomorrow, Bread and Circuses.* 1968: **Ironside**/*Girl in the Night, Return of the Hero.* 1969: **Star Trek**/*Is There No Truth in Beauty?, The Tholian Web.* 1970: **Dan August**/*Death Chain, The Law, Dead Witness to a Killing.* 1971: **Dan August**/*Bullet for Hero, Days of Rage.* 1972: **Banyon**/*Dead End, The Decent Thing to Do, The Graveyard Vote.* 1973: **Search**/*Ends of the Earth;* **A Dream for Christmas.** 1974: **Death Cruise.** 1975: **The Family Nobody Wanted; Medical Story**/*An Air Full of Death;* **The Family Holvak**/*Stranger in a Strange Land, Remembrance of a Guest;* **Blue Knight**/*Triple Threat.* 1976: **The Waltons**/*The Fire Storm, The Pony Cart;* **City of Angels**/*Match Point.* 1977: **The Waltons**/*The Grandchild* (2 pts); **Westside Medical**/*The Sound of Sunlight.*

From the emotional disturbance of construction worker James Whitmore, in *My Name Is Martin Burnham*, to the problems attendant upon Season Hubley recovering her hearing in *The Sound of Sunlight*, Senensky seems always to have been interested in, and particularly gifted in exploring, the inner tensions and mental fears of the characters who populate the scripts he accepts. Even in the more formula-based series, his successes are when he has time and room to get close to the characters. This sensitivity has surfaced in more obvious ways, in series like **The Waltons** and **The Family Holvak**: telefeatures such as **A Dream for Christmas** (written by **Walton**'s creator, Earl Hamner), the domestic triumph of a black minister's family in a '50s ghetto; and **The Family Nobody Wanted**, where a white minister and his wife adopt a family of multi-racial rejects.

This Senensky sensibility even surfaces in **Star Trek**, particularly in *Metamorphosis*. One of the strangest stories to come out of the series, it involves an alien life-form having a love-affair with a shipwrecked space pilot, and thereby keeping him alive and animate. It is one of the gentlest stories, its roots seemingly controlled by religious orthodoxy. By contrast, as if to prove something to himself, Senensky made *The Tholian Web* into one of the most suspenseful and thrilling **Star Treks** which maintains a hold on the viewer, the way a good wire-walker does even with a net. The 'Enterprise' has intruded into Tholian space and is slowly being 'webbed in' by the spider-like actions of the Tholian space vessels. It is a matter of time before the crew are cocooned forever. With no guest-stars to accommodate, Senensky can concentrate on character-under-stress and keep the pace simmering.

A simmering pace is, however, an exception in the nonetheless confident and understanding world of this 'humanist', who prefers to communicate joy and the triumph of the human spirit rather than shoot off strings of fireworks. Such moving performances as Season Hubley's in *The Sound of Sunlight* are, however, harder to encourage and accommodate but Senensky always tries to find a way to do so.

Nick Sgarro

1976: **Benny and Barney: Las Vegas Undercover** (exec pr + wr); **Kojak**/*A Separate Peace, I Was Happy Where I Was.* 1977: **The Man with the Power; Kojak**/*Laid Off, Once More from Birdland, An Unfair Trade, Case Without a File, Letters of Death.*

The director who brought you THE HAPPY HOOKER is now plying his trade in TV, and has turned out some superior segments. The best is *Once More from Birdland*, a **Kojak** set in a jazz milieu starring Andrea Marcovicci. Sgarro neatly welded together the investigative layers with the jazz elements. It suggests that if he stays in TV, he won't be practising for long.

James Sheldon

1950-1959: **Robert Montgomery Presents; Schlitz Playhouse of Stars; Mr Peepers; Armstong Circle Theatre; The Millionaire; West Point; Zane Grey Theatre; Desilu Playhouse** (multiples). 1960: **The Twilight Zone**/*The Whole Truth, A Penny for Your Thoughts.* 1961: **The Twilight Zone**/*Long Distance Call, It's a Good Life, Still Valley;* **Naked City**/*The Sweet Smiling Face of Truth;* **Route 66**/*The Mud Nest, You Never Had It So Good;* **Alcoa Premiere**/*The Boy Who Wasn't Wanted;* **The Twilight Zone**/*I Sing the Body Electric;* **Naked City**/*King Stanislaus and the Knights of the Round Table, Spectre of the Rose Street Gang;* **The Nurses** (multiples). 1963: **The Defenders**/*Fugue for Trumpet and Small Boy;* **The Fugitive**/*The Other Side of the Mountain, Where the Action Is;* **Espionage**/*The Light of a Friendly Star, Festival of Pawns;* **Naked City**/*Barefoot on a Bed of Coals, Carrier, The Highest of Prizes;* **Alfred Hitchcock Hour**/*I'll Be Judge–I'll Be Jury;* **Route 66**/*Hey Moth, Come Eat the Flame, The Cruelest Sea of All, To Walk with a Serpent, Aren't You Surprised to See Me?* 1964: **Suspense**/*Web of Circumstances, Date for Tomorrow;* **Bing Crosby Show** (multiples); **Perry Mason**/*The Case of the Lavender Lipstick.* 1965: **Trials of O'Brien/Goodbye and Keep Cool; The Man from UNCLE**/*The Man from Thrush Affair;* **Perry Mason**/*The Case of the Carefree Coronary.* 1966: **The Fugitive**/*The Chinese Sunset, Echo of a Nightmare;* **Family Affair**/*Buffy* (1st ep + multiples); **Batman**/*The Purrfect Crime–Better Luck Next Time.* 1967: **The Virginian**/*Good Hearted Badman.* 1968: **Ironside**/*Barbara Who?, Officer Bobby;* **The Virginian**/*The Girl in the Shadows, The Wind of Outrage, The Orchard, The Land Dreamer, Big Tiny;* **Felony Squad**/*Bed of Strangers.* 1969: **My World and Welcome to It**/*Maid in Connecticut, Rally 'Round the Flag, The Wooing of Mr Monroe;* **Love American Style** (multiples); **Gidget Grows Up.** 1970: **The Virginian**/*Train of Darkness;* **To Rome with Love** (multiples). 1971: **Owen Marshall, Counselor at Law**/*A Lonely Stretch of Beach, Warlock at March 3;* **Room 222** (multiples); **Gidget Gets Married.** 1972: **Owen Marshall, Counselor at Law**/*The Color of Respect, Journey through Limbo, Sigh No More Lady, Starting Over Again;* **MASH**/*Edwina.* 1973: **Owen Marshall, Counselor at Law**/*The Second Victim, The Pool House, A Killer with a Badge, House of Friends;* **Apple's Way** (multiples). 1974: **Owen Marshall, Counselor at Law**/*The Ghost of Buzz Stevens;* **MacMillan and Wife**/*The Deadly Cure, Buried Alive.* 1975: **Ellery Queen**/*The Adventure of the Mad Tea Party;* **Doc Elliott** (multiples); **Petrocelli**/*By Reason of Madness, Counterploy, A Covenant with Evil.* 1976: **Ellery Queen**/*The Adventure of Miss Aggie's Farewell;* **MacMillan and Wife**/*Coffee Tea or Cyanide.* 1977: **MacMillan and Wife**/*Have You Heard About Vanessa?*

James Sheldon comes from that live/film-New York/Hollywood period of

American TV generally referred to as the 'golden age' of Television. He spent almost a decade working among the prestigious playhouses, and had opportunities to work with some of the best TV talents and early-film series—with Robert Montgomery and Dick Powell, who were actively producing some of the most interesting TV of the period, and the **Mr. Peepers** series, remembered, perhaps, more affectionately, by the generation that grew up with the Wally Cox comedy show. It is in Sheldon's early TV work that the real fruits of his talent lie; the period from '60 to '65 reflects an area of accurate evaluation on the Sheldon tele-film. The **Owen Marshalls**, **Petrocellis**, and **Ellery Queens**, despite their own qualities, are really no more than distant echoes of the work Sheldon was doing some ten years before.

Paul Stanley

1959: **The Third Man**/*The Man Who Died Twice, The Indispensable Man, Sparks from a Dead Fire, Hollywood Incident.* 1961: **Adventures in Paradise**/*Walk through the Night* (+ pr), *The Pit of Silence;* **The Defenders**/*The Best Defense;* **Desilu Playhouse**/*Cry Ruin.* 1962: **Adventures in Paradise**/*Haunted, Judith, The Lady from South Chicago;* **The Untouchables**/*The Economist, The Pea;* **Naked City**/*Five Cranks for Winter . . . Ten Cranks for Spring, Without Stick or Sword.* 1963: **The Richard Boone Show**/*Captain Al Sanchez;* **The Great Adventure**/*The Hunley;* **The Defenders**/*Climate of Evil.* 1964: **The Outer Limits**/*Second Chance* (aka *Joy Ride), The Guests;* **The Reporter**/*Rope's End, He Stuck in His Thumb;* **Bob Hope Chrysler Theatre**/*Escape Into Jeopardy;* **Profiles in Courage**/*The General Alexander Doriphan Story.* 1965: **The Outer Limits**/*Counter-weight;* **Lost in Space**/*My Friend Mr Nobody;* **Laredo**/*Lazyfoot Where Are You?, Jinx;* **The Virginian**/*The Nobility and Kings, Inchworm's Got No Wings at All.* 1966: **The Virginian**/*Harvest of Strangers, The Wolves in Front, The Jackals Behind;* **Mission Impossible**/*The Money Machine, The Junior;* **Tarzan**/*The Ultimate Weapon, The Prodigal Puma;* **The Time Tunnel**/*The Night of the Long Knives.* 1967: **High Chaparral**/*Gold is Where You Leave It.* 1969: **It Takes a Thief**/*Boom at the Top;* **Sole Survivor; Gunsmoke**/*Hidalgo, The Good Indian;* **River of Mystery**. 1970: **Mission Impossible**/*The Spy;* **Gunsmoke**/*Drago.* 1972: **Ghost Story**/*The Dead We Leave Behind, Legion of Demons;* **Search**/*Flight to Nowhere.* 1973: **Kojak**/*The Corruptor.* 1974: **Streets of San Francisco**/*I Ain't Marchin' Anymore, False Witness;* **Petrocelli**/*Music to Die By, An Act of Love;* **Murder by Proxy**. 1975: **Streets of San Francisco**/*Underground;* **Cannon**/*Revenge, The Wrong Medicine, Nightmare.* 1976: **Six Million Dollar Man**/*The Ultimate Imposter;* **Westside Medical**/*Risks;* **Baretta**/*Nuthin' for Nuthin';* **Rich Man Poor Man–Book II**/*Chapter 16.* 1977: **Stedman; Dog and Cat**/*Family Feeling, A Dude is a Dude;* **Hawaii Five-O**/*The Cop on the Cover.*

Stanley's credits are scattered with too many conflicting characters and genres, forms and feelings, to be collectively assessed and evaluated. The influence, of too many masterful producers (Brodkin, Martin, Leonard, Stefano, Geller, etc.) along the line prohibits true appraisal. On a driving test, Stanley would do well, he has the skill and ability to shift from fourth gear (**The Defenders, Naked City**) down to first (**Lost in Space, Time Tunnel**) and back up to third (**Baretta, Hawaii Five-O**) without losing speed. Tenacity actually may be a quality of reputable series; it is safe to assume that his presence has contributed to, rather than detracted from, their quality.

E.W. Swackhamer

1964: **Tom, Dick and Mary**/*And Baby Makes Four, Dick and the Beanstalk, Hail! Dick the King.* **Bewitched**/*Cousin Edgar.* 1965: **Bewitched**/*My Grandson the Warlock, The Joker Is a Card, Trick or Treat, . . . And Then I Wrote, Aunt Clara's Old Flame, A Strange Little Visitor.* 1969: **Mr Deeds Goes to Town** (pilot) *The Pixilated Man, A Ransom in Small Unmarked Flowers;* **In Name Only.** 1972: **Owen Marshall, Counselor at Law**/*The Trouble;* **MASH**/*Chief Surgeon Who?,* **Gidget Gets Married.** 1974: **McCloud**/*Sharks!;* **MacMillan and Wife**/*Requiem for a Bride.* 1975: **Switch**/*The James Caan Con, Body at the Bottom;* **McCloud**/*Park Avenue Pirates, The Day New York Turned Blue, Our Man in the Harem* (aka *The Sheik of Arami).* 1976: **Best Sellers: Once an Eagle** (pts 1, 4, 5 & 6); **Nancy Drew Mysteries**/*The Mystery of the Pirate's Cove,* **Quincy**/*Go Fight City Hall—to the Death;* **Death at Love House.** 1977: **Night of Terror; Spiderman.** 1978: **The Dain Curse.**

There are 8 million Swackhamers in the TV city, and this is one of them. E. W. Swackhamer, to be precise (if not respectful), is a director who has emerged from the side-lines of the sit-com industry to the full-blown opera of prime-time Television. His **Tom, Dick and Mary/Bewitched/Mr. Deeds Goes to Town** period can be by-passed in favour of exploring the potential among the avenues of **Switch, McCloud, Once an Eagle**, etc. In the field of adapting comic-strip characters to screen, one of Swackhamer's most noble TV effects has been the **Spiderman** tele-features—usually regarded as a territory too dangerous to tread on network TV. **Spiderman** does not turn out to be one of the best examples in this sub-division, having something of a hurried look about it, but it does make its mark in the cutting and effects departments. Swackhamer's roulette-wheel is still spinning and has yet to pay out.

Robert Totten

1960: **Hawaiian Eye**/*Lament for a Saturday Warrior.* 1962: **The Dakotas**/*Justice at Eagle's Nest, Reformation at Big Nose Butte;* **The Gallant Men**/*Advance and Be Recognised.* 1963: **Temple Houston**/*Gallows in Gallilee, Letter of the Law, Seventy Times Seven, Jubilee.* 1964: **Bonanza**/*Dead and Gone, The Natural Wizard;* **The Virginian**/*Secrets of Brynmar Hall.* 1965: **Legend of Jesse James**/*The Celebrity, Reunion.* 1966: **The Monroes**/*The Adventure, War Arrow* (aka *Wahkonda), Lost in the Wilderness;* **Iron Horse**/*Cougar Man;* **Gunsmoke**/*The Good People, The Wrong Man, The Newcomers, Saturday Night, Mail Drop.* 1967: **Gunsmoke**/*Mistaken Identity, Tiger by the Tail* (2 pts), *The Wreckers, A Hat, Major Glory.* 1968: **Gunsmoke**/*Blood Money, Hill Girl, The First People, Waco;* **Mission Impossible**/*The Recovery.* 1969: **Gunsmoke**/*Stryker, A*

Matter of Honor. 1970: **Gunsmoke**/*Stark, The Scavengers, Jenny, Murdoch;* **Dan August**/*When the Shouting Dies.* 1971: **Gunsmoke**/*The Lost.* 1973: **Doc Elliot**/*And All Ye Need to Know, The Touch of God;* **Kung Fu**/*The Tong, The Hoots.*

Robert Totten freewheels quite unemotionally from frontier gunfighters to placid ranch life to Dodge City misdemeanours without ruffling his suit. **Gunsmoke** presents itself as the most regular Totten centre of activity, and if there is a style, a presence to define his status, it is somewhere in this area. It eludes us and Totten remains something of a dubious drifter.

Virgil W. Vogel

1958: **Wagon Train**/*The Mary Ellen Thomas Story, The Old Man Charvanaugh Story, The Duke le May Story* (+co-wr), *Chuck Wooster, Wagonmaster, The Andrew Hale Story, The Rodney Lawrence Story, The Cappy Carrin Story;* **M Squad**/*The Crush Out.* 1959: **Wagon Train**/*The Colonel Harris Story, The Benjamin Burns Story, The Maudie Brant Story, The Clayton Tucker Story, The Joshua Gilliam Story, The Jonas Murdock Story, Trial for Murder* (2 pts), *The Doctor Swift Cloud Story, The Charlene Brenton Story;* **Laramie**/*Circle of Fire.* 1960: **Wagon Train**/*The Bleymier Story, The Jeremy Dow Story, The Sam Elder Story, Path of the Serpent, The Beth Pearson Story, The Jose Morales Story* (co-wr), *The Jed Polke Story, The Nellie Jefferson Story.* 1961: **Wagon Train**/*The Duke Shannon Story, The Ah Chong Story, The Chalice.* 1964: **Bonanza**/*To Own the World, The Return.* 1965: **Bonanza**/*Devil on Her Shoulder;* **The Big Valley**/*The Murdered Party, Last Train to the Fair, Into the Widow's Web, By Force and Violence.* 1966: **Amos Burke–Secret Agent**/*Steam Heat, A Very Important Russian is Missing, Or No Tomorrow;* **A Man Called Shenandoah**/*Rope's End;* **Bonanza**/*Her Brother's Keeper;* **The Big Valley**/*The Great Safe Robbery, Pursuit, Legend of a General* (2 pts), *Tunnel of Gold, Caesar's Wife, A Day of Terror.* 1969: **Mission Impossible**/*Squeeze Play;* **Lancer**/*The Experiment, Splinter Group.* 1970: **High Chaparral**/*Too Many Chiefs.* 1971: **Dan August**/*Prognosis: Homicide.* 1972: **Streets of San Francisco**/*The Unicorn, Beyond Vengeance.* 1973: **Caribe**/*Murder in Paradise, One Second to Doom, Counterfeit Killer, Assault on the Calavera;* **Cannon**/*Dead Lady's Tears;* **Streets of San Francisco**/*For the Love of God, Harem, Blockade, The Hard Breed, Inferno, Death and the Favoured Few.* 1974: **Six Million Dollar Man**/*Dr Wells Is Missing;* **Streets of San Francisco**/*Bird of Prey, The 25 Caliber Plague, Flags of Terror, License to Kill, No Place to Hide, Murder by Proxy, Merchants of Death, Dead Air.* 1975: **Return of Joe Forrester; The Streets of San Francisco**/*Deadly Silence, The Most Deadly Species, Letters from the Grave, Web of Lies, Superstar;* **Bert D'Angelo Superstar**/*Cops Who Sleep Together, Flannagan's Fleet.* 1976: **The Streets of San Francisco**/*Alien Country, The Cat's Paw, Police Buff, Judgement Day, Clown of Death, The Thrill Killer* (2 pts), *Hot Dog;* **Oregon Trail**/*Waterhole;* **Most Wanted**/*The Slaver, The Corruptor, The Two Dollar Kidnapper, The Torch, The White Collar Killer, The Pirate, The Natural Killer, The Insider, The Driver;* **Fantastic Journey**/*An Act of Love.* 1977: **Man from Atlantis**/*Melt Down, The Mudworm.* 1978: **Colorado C.I.**

Virgil Vogel hovers somewhere between the TV westerns of Tony Leader and Richard Bare. Devoting almost two decades to the small-screen prairie, Vogel still remains something of an unresolved talent—he tends to blend a Leader pioneer with a generous dash of the Bare adventurer. At times he resorts to a

Claxton-like family brew. Vogel's **Wagon Train** segments tend to maintain the 'frontier' spirit but are, in effect, little more than consistent in a series that wallowed in consistency—it usually took the determined power of someone like a John Ford to shake the structure of the series and actually make it jump. The **Bonanzas** and **Big Valleys** are areas best left to the likes of William Claxton, who appears suitably equipped to handle stagnant situations. When the TV western phase started to dry up, and most active directors became involved with the growing wave of wailing-siren shows, Vogel also turned his hand to the genre, rotating between the still-born (**Dan August, Caribe, Bert D'Angelo**, etc.) and the senior citizens (**Streets of San Francisco**, etc.). A sudden return to the Western—by both TV and Vogel—was **Oregon Trail** and Vogel's *Waterhole* segment. The series itself must be one of the all-time non-starters, but Vogel's segment is the only one in the history of television to have caused terminal boredom. It is a sad reflection on a director who could at one time energize an entire wagon train yet now appears to struggle with a cart.

William Wiard

1965: **Mister Roberts**/*Dear Mom, Black and Blue Market, The Replacement.* 1966: **Get Smart**/*Casablanca.* 1967: **The Monroes**/*The Ghosts of Paradox, Gun Bound;* **Tarzan**/*Jungle Dragnet.* 1969: **High Chaparral**/*The Lieutenant.* 1972: **Search**/*The Bullet, The Clayton Lem's Documents, The Mattson Papers;* **MASH**/*Henry–Please Come Home, The Long John Flap;* **Cannon**/*Death of a Stone Seahorse.* 1973: **Chase**/*Sizzling Stones;* **MASH**/*Sometimes You Hear the Bullet, Tuttle.* 1974: **Cannon**/*Duel in the Desert, Blood Money, Kelly's Song, The Hit Man, Voice from the Grave, The Lady in Red, Flashpoint, The Prisoner;* **The Rockford Files**/*Claire, Slight of Hand.* 1975: **Bert D'Angelo Superstar**/*A Concerned Citizen;* **Cannon**/*Tomorrow Ends at Noon, Perfect Fit for a Frame, Missing at FL 307, Madman, Quasar Kill, The Man Who Died Twice, The Iceman;* **The Rockford Files**/*The Gear Jammers* (2 pts). 1976: **Sara**/*The Visit;* **The Rockford Files**/*Just Another Polish Wedding, The Fourth Man, Family Hour, To Protect and Serve* (2 pts); **Baa Baa Black Sheep**/*Love and War;* **Scot Free.** 1977: **The Rockford Files**/*Trouble in Chapter 17, Requiem for a Funny Box, The Deadly Maze;* **Big Hawaii**/*Blind Rage.*

In a fairly uneventful TV career, William Wiard exists as a director who appears unable to overcome the themes and concepts with which he has to deal. Earliest records of Wiard show that he was working in the editing department of **77 Sunset Strip** during its last season, when William Conrad was producing and directing the show. This early association with Conrad led to him directing several episodes of **Cannon**. It is also from this point that the on-off career of Wiard begins. *Quasar Kill* is probably the worst, the most tedious, example of filmed Television to ever appear. *Just Another Polish Wedding*, however, comes out as one of the best (and funniest) in its field. Where this actually places Wiard as a directing force is anyone's guess. However, it seems obvious that Wiard's ability to control his material is largely dependant on the strength and alent of the producers and writers with whom he is working—as Huggins and Cannell proved with *Just Another Polish Wedding*.

6/Not Just a Poor Player

Though they may still strut and fret occasionally in front of the camera, these are the actors who have successfully traded in their makeup boxes for megaphones or have, by the sheer power of their position as stars, become part of the creative TV process, influencing and dictating the course of their affairs, and therefore demanding recognition as more than mere puppets.

Lou Antonio

1968: **Gentle Ben**/*Ben the Champ, Knights of the Road.* 1971: **McCloud**/*Showdown at the End of the World;* **Owen Marshall, Counselor at Law**/*Nothing Personal.* 1972: **Owen Marshall, Counselor at Law**/*Smiles from Yesterday, Lines from an Angry Book, The First Day of Your Life, Seed of Doubt.* 1973: **Griff**/*The Framing of Billy the Kid;* **Owen Marshall, Counselor at Law**/*A Girl Named Tham, Once a Lion;* **McCloud**/*The Solid Gold Swingers.* 1974: **Owen Marshall, Counselor at Law**/*To Keep and Bear Arms;* **Rockford Files**/*The Kirkoff Case Roundabout;* **MacMillan and Wife**/*Love Honour and Swindle, Down Shift to Danger;* **McCloud**/*The Man with the Golden Hat;* **Sons and Daughters**/*The Invitation, The Accident.* 1975: **The Rockford Files**/*The Aaron Ironwood School of Success, The No-Cut Contract Foul on the First Play;* **Fools, Females and Fun**/*Doctor in the House, Gotta Believe Me;* **MacMillan and Wife**/*Point of Law, Deadly Inheritance;* **McCloud**/*Fire!* 1976: **MacMillan and Wife**/*Philip's Game;* **Lannigan's Rabbi** (pilot); **Something for Joey; Rich Man Poor Man: Book II** (pt 4).

Unlike the majority of other actors-turned-directors represented here, Antonio has not relinquished one career for the other, but has kept active in both. In front of the cameras his shaggy, sometimes bewildered, but always dogged persistence gives him an 'everyman' quality, and this is reflected in his directorial work. He is closer to his players than to his camera and is, therefore, more than usually dependent on the possibilities of the script. The rapport that he has with his characters can give an extra degree of warmth and understanding to formula antics, and **Lannigan's Rabbi**, with Art Carney and Stuart Margolin, plus assorted friends and wives (Janet Margolin, Barbara Carney, Barbara Flicker) was a quietly civilised pilot. His sensitivity helped divert the sticky problems of **Something for Joey** (leukemia, say no more . . .) into emotional truth. If we must have tear-jerkers, Antonio is the man to make them.

John Astin (1930-)

1970: **Four-In-One: Night Gallery**/*The House.* 1971: **Rod Serling's Night Gallery**/*A Fear of Spiders, The Dark Boy;* **MacMillan and Wife**/*Murder by the Barrel.* 1976: **Holmes and Yoyo**/*K-9*

Caper, The Hostages, Dead Duck, Connection Correction.

John Astin may be more familiar as Gomez Addams, in **The Addams Family**, or even as Harry Dickens, in **I'm Dickens . . . He's Fenster**, than a director of the small-screen. His most interesting work can be seen in two segments of **Night Gallery**: *The House* and *The Dark Boy.*

The House, first telecast as part of the **Four-in-One** package, is a haunting psychological drama, conveyed in a pleasantly relaxed fashion, while *The Dark Boy* emerges as an eerie excursion into the supernatural pastures of Henry James's *The Turn of the Screw*. The most pleasing factor, perhaps, with both these segments, is the superb dream-like quality that Astin achieves, almost something that could be termed a 'misty reality'.

The **MacMillan and Wife** series was, at most times, as much a caricature of drama as **Holmes and Yoyo** was forced laughter in a heavily contrived situation. Astin's intentions as a director are still unclear, though his occasional sparks of excellence are worth noting and applauding.

Bill Bixby (1934-)

1975: **Barbary Coast**/*Jessie Who?;* **Bert D'Angelo–Superstar**/*A Noise in the Street.* 1976: **Spencer's Pilots** (multiples); **Rich Man, Poor Man: Book II**/*Chapters 3 & 18.* 1977: **Oregon Trail**/*Scarlet Ribbon;* **Charlie's Angels**/*Dirty Business.*

Bixby is currently appearing as the 'lighter' side of **The Incredible Hulk.** He has had a rather fragmented career behind the camera. Since appearing in the popular sit-coms, **My Favourite Martian** and **The Courtship of Eddie's Father,** Bixby has taken to directing such mixed flavours as **Barbary Coast, Spencer's Pilots** and **Charlie's Angels.** His title-role **Magician** series, alternatively, was a carefully concocted cocktail of Harry Houdini and Ellery Queen, a somewhat unique brew with much creative potency. However, it projected him into the sterile hostship of ABC's **Wonderful World of Magic** specials. If there is a gleam of creative light shining from Bixby's directorial work, it is heavily masked by a filter of indecision.

Richard Boone (1917-)

1960: **Have Gun-Will Travel**/*The Night the Town Died, Ambush, Black Sheep, The Campaign of Billy Banjo, Ransom, The Search, Out at the Ball Park, The Calf, The Shooting of Jesse May, The Marshal's Boy, The Mountebank.* 1961: **Have Gun-Will Travel**/*The Princess and the Gunfighter, The Tax*

Gatherer, Fandango, The Broken Image, The Education of Sarah Jane, A Proof of Love, The Hanging of Aaron Gibbs. 1962: **Have Gun-Will Travel**/*Squatters' Rights, Justice in Hell, Dream Girl, The Bandit, Taylor's Woman.* 1963: **Have Gun-Will Travel**/*Be Not Forgetful of Strangers, The Walking Years, Sweet Lady of the Moon, Lady of the Fifth Moon.* 1964: **The Richard Boone Show**/*All the Blood of Yesterday.*

The craggy Boone took advantage of the way TV turned movie character actors into 'heroes' (their non-beautiful faces were more effective than those of matinee idols; their talent, too, was more apparent, with the camera boring in close) and established himself as an actor with the **Medic** series. He became an 'artist' with **Have Gun-Will Travel**, although one with mannered pretensions. The **Richard Boone** show was a repertory-company framework which allowed the company to interchange roles with the scripts (some by Clifford Odets) carried rather heavy 'messages'.

It seems strange to enthusiasts, who treasure the wealth of potential subversion, moral dramas, suggestion and myth in the great western, thriller and other genres, that their practitioners seem always to need 'significance'. Boone had it all, but was found wanting; **The Richard Boone Show** was cancelled. Apart from **Hec Ramsey** — another short-lived show, with Boone as a shambling western detective — Boone's TV series career ended there; he seems to have directed nothing else. If he had anything to say, it was best expressed in **Have Gun-Will Travel**, but simply watching him work was its own reward.

Georg Stanford Brown

1976: **Charlie's Angels**/*The Big Tap Out, The Blue Angels.* 1977: **Starsky and Hutch**/*The Crying Child, The Heroes, Starsky's Lady;* **Charlie's Angels**/*Angels in the Outfield, Angel Blue.* 1978: **Charlie's Angels**/*Little Angels of the Night.*

Stanford Brown has doubled as actor and sometime director on **The Rookies, Roots, Charlie's Angels** and **Starsky and Hutch**. Working mainly under the Spelling-Goldberg banner, he has helmed two of the company's most popular and successful shows. If his turn behind the cameras is intended as something of a foothold in TV directing, then he appears to have made an interesting start. His *Angel Blues* segment, in a general format dominated by glamour gals and gratuitous 'jeopardies', is a notable exception to the routine. *Angel Blues* sets the heroines in a rock-music milieu, and manages to develop the standard **Angels** presentation into an above-routine programmer. Whether Stanford Brown justifies his being in the director's chair depends on his integrity in the creative field. No one can evaluate it on the basis of his working on **Charlie's Angels**, although there are signs of a discomforting talent even here. *Little*

Angels of the Night had the trio doubling as prostitutes in a brothel and came near to edging the programme away from the comic strip and into the bedroom.

Richard Carlson (1912-1978)

1960: **Thriller**/*Choose a Victim.* 1972: **O'Hara–US Treasury**/*Operation: Spread, Operation: Mr Felix* (both wr only).

ZIV's **I Led Three Lives** was Carlson's first, and only, big TV show, in an acting capacity. The communist-blacklisting paranoia of the early fifties that spawned **I Led Three Lives** faded soon afterwards, along with the series. Carlson directed three features for the big-screen (RIDERS TO THE STARS, FOUR GUNS TO THE BORDER, and THE SAGA OF HEMP BROWN) during the fities, and then turned up again, in '58, with another continuing series, **Mackenzie's Raiders**, but elusive records fail to list if he actually directed any of these. **Thriller**'s *Choose a Victim* was one of the show's earlier segments, made at a time when the producers were not sure which path the series should take, it remains more in keeping with the Hitchcock strain of *thriller* than with what eventually became the supernatural **Thriller**. The Webb **O'Hara** series was simply a variation of Quinn Martin's **The FBI**, with David Janssen slotting into the Zimbalist groove. Carlson's writing credits for this show remain as odd a creative venture as his directing credits.

Jackie Cooper (1921-)

1955-1957: **People's Choice** (multiples). 1959-1962: **Hennesey** (multiples). 1972: **MASH**/*The Ringbanger, Showtime.* 1973: **MASH**/*Dear Dad . . . Again.* 1976: **The Feather and Father Gang**/*Murder at F-Stop 11, The Big Frame, The Mayan Connection.*

Outgrown member of the OUR GANG comedies, and one-time production head of Screen Gems, Jackie Cooper seems to have lost none of that stubborn drive which characterised him so endearingly in Vidor's THE CHAMP. With his long-running **People's Choice** and **Hennesey** series Cooper found time to crank out over 160 episodes.

Dear Dad... Again is a particularly well-made episode concerning Alda's letter home, in which the crazy events that he relates are shown. The whole **MASH** show is a splendid series of fast gags, but this particular segment rounds-off and polishes it into a grade-A routine. **The Feather and Father Gang** slides along on a slick surface of tongue-in-cheek capers, but somehow falls short of expectation due to the jousting for character dominance by Harold Gould and Stephanie Powers. Cooper's segments are as efficient under the circumstances, though they lack any exceptional merit.

Jeff Corey (1914-   )

1970: **Four-In-One: Night Gallery**/*Certain Shadows on the Wall;* **Rod Serling's Night Gallery**/*The Academy, The Late Mr Peddington;* **Four-In-One: The Psychiatrist**/*Ex-Sgt Randell File USA.* 1971: **Rod Serling's Night Gallery**/*The Dear Departed, Deliveries in the Rear, Quoth the Raven, Lindemann's Catch, Tell David, You Can't Get Help Like That Anymore;* **Alias Smith and Jones** (multiples); **Owen Marshall, Counselor at Law**/*The Triangle.* 1972: **Rod Serling's Night Gallery**/*Fright Night;* **The Sixth Sense**/*Eye of the Haunted.* 1973: **Hawkins** (multiples); **Police Story** (multiples); **The Bob Newhart Show** (multiples).

Making his feature-film acting debut in 1941 with ALL THAT MONEY CAN BUY, Jeff Corey has spent over three decades refining the character roles of convict, policeman, hoodlum, etc., (in movies like THE KILLERS, SECONDS, THE BOSTON STRANGLER and TRUE GRIT), before taking the director's chair on Universal's **Four-in-One** series.

Corey's most continuous output was for **Night Gallery.** *Lindemann's Catch* and *You Can't Get Help Like That Anymore* remain in the memory. The former segment is an outlandish piece of fairy-tale *fantastique*, where a sea captain nets a mermaid; the latter features a bravado performance from Broderick Crawford and Cloris Leachman, as a destructive couple. On the negative side, material like *Quoth the Raven* and *Tell David* reduce Corey's high points-score; he tries too hard to be either clever, witty, or weird and succeeds only in creating indulgent nonsense. With Serling's continual battle over creative freedom, it may be interesting to consider just how tightly-reined Corey may have been under the Universal executive watch. Consequently, Corey's directorial output places him somewhere between the journeyman efforts of a Paul Steward and the 'strained seriousness' of an Ida Lupino.

Ray Danton (1931-   )

1977: **Quincy**/*A Question of Time, Tissue of Truth, Main Man* (+st), *Last of the Dinosaurs;* **Switch**/*The Tong.*

Actor Danton began his film career in the middle '50s, and never really found a niche for himself in a Hollywood which was in the process of dying. He arrived too late to step into a Tony Curtis mould, never conveyed the warmth necessary to emulate a Robert Wagner, never appeared to have the dedication and commitment of a Paul Newman, or the sheer screen chemistry to turn himself into a true original. He shuffled around in a myriad of routine roles in middle or low budget movies before disappearing from the screen, but not before he had secured a place in the heart of cultists with Boetticher's RISE AND FALL OF LEGS DIAMOND.

Legs, from his first day dodging traffic to his last day daring death, is perpetually on the move. His agility, his cat-like movements and sheer physical charm become part of Boetticher's camera choreography, itself full of sharp planes and incursive angles, of sepulchral blacks and rich daunting whites. The film is a helter-skelter fashioned into something meticulous, exhilarating and deadly funny; Boetticher and Danton make Legs one of the most sophisticated and disturbingly ambiguous of all screen gangsters.

It would have been impossible for Boetticher to have made such a film without the total understanding and collaboration of his actor; indeed a certain hostility exists between them, based apparently on Danton's claim that *he* is really responsible for the film. Such squabbling, even if true, would normally only be of interest as trivia—except that Danton has himself now begun to direct.

There is a certain pleasurable symmetry to this, in that the majority of his erstwhile directors—Abner Biberman, Joseph Pevney, Jesse Hibbs, Charles Haas, Paul Wendkos, Vincent Sherman and the ubiquitous Mr Martinson—themselves, all prolifically, worked the TV mine. So can we now expect a vision in some way compatible with that expressed in LEGS DIAMOND?

Any vision is unlikely to emerge from **Quincy** segments, though **Switch** has a concept conducive to irony, wit, doublecross and deception. Tracking down Danton segments may, therefore, turn out to be rewarding, more rewarding than might have been expected.

Joan Darling

1975: **Doc** (pilot), *Doc Heal Thyself, Benson Hedges;* **Mary Tyler Moore Show**/*Chuckles Bites the Dust;* **Phyllis**/*All Together Now, So Lonely I Could Cry, A Man and a Woman and Another Woman.* 1976: **Rich Man, Poor Man: Book II** (pt 5).

One of the few women who had managed to surface behind the American TV camera, her comedy credits are an extension of her own career in Chicago's Second City productions and as the star of Theodore Flickers' THE TROUBLE-MAKER. **Rich Man Poor Man**: Book 2 part 5 took her—along with Karen Arthur—into a more serious mainstream. Her career will be worth watching, as much out of a sense of sociological curiosity as to see how her oddball sensibility survives.

Ivan Dixon

1971: **Nichols**/*Sleight of Hand, Wings of an Angel, Zachariah, Away the Rolling River.* 1974: **Get**

Christie Love/*Highway to Murder.* 1975: **Starsky and Hutch**/*The Bait;* **The Waltons**/*The Fighter.* 1976: **Quincy**/*Strangers in Paradise;* **McCloud**/*The Great Taxi Cab Stampede.* 1977: **Hardy Boys Mysteries**/*The Flickering Torch Mystery;* **Rockford Files**/*Battle of Canoga Park, The Major's Committee from Deer Lick Falls;* **Switch**/*Whatever Happened to Carol Harriday?;* **Richie Brockleman**/*Junk It to Me Baby.* 1978: **Love Is Not Enough.**

One of the first black actors to turn to TV directing, his segments have little to distinguish them, but when the foundation of a series is sound, Dixon can do a fine job. His four **Nichols** segments are among the best of the series. **Love Is Not Enough**, his first telefeature, seems also to be his first work to deal with 'the black experience', a family drama about a widower (Bernie Casey) and his five children (aged from 19 to 6) who pull up stakes in Detroit and try to make a better life in Los Angeles. The dramatic problems they inevitably encounter are given an extra layer of sharpness by their particular nature; Dixon's work reflects major contemporary interests. As a pilot for a series, reactions to **Love Is Not Enough** were rather patronising; but they did imply that with its 'good intentions' it should be shown by NBC. It might well have good ratings.

Lawrence Dobkin

1961: **Trackdown**/*Every Man a Witness;* **Sam Benedict**/*Too Many Strangers;* **The Detectives** (multiples). 1962: **Dr Kildare** (multiples); **The Rifleman** (multiples); **Ensign O'Toole** (multiples). 1963: **77 Sunset Strip**/*By His Own Verdict, Lover's Lane, The Toy Jungle, Alimony League, The Fumble, Not Such a Simple Knot, Queen of the Cats, The Target;* **Alcoa Premiere**/*Chain Reaction;* **The Eleventh Hour** (multiples); **The Donna Reed Show** (multiples). 1964: **Tom, Dick and Mary**/*The Touch of Your Hand;* **Burke's Law**/*Who Killed Supersleuth?;* **Seaway**/*Dead Reckoning, Gunpowder and Paint* (2 pts); **My Living Doll** (multiples). 1965: **Mr Roberts**/*Old Rustysides, Carry Me Back to Cocoa Island;* **Trials of O'Brien**/*Picture Me a Murder, The Partridge Papers;* **Laredo**/*Anybody Here Seen Billy? A Medal for Reece, The Calico Kid;* **The Munsters**/*Autumn Croakus, Family Portrait, Knock Wood Here Comes Charlie, Munster Masquerade.* 1966: **The Fugitive**/*Nobody Loves All the Time;* **Star Trek**/*Charlie X.* 1967: **Custer**/*Accused, The Glory Rider, Under Fear;* **Felony Squad**/*The Fear Merchant, Debt of Fear.* 1971: **Emergency**/*Mascot;* **O'Hara–US Treasury**/*Operation: Time Fuse, Operation: Dorais, Operation: Latisse.* 1972: **Emergency**/*Helpful, Hangup, Weird Wednesday;* **Cannon**/*Hounds of Hell, Moving Target.* 1973: **Cannon**/*Valley of the Damned;* **Intertect.** 1974: **Six Million Dollar Man**/*The Pal-Mir Escort;* **Cannon**/*Bobby Loved Me, The Stalker.* 1975: **The Manhunter**/*Day of Execution, Trial by Terror, Death Watch;* **Cannon**/*The Victim, Fall Guy, Cry Wolf;* **Emergency**/*Virus.* 1976: **The Waltons**/*First Edition, The Wedding* (2 pts), *The Best Christmas, The Ferris Wheel, The Go-Getter, The Quilting;* **Sara**/*When Gentlemen Agree.* 1977: **The Waltons**/*The Children's Carol, The Seashore.*

Mainly a supporting actor during the 1950s, Lawrence Dobkin turned to directing for TV in the early '60s, and gracefully travelled through 18 years of TV production without causing the slightest ripple. A most lauded segment, **Star Trek**'s *Charlie X* appears almost extraneous to the Dobkin credits and is mainly a consequence of the great praise lavished on the show's first season. The lightweight, action and comedy **Laredo** series excites pleasant memories of a grizzled Neville Brand of the less-than-determined Rangers. **The Munsters**, on the other hand, are a sore reminder of just how invalid cheap imitation can be, particularly in the sit-com field. Nevertheless, Dobkin's time has been spent under the roofs of many studios where some above-average material has been put together.

Robert Douglas (1909-)

1960: **Maverick**/*Dutchman's Gold, Kiz;* **77 Sunset Strip**/*The Valley Caper, The Rice Estate, The College Caper;* **The Roaring 20's**/*Red Carpet.* 1961: **Hawaiian Eye**/*The Pretty People, Point Zero, Total Eclipse;* **77 Sunset Strip**/*Face in the Window, The Legend of Leckonby, The Eyes of Love, The Desert Spa Caper, The Chrome Coffin.* 1962: **77 Sunset Strip**/*Wolf! Cried the Blonde, Baker Street Caper, Flight from Escondido, Nightmare.* 1963: **Kraft Suspense Theatre**/*Kill Me on July 20th;* **The Virginian**/*The Final Hour.* 1964: **Alfred Hitchcock Hour**/*You'll Be the Death of Me* (+ pr), *Behind the Locked Door* (+ pr), *The Long Silence.* 1966: **Court Martial**/*Where There Was No Echo* (+ pr), *A Date with Celeste* (+ pr), *Flight of a Tiger* (+ pr); **Lost in Space**/*The Toymaker.* 1967: **The Invaders**/*The Prophet;* **The Monroes**/*Manhunt.* 1968: **The Invaders**/*Counterattack.* 1969: **Mission Impossible**/*The Diamond.* 1970: **Dan August**/*Invitation to Murder.* 1972: **Cannon**/*Endangered Species, The Shadow Man.* 1973: **Cannon**/*Murder by Proxy, Perfect Alibi, Trial by Terror.* 1975: **Baretta**/*When Dues Come Down, A Bite of the Apple, Pay or Die, Dead Man Out, Left Hand of the Devil;* **The Streets of San Francisco**/*Asylum.* 1976: **Baretta**/*Dear Tony, Runaway Cowboy, Can't Win for Losing, Why Me?;* **Columbo**/*Old Fashioned Murder;* **City of Angels**/*The Castle of Dreams, The House on Orange Grove Avenue;* **Future Cop.** 1977: **Big Hawaii**/*Tightrope;* **Man from Atlantis**/*The Naked Montague.*

The suave, polished villain of THE NEW ADVENTURES OF DON JUAN, THE PRISONER OF ZENDA, THE SCARLET COAT, etc., Robert Douglas started directing in TV with the early Warner Brothers shows: **Maverick, 77 Sunset Strip, Roaring '20's,** and **Hawaiian Eye**. His term under the Hitchcock aegis gave warnings of a growing technique and some promise, producing and directing the **Alfred Hitchcock Hour** shows. Midway through the '60s he switched to more frivolous fare, beginning with the silly **Lost in Space**, through the bland **Monroes**, the ineffective **Dan August**, to the tedious **Cannon** series. In 1975 Douglas's work took a swing in a creative direction—the **Streets of San Francisco, Columbo** and the **Barettas** are series of significant force and creative scope, enabling Douglas to, presumably, regain his stance. More recently, he has wandered slightly off path but, then, Douglas always seems to wait around for someone to blaze the trail before him, moving only when the smoke has cleared.

Peter Falk (1927-   )

1971: **Columbo**/*Blueprint for Murder.*

Falk has been before the **TV** cameras since the late '50s, appearing in **Robert Montgomery Presents, Studio One, The Untouchables, The Islanders**, etc. He first scored with his **Trials of O'Brien** series ('65-'66), developing the sloppy, apparently absent-minded characterisation that was to later emerge as **Columbo.** That was for NBC's **Sunday Mystery Movie. Trials of O'Brien** was a modest series with a peculiarly pleasurable aura, in which Falk developed a delightful, almost Watsonian quality. **Columbo** collated these elements; it is a slick version of **O'Brien** extending itself into caricature. The somewhat unique Falk characterisation sustained the earlier series, but it monopolises **Columbo.** Colleague, Ben Gazzara, has taken shots at directing the Falk series, but this is more a function of the Cassavetes circus. Of this circus (HUSBANDS, etc.), Falk appears the least directorially/creatively inclined.

Mel Ferber (1917-   )

1971: **Alias Smith and Jones**/*20 Days to Tenstrike.* 1972: **MacMillan and Wife**/*Reunion in Terror.* 1976: **Sirota's Court** (pilot), *The Split Up, The Reporter, Snake and the Old People, Sirota's Car, The Election, Court Fear, The Hooker, The Old Friend, The Vacation, The Alien, The Judge.*

Ferber is a somewhat shadowy figure and as with many of his contemporaries who have yet to build up any sizeable body of work, it is far too early to make anything like a definite statement about him. Indeed, currently, he seems to be edging out of the director's chair into production (THE CLONE MASTER). Be that as it may, **Sirota's Court** appears to have been his only area of commitment, having directed multiple episodes since the show's pilot. **Sirota's Court** is an oil and water comedy series, which attempts to combine comic strip characters in a semi-serious setting (a night-court judge who appears to be a cross-pollination of Neil Simon's Felix Ungar and Oscar Madison). In trying to be unusual for all the good reasons, the show has merely succeeded in being unorthodox for all the bad reasons. In a directorial span that appears, overall, to lack any significant areas of responsibility, Ferber remains on the threshold of influencing his programmes.

James Garner (1928-   )

1976: **Rockford Files**/*The Girl in the Bay City Boys Club.*

TV and **Maverick** turned Garner from a Warner Bros. contract player into a star, but it wasn't generally recognised how much his talent was relevant to their success. On leaving the series, he spent a decade trying to find the right material on the big screen. Much of his resulting work is excellent, but the best directors somehow eluded him; he never became part of a 'world' the way Cary Grant or James Stewart had been for Hawks, Hitchcock and Mann. The relative indignity of appearing in Disney features, although he performed well in them, must have encouraged him to go back to TV—but on his own terms and through his company Cherokee Productions.

Nichols was the initial result, which seems to be as personal to Garner as **The Prisoner** is to Patrick McGoohan. Although the series built up a considerable following, it wasn't large enough to dent the ratings and was cancelled. (It is now beginning to enjoy the cult status of **The Prisoner** and **Star Trek.**)The next project reunited Garner with Roy Huggins, who between them had delineated **Maverick. The Rockford Files**, which has many affinities with the earlier series, is now entering the magic fifth season (when enough segments will have been filmed to enable the series to reap the rewards of future non-network syndication).

Garner's role is plainly much more than that of 'mere' actor. Around him have grown a number of small cottage industries, composed of writers, directors and producers who have cut their teeth on the various series; he is as much the creative heart of his current activities as anyone can be. His one directorial effort is relatively undistinguished. His overall career, and its creative associations, is, however, of the highest order.

Ben Gazzara (1931-   )

1966: **Run for Your Life**/*Tell It Like It Is, The Killing Scene.* 1970: **The Name of the Game**/*Appointment in Palermo.* 1974: **Columbo**/*Troubled Waters, A Friend in Deed.*

It is only right that Ben Gazzara should have taken a turn in the director's chair when he was doing **Run for Your Life**, but his later directorial stints appear as vehicles without a destination. It could, however, be said that there is more than a passing influence here from comrade Cassavetes; the **Columbo** segments also tie-in with the Cassavetes/Gazzara/Falk triumvirate. It remains to be seen which route Gazarra will take, although we do not believe that the wait will be worth it.

Paul Michael Glaser & David Soul

1976: **Starsky and Hutch**/*Bloodbath* (Glaser), *Survival* (Soul).

The Spelling-Goldberg **Starksy and Hutch** series came along with the wave of police actioners that hit the small-screen during the mid-1970s; with its two young, somewhat unorthodox, cop-heroes it struck gold in the ratings: Paul Michael Glaser (as Starsky) and David Soul (as Hutch). Though Soul appeared content with the series, later moonlighting as a teeny-bop-market warbler, Glaser remained as uneasy participant, wanting, eventually to sever his contractual commitments and explore new areas. Glaser proved himself a more than durable actor when he appeared in Melville Shavelson's **The Great Houdinis.** Their spots at helming an episode of the series would appear to be little more than an exploration but Glaser is, maybe, the more ambitious and wants to move on.

Paul Henreid (1905-)

1958: **Maverick**/*Passage to Fort Doom.* 1959: **Sugarfoot**/*The Mysterious Stranger;* **Cheyenne**/*Reprieve;* **Maverick**/*The Brasada Spur;* **Alfred Hitchcock Presents**/*The Crooked Road, Out There—Darkness, A Personal Matter, Vicious Circle;* **Johnny Staccato**/*The Mask of Jason.* 1960: **The Third Man**/*Happy Birthday, Diamond in the Rough, Queen of the Nile, Meeting of the Board, Calculated Risk, The Luck of Harry Lime.* 1961: **Thriller**/*Terror in Teakwood.* 1962: **Sam Benedict**/*Run Softly Oh Softly.* 1964: **Bonanza**/*A Time to Step Down;* **Alfred Hitchcock Hour**/*Annabel.* 1965: **The Virginian**/*Long Ride to Laird River;* **The Big Valley**/*Earthquake, The Fallen Hawk, My Son My Son;* **The Loner**/*One of the Wounded.* 1966: **Hawk**/*The Man Who Owned Everyone, Ulysses and the Republic.* 1967: **Iron Horse**/*Grapes of Gran Valley.* 1969: **The Survivors**/*Chapter II.* 1971: **The Man and The City**/*The Handwriting on the Door, The Cross-Country Man, Running Scared, I Should Have Let Him Die.*

Paul Henreid has been an actor-director in movies and TV for over two decades. Among his feature films, Henreid has directed FOR MEN ONLY in 1952 (also produced), DEAD RINGER in '64, and BALLAD IN BLUE in '65. His TV-direction began in the late '50s with Warner material. His TV credits, however, are etched with enough also-rans (**The Third Man, The Loner, The Survivors, Man and the City**) to cast doubt on the segments in more-prestigious pastures. Henreid's best work, perhaps, stirs fond memories of a bygone era of TV, (**Alfred Hitchcock Presents, Maverick, Staccato**, etc.), whilst most of his later stuff, with few exceptions, is decidedly dull and virtually anonymous.

Fernando Lamas (1926-)

1967: **Run for Your Life** (multiples). 1968: **Mannix** (multiples). 1969: **Mission Impossible** (multiples); **Alias Smith and Jones**/*The 5th Victim.* 1971: **Alias Smith and Jones**/*Smiles with a Gun.* 1972: **The Bold Ones** (multiples). 1975: **Starsky and Hutch**/*Shootout.* 1976: **Starsky and Hutch**/*Tap Dancing Her Way Right into Your Hearts, The Specialist;* **The Hardy Boys Mysteries**/*Mystery of the Disappearing Floor;* **Starsky and Hutch**/*Shootout, The Specialist.*

Run for Your Life, Mannix and **Mission Impossible** set Lamas on a promising path, since picking up the megaphone for TV in 1967. The **Starsky and Hutch** episodes as quite efficiently directed and *Tap Dancing Her Way Right Back into Your Hearts* is exceptionally pleasing. One suspects that there may be more to Lamas than an actor's preoccupation with small-screen production. He is especially interesting when he works under such creative talents as Roy Huggins and Bruce Geller.

Norman Lloyd (1914-)

1957: **Alfred Hitchcock Presents** (assoc pr). 1959: **Alfred Hitchcock Presents**/*The $2,000,000 Defence, Six People No Music, Safety for the Witness.* 1960: **Alfred Hitchcock Presents**/*Human Interest Story, Your Witness.* 1963: **Alfred Hitchcock Hour** (exec pr), *Final Vow, The Jar.* 1968: **Companions in Nightmare.** 1971: **Columbo**/*Lady in Waiting;* **What's A Nice Girl Like You** (pr).

Norman Lloyd immediately comes to mind as the unfortunate fellow who fell from the Statue of Liberty in Hitchcock's SABOTEUR, Lloyd also appeared in SPELLBOUND, and later re-surfaced on the production side of the Hitchcock TV shows. Alternating the associate producer credits with Joan Harrison and Gordon Hessler, Lloyd's term on both **A. H. Presents** and **A. H. Hour** remains too hazy to be of any notable value. Hitchcock brought a lot of his favourite players into the series, as well as assistants like Joan Harrison. Lloyd was merely part of the entourage.

Ida Lupino (1918-)

1959: **Four Star Playhouse** (multiples). 1960: **Alfred Hitchcock Presents**/*Sybilla, A Crime for Mothers;* **Have Gun-Will Travel**/*The Trial, Lady with a Gun.* 1961: **Have Gun-Will Travel**/*The Gold Bar;* **Dick Powell Theatre** (multiples). 1964: **Bewitched**/*'A' Is For Aardvark;* **Fugitive**/*Glass Tightrope, Garden House.* 1965: **The Rogues**/*Huager-Mugger by the Sea, Bow to a Master;* **Dundee and the Culhane**/*Thy Brother's Keeper Brief.* 1966: **The Virginian**/*Deadeye Dick;* **The Big Valley** (multiples).

Sarris merely observes that 'her directed films express much of the feeling if little of the skill which she has projected so admirably as an actress.' He then uses the rest of his entry on Ms Lupino to thumbnail together some score of other directors whose sex is not male. Her TV work is a disappointingly amorphous collection, although such female-oriented-series as **Bewitched** and **Big Valley**, and such segments as *Sybilla, A Crime for Mothers,* and *Lady with a Gun* reveal more personal touches. Her involvment with the **Four** Star Company and her marriage to the producer Collier Young (**One Step Beyond, The Rogues**) place her in the role of businesswoman as much as actress/director.

Feminist cineastes who take a particular interest in Lupino's career, are likely to find that the small screen has provided her with more scope than the large screen ever did, as well as the opportunity to express a personal viewpoint.

Darren McGavin (1925-)

1959: **Riverboat**/*Blow-Up*. 1974: **Kolchak: The Night Stalker** (series exec pr and star: 20 eps).

McGavin has a sincere, almost over-serious, approach to his work—in a medium that needs, yet fears, sincerity. The success of **The Night Stalker** feature (1st pilot) sowed the seeds for the later series; the 2nd pilot, **The Night Strangler,** was weaker, though it maintained it own distinct flavour. McGavin's involvement with both these pilots, plus his confidence in the concept, eventually spawned the **Kolchak: The Night Stalker** series (under McGavin's own company banner, Francy Productions). However, he was unable to retain the writing talents of Richard Matheson, and the show suffered because of it; David Chase, filling the Story Consultant slot, was an able accomplice but somewhere lacked the drive and sense of pace that Matheson had instilled in the earlier productions.

Patrick McGoohan (1928-)

1962: **Danger Man**/*The Paper Chase, To Our Best Friend.* 1967: **The Prisoner**/*Once Upon a Time* (+ wr), *Fall Out* (+ wr). 1975: **Columbo**/*Identity Crisis.* 1976: **Columbo**/*Last Salute to the Commodore.*

The Prisoner confirmed McGoohan's thirst for esoteric subjects and complex plots. His **Danger Man** (aka **Secret Agent**) series was a successful avenue of double-dealing and triple-faced characters, and led indirectly to **The Prisoner**, which he created, produced and starred in. McGoohan resolutely had his way when making **The Prisoner**, and never allowed interference from the more commercially-minded forces. The show is still seriously discussed, mainly because its objectives and style were always slightly out of focus and were never fully resolved. McGoohan himself wrote the final two segments, which were designed to solve the whole puzzle and bizarre set-up. As a creative force, McGoohan prefers—almost demands—to operate in an unlimited and unrestricted area. He functions with a cool precision only when *he* is calling the shots; **The Prisoner** stands as exhibit 'A' of this determined pursuit.

Randolph Mantooth & Kevin Tighe

1974: **Emergency**/*Gossip, Inventions.* 1975: **Emergency**/*Equipment.* 1976: **Emergency**/*Fair Fight, The Nuisance* (Mantooth), *Insanity Epidemic* (Mantooth).

Manooth and partner Tighe are the anchor–men on the **Emergency** series (from Jack Webb's Mark VII stable); they have both directed the occasional episode. **Emergency** operates on the basic concept of three incidental plots and a sub-plot—directing any given episode simply becomes a routine chore, which, one suspects, is why both lead players have taken turns in the director's chair. Their respective episodes, within their obvious limitations, are as well made, certainly, as the episodes helmed by the more experienced directors (Joe Pevney, Alan Crosland) etc. Their sincerity as directors is still somewhat dubious, and their stint behind the cameras may have been nothing more than a case of a cure for boredom.

Harry Morgan (1915-)

1972: **Hec Ramsey**/*The Mystery of Chalk Hill, Only Birds and Fools.* 1974: **MASH** (multiples).

Morgan's **Hec Ramsey** segments may possibly be the result of previous associations with star Richard Boone (particularly in the latter's '63-'64 show), and as such suggest a collaborative effort. **MASH** is a tightly-paced, high gear sit-com, more dependant on the stamina of its actors than on directorial decision—even with Morgan's apparent, though unremarkable, control over the insane proceedings.

Gene Nelson (1920-)

1964: **The Reporter**/*No Comment;* **Burke's Law**/*Who Killed Vaudeville?, Who Killed the Richest Man in the World?* 1967: **Star Trek**/*The Gamesters of Triskelion;* **Felony Squad**/*Echo of a Killing;* **Iron Horse**/*The Return of Hod and Avery, Wild Track.* 1968: **Lancer**/*Blood Rock, Glory.* 1969: **Wake Me When the War Is Over.** 1972: **Cannon**/*Target in the Mirror.* 1973: **Ironside**/*Mind for Murder;* **The Letters.** 1974: **Get Christie Love!**/*The Longest Fall, Market for Murder.* 1976: **McNaughton's Daughter**/*The Smashed Lady.*

Dancer-actor-director Gene Nelson has wearily advanced through directing such big-screen trivia as KISSING COUSINS, HAREM SCAREM, and THE PERILS OF PAULINE to the non-committal TV-land of **Lancer, Cannon, Get Christie Love!** and **McNaughton's Daughter**. His TV directing appears to be little more than a footnote to his actor-dancer career and, as such, remains adrift somewhere between the poles of competence and absurdity.

Paul Newman (1925-)

1977: **See How She Runs.**

The 'Movie of the Week' syndrome really came of age when superstar Newman directed his fourth feature expressly for the small screen. Of course, he owned the production company behind it.

Leonard Nimoy

1972: **Rod Serling's Night Gallery**/*Death on a Barge.*

Leonard Nimoy deserves an honorable place in this category purely on the strength of his superb *Death on a Barge* segment. *Death on a Barge* is an excellent piece of fantasy Television delivered in a soft, gentle style. Even more alluring is Lesley Ann Warren's vampira. Sadly, the grotesque finale is as jarring to the smooth rhythm of the film as it is (intentionally) to the story. One suspects that this may be the result of executive action for it would be consistent with the general mayhem that Universal enforced on the show. Nevertheless, this segment remains a most memorable achievement, in a series that had little about which to boast.

Lee Philips

1969: **The Survivors** (pt 9). 1971: **Man and the City**/*Run for Daylight.* 1972: **Getting Away from it All.** 1973: **The Girl Most Likely to . . .** 1974: **Red Badge of Courage.** 1975: **Sweet Hostage.** 1976: **Wanted: the Sundance Woman; James Michener's Dynasty; Louis Armstrong–Chicago Style.** 1977: **The Spell; The War Between the Tates.** 1978: **The American Girls** (pilot).

A young Fox contract artist, Lee Philips appeared in **Peyton Place** and other TV shows before throwing in the towel and beginning a career as director. His credits now include an enviable string of successes. **Getting Away from It All** is a comedy about two city couples who do what the title says by buying an island in Maine. Barbara Feldon, too little seen since **Get Smart**, is one of the reasons for the project's charm; Stockard Channing is another in the **Girl Most Likely to . . .**, (plastic surgery transforms her from plain Jane to a delectable siren and she is able to take revenge for all the wounds she suffered with her pre-accident image). The underlying chaos here escalates to the surface in **Sweet Hostage**, with Martin Sheen as a runaway from a mental hospital, kidnapping Linda Blair and hiding out in the mountains. There are reverberations from **Getting Away from It All**—but there are no happy endings. There are echoes of **The Girl Most Likely to . . .** in **The Spell**, a TV spinoff of CARRIE with Susan Myer as a frustrated, humiliated young girl, taking paranormal revenge on her enemies.

A quartet of historical projects show Philips's range. **Red Badge of Courage** is a brave attempt to re-film Stephen Crane's story, and **Wanted: the Sundance Woman** is an interesting sequel to BUTCH CASSIDY AND THE SUNDANCE KID, with Katherine Ross in her original role as Etta Place being hunted by the Pinkertons and getting involved with Pancho Villa. **James Michener's Dynasty**, is a family saga with Sarah Miles and Stacey Keach, while **Louis Armstrong—Chicago Style** features the excellent Ben Vereen as the jazz immortal and his struggles in the '30s.

Philips's affinity with his players is greater than that with the form and technique of the medium, but virtually all his work repays attention.

Telly Savalas (1924-)

1974: **Kojak**/*The Betrayal, I Want to Report a Dream . . .* 1976: **Kojak**/*Kiss It All Goodbye.* 1977: **Kojak**/*In Full Command.*

Since he shot to small-screen stardom, via **Kojak**, Savalas appears to have taken directing seriously, having since indulged himself with the Mati production. There is a distinct accent, a certain quality that gives Savalas-directed episodes their own individual charm. Certainly, they generate emotion. The themes that his episodes deal with are more personal and consequently, more honest. Immigrant families, Greek old country comeraderie, even the relationship and play-off between the Kojak character and Stavros (Savalas's brother, George Demosthenes), are all fashioned in a gentle moist-eyed manner. Interestingly, his lively use of the camera, picking up angled shots from somewhat elaborate set-ups may be another token in the direction of serious direction. His curiosity may exceed his caution, though Savalas may never take up a post permanently behind the cameras, but the faint trickle of films in **Kojak** which culminates in *In Full Command*, a reworking of THE CAINE MUTINY for the police force, shows that he is no nonentity.

Paul Stewart (c.1908-)

1952-1954: **Climax; Playhouse 90; Top Secret; Inner Sanctum; Reader's Digest** (multiples). 1955: **King's Row**/*Lady in Fear, Two of a Kind, Mail Order Bride, Introduction to Erica.* 1956: **King's Row**/*Carnival, Ellie;* **Warner Brothers Presents**/*Survival, Siege.* 1957: **Meet McGraw** (multiples). 1958: **Peter Gunn** (multiples). 1959: **Lawman**/*The Prodigal;* **Phillip Marlowe** (multiples); **Alcoa Theatre** (multiples); **Deadline** (multiples); **The Californians** (multiples). 1960: **Hawaiian Eye**/*Stamped for Danger;* **Michael Shayne**/*Murder in Wonderland, A Night with Nora, This Is It, Michael Shayne, Call for Michael Shayne, Dolls Are Deadly, Shoot the Works, The Poison Pen* 1961: **Coronet Blue**/*Where Are You from and What Have You Done? Man Running, The Rebels* (2 **The Asphalt Jungle** (multiples); **87th Precinct** (multiples); **The Investigators** (multiples). 1962: **The Twilight Zone**/*Little Girl Lost;* **The Defenders**/*The Eye of Fear;* **Going My Way** (multiples). 1963: **The Nurses** (multiples); **Alcoa Premiere** (multiples). 1964: **Bob Hope Chrysler Theatre** (multiples).

Making his screen acting debut with Welles in CITIZEN KANE, Paul Stewart went on to a Jekyll and Hyde existence in TV. It is still not clear what his objectives were; the ambitions behind Cassavetes and Newland, for instance, were obvious. Stewart's TV directing credits go back to the early '50s (**Climax, Inner Sanctum, King's Row**, etc.), a time when he was still very much active in *front* of the cameras. His list of directorial credits makes impresssive reading (**Peter Gunn, M Squad, Lawman, 87th Precinct, Twilight Zone, Defenders**) but, despite being on both sides of the camera during some of Television's more memorable moments, the entire collection somehow adds up to an odd pattern. The short-lived **Michael Shayne** series, in 1960, was a strange collaborative affair with Robert Florey. Certain traces of this collaboration show up in Stewart's *Little Girl Lost* segment for **The Twilight Zone,** which is his best and most effective work for the small-screen. This episode is a beautifully staged piece of atmospheric storytelling (not surprisingly, story and script came from Richard Matheson), although it is not strictly the narrative that makes *Little Girl Lost* such a fine example of filmed television. Composition is maintained as carefully as the pacing, neither suffers at the hands of the other. The entire 30 minute episode is handled in such a gentle and unobtrusive fashion that the incredible seems almost delightfully domestic. In the stream of actor-directors, Paul Stewart remains somewhere out in deep water; although his feet do not touch solid ground, he does not sink.

Sam Wanamaker (1919-)

1964: **Coronet Blue**/*Where Are You from and What Have You Done?, Man Running, The Rebels* (2 pts), *The Presence of Evil;* **Court Martial**/*Bitter Wind.* 1965: **Dundee and Culhane**/*The Jubilee Raid Brief;* **For the People**/*Act of Violence;* **Defenders**/*Eyewitness.* 1966: **Hawk**/*Games with a Bitter End, How Close Can You Get?, Do Not Mutilate on Spindle;* **Legend of Custer**/*Sabres in the Sun* (pilot). 1967: **Lancer**/*The High Riders* (pilot + pr); **Cimarron Strip**/*Broken Wing.* 1977: **Columbo**/*The Bye-Bye Stay High I.Q. Murder Case.*

As actor, producer, director, actor-manager, Wanamaker has leap-frogged from the theatre to TV, from cinema to opera, in a bewildering fashion.

For a few years from 1964 it seemed as though Wanamaker had a career in TV as a director and **Defenders, Hawk, Coronet Blue** all had the benefit of his energy and dramatic conviction. Being assigned the pilots of **Lancer** and **Legend of Custer** would have helped anyone's career to take off—but being Wanamaker, he took off instead, perhaps starved of cultural relevance. You never know when Wanamaker is going to jump into view—he bounced in with the oddball **Columbo**, *The Bye-Bye Stay High I.Q. Murder Case.*

7/Paso Por Aqui

Ragtags and bobtails who passed through TV on their way to or from more substantial work in other areas, but who occasion a little twinge of delight in the teleaste's soul at their mere presence on the small screen.

They are listed here in the interests of completeness, and also to indicate the range of surprises a closer look at TV can—and hopefully will continue to provide.

There may be more where these come from—or went—which further researches will illumine.

John Berry (1917-)

1964: **Seaway**/*Mutiny, Port of Call: Paradise;* **Mr Broadway**/*Smelling Like a Rose.*

Dalton Trumbo, Carl Foreman, Joseph Losey and other victims of the McCarthy witch hunts subsequently became something like heroes to liberal critics. They bit their tongues rather than be too rude to the first named, they perhaps over-praised the last. Yet, strangely, John Berry, who filmed HE RAN ALL THE WAY, FROM THIS DAY FORWARD (and, perhaps, CASBAH) and who showed a most estimable talent, has become something of a forgotten man. He roamed around Europe during the '50's and early '60's, making films like TAMANGO which are neither as fine nor as interesting as before nor yet to be despised.

Where Losey, Foreman and Cy Enfield (another unduly unrecognised McCarthy victim) found a home in England, it was in Canada that Berry returned to English language film making, with the **Seaway** series, joining Abraham Polonsky and Ring Lardner Jr. in a situation reminiscent of so many gangster movies—the boys gathering across the border, waiting their chance to sneak back in.

Berry made it back first, on to **Mr. Broadway**, and finally, through into his commerically successful but critically thumbs-downed black movies, before Lardner with **MASH** and Polonsky with WILLIE BOY ended their professional exiles too. Did Berry work on other Canadian projects? If he did we have not discovered them. It would be good to find that his television shows recaptured the flair and imagination of his earlier films. Either way, TV provided a lifeline.

Noel Black

1976: **Nancy Drew Mysteries**/*Mystery of the Diamond Triangle, Mystery of the Fallen Angels;* **Quincy**/*A Star Is Dead;* **McCloud**/*London Bridges;* **Kojak**/*The Condemned.* 1977: **Switch**/

Maggie's Hero; **Big Hawaii (Danger in Paradise)**/*Red Midnight.*

Black made what must be one of the most commercially profitable of all short movies—SKATERDATER— a piece of grade A eccchhh which a few years back was inescapable on supporting programmes, and with the skateboard boom, has probably gone into even bigger profit.

This must seem ironic to Black, for his next film and first feature PRETTY POISON is stunningly good, an alert, intelligent and extremely disturbing thriller, capitalising brilliantly on our memories of Anthony Perkins in PSYCHO and at last revealing Tuesday Weld as a profoundly adept movie actress. But by all reliable accounts, Black's next film JENNIFER ON MY MIND is a pompous exercise in self-gratification and a resounding flop.

Black has recently accepted the inevitable and begun to take TV assignments. *The Condemned* was up to par **Kojak**, *Red Midnight* an interesting INFERNO—like ordeal on a volcano which brought a temporary breath of life to a terminally ill series. Black's other segments could all prove to be of interest.

Even so, one's immediate response is to regret this turn of events, and wish that he were more active in motion pictures. Such an attitude is, paradoxically, not a denial of the purpose of this book. For PRETTY POISON is, in many respects, an ideal TV project—smallscale, intimate etc.—and if it is any kind of clue to Black's aspirations and real impulses, perhaps TV could successfully accommodate them.

It remains to be seen whether he will gravitate toward the big screen again or take part in what, to the observer, at least, appears to be important creative shifts of direction with TV. Enthusiastic talents will be needed to make the changes work and last—Black has shown that he would be one of the best.

He may not, therefore, just be passing through, and his sense of intimacy with freaky characters, the quirks of their souls, the contrasting elegance of his style, may all grace future TV and steer the small screen in more unique and personal areas.

Budd Boetticher (1916-)

1951: **The Three Musketeers** (pilot: released theatrically as SWORD OF D'ARTAGNAN). 1957: **Maverick**/*The War of the Silver Kings* (pilot), *Point Blank, According to Hoyle.* 1958: **The Dick Powell Show** (multiples). 1959: **Hong Kong**/*Captain Cat.*

The Stranger, dirty, dust-covered, bearded, surely a saddletramp, rides into an equally seedy mining town and lugs a battered suitcase into the hotel.

The desk clerk is busy, so doesn't see The Stranger pick up a newspaper, wander to the end of the counter, extract a $1,000 bill from inside the lining of his coat, take a penknife and fashion a stack of bill-sized paper from the old newspaper, then tuck this and the $1,000 bill into an envelope and write $5,000 on it before turning to register.

The Stranger asks for the best room in the house. The desk clerk coldly informs him that there is no room, but The Stranger ignores him, registers, and extends the envelope. The sight of the $5,000 printed on it instantly fills the clerk with respect. But before he can take the envelope to lodge in the safe, The Stranger draws it back, takes out the lone $1,000 bill, seals the now-worthless, paperfilled envelope, changes the figure to $4,000 and gives it back to the clerk, who personally escorts his well-heeled guest to the best room in the hotel . . .

That was the first of many such sneaky dodges practised by The Stranger—who was of course Bret Maverick as incarnated by James Garner—in the opening sequence of what had been known only as 'Special Project 6906' at Warner Bros. TV and became the pilot for **Maverick**. Under Budd Boetticher's direction, a hit was instantly recognised, a series was born and Boetticher directed the next two segments, *Point Blank* and *According to Hoyle*, before returning to his motion picture career, which at the time included only one of the Randolph Scott westerns which are the cornerstone of his reputation (7 MEN FROM NOW).

Almost parenthetically, he had helped establish the style and character of what has become a legendary TV series. If it is not the most popular or commerically successful, arguably it is the most artistically successful. It is being syndicated again after almost a decade on the shelf, while a new pilot, **Maverick's Return**, is imminent.

There is no way of minimising the importance of Roy Huggins in all this—having created the show, scripted it, and produced the first two seasons. But a series stands or falls on its initial impact, and obviously Boetticher's affinity for the subject and style, his own laid back humour, must have significantly coloured those initial segments.

Probably it could as easily have been **Cheyenne**, or **Bronco** or **Sugarfoot**, or indeed any Warner TV show, for Boetticher was then contracted to the company, but there is something marvellously appropriate that **Maverick** should represent his most important TV work, for Boetticher is Hollywood's most intransigent figure. Yet his very intransigence is a perpetual source of sadness to his admirers.

Unable to emulate Aldrich, Siegel, or Peckinpah in consolidating his motion picture career, it would have been logical for him to settle down like Wendkos or Singer, with a TV contract and the opportunity to 'transform from within' which, after all, Boetticher had been doing with his 17 day Scott westerns.

But this resolute personality would find it easier to become a computer operator. It is unlikely that he'll pass through TV again, so it would be appropriate if his trio of **Mavericks** could be made more generally available. They are fragments of TV history and would add an extra little sparkle to a glittering, if wilfully abortive, career.

Gilbert Cates (1934-)

1972: **To All My Friends on Shore** (+ pr). 1973: **The Affair.** 1974: **After the Fall.**

Cates has had a most curious career. While many directors began in minor positions—gophers, messenger boys etc., few can have started as studio guides. Cates did just that at NBC in New York. Perhaps this chance for intimate observation of human behaviour helped as he worked his way up to become producer and director of game and quiz shows. He then created **Hootenanny,** packaged and directed many specials, and from 1963 to 1966 produced/directed variety shows such as **International Showtime** and **Electric Showcase.**

His first dealings with film were with the short THE PAINTING and then RINGS AROUND THE WORLD which was, what else?, a circus documentary narrated by, of course, Don Ameche.

Before, during, or after such flirtations with raw entertainment, Cates directed many stage plays, including I NEVER SANG FOR MY FATHER which became his first dramatic feature and received moderate and respectful praise.

His TV work is in a similar vein of intimate, emotional drama, teetering on the edge of melodrama: **To All My Friends On Shore** reprises the father/son relationship, with Bill Cosby discovering that his son has an incurable disease; **The Affair** concerns Natalie Wood—as a polio-stricken songwriter—and her first love affair with lawyer Robert Wagner; while **After the Fall** is a version of the Arthur Miller play which thinly disguises his own relationship with Marilyn Monroe.

Those who admire I NEVER SANG FOR MY FATHER and the later SUMMER WISHES, WINTER DREAMS would therefore be advised to take note and lobby for a more general availability of these films. Those who have reservations might hope that Cates could meld the two halves of his professional character, to produce, say, a SMILE of the game shows, or something a little closer to the vulgarity and gusto of the circus ring.

After all, that's entertainment too, and Cates has known that all along.

James Clavell (1924-)

1961: **Detectives**/*Eye for an Eye;* **Rifleman**/*The Queue;* **Whiplash**/*Love Story in Gold* (st only).

We cannot pretend that this sorry excuse for a list is in any way complete, and self-protection might have advised not including Clavell at all. But he is an interesting figure, and THE QUEUE presents obvious connections with his weird western WALK LIKE A DRAGON, both of which concern the problem of identity and the assimilation of races, played out around the symbol of the Chinese queue.

Clavell has virtually abandoned directing for the writing of mammoth novels (*King Rat, Tai Pan, Shoegun*) but he is not as easily dismissed as those who abhor TO SIR WITH LOVE would hope.

His best screen work is admittedly minor—his other TV work (there must be more) may be on a similar level of curious obsession, and therefore fascination to the cultist.

Francis Ford Coppola (1939-)

1971: **The People** (pr). 1977: **The Godfather Saga.**

The Godfather Saga qualifies as an entry in its own right, for it is Coppola's own re-editing of the 175 minute GODFATHER and 200 minute GODFATHER2, with the addition of some 60 minutes of 'new' material—sequences impossible to include, because of length, in either feature format. It is all arranged chronologically, and charts the Corleone history in what is essentially a **Roots** pattern; It is being aired in 3 two hour segments with a three-hour conclusion. Ratings were not as high as expected, largely because the first section is almost entirely in Italian dialogue with English subtitles, a method of presentation not conducive to prime-time success.

Nobody can say that they have seen **The Godfather** now unless they have seen this definitive version. It is Coppola's masterpiece, and all for TV.

Michael Crichton

1972: **Pursuit.**

'Get in, get it done, get out' as Jason Robards growls in BALLAD OF CABLE HOGUE. Certainly Crichton agrees, if his whirlwind career is to be believed. He passed through TV so quickly that nobody seems to know he was ever there.

An extraordinarily prolific writer (15 novels under four different pseudonyms), having graduated from Harvard Medical School and done post-graduate work at the Salk Institute, he has a first-hand base to unreel the technological nightmares and eroding human relationships so cunningly presented in THE CAREY TREATMENT, ANDROMEDA STRAIN, TERMINAL MAN, COMA etc.

WESTWORLD, the first feature Crichton directed from his own script, delighted cultists by its ideas and the brilliant coup of having Yul Brynner reprise his MAGNIFICENT SEVEN persona, complete with same wardrobe, this time (this time?) as a robot. But in fact, though technically a first feature, Crichton had polished his megaphone with the TV film **Pursuit**, where Ben Gazzara attempts to track down a madman threatening to destroy a city with lethal nerve gas.

Pursuit is more thriller than nightmare, perhaps, but it should surely be fitted into the Crichton canon as quickly as possible, if only out of respect for the speed of this unique talent's ideas and rush to success.

André De Toth (1913-   )

1959: **Maverick**/*Cruise of the Cynthia B;* **Hawaiian Eye**/*Beach Boy, A Dime a Dozen;* **77 Sunset Strip**/*Six Superior Skirts;* **Bourbon Street Beat**/*Secret of Hyacinth Bayou.* 1960: **Hawaiian Eye**/*Kikiki Kid, Fatal Cruise;* **Bronco**/*Legacy of Twisted Creek;* **77 Sunset Strip**/*Starlet;* **The Westerner**/*The Old Man, School Day;* **DuPont Theatre** (multiples).

Though De Toth has the votes of such influential observers as Sarris and David Thomson, and has long been an admired figure by the more discerning Continental critics, there is a distinct lack of urgency about the more establishment organs and institutes realising that he is a director of vision, personality and intelligence; so that it is unlikely that this small collection of TV work will suddenly become common property.

De Toth was, however, a favoured Warner Bros. director at the period when the majority of the above titles were made, and had a great degree of freedom and respect, so it is unlikely that this work is merely minor. Shortly after completing this TV stint, De Toth exiled himself from the United States and his subsequent career has found him based largely in England. It does not seem probable that our list will be added to in future. But when a final check is made of De Toth's films, these TV segments must not be ignored.

Stanley Dragoti

1975: **McCoy**/*In Again out Again.*

An ex-commercials director, like Dick Richards with CULPEPPER CATTLE COMPANY Dragoti made an offbeat western, DIRTY LITTE BILLY as his first feature. Its mean and moody attempt to invest the Billy the Kid myth with some much needed realism ultimately floundered on Michael J. Pollard's cutesypie lunatic performance, but suggested that Dragoti, once confidence was established in a form longer than sixty seconds, would have a career worth watching. But as far as we can discover, one lonely **McCoy** segment is the only addition to his oeuvre.

Cyril Raker Endfield (1914-)

1952/1954: **Colonel March of Scotland Yard** (multiples).

Endfield's extraordinary SOUND OF FURY is unaccountably undervalued (if known about at all) by critics of all persuasions, and his subsequent flight to England with the McCarthy wolves howling at his heels (it is tempting to picture him on the same plane out as Joseph Losey) failed to alert liberal interest to his undeniable talents. The Losey parallels continue, for Endfield also made pseudonymous English 'B' films (it is of paranthetic interest to note that Lloyd Bridges, star of SOUND OF FURY, was willing to appear in THE LIMPING MAN, and thereby risk possible career repercussions back home) before his real name was lettered again on the credits of THE SECRET.

But this blight on his career has never really lifted, critically or professionally, and had he not forged a close relationship with actor Stanley Baker (CHILD IN THE HOUSE, HELL DRIVERS, SEA FURY, ZULU, SANDS OF THE KALAHARI) his subsequent work might have been bereft of a single highspot. Critical disdain for the best of these films (ZULU is a masterpiece to rank with SOUND OF FURY) seems equally inexplicable, especially given the similar relationship that developed between Baker and Losey which has itself been well-marked. Undoubtedly Endfield's career is the more minor, but who can deny the power of publicity?

Endfield's TV work consists entirely, it seems, of segments of a strange series made in the first stages of his English exile, starring Boris Karloff as **Colonel March of Scotland Yard,** head of the Department of Strange Cases. Students of Karloff would doubtless like the chance to reappraise their man's first smallscreen series, while Endfield's admirers would like to see whether the dark shadows of the series, subtle spookery, and altogether disorienting mood, compared to the complacency of mid-50s TV, lie solely in the vaults of memory or are indeed filtering through the celluloid. Another element of mystery surrounds Endfield's involvement—this being his period of low profile—for the segments we have checked in the records list such directors as Terence Fisher, Arthur Crabtree and Bernard Knowles, with only 'Phil Brown' as a disturbing intruder. Was this Endfield? Did the other regular directors sign his segments as others had his features? Or was his involvement more elusive? Ultimately of course, the series may add nothing at all for Endfield's stature—but it does provide a reasonable excuse to lobby for his critical rehabilitation.

Theodore J. Flicker (1930-   )

1964: **The Rogues**/*Grave Doubts;* **The Dick Van Dyke Show**/*Show of Hands, 100 Terrible Hours.* 1965: **Run Buddy Run**/*It's a Wild Wild Wake.* 1970: **Night Gallery**/*A Question of Fear* (wr only), *Junior, Hell's Bells;* **Nichols**/*The Indian Giver* (wr only). 1972: **Banacek**/*The Greatest Collection of Them All* (wr only); **Banyon**/*The Old College Try* (co-wr only); **Streets of San Francisco**/*The Locusts* (wr only); **Playmates.** 1973: **Guess Who's Sleeping in My Bed.** 1977: **World Premiere**/*Just a Little Inconvenience* (+ co-wr).

Flicker was a member of Chicago's Second City group and made his first feature THE TROUBLEMAKER in 1964. That same year a segment of **The Rogues** found him realising the cineaste's dream of using virtually every optical transition in the laboratory catalogue (spiral wipes, Stars & Stripes mixes, ripple dissolves etc.) either out of sheer delight or as a desperate attempt to justify the assignment. Such visual devices were at least used with some wit and are, anyway, refreshing in a medium geared to the visually conventional. A brief tenure with the Dick Van Dyke company could only have been an engaging way to spend some time, while **Run Buddy Run**, a kind of funny **Fugitive**, allowed Flicker to tune up his technique, and is a partial precursor of his best work THE PRESIDENT'S ANALYST, which indicated that he might be the long-awaited reincarnation of Preston Sturges. But sadly comedy seems to be the hardest genre to perpetuate in the cinema of the '70s, unless for a performer/director like Allen, Brooks, or Wilder or a Gene Saks, content to bring Broadway comedy to the screen.

Throughout the '70s then, Flicker's career has itself flickered fitfully, first with amusing pastiches for **Night Gallery** (*Hells Bells* has the oddball bonus of Flicker himself portraying The Devil) and formula writing chores to, presumably, pay the bills.

There were indications however that with the development of the Movie of the Week syndrome and in projects like **Playmates** and **Guess Who's Sleeping in My Bed**, Flicker's mordant and satiric personality had found an ideal niche at last.

Not only does his oeuvre cry out for wider exposure and recognition, but also surely, audiences need the kind of humour he is most fond of exhibiting. We fervently hope that one of the few originals we have among us will be gainfully accommodated within a system which could only benefit from his therapeutic ideas. Recently he appears to have gone 'serious' with **Just a Little Inconvenience**, Lee Majors's first non-Bionic vehicle for his own production company. This association with a smallscreen supermensch might thrust Flicker's career forward into more consistently active realms.

Samuel Fuller (1911-)

1962: **The Virginian**/*It Tolls for Thee* (+ wr); **Dogface** (pilot); **The Dick Powell Show**/*Independence S.W.* 1966: **The Iron Horse**/*High Devil* (+ wr), *The Man from New Chicago, Hellcat* (+ co-wr), *Banner with a Strange Device, Volcano Wagon, Red Tornado.*

Fuller has passed through TV at a couple of times of crisis in his motion picture career, and his work for the small screen is more a matter of record than of consuming interest for, in essence, it comes virtually at the end of his career. Thus there is none of the energy, ambition or drive which fuels the work of the younger talents trying to make their mark.

The Iron Horse segments seemed particularly disappointing a decade ago, but then the critical mind was more innocent, and truly believed in the absolute autonomy of any favourite auteurs. Certainly familiar themes abound. Both *Hellcat* which Fuller co-wrote and *Red Volcano* picked up the Indian preoccupation of RUN OF THE ARROW, there are beautiful and/or ruthless lady protagonists in *High Devil* and *The Man From New Chicago* (which also has strong overtones of FORTY GUNS) while, if memory is correct, *Volcano Wagon* is an unusually extensive action vehicle. Expecting little, these segments may reveal more when looked at today.

Independence S.W. got a little closer to pure-Fuller, involving William Bendix in some kind of subversive war with a trucking Mafia and, stylistically, showed the director perfectly at home with TV techniques, using the zoom lens not for flashy emphasis but as a substitute for the tracking camera in typical long-take, travelling conversation scenes.

Dogface is an unknown quantity, but might be vintage Fuller, as is *It Tolls For Thee.* Working from his own script, and with Lee Marvin as, 'natch, a violent outlaw who escapes from the Pen and is out for revenge on Lee J. Cobb who sent him there in the first place, it successfully manages to fuse Fuller's preoccupations with the necessities of the series format. Though, ultimately, it is never more than an exercise, it is among the best **Virginian** segments, perhaps because it came before the 'family' nature of the series asserted itself over the more classical 'loner' nature of the western genre. Fuller seems more committed to it than to the **Iron Horse** segments (though Charles Marquis Warren was paying the salaries on both series), and, perhaps the fact that it could never be his—even though it is usually frenzied with incipient violence—soured Fuller for similar commitment of future TV work.

Is it now too much to hope that the medium can accommodate his brand to 'love—death—hate—in a word EMOTION' and that some future volume will have a post-1978 list of Fuller titles? After the abortive fiasco of THE DEADLY TRACKERS it seems that TV is the only way we'll get an update on the wild world of this splendid figure who seems otherwise doomed to acting parts as a film director as in Dennis Hopper's LAST MOVIE, or figuring in another film obssessed with the end of cinema—Wim Wenders's THE AMERICAN FRIEND.

Curtis Harrington (1928-)

1966: **Legend of Jesse James**/*A Lonely Place, A Burying Place for Rosie.* 1970: **How Awful About Allan.** 1973: **The Cat Creature.** 1974: **The Killer Bees; The Dead Don't Die.** 1975: **Baretta**/*Set-Up City, Murder for Me.* 1976: **Tales of the Unexpected**/*A Hand for Sonny Blue.* 1977: **Logan's Run**/*Stargate;* **Lucan**/*Pariah.*

Harrington is one of the few obvious oddballs in Hollywood. The man who could get a Bachelor of Arts degree from U.S.C., write the first true auteur studies of Joseph von Sternberg, make freaky shorts and get Roger Corman to produce NIGHT TIDE, (a film involving Dennis Hopper's love affair with a mermaid) is plainly deserving of any amount of a teleaste's time.

Unfortunately privileged moments seem rather rare for (whether voluntarily, or bowing to commercial reality) Harrington has discarded the voluptuous world of von Sternberg and his own earlier flirtations with surrealism for the labyrinthine landscape of Gothic horror, turning increasingly to parody and pastiche in lieu of genuine obsession. None of his known TV work shapes up to GAMES, or his most consistently successful blend of nostalgia and the pain of madness WHAT'S THE MATTER WITH HELEN? Indeed his **Lucan** segment was, unforgivably, low on even basic conviction, and was technically sloppy.

There are, however, marvellously evocative moments of pure cinema, enhanced by lustrous lighting by Charles Rosher (senior, presumably) in the otherwise silly **Cat Creature**, *Stargate* with swamp monsters and aliens teleporting down to Earth looked like a cheerful homage to Cormanesque capers of the mid-50s, while *A Hand for Sonny Blue* sounds like an interesting modern variant of THE HANDS OF ORLAC, with major league pitcher Rick Nelson the recipient of a transplant from a vicious young hoodlum. Harrington has also visited non-fantasy genres with **Legend of Jesse James** and **Baretta**.

Harrington is, then, undoubtedly an original, if a rather woolly one, an enthusiast, perhaps, rather than a career professional, delighted merely to give direction to favourites such as Gloria Swanson and shape to his fantasies. A more thorough review of his smallscreen work helps to make sense out of an apparently random and unsatisfactory career.

Anthony Harvey (1931-   )

1975: **The Disappearance of Aimée.**

Ex RADA-trained actor, ex-editor (Boulting Brothers comedies, LOLITA, DR. STRANGELOVE etc.), Harvey has shown enough in his films to reveal a sound technique and a superb way with extrovert actors (Peter O'Toole, George C. Scott, Katherine Hepburn), as well as a rare ability to communicate pain, tenderness, vulnerability. Though rather swamped by **The Disappearance of Aimée,** his talents seem suited to the smallscreen and, with luck, he may pass this way again.

Seth Holt (1923-1971)

1966: **Court Martial**/*Saviour of Vladik, La Belle France.*

Having known and worked professionally with him, it is impossible for any critical objectivity to permeate memories of one of England's finest film-makers; he was essentially an English Jean-Pierre Melville. It is Holt's tragedy—the tragedy too of English cinema—that such a parallel exists only in the *'musée imaginaire'*.

Holt worked his way up through the Ealing film school, from 'junior' in the cutting rooms (he was literally the voice of the blizzard in SCOTT OF THE ANTARCTIC), to prefect in the production department, to head boy in the year that Mr Balcon's academy finally closed down. NOWHERE TO GO, his first film as a director, was the last made by an autonomous Ealing—and it had, retrospectively, an awesomely prophetic title. There was nowhere to go—except perhaps to America (whose spirit animated Holt) for someone so resolutely disdainful of all that was revered and respected in 'British Cinema' (the Leans and Reeds *et all*). After all, his inspiration at 19 had been CITIZEN KANE (which he saw a dozen times in its first week of opening) which impelled him to try and emulate such a work of original cinema, rather than aspire to make the definitive HAMLET or IMPORTANCE OF BEING EARNEST or DOCTOR ZHIVAGO. To want to create was, probably, his original sin.

In his fifteen years as a director, the films that made the most impression of those he worked on were, ultimately, not his own—Karel Reisz's SATURDAY NIGHT AND SUNDAY MORNING and Tony Richardson's THE ENTERTAINER.Both, by reliable reports from people concerned with their production, were virtually unshowable until Holt, pure film-maker, agreed to help the young turks and brought his exquisite technique and skill to bear in the cutting rooms, shaping each mess to such a point that the films were heralded by an ignorant critical fraternity as 'significant directorial works'.

Although Godard, Truffaut, Rivette, Chabrol etc. could swop ideas, rôles and identities in the heady early days of the French new wave, such *esprit* somehow backfired on Holt, for the equivalent talents of the English 'new wave' seem to have been ashamed of their lack of basic talent and a hostile curtain came down. Naturally, public honesty would have been out of place—but private gratitude might not have been. Holt was never offered the opportunity to work under the Woodfall banner.

His misguided comradeship had become a career mistake. This was 1960, Holt had not directed in four years, holding out for finance to make his own personal films. An industry, geared to singularity not originality, supposed that his return to the cutting rooms indicated that he had lost his nerve, and his credibility suffered. Equally, the rest of us were doomed to an interminable series of film abortions masquerading as 'new British cinema'. Would there have been a wholly different 'new wave' had Holt not wielded the scissors and splicing tape? Would there have been none at all?

Although Holt's attempts to fashion his own kind of cinema in virtually an alien country were doomed, he resisted any long-term relationship with TV. Colleagues such as John Moxey and Robert Day were happy enough to direct **Danger Man**, steer **The Saint**, guide **Gideon's Way** and the other hybrid 'mid-Atlantic' teleseries of the '60s, but Holt remained as proudly aloof from such commitment as he did from any flirtations with the theatre of 'prestige' TV (**Armchair Theatre, Play of the Month** etc.). The few TV segments which he was involved with–animated primarily by the desire to pay bills—have only his technique to commend them. However, as his actual output in film and TV is less than his gigantic talent could have offered, the temptation is to welcome any strip of celluloid in which he had a hand.

Harry Horner (1910-   )

1955: **Gunsmoke**/*The Guitar.*

Horner is best known as a superb art director (he was nominated for six Oscars and won two), who trained with Max Reinhardt's company in Vienna and came to America as the legendary figure's assistant. He worked on the New York stage for ten years, before making his first film as production designer, OUR TOWN, in 1938, sharing a credit with his even more illustrious colleague, William Cameron Menzies, who curiously had a similar parallel career as a director.

While Horner has nothing like THINGS TO COME to his name, overall his work is far more consistent than Menzies's and there are a number of very interesting genre pictures (in particular THE MAN FROM DEL RIO) worth seeking out—as would be his **Gunsmoke** segment written as it was by Sam Peckinpah. Other Horner credits currently elude the historian's desire for completeness hidden as they are in the records of **Omnibus, Cavalcade, Readers' Digest, Author's Playhouse, Four Star Theatre** and **DuPont Theatre** anthologies. If we ever get a real TV museum, Horner's exhibits might be more than curios.

James Wong Howe (1899-1976)

1961: **Checkmate**/*State of Shock.*

The celebrated Chinese cinematographer, a permanent Hollywood fixture since 1917, directed one movie—GO MAN GO about the Harlem Globetrotters with a young Sidney Poitier—which would be almost incidental to his multi-award-winning career were it not for the discovery of this **Checkmate** segment, directed nearly a decade later. We can only speculate for the moment about other possible TV work, but it would seem likely that there is more. It, anyway, provides a unique postscript to an already illustrious career.

Garson Kanin (1912-   )

1956: **Hallmark Hall of Fame**/*Born Yesterday.* 1958: **Playhouse 90**/*The Right Hand Man* (wr only). 1959: **Alfred Hitchcock Presents**/*Six People No Music* (st only). 1964: **Mr Broadway** (series cr), *Keep an Eye on Emily* (wr/dir), *The He She Cheating* (wr only), *Something to Sing About* (wr-pr).

It must be marvellous being Kanin's telephone operator, eavesdropping on scintillating calls to and from wags and wits, or his mailman, secretly steaming open missives to show business legends. Social intercourse, Hollywood, Broadway and literary careers have kept Kanin (and wife Ruth Gordon) far too busy to have much to do with parvenu TV, though it would be interesting to catch and compare the smallscreen version of *Born Yesterday*.

In 1964 Kanin created the **Mr Broadway** series, which on paper must have seemed a wondrous way to harness all the Kaninesque show-knowledge, built as the series was around Craig Stevens as a New York PR man and his 'distinguished clients' (such guest stars as Tuesday Weld, Art Carney and the young Liza Minnelli). Kanin's actual involvement was limited to writing and directing the premier segment, and contributing two other scripts; overall the show was a colourless disappointment. Any teeth it may have had, any oblique wit or offbeat stride, must have been trodden on by the powers that be—although as Kanin later wrote and directed two inexplicably poor features (WHERE IT'S AT, and SOME KIND OF A NUT) perhaps he was just out of touch. He has now settled for the nostalgia of his biographies and memoirs. One should be grateful.

Phil Karlson (1908-)

1959: **Desilu Mystery Theatre**/*The Untouchables* (2 pts). 1964: **Alexander the Great.**

After so excellently empathising and exploring mob mentality in KANSAS CITY CONFIDENTIAL and BROTHERS RICO, and simultaneously creating bewildered, revenge-seeking heroes incarnated by the likes of John Payne and Richard Conte, to bring both sides together in a plethora of stunning, sense-numbing collisions, Karlson had impeccable credentials for directing the two-part **Desilu Mystery Theatre** which became **The Untouchables** pilot (and a feature THE SCARFACE MOB for theatrical release). As perfect a match as Boetticher and **Maverick** (incidentally indicating that executives instinctively know something about auteur theory), Karlson's work virtually guaranteed the success of the series as well as creating a sequence for a myriad of other directors to incorporate into their own footage (the orgy of destruction when the ambivalently pious Ness and Co. annihilate a liquor warehouse).

A style was set—if rarely as well matched—which posed problems for executive producer Quinn Martin. Audiences continually demanded even more violence—censors constantly ordered its diminution. It is too fanciful to suggest that Karlson ushered in the brutal early 60s shows like **M Squad, Johnny Staccato** and **Tightrope** singlehanded—but he certainly attached the weights and pushed them off the pier.

His only other TV work seems to be a most unusual oddity—William Shatner as **Alexander the Great** (apparently a pilot for an abortive series) which opens with the great historical warlord galloping through western locations pursued by Persian Indians, the Karlson cameras tracking furiously the while. John Cassavetes, Joseph Cotten, the delectable Ziva Rodann and even a young Batman, Adam West, all thesp uneasily, but as the segment details the one hour, thirteen minute Battle of Issus between the Greeks and the Persians (death toll 1800 to 3500 respectively), Karlson remains in his frantic element.

Howard W. Koch (1916-)

1959: **Miami Undercover** (multiples); **The Untouchables**/*The St Louis Story, Unhired Assassin* (2 pts—aka *A Gun for Zangara).*

Koch began his working life as a runner on Wall Street—apparently giving up dreams of financial magnitude to become an assistant editor, then assistant director, then 2nd unit director before working as producer of the Aubrey Schenk company's oddball B feature output in the 50s.

He directed BIG HOUSE USA and THE LAST MILE himself, and built a cult reputation with these above average gangland gallivantings which nurtured a brutal callousness perfectly attuned to such lowlife subjects and to an audience tired of the plastic unreality of conventional codes. UNTAMED YOUTH, sweaty eroticism with Mamie Van Doren in reform school, shared the same crude energy. Koch plainly was destined, therefore, to help **Untouchables** segments—indeed they seemed made for him.

But seemingly Wall Street was not a distant memory—for his subsequent career has found him as Frank Sinatra's executive producer and then with that excellent appellation 'vice president in charge of production' at Paramount. Koch has not had to run anymore; he can look down on lesser mortals from a penthouse suite. Perhaps through nostalgia for all that lowlife of the past, he produced and directed BADGE 373 in 1973, an unjustly neglected if still minor reprise of Koch's earlier work, but now with Robert Duvall singlehandedly fighting the mob. Teleastes prefer the way Koch did it with Ness.

Jerry Lewis (1926-)

1970: **The Bold Ones: The Doctors**/*In Dreams They Run.*

TV played a big part in the Martin/Lewis rise to success, and since then a solo Lewis has returned, usually to disastrous notices and ratings, with a variety of autocratic spectaculars. Now too his unique vein of love/hate comedy seems to have dried up and as performer and director he has been silent (mercifully, for some) for several years, apart from an unseen collaboration with Pierre Etaix in France.

His one non-comic credit as director dates from his last really active year in Hollywood (WHICH WAY TO THE FRONT) and is a fascinating footnote for admirers and detractors alike. Does his skill with and understanding of the camera shine in a dramatic context? Does his incurable penchant for didactic sentimentality have free rein in such a context? Do enough people still care one way or another.

Alexander Mackendrick (1912-)

1964: **The Defenders**/*The Hidden Fury.*

The title of his one TV segment is perhaps an echo of Mackendrick's own feelings towards a medium which is happier for him to teach it than make it. Like Seth Holt, he never really came to terms with the severing of Ealing's umbilical cord (SWEET SMELL OF SUCCESS and HIGH WIND IN JAMAICA notwithstanding) and it is to be hoped that those students who sit at the master's feet savour his enthusiasm and love for the medium rather than run scared into dentistry.

Michael Miller

1978: **Outside Chance.**

Produced and financed by Roger Corman's New World Pictures, **Outside Chance** is the sequel to JACKSON COUNTY JAIL, and again teams Yvette Mimieux with Miller. Planned as a telefilm for CBS, new footage was shot to expand the project into a theatrical feature—but at the time of writing CBS was holding its options. If the film is initially released theatrically, it would be the first time CBS has gone this route. Though producer Jeff Begun told *Variety*—'It's not just a movie of the week, but a fullblooded feature film', the project will in the fullness of time find its way back to its original source. It is listed here as a counterpoint to **The Godfather Saga**.

Robert Parrish (1916-   )

1960: **Twilight Zone; Johnny Staccato.**

Like Boetticher, Parrish is a miniaturist—though we should firmly resist the idea that being so in some way makes a talent 'minor'. Can there really be 'minor masterpieces'? As farmer Anthony Caruso tells fugitive Robert Mitchum in WONDERFUL COUNTRY when the latter wonders why a total stranger would help him—'A man is measured in a minute', and so it is with Parrish's best films and his book of memoirs, *Growing up in Hollywood*.

Parrish is not interested in earth-shattering conflicts, in pompous didacticism, in glib liberalism; he could not have been involved with a WILD BUNCH, a DIRTY DOZEN, a STING, an EXORCIST or any of the kind of 'projects' which become box office champs.

TV would, one feels, have proved a conducive framework for Parrish's gentle, subtle understanding of the human spirit—and arguably his urbanity and well-honed technique (his editing Oscar for BODY AND SOUL, his years working with John Ford) would have been a touchstone to help shape the medium in the '60s.

Indeed the history of various things—not least Parrish's own career—would have been different had his involvement with **Twilight Zone** come to the fruition originally forseen. Parrish was developing the project with Rod Serling as an hour-long anthology series, and the two men were slated to co-produce it. But executive decisions decreed that it became a half-hour series instead and Parrish politely bowed out, not being interested in the new format. He merely directed the above segment to honor his friendship with Serling. An interesting series of 'what if's are posed therefore. What if the series had gone ahead as planned? Would Parrish be a far more successful film maker than he has become? For with the exception of UP FROM THE BEACH, Parrish's last consistently fine work is the exquisite WONDERFUL COUNTRY—made the year before **Twilight Zone** occupied his time.

The small body of work he has actually made for the small screen (**Johnny Staccato** representing more his friendship with John Cassavetes than a commitment to the series) is both a reminder of one of the most lyrical artists of post-war American cinema, and a tantalising moment when paths crossed but did not join.

Frank R. Pierson

1960: **Have Gun-Will Travel**/*The Search* (co-wr), *The Fatalist* (pr), *Love's Young Dream* (pr), *A Head of*

Hair (pr), *Out at the Old Ball Park* (wr/pr). 1962: **Have Gun-Will Travel**/*The Trap* (dir + co-wr). 1971: **The Neon Ceiling; Nichols** (series cr + pr + pilot: wr/dir), *Where Did Everyone Go?* (wr/dir), *Wonder Fizz Flies Again* (dir only), *All In the Family* (st only), *Eddie Joe* (co-wr only), *The Specialists* (dir only), *Gulley vs Hansen* (dir only), *The Indian Giver* (dir only). 1972: **The Bold Ones: The Doctors**/*And Other Springs I May Not See* (co-wr/co-pr/dir).

Pierson had a pretty distinguished career as a screenwriter (CAT BALLOU etc.) and fought to direct his script of LOOKING GLASS WAR, winning the fight but few admirers. He donned the gloves again to step into another kind of battle, the Streisland/Kristofferson STAR IS BORN—writing the final rewrites and becoming the final, and credited, director. Although this already notorious encounter entitles him to at least a points decision, on the big screen evidence Pierson remains an unranked challenger for the *Made It, Ma* . . . title. His TV work is something else. **The Neon Ceiling** is weird, self-consciously arty, pretentious in a peculiarly American way; yet it still manages to be moving and powerful. Young and old losers sort out their lives, look for second chances, circle like moths round a desert gas station, where the flame is the neon ceiling—a collection of neon signs in alcoholic Gig Young's room—an extremely potent idea like a modern magic wishing pool; Pierson is more than alive to the haunting challenge of the imagery.

His work here helped win Emmys for Carol Sobieski/Henri Simoun (script) and Lee Grant (acting) and without being an unqualified success it remains firmly and tantalisingly in the mind. So too does **Nichols**, the series which brought James Garner back to TV, a turn-of-the-century western, with 'modernity' colliding with 'the old values'. It is a strangely flavoured comedy which Pierson created, produced and contributed to (either as writer, director or both) eight segments. There is perhaps an extension here of interests which surfaced during his stint on **Have Gun-Will Travel**, and the series is approaching cult status.

Ernest Pintoff (1931-   )

1975: **Hawaii Five-O**/*Turkey Shoot;* **Ellery Queen**/*Adventure of the Chinese Dog, Adventure of the Blunt Instrument;* **Six Million Dollar Man**/*Clark Templeton O'Flaherty;* **Kojak**/*A Long Way from Times Square.* 1976: **Hawaii Five-O**/*Practical Jokes Can Kill, Assault on the Palace;* **Kojak**/*Monkey on a String, Sister Maria;* **The Wild Wild East; The Shoes; Spencer's Pilots**/*The Match Book.* 1977: **The Kowboys; Blade; The Feather & Father Gang**/*The Apology;* **Kojak**/*No License to Kill;* **Bionic Woman**/*Sanctuary Earth;* **Hawaii Five-O**/*When Does a War End?*

Pintoff is a genuine original, his cartoon collaborations with Mel Brooks (THE CRITIC and OLD MAN AND THE FLOWER) having become art house favourites.

After oddball features, low-budgeted and poorly distributed (such as HARVEY MIDDLEMAN FIREMAN and WHO KILLED MARY WHAT'SERNAME?) he became involved in series TV and, purists would say 'sold out'.

Maybe he has—yet series TV is all the richer for the injection of doses of his quirky humour and sense of humanity into the increasingly bland formulas. *A Long Way from Times Square* is one of the most idiosyncratic **Kojaks** (the 'hero' being a nosy old mid-west grandma) while *Assault on the Palace* shows that Pintoff can plot action and plan mechanics as skilfully as any seasoned veteran. Further investigations are necessary before we can know to just what degree he had been able to impose his ideas (though it might be noted in passing that he cast Season Hubley, the daughter of his late colleague, animator John Hubley, as *Sister Maria*) and how successful and rewarding the new continuity of his career will prove to be.

Abraham Polonsky (c.1910-)

1965: **Seaway** (cr + sup), *A Medal for Mirko* (wr + dir), *Nothing but a Long Goodbye* (wr only), *The Only Good Indian* (wr only); **Kraft Suspense Theatre: Crisis**/*The Last Clear Chance* (wr only).

Along with Dalton Trumbo, Polonsky was the most relentlessly unforgiven of the blacklisted talents of the McCarthy period—or perhaps it merely seems that way today as both of them 'survived' and remained in at least a corner of the consciousness where others (Herbert Biberman for instance) appeared to be broken by the treatment. Polonsky took a perverse delight in writing pseudonymous screenplays during his long (1951-1968) period of outlawry from the big screen, usually for higher and higher salaries, until his name officially appeared again on the MADIGAN titles.

Canadian TV had given him a platform some years earlier, with **Seaway.** He 'created and supervised' the series and, as well, wrote three scripts and directed for the first time in seventeen years. The whole affair looks like a blacklist rehabilitation programme, for Polonsky drafted in such other erstwhile victims as Paul Jarrico, Ring Lardner Jr. and John Berry.

Ostensibly the series was about 'smuggling, crime, romance and the eternal battle with the elements on the great St. Lawrence Seaway'—but it is impossible to ignore the undercurrents which creep in. In Polonsky's segments, we find the long hand of fate/revenge closing on a victim from half way round the world in *A Medal for Mirko.* We discover the death wish of a blinded river pilot in *Nothing but a Long Goodbye*. Most interestingly, *The Only Good Indian* looks forward (as a kind of emotional rough sketch) to TELL THEM WILLIE BOY IS HERE, as an

Indian wages a one man fight against 'progress'.

Having proven presumably with this series that he was not 'dangerous', Polonsky was slowly assimilated back into the Hollywood mainstream—Universal, in particular, making positive first moves, evidenced by *The Last Clear Chance* for the studio's **Kraft Suspense Theatre** anthology. A junior auteurist watched vainly for any signs of personal themes or obsessions in this study of a day and two nights in the lives of Glenn Corbett and Barry Sullivan working behind the German lines in 1942 France. It will take an update to be sure that this merely represents the triumph of an overground assignment, the enemy weakening, the hero on the verge of triumph.

Since then, WILLIE BOY and ROMANCE OF A HORSE THIEF, Polonsky has fallen into a different kind of silence. In view of the enforced contraction of his career, a detailed study of his TV material (there may be more in Canada) will be necessary when making definitive judgements.

Michael Powell (1905-)

1964: **Espionage**/*Never Turn Your Back on a Friend, A Free Agent;* **Bluebeard's Castle**. 1965: **The Defenders**/*The Sworn Twelve;* **Doctors and Nurses** (one segment). 1978: **Return to the Edge of the World**.

Perhaps the greatest British director of his generation (with the exception of the Cockney-American Alfred Hitchcock), Michael Powell was bypassed by critics in the '60s, after making three insubstantial features.

PEEPING TOM, his romantic masterpiece, has Karl Boehm kissing the camera lens and indicated the love that Powell himself, (who appears in the film on a home-movie) has for the cinema. His famous films with Emeric Pressburger, BLACK NARCISSUS, A MATTER OF LIFE AND DEATH and THE RED SHOES (the only Rank film to make real money in the U.S.) etc. won Oscars and awards for everyone but Powell and Pressburger, and had an impressive range of artists and technicians working on them. Powell was intermittently pretentious and showed an incapacity to control the shape and structure of his films, and, consequently, found it increasingly difficult to finance his best concepts. Nevertheless, his stable stayed faithful and one sees the same technicians, actors, composers and designers in his later work, for television or otherwise. **Return to the Edge of the World** is merely his first major film (THE EDGE OF THE WORLD) with a colour epilogue, but has many of his old associates and actors on it.

PEEPING TOM was hated by the British Press, but was seen by the French critics for the superb film it is. Later, another Powell enthusiast mounted, not without resistance, Powell's first retrospective at The National Film Theatre in London, and he was quickly seen to be a major talent. Retrospectives, booklets, and honorary degrees have followed in Europe and America, and the British Film Institute itself, has now, to everyone's amusement, 'discovered' him again.

He dismisses most of his TV work, most of which was for Herbert Brodkin. His US work 'one **Defenders**, one **Doctors and Nurses**, both of them routine soap-operas but with good actors like J-P Aumont', seems to him worst. He is probably unfair to himself and his vision, which he pursues relentlessly through the theatre, his writings and through film. One cannot help noticing that talent and beauty follow him: Hein Heckroth, his designer, worked on **Bluebeard's Castle** (a superb Powellish reading of the Bartok opera, with Norman Foster as Bluebeard, made for German television); Leo Marks, the writer of PEEPING TOM turns up on *A Free Agent* (which starred Anthony Quayle and Sian Phillips); Brian Easdale, his composer since BLACK NARCISSUS worked on **Return to the Edge of the World**; Pamela Brown, with him since I KNOW WHERE I'M GOING (1945) stars with Julian Glover in an **Espionage** segment (especially rewritten for Powell by Larry Forrester) *Never Turn Your Back on a Friend*, something, indeed, that Powell himself never does.

Return to the Edge of the World is a BBC documentary project taking Powell back to the scene of his 'first' film, THE EDGE OF THE WORLD, which may prove to be an unduly symmetical way to close a gloriously irregular artistic life.

Richard Quine (1920-)

1971: **The Jean Arthur Show** (multiples). 1972: **Columbo**/*Requiem for a Falling Star, Dagger of the Mind.* 1973: **Columbo**/*Double Exposure.* 1974: **World Premiere**/*The Specialists.* 1975: **McCoy**/*Double Take.*

Of all the oddball auteur favourites of the early 60s, only Don Weis has been deserted by his admirers so completely as Quine who, if he took the earlier attention at all seriously, must be reeling from the abrupt shift of critical fortunes, paralleled by the drying-up of feature projects and the switch to TV.

All his small screen work is at least on the same level as the kind of features he made in the '50s and '60s, and though he relies more on scripts than a Hawks or a La Cava, he is a test case in the study of TV, for Quine is such an obviously proven stylist outside it.

As an opening shot, let it be said that even with Anne Baxter as a murderous screen ikon, *Requiem for a Falling Star* owes more to formats than fickle inspiration. Quine drives a crooked road.

Denis Sanders (1929-)

1955: **The Day Lincoln was Shot** (co-wr only). 1959: **Have Gun-Will Travel**/*The Wager* (co-wr only). 1961: **Naked City**/*Kill Me While I'm Young So I Can Die Happy!, The Horse has a Big Head—Let Him Worry.* 1962: **The Great Adventure**/*The Testing of Sam Houston.* 1963: **The Defenders**/*The Hidden Jungle.*

Sanders, and young brother Terry, were documentarists who broke into overground fiction cinema with A TIME OUT OF WAR, winning the 1954 short subject Oscar and becoming the darlings of the film society set. Of their subsequent features, CRIME AND PUNISHMENT USA is more interesting to read about than to see, although WARHUNT is a truly excellent and disturbing film.

One sought in vain for further movies, until Sanders returned to the documentary field with ELVIS—SOUL TO SOUL; the TV work actually represents a more enduring flirtation with fiction than the cinema did.

We're back in mists of memory, however, with the outrageously titled **Naked City** segments, (both holding up in the mind as among the best of an already brilliant series) and *The Testing of Sam Houston* which brought an unusually real quality to an equally ambitious series. Although Sanders remains an enigmatic figure, his work may prove to be more representative of the possible achievements of series TV than that of many more committed professionals.

Melville Shavelson (1917-)

1971: **Make Room for Daddy** (cr). 1972: **My World and Welcome to It** (cr). 1975: **The Legend of Valentino** (wr/dir). 1976: **The Great Houdinis** (wr/dir).

Shavelson's best achievements are as writer/director for Bob Hope in the '40s and '50s; his career declined in interest with projects such as IT STARTED IN NAPLES and THE PIGEON THAT TOOK ROME where he began to forsake the raucous world of vaudeville screen comedy. But we have to cheer **My World and Welcome to It**, a brave attempt to transfer James Thurber to TV, and admit that his two biopics are often engaging reminders of the old Warner school ('Don't call me boy, my name's Harry Houdini'), resolutely old-fashioned yet infinitely more evocative than the kind of hysterical surrealism promulgated by the Ken Russell school.

If Shavelson continues to work in this particular vein, and remains in TV, he will, perhaps enter the 'Elephant's Graveyard'. But for now he is just passing this way—and, damn it, it's nice to see him.

Don Siegel (1912-)

1953: **The Doctors** (three segments); **US Steel Hour**/*The Bogeyman* (wr + orig st only). 1954: **The**

Lineup (pilot). 1961: **Frontier**/*Out from Taos* (title unconfirmed); **Code Three** (pilot) (+co-wr); **Man from Blackhawk** (pilot: co-wr only). 1962: **The Visitor**/*Those Who Wait.* 1963: **Bus Stop** (pilot); **Breaking Point**/*There Are the Hip and There Are the Square;* **Twilight Zone**/*Uncle Simon.* 1964: **The Lloyd Bridges Show** (unidentified segment); **The Killers**; **The Hanged Man**; **Twilight Zone**/*The Self-Improvement of Salvadore Ross.* 1965: **Destroy** (pilot). 1966: **Convoy** (pilot + pr); **The Legend of Jesse James** (pilot + series pr all 34 segments); **World Premiere**/*Stranger on the Run.*

'None of this was any good. Television is about equal to the worst B pictures that one can make. I think you're in Television for one reason, and that's to make money. There's very little good work in television. Outside of the one-twenties (the three features) that I did, I don't think that my work was good in the pilots that I've directed. **Bus Stop** was pretty good, but that was based on the play. Tuesday Weld, Joe Cotten were in it. The pilots have very little resemblance to what comes out of the series. The only good thing about the pilots that I've directed and I've done about eight, I guess, has been that they sell, that's all—I make them so that they sell. I don't have to do them with any idea of artistic work.

'I felt that if I was going to do TV that the only way to make any money was to be a producer, not a director. So I decided to become a producer for television. I produced and directed the pilot on **Jesse James** and became the series producer, a very stupid job, that I'm not equipped to do—an enormous amount of detail. There's no time to direct if you're going to be a producer. If you're going to be in television there's only one reason to be in it, although a great many people in television would take umbrage at this: I think you're in it to make money. They way to make money, is to be a producer. So I was honest about it . . .'

Interview with Peter Bogdanovich *Movie* no. 15.

Robert Siodmak (1900-)

1957: **O.S.S.** (multiples).

Siodmak's always interesting if rarely totally fulfilled career came to a spluttering close with weird and far from wonderful projects in England and Germany. Oddly, his **O.S.S.** segments might prove to be a swan song for the kind of melodramatic intensity he purveyed at his best in SPIRAL STAIRCASE, PHANTOM LADY *et al*, for this series based (purportedly) on true O.S.S. cases, was (so the memory bank reminds us) not only one of the best 'Mid-Atlantic' hybrids of the period, but a consistently exciting and suspenseful one. Siodmak's shows are amongst the best in the series.

Jack Starrett

1970: **The Night Chase.** 1974: **Planet of the Apes/***The Horse Race;* **Starsky and Hutch/***Savage Sunday.* 1977: **Nowhere to Hide.**

Starrett (an erstwhile actor) graduated from the AIP school of hard knocks and broken dreams, and won auteur support, most decidedly with RACE WITH THE DEVIL. His TV work would seem to be a consistent obsession with similar themes of pursuit—**The Night Chase**, with fugitive David Janssen (a murderer for real, this time) fleeing in a cab with driver Yaphet Kotto to Mexico; **Nowhere to Hide** reprising the old standby plot of gangland witness, Tony Musante, trying to survive assassination attempts by former confederates, before he can spill the beans at the trial. Written by Edward Anhalt, (who does a John Houseman and plays the syndicate boss) this, and **Night Chase**,may prove to be among Starrett's very best work. They should not languish in TV vaults, when such fare as SLAUGHTER and CLEOPATRA JONES is widely available.

The Great Shows

Alfred Hitchcock Presents (1955-1962)

Anthology series of bizarre and off-beat stories, usually with a 'snapper'-ending, to tie-in with the Hitchcock mode of story-telling. Hitchcock hosted the series, introducing each episode and turned up at the end to add a final twist. Most of the episodes usually allowed the bad-guy to get away at the end, but it was always implied that justice was later served in one way or another. Hitchcock returned with an hour-format series (**Alfred Hitchcock Hour**) in late '62, which ran for a further three years.
See: John Brahm, Herschel Daugherty, Robert Douglas, Alfred Hitchcock, Alf Kjellin, Robert Stevens.

Alias Smith and Jones (1971-1973)

Obviously inspired by the popularity of BUTCH CASSIDY AND THE SUNDANCE KID, this tongue-in-cheek western series featured some interesting exterior photography and near-narrative dialogue. Ben Murphy and Pete Duel played the two free-wheeling characters—though Roger Davis later replaced Duel, following the latter's death midway through the series.
See: Jack Arnold, Roy Huggins, Glen Larson, Alexander Singer.

Arrest and Trial (1963-1964)

This courtroom-based series heralded the 45-minute drama programme, featuring the process from crime to court. The first half of the show was taken up with the crime and subsequent arrest, and the second played itself out in the courtroom. Ben Gazzara and Chuck Conners played on opposite sides of the fence, inside the law.
See: Lewis Milestone, Jack Smight.

Baretta (1975-1978)

Colourfully-produced police actioner, featuring Robert Blake as Tony Baretta, an undercover police officer with a unique style. The concept was originally derived from the **Toma** series (which fronted Tony Musante). When **Toma** suddenly terminated, Blake was brought in to continue the theme, and the show was retitled **Baretta.** As it stands, it is a well-balanced series, paying equal time to character, pace, and action.
See: Bernard Kowalski, Roy Huggins, Stephen J. Cannell, Don Medford, Curtis Harrington.

Ben Casey (1961-1964)

A fast-paced medical-drama series, countering **Dr Kildare** on the wave of early '60s hospital programmes. Like **Kildare**, Casey (played by Vince Edwards) was a young intern under the guidance of an elderly mentor, Dr Zorba (Sam Jaffe). The general theme of the series was taken up with Casey battling it out with the hospital authorities. The show's overall formula harks back to the crusading days of **Medic**.
See: Fielder Cook, James E. Moser, Sydney Pollack.

Best Sellers (1976-)

With the incredibly high ratings of **Rich Man, Poor Man,** in late '75, the studios and networks turned their eyes towards serialising novels. This created the series' package title, **Best Sellers,** and some interesting TV followed, in the form of Taylor Caldwell's **Captains and the Kings**, Anton Myer's **Once an Eagle**, Robert Ludlum's **The Rhinemann Exchange**, and Norman Bogner's **Seventh Avenue**.
See: Douglas Heyes, Burt Kennedy, Jerry London, Allen Reisner, Paul Wendkos.

Bonanza (1959-1973)

The first of the sprawling western family sagas. Featuring the noble Cartwright family (Lorne Greene, Pernell Roberts, Dan Blocker and Michael Landon), the show mainly hovered around their vast family ranch, the Ponderosa. Notable mainly for its original form of story-telling (in the TV western genre) and its influence on many similar shows during the '60s and early '70s.
See: William F. Claxton, Tay Garnett, Michael Landon, Joseph Sargent, William Witney, Gerd Osward.

Charlie's Angels (1976-)

Prime network show, featuring a 'trio of glamorous detectives', who work for a faceless private-eye in exotic, often lavish, surroundings. Kate Jackson, Farrah Fawcett-Majors, and Jaclyn Smith supplied the smiles and statistics, with Cheryl Ladd later replacing Fawcett-Majors. The series has its significance in successfully achieving an all-female-fronted show in an area, and genre, generally dominated by hard-nosed macho private-detectives.
See: George McCowan, Georg Stanford Brown, Richard Lang.

Cheyenne (1956-1963)

This emerged from **Warner Brothers Presents**, and went on to outdistance most

of its contemporaries. It also created the great TV rush into Western-programming. It led the WB output and inspired other production companies to follow suit. It marked the first, notable, independent western adventurer (played by Clint Walker), *sans* Indian, Mexican, or Old-Timer sidekick.
See: Richard L. Bare, Roy Huggins, Leslie H. Martinson, Lee Sholem, George WaGGner.

Columbo (1971-)

A part of the Sunday Mystery Movie format of 90-minute thrillers, this series showcased the very individual talents of Peter Falk as an almost over-slovenly police Lieutenant solving complex crimes, usually, in society circles. Slick production and odd-but-interesting characterisations elevated this series above the other Mystery Movie entries.
See: Ben Gazzara, James Frawley, Levinson & Link, Richard Irving, Peter Falk, Bernard Kowalski

---

Combat (1962-1967)

It featured the day to day events of a battle-weary group of U.S. Infantrymen, led by Vic Morrow, in World War Two, Europe. The series had, on occasion, flashes of stark realism, particularly when dealing with individual characters. Morrow's presentation, of front-line military activity (coupled with some exceptional photography) was more true to its subject than most later WW2-based series.
See: Burt Kennedy, Gene Levitt, Robert Altman.

The Defenders (1961-1965)

Created by Reginald Rose, this legal-drama series goes down in TV history as one of the major achievements of small-screen producing, directing, writing and acting. The scripts and their controversial topics were almost a well-polished return to the excellent anthology-play heyday of **Studio One** and the Philco-Goodyear series. A masterful example of high-powered Television.
See: Paul Bogart, David Greene, Buzz Kulik, Michael Powell, Stuart Rosenberg, Franklyn Schaffner, Elliot Silverstein.

Dick Powell Theatre (1961-1963)

Always opening with Powell entering the sound-stage through gigantic doors, the anthology series was a fine mill for various TV talents, to develop, in both the writing and directing departments. It was probably the last of the classic

anthology shows introduced by and hosted by a notable Hollywood star.
See: Arthur Hiller, Sam Peckinpah, Samuel Fuller, Buzz Kulik.

The Dick Van Dyke Show (1961-1966)

Elevated to classic status, among the 1960's sit-com programmers, Dick Van Dyke commanded an impressive line-up of talent on this popular series: Mary Tyler Moore, Morey Amsterdam, Rose Marie, and Richard Deacon. The final stamp of quality was central writer-creator, Carl Reiner. Van Dyke returned with the **New Dick Van Dyke Show** in the early '70s.
See: Theodore J. Flicker.

Dr Kildare (1961-1966)

MGM TV's capitalisation on the Lew Ayres/Lionel Barrymore movie series of the 1930s. More concerned with the trials and tribulations of the young intern (Richard Chamberlain) than with serious medical issues or dramatic story-telling, this series revolved around the almost-paternal relationship of Kildare's mentor, Dr Gillespie (played by Raymond Massey), and the coming-of-worldly-wisdom to the intern. A well-produced series, that, along with **Ben Casey** and **The Nurses**, almost caused a TV deluge of scalpel and stethescope shows.
See: Michael Ritchie, James Goldstone.

Dragnet (1951-1959)

The foundation-stone of all TV police dramas, **Dragnet** was created by Jack Webb, who fashioned it into a tightly-wrapped package of LA Police Department case histories, delivered in a semi-documentary style. Webb re-introduced the show in '67, and it ran for three more years. The earlier series was run in syndication under the title **Badge 714.**
See: Jack Webb, James E. Moser.

East Side/West Side (1963-1964)

Social workers were the subject of this notable series. It allowed more controversial issues and social comments to be aired in a dramatic form. George C. Scott was the central character, and the series as a whole provided early '60s TV with some of its more sparkling moments.
See: Tom Gries.

The FBI (1965-1974)

Probably the last of the 'big' Quinn Martin action dramas, the show enjoyed a long and successful run before absorbing itself in cold-war paranoia themes. Fronting Efrem Zimbalist Jr. and William Reynolds, as the department agents, the show was also well-received by then-FBI chief Edgar Hoover, who heartily endorsed the programme.

See: William A. Graham, Don Medford.

Four-In-One (1970-1971)

In an attempt to devise new ways to present series drama, this was an overall title for four revolving shows: **McCloud, Night Gallery, The Psychiatrist** and **San Francisco International Airport.** Both **McCloud** and **Night Gallery** became spin-offs and continued to run under their own banner, but unlike the **Mystery Movie** slot with its revolving crime-busters, the format was unsuccessful.

See: Russ Mayberry, Douglas Heyes, Don Taylor, Steven Spielberg, Rod Serling, Jerrold Freedman, Jeannot Szwarc, Daryl Duke, Boris Sagal.

The Fugitive (1963-1967)

Created by Roy Huggins, this series must go on record as the longest chase-sequence in TV history. David Janssen was the hunted figure, wrongly accused of murdering his wife, and Barry Morse was the fanatically-determined police Lieutenant. For four years, Janssen managed to remain one step ahead of the law, whilst pursuing the trail of the mysterious 'one-armed man' (the real killer); the final two segments galvanised viewers to their sets, world-wide, in April 1967.

See: Roy Huggins, James Goldstone, Mark Rydell, Walter Grauman.

Gunsmoke (1955-1975)

If Webb's **Dragnet** is the grand old man of TV police actioners, then Charles Marquis Warren's **Gunsmoke** is undoubtedly the grandfather of the 'adult' TV western. The series, mainly set in Dodge City, made legendary figures out of Matt Dillon (played by James Arness), Kitty (Amanda Blake), Chester (Dennis Weaver), and Doc (Milburn Stone). The show became TV's longest running western series and Arness eventually assumed ownership of the show. It wore out Dillon's deputy (Ken Curtis took over as Deputy Festus in 1964). The early series were also shown in some areas as **Gun Law.**

See: Marvin Chomsky, Charles Marquis Warren, Andrew V. McLaglen, Bernard McEveety, Vincent McEveety, Philip Leacock, Sam Peckinhah, Clyde Ware, Arthur Hiller, Ted Post, Mark Rydell.

Have Gun-Will Travel (1957-1963)

Operating out of the 'Carlton Hotel, San Francisco', Paladin (played by Richard Boone) was almost a western private-eye. The series maintained an adult approach, intelligent and serious stories were aired. When gunplay came into it, the hero aimed to kill. The show was something of a turning-point in the TV western genre.
See: Richard Boone, Andrew V. McLaglen, Gary Nelson, Lewis Milestone, Lamont Johnson, Frank R. Pierson, Richard Donner.

Hawaii Five-O (1968-)

Crime drama in colourful surroundings is the mainstream of the series' activities, from local dope peddlers to Ninja assassins, and from crazed rooftop snipers to Red Chinese agents. Jack Lord (as Steve McGarret) plays the central character, assisted somewhat naively by James MacArthur, as officers of the Hawaiian Islands' special police division. Visually exciting locations played a significant role in the production of the show, allowing for some exceptional photography.
See: Philip Leacock, Michael O'Herlihy, Ernest Pintoff, Marvin Chomsky, Sutton Roley.

Hawk (1966)

Unique concept featuring a Red Indian cop (played by Burt Reynolds) amidst the concrete canyons of New York City. Unusual and exciting for its approach to racial, if not cultural, relations in an action-thriller format. Perhaps a forerunner of the later, faint-hearted, **Dan August** series, in terms of cultural clashes in a racially-heated environment.
See: Alexander Singer, Paul Bogart.

High Chaparral (1967-1971)

A superbly-produced, and authentically presented, family-ranching saga, set in the remote locale of 1880s Arizona. Leif Erickson portrayed the patriarch, Frank Cannon, trying to live in harmony with the land and the Apaches. Linda Cristal, Cameron Mitchell, Mark Slade and Henry Darrow made up the other members of the Cannon clan. The depiction of the Apache, and excellent use of the desert region, made this series top-drawer programming.
See: Richard Sarafian, William Witney, Joseph Pevney, William F. Claxton.

I Spy (1965-1968)

Coming in on the surge of spy series, this show was one of the slickest of its period. Robert Culp and Bill Cosby were the agents, fronting as pro-tennis player and trainer. The series was also one of the first to feature an inter-racial partnership. Good scripts and some excellent locations made this show one of the best in its field.
See: David Friedkin and Mort Fine, Tom Gries, Paul Wendkos, Mark Rydell, Richard Sarafian.

Johnny Staccato (1959-1960)

A fast-moving private-eye series, featuring John Cassavetes, as Staccato, a character originally intended as a jazz-piano player. An imaginative deviation from the well-worn solo-sleuth actioner. Elmer Bernstein created a particularly effective music score for the show.
See: John Brahm, John Cassavetes, Bernard Girard, Paul Henreid, Robert Parrish, Joseph Pevney, Boris Sagal.

Kojak (1973-1978)

Conceived by Abby Mann, the hard-nosed, cynical NY police Lieutenant, Theo Kojak (Telly Savalas), has amassed a large following. Interesting, often emotional, themes developed during the course of the series, thus making the whole premise all the more acceptable.
See: Telly Savalas, Jeannot Szwarc, Ernest Pintoff, Jack Laird, Gene Kearney, William Hale.

Kung Fu (1972-1973)

Warners really set the machinery rolling when they made this oriental/western drama. The show sparked interest in the Martial Arts and led the way for countless KUNG FU films to be shown in the West. The series, itself, featured David Carradine (as Caine), martial arts expert from China, searching for his long lost brother in the early American West. Some superb colour photography high-lighted the show.
See: Jerry Thorpe, Richard Lang, John Llwellyn Moxey.

M Squad (1957-1960)

One of the most active, and brutal, of the late '50s police shows, headlining Lee

Marvin as a tough Chicago police lieutenant. Gritty black and white actioner that might have blue-printed the later **Untouchables** style of hard-hitting violence. It certainly defined the lunatic single-mindedness of the Marvin persona.
See: Robert Altman, David Butler, John Brahm, Bernard Girard, Allen H. Miner, Don Taylor, Don Weis.

McCloud (1971-)

Spinning out of the **Four-In-One** series, this cowboy-marshal-in-the-big-city series soon made an impact on viewers. Sam McCloud was played by Dennis Weaver, not too distantly related from his early Deputy Chester role, and involved the hero in urban criminals and NY city police procedures. Inspired, albeit vaguely, by the COOGAN'S BLUFF feature.
See: Richard A. Colla, Douglas Heyes, Glen A. Larson, Bruce Kessler.

The Man from UNCLE (1964-1968)

Coming in on the wave of spy and espionage actioners, this lush Metro series related the adventures of two **UNCLE** agents, Napoleon Solo (played by Robert Vaughn) and Ilya Kuryakin (David McCallum), in their fight against the villainous operatives from Thrush. Leo G. Carroll (as their chief, Mr. Waverley) was their anchor-man. The series rapidly built a large cult following. It also spun off a companion series **The Girl from UNCLE**, toplining Stefanie Powers.
See: Richard Donner, John Newland, Mitchell Leisen, John Brahm, Barry Shear.

MASH (1972-)

Based directly on the Robert Altman feature, this Mobile Army Surgical Hospital comedy series may go down on record as one of the most cynical of U.S. TV shows. It should also be recorded as one of the most rapid-fire, hysterical comedy shows ever telecast. Alan Alda (as Hawkeye), Wayne Rogers (as Trapper), and McLean Stevenson featured in the sizable cast; Rogers and Stevenson were later replaced by Mike Farrell and Harry Morgan.
See: Harry Morgan, Don Weis.

Maverick (1957-1962)

Not understood at the time, this Warner Brothers western may be regarded as one of the cleverest, or as one of the most subversive, of series. Roy Huggins produced the early seasons of the show, about two itinerant gamblers (James Garner and Jack Kelly) who live by lying, cheating, stealing, and generally using any underhand method available. A unique western capable of being enjoyed on several different levels.
See: Robert Altman, Richard Sarafian, Budd Boetticher, Roy Huggins, James Garner.

Mission: Impossible (1966-1973)

'This tape will self-destruct in ten seconds' always ended the message given to Jim Phelps (played by Peter Graves) as an instruction to put his I.M.F. operatives into action. Focusing on the activities of a special group of freelance agents, this series may possibly be one of the most pro-CIA shows ever made, involving itself in international espionage, sabotage, assassinations, and all-round duplicity. However, the excellent, though complex, scripts also made it one of the most exciting.
See: Bruce Geller, Lee H. Katzin, Bernard Kowalski, Allen H. Miner, Alexander Singer.

Naked City (1958-1963)

Based on Mark Hellinger's 1949 movie, this series was one of the first to actually take the TV cameras out onto the sidewalks of Manhattan. The '58-'60 period of the show (30-minute segments) was mainly routine police drama, but the second ('60-'63) format 60-minute segments and was remarkable for its fine scripts and photography.
See: Buzz Kulik, Arthur Hiller, James Sheldon, Elliot Silverstein, Walter Grauman, Stuart Rosenberg, Tay Garnett, William Conrad, John Brahm, Laslo Benedek, David Lowell Rich, Lamont Johnson, Jack Smight, Paul Wendkos, William A. Graham.

The Name of the Game (1968-1971)

A lavish production from Universal, which centered on the affairs of three characters (mainly run in rotation) working for a large publishing corporation. Gene Barry, as head of the organisation, assigned newshounds, Robert Stack and Tony Franciosa, to their various, usually hazardous, projects. The series rises above the majority of 90-minute programmers due to its sizable budget allowance and utilisation of talented personnel.
See: Steven Spielberg, Leslie Stevens, Robert Day, Barry Shear.

Nichols (1971)

An odd western adventure, set around the 1910 period, with James Garner almost reworking his Maverick role. A curious and off-beat enterprise, with a wide cult audience; the final segment had the Garner title-character shot dead midway through the episode and followed-up with Garner doubling as his twin brother arriving to replace him. The series was re-run under **The James Garner Show.**
See: Meta Rosenberg, Frank Pierson, James Garner, Gerd Oswald, William Wiard, Paul Bogart.

Night Gallery (1971-1973)

Rod Serling's last tele-series in the *fantastique* vein. Beginning as part of the **Four-In-One** compendium, the show skipped between serious, often Lovecraftian, horror-fantasy episodes and serio-comic playlets. Although it was something of a sad departure from series activity for Serling, the show did contain moments of true horror and mood-drenched atmosphere. Original, and actual, title of the show was **Rod Serling's Night Gallery.**
See: John Badham, Steven Spielberg, Jeannot Szwarc, Theodore J. Flicker, Jerrold Freedman, Rod Serling, Jack Laird.

One Step Beyond (1959-1961)

Psychic phenomena were the central subject of this popular series, hosted by John Newland. The stories were all, apparently, based on real-life incidents, and were depicted as convincingly as possible. Effectively eerie segments and a determined authenticity place this show among the more notable examples of the genre.
See: John Newland.

The Outer Limits (1963-1965)

Created by Leslie Stevens (originally entitled **Please Stand By**) and mainly controlled by Joseph Stefano, this remains one of the supreme examples of 1960's s-f anthology drama. Presenting the strangest of weird s-f stories, the series brought a certain serious distinction to TV fantasy, and catered for both the adult and juvenile audience.
See: James Goldstone, Leonard Horn, Leslie Stevens, Gerd Oswald.

Perry Mason (1957-1965)

Taking the Erle Stanley Gardner courtroom character, and his trusty associates, TV created a memorable figure and series. Raymond Burr played Mason, while William Hopper and Barbara Hale were his assistants. It was an exceptionally

popular show during its early days; an unsuccessful attempt was made in the '70s to revive the character but, Perry Mason truly belongs to the earlier TV period.
See: Richard Donner, Andrew V. McLaglen, Ted Post.

Peter Gunn (1958-1959)

Craig Stevens was the private-eye in this Blake Edwards-created series, which contained a somewhat unique style of presentation. Elaborate camera-angles and some stunning music elevated the show to an above-average level. Edwards also produced and directed a feature version in 1967, though it came in too late to create sufficient interest in the character.
See: Lamont Johnson.

Police Story (1973-)

Police officer-turned-novelist Joseph Wambaugh created this exceptionally well-made anthology series, depicting the activities of various LA Police Departments. In trying to avoid the 'taken from the files of the LA Police Department' situation, producer Liam O'Brien personally interviewed police officers for story material. **Police Woman** and **Joe Forrester** were spin-offs from this show.
See: Edward Abroms, William A. Graham, Robert Collins, John Llewellyn Moxey, Gary Nelson, Alvin Ganzer, David Moessinger.

Rawhide (1958-1966)

Legendary TV western series, depicting a lengthy cattle-drive and the characters involved. Trial-boss Gil Favor was played by Eric Fleming, while Ramrod Rowdy Yates was played by a young Clint Eastwood. Contrary to popular opinion, they did finish their original drive, and went on to other cattle-drive related adventures. Eastwood, needless to say, went on to achieve greater fame and fortune, and left the TV trail forever.
See: Andrew V. McLaglen, Ted Post, Stuart Rosenberg, Charles Marquis Warren.

Rich Man, Poor Man (1976)

Based on Irwin Shaw's best-seller, this 12 part series cemented the format we know today as the 'mini-series'. Relating the life-stories of two brothers, from an immigrant family, and their separate paths, the series scored a big success—and was later followed-up by **Rich Man, Poor Man**—Book II. This also set the

pattern of limited-episode story-telling that was effectively used by **Roots, Washington: Behind Closed Doors**, and has now become a virtual film industry of its own.
See: David Greene, Boris Sagal.

The Rockford Files (1974-)

A superbly blending of Chandleresque themes and characters into TV-style programming, featuring James Garner (as Jim Rockford) who, mainly by accident, becomes involved in outrageous (and complex) plots, alongside some extremely bizarre characters. It would be unfair to simply suggest that the series succeeded solely on the strength of Garner's characterisation and the excellent, sometimes brilliant, teleplays, but it would be an accurate indication of the particular flavour the show pursues.
See: James Garner, Roy Huggins, Meta Rosenberg, William Wiard, Stephen J. Cannell.

Route 66 (1960-1964)

Over the years this foot-loose series has been accorded a place among the classic shows of early '60s TV. A fast-moving adventure, effectively stirred but not shaken by Stirling Silliphant, it featured two free-wheeling characters, Buzz and Tod (Marty Milner and George Maharis), who drive the show's convertable around the country.
See: Robert Altman, Richard Donner, Arthur Hiller, Sam Peckinpah, Ted Post.

---

77 Sunset Strip (1958-1964)

Notable forerunner of the small-screen private-investigator team shows, based on Hollywood's exotic Sunset Strip. The series was a direct influence on such similar fare as **Hawaiian Eye** and **Bourbon Street Beat**, which at times exchanged characters.
See: Richard L. Bare, Leslie H. Martinson, George WaGGner, Robert Douglas, Irving J. Moore, André De Toth, William Conrad.

The Six Million Dollar Man (1973-1978)

Initially one of the strangest heroes to continue a TV series, Lee Majors (as Col. Steve Austin) portrayed a near-fatally crashed astronaut who is 'rebuilt' into a bionic man, with some remarkable powers of strength and sight. Created from Martin Caidin's novel, the show and character took off in a big way, hitting high

in the ratings and creating a deluge of merchandising. The early years of the show reflect a more imaginative format and pace. It began to slow down toward the end until the creative machinery finally ground to a halt.
See: Jerry Jameson, Alan J. Levi, Russ Mayberry.

Star Trek (1966-1969)

Something of a TV phenomenon, by way of production and later audience reaction. The show dealt with science-fiction from a respectable standpoint and managed to deliver intelligent stories without resorting to the accepted juvenilia. For a while, the show succeeded in delivering top notch material in an area usually established as 'pre-team terrain.'
See: Joseph Pevney, Ralph Senensky, Marc Daniels, Gene Roddenberry, Gene L. Coon, James Goldstone.

Tarzan (1966-1968)

The popular Edgar Rice Burroughs character came onto the small-screens in the form of Ron Ely, and saw only a few exciting seasons of jungle adventure. Primarily aimed at a more juvenile market, this series did take on social/political themes and succeeded in supplying TV with some visually superb moments.
See: William Witney, Barry Shear.

The Twilight Zone (1959-1964)

One of the classics of the small-screen sf/fantasy genre. Created by Rod Serling, and running for over five years, the show never achieved much critical or aesthetic acclaim. Its popularity lay in its style of presenting fantasy in a highly competitive medium. All the segments (excepting one season) were half-hour, and all contained a twist-of-fate ending. The series was, from a creative angle, a remarkable showcase for various TV writers and directors.
See: Rod Serling, Robert Stevens, Stuart Rosenberg, Alvin Ganzer, John Brahm, Douglas Heyes, Buzz Kulik, Richard L. Bare, Paul Stewart, Abner Biberman, Jacques Tourneur.

The Trials of O'Brien (1965-1966)

With Peter Falk as the title character, a NY-based lawyer, this unusual and expertly played series was almost a basic groundwork for Falk's later Columbo characterisation. A continuing, yet amusing, sub-plot concerned Falk's attempts at trying to reconcile, thus re-marry, his ex-wife (Joanna Barnes). A fondly-remembered series, with many incredible moments.
See: Stuart Rosenberg, Richard Sarafian, Paul Bogart.

The Untouchables (1959-1963)

Just about the most classic and notorious, of crime dramas in TV history. Beginning its life on **Desilu Playhouse**, it immediately gained popularity as a regular series for ABC-TV. It featured the continuing struggle between government agents, headed by Eliot Ness (Robert Stack), and Chicago's gangland, during the 1920s and '30s. Producer Quinn Martin pushed for both sadism (from his writers) and authenticity (from Desilu Studios), achieving a superb blend of Capone-era action/drama.
See: Walter Grauman, Tay Garnett, Phil Karlson, Howard Koch.

The Virginian (1962-1970)

Long-running western series and the first TV show to expand to 90-minutes. Photography and design on the show was well above the average western programme, and some of the earlier stories ranked among the best ever presented on Television. James Drury was the anonymous title character, while Doug McClure played sidekick Trampas. Original owner of the Shiloh ranch, the series's base, was played by Lee J. Cobb, but John McIntire eventually took over for the latter part of the series. The show reappeared for one season ('70-'71) as **Men from Shiloh**, with Stewart Granger as owner of the ranch.
See; Richard A. Colla, Burt Kennedy, Samuel Fuller, Stuart Heisler.

Wagon Train (1957-1965)

Loosely based on Ford's WAGONMASTER, this show was MCA's contribution to the western deluge during the genre's early days. The series central theme was an East to West trek. It utilised all the classic western ingredients, and each episode unfolded the story of some individual character. Ward Bond played the wagonmaster for the first three years and John McIntyre took over the remainder.
See: Richard H. Bartlett, Virgil Vogel, Tay Garnett, Ted Post, Allen H. Miner.

Warner Brothers Presents (1955-1956)

An umbrella-title for three separate series: **King's Row, Casablanca** and **Cheyenne**. Initially, there was a 10-minute WB promo-film included, called **Behind the Cameras**, but this was later dropped. All were based on previous Warner properties, **King's Row** and **Casablanca** ran only one season apiece, while **Cheyenne,** the least prestigious, went on to achieve fame and success in its own right.
See: Paul Stewart, Don Weis, John Peyser, Richard L. Bare.

The Westerner (1960-1961)

Cult-classic, if not a TV classic, this Peckinpah-created show offered early '60s Television some of its finest moments. The series headlined Brian Keith (as Dave Blassingame), his dog (Brown), and his specialised Winchester rifle. The show came from a pilot originally aired via the **Zane Grey Theatre**, and ran only one season. However, the series has attained legend status with teleastes, and represents one of the true peaks of TV-western production.
See: Tom Gries, Sam Peckinpah, André De Toth, Bruce Geller.

Wild Wild West (1965-1969)

A curious mixture of chapter-play, comic-strip, and swashbuckling adventure, this 'western' series remains remarkable purely on the strength of this unique blending. The show followed the hazardous, usually Gothic, route of agents James West (Robert Conrad) and Artemus Gordon (Ross Martin), who worked undercover for President Grant. Michael Dunn (as Dr Lovelace) appeared frequently as one of their main adversaries, styled in his own individual fashion. Although something of an irregular format, split between genres, the series demonstrated that there are no limitations in TV production and programming.
See: Mark Rydell, Richard Sarafian, Irving J. Moore.

Index